A SPECIAL WORD TO THE SELF-STUDY STUDENT

Below is a study plan for you if you are working without a teacher. You will probably spend many more hours than the time suggested. The more time you spend studying, the better your score will be. You must spend at least 45 minutes to an hour becoming acquainted with the organization of the **Prentice-Hall TOEFL Book** itself as well as the organization of the TOEFL exam before you even begin to study.

Note:
If you are preparing for a TOEFL given on or after July 11, 1986, you should study the new Essay Target section.

Self-Study Time Schedule

15 minutes
30 minutes
120 minutes
Time: Open
	1. Survey this book to learn its organization.
	2. Read the introduction to the diagnostic tests.
	3. Take a diagnostic test.
	4. Review your answers and prepare your Personal Study Plan.
	5. Read the introduction to the Listening section.
	6. Read the introduction to the Structure section.
	7. Read the introduction to the Vocabulary section.
	8. Read the introduction to the Reading section.
	9. Read the introduction to the Essay section.
	10. Determine your available study time.
	11. Study the most difficult items from your Personal Study Plan.
	    For each Listening and Structure exercise, allow 20 minutes.
	    For each Reading passage, allow 15 minutes.
	    For each Essay exercise, allow 30 minutes.
	12. After you have done about 20 Target exercises, or when you feel you are ready, take another diagnostic test.
	13. Prepare a new Personal Study Plan; repeat steps 9 through 11.

Personal Study Plan
The *Personal Study Plan* (PSP) is your record of your own strengths and weaknesses in English. Each question on a diagnostic test is keyed to a Target exercise. If you miss a test question, you are referred to the Target exercise that gives you extra practice on that particular problem.

In preparing to study for the TOEFL, first take a diagnostic test and complete your PSP. The directions for completing the PSP are in the section titled *How to Take the Diagnostic Tests*. The Personal Study Plan is located with the answer sheets at the back of the book.

Answer Sheets
The **Prentice-Hall TOEFL Prep Book** uses answer sheets similar to those used on the TOEFL exam. Using these answer sheets for both the diagnostic tests and the Target exercises will help you develop the coordination necessary to move your eyes quickly from the test booklet to the proper spot on the answer sheet. The answer sheets are at the back of the book.

A SPECIAL WORD TO THE TEACHER

The **Prentice-Hall TOEFL Prep Book** contains more material than could ever be taught in an average course. This extra material is provided to give you the flexibility you need to develop an appropriate TOEFL preparatory course for the special needs of your class. This section is your guide to help you use the exercises in this book effectively. Below are some suggestions to assist you in preparing your lessons.

Time Schedules
The **Super TOEFL Book** may be used in a variety of learning situations: short 4-hour workshops, an all-day session, or a 15-week course. The following timetables are guides for lesson planning. They are only approximate and do not account for administrative considerations (holidays, break periods, and so forth).

Note:
If you are preparing students for a TOEFL on July 11, 1986 or after, you should include the Essay Target section in your lesson plans.

Four-Hour Class

30 minutes	Explain TOEFL question types.
120 minutes	Administer a diagnostic test.
30 minutes	Correct the diagnostic test.
15 minutes	Discuss the use of the Personal Study Plan.
15 minutes	Explain self-study Vocabulary skills.
15 minutes	Explain self-study Reading Comprehension skills.
15 minutes	Explain how to organize an essay.

Eight-Hour Class

30 minutes	Explain TOEFL question types.
120 minutes	Administer a diagnostic test.
30 minutes	Correct the diagnostic test.
30 minutes	Discuss the use of the Personal Study Plan. Compute the Class Study Plan (CSP).
50 minutes	Do top two Listening Targets from CSP.
50 minutes	Do top two Structure Targets from CSP.
50 minutes	Do Reading Target introduction. Discuss the reading theories outlined.
30 minutes	Explain how to organize an essay. Discuss the discourse styles outlined.
30 minutes	Discuss the self-study Vocabulary-Building skills.

2. Encourage the students to keep a Word Notebook as suggested in the Vocabulary Target introduction. Establish a minimum number of words per day for them to study.

In the Classroom

1. Discuss the words the students have collected in their Word Notebooks. Have each student quiz one another on the words they collected. Every other week use their words as part of a vocabulary quiz.

2. Have the students tell the others about the passages they read. Have them discuss the specific areas (science, arts, humanities, and so forth) that they read about. This will turn their passive vocabulary into an active one.

3. Discuss contextual clues. Choose a reading passage and have them scan the passage and circle all noun markers (or circle other contextual clue markers discussed in the Reading Target introduction). Have them compare their passages with one another. Then have them scan the passage again and circle all verb markers. Once more, ask them to scan the same passage or another passage, circling adjective and adverb markers. Each time they finish scanning a passage, have them compare their findings with their classmates.

4. In discussing adjective and adverb markers, refer the students to the Structure Target section on adverbs and adjectives.

5. To illustrate the prefix and root clues, write a prefix (or a root) on the board. Have the students try to provide a new vocabulary word from their notebooks using the prefix or root.

6. Show them how to use the dictionary to find a root and a prefix. Have them do some dictionary work at home by researchng word roots beyond those given in this book.

Vocabulary Exercises

7. The students should do the vocabulary exercises at home on their own time and at their own pace. Have them circle every word they do not know and add it to their Word Notebook or flash cards. You need not spend class time discussing the answers since the students should be able to look the answers up in the key and find further clarification in a dictionary.

READING TARGET

Overview

The Reading Target introduction is written as if it were a TOEFL reading passage. The students will get practice with the TOEFL format and will learn the skills necessary to be a good reader. Then they must read, read, and read some more.

Outside the Classroom

1. Tell the students that reading is a very private activity; they can improve only by reading, reading some more, and then reading even more.

2. The students must develop a conscientious reading plan. Have the students keep a record of *when* they read and *why* they read. Have them notice what they read (magazines vs. texts) and when they most frequently read. They should set definite times aside (after lunch, before dinner, before bed) to read even if only for 5 to 10 minutes per session.

3. They should try to use SQ3R everytime they read. (SQ3R is a reading technique that is summarized below and explained in detail in the Reading Target introduction.) The students should never read anything without first trying to guess *Who? What? When? Where?* and *Why?*

In the Classroom
1. You can help your students read more efficiently by using the following techniques.

   A. SQ3R
   Survey: Have the students survey the **Prentice-Hall TOEFL Prep Book**, a newspaper, or a textbook and let them try to form the five *wh* questions: *Who? What? When? Where?* and *Why?*

   Question: The five *wh* questions are only a beginning. Teach the students to develop their own personal questions about a passage. The more personally involved in a reading passage they become, the more they will learn from it.

   B. Skimming and Scanning
   Have the students skim for the general idea; have them scan for specific details. These specific details should include the various contextual markers discussed in the Reading Target introduction. For example, have the students scan for transition words. Point out how these transition words might change the meaning of a reading passage and thereby influence the answer choice.

   C. Speed Reading
   Most people have lazy eyes; you must train the students' eyes and minds to move faster. To train the students to move their eyes quickly, give them 5 minutes to skim a passage; then give them another 2 minutes to skim the same passage from the beginning; finally, give then only 1 minute to skim the same passage. This technique will not be easy for them; they will try to read every word. Pushing them faster forces them to read in phrases and groups of words. Another speed technique is to give the students 1 minute to read as far as they can. After 1 minute, say "Stop!" Have them put their fingers on the words they were reading when you said "Stop!" Then tell them to start again at the beginning and give them 1 minute to see if they can read beyond where they stopped previously. Again you will say "Stop" after 1 minute and they will put their fingers on the words they were reading when you said "Stop."

   Do the drill one more time. They will see how they read faster and faster and, since they are reading the same passage, understand more of what they read. They will discover that it may be better for them to read the passage several times in 2 minutes than only once in 2 minutes.

2. Analyze the Comprehension Questions
   What kind of information do the questions that follow the reading passage want from the students?

   An inference?   A specific detail?
   An opinion?   A restatement?
   A definition?   A general piece of information?

   The reading test items are coded in the *Diagnostic Test Answer Keys* according to what the question required the student to be able to do. However, there is no

Personal Study Plan (PSP) for the Reading Target section. The target areas (facts, inferences, restatements, and definitions) are specific enough that a student can learn how to recognize these questions by carefully studying the examples in the diagnostic tests and by doing the additional readings in the Reading Target section.

3. Guess at the Answers
Occasionally, let the students try to answer the questions *before* they read the passage. Then let them read the passage and correct their guesses.

Point out the value of previewing the questions before reading the passage.

4. Vary Your Teaching Activities
Each hour you might do three passages focusing on a particular skill. Below are some examples:

   A. In one passage, you could help the students identify referents. Have them scan the passage and circle all pronouns. Then have them, in pairs, identify the referents for the pronouns.

   B. In one passage, you could help the students identify discourse style. Have them scan a passage and circle any discourse markers they find. Have them compare their results with a classmate and then with the class as a whole.

   C. In one passage, have the students scan and circle all transition markers. As a class, have them discuss the particular markers and the kind of transitions they found.

ESSAY TARGET

Overview

The Essay Target section should be studied by those students taking the TOEFL on or after July 11, 1986. There are no essay exams on the diagnostic tests in the **Prentice-Hall TOEFL Prep Book**. The students should use the essay questions in the Essay Target section for practice.

The Essay Target exercises stress the importance of organization. No written essay models have been provided. This will prevent students producing carbon copy essays on the actual TOEFL. Students should develop their own unique styles of introduction and conclusions. For additional writing practice, students should be referred to the Prentice-Hall, Inc. writing texts listed in the back of the book.

Outside the Classroom
There is no need for the students to take precious class time to compose a 250 to 300 word essay. This work should be done at home. Homework should consist of using the Reading Target passages to practice outlining and using the Essay Target exercises to write their essays.

The students should be encouraged to edit their own essays and those of their classmates. This can also be done at home. The teacher should read only one of every four essays a student writes (depending on available class time and teacher preparation time.)

In the Classroom
 1. Explain the format of the Essay section.
 2. Discuss the structure of an essay.

3. Discuss the linear style of essay organization.
4. Explain the organization of a paragraph.
5. Discuss the four rhetorical styles.
6. Develop sentences using the vocabulary of the four styles.
7. Explain how to outline.
8. Outline a reading passage with the class.
9. Discuss the concept of general statements and facts.
10. Locate general and specific statements in the reading passages.
11. Assign Reading Target passages to be outlined every night.
12. Discuss in class the first few outlines done as homework.
13. Assign one essay to be written every two days.
14. Discuss in class the first few essays done as homework.

PRENTICE-HALL TOEFL PREP BOOK

THE TOEFL: WHAT IS IT?

The TOEFL, the Test of English as a Foreign Language, measures the English proficiency of nonnative English speakers. It tests their ability to understand spoken English, recognize correct grammatical constructions, identify synonyms, and comprehend reading passages.

The test is divided into three sections. (On July 11, 1986, a fourth section will be added to the TOEFL. See *Note* below.) Each section is timed. The chart below gives a general outline for the exam. The exact format of the exam may vary; the number of questions and the time given may occasionally differ from test to test. The TOEFL uses several different forms, some of which may include 50 experimental questions. These questions look like the other test questions but will not be counted in your score. The experimental questions and the respective time allotted are in parentheses in the chart.

SECTION		QUESTIONS	MINUTES
Section One **Listening Comprehension**		50	40
Part A: Short Statements	20		
Part B: Short Conversations	15		
Part C: Mini-Talks	15		
Section Two **Structure and Written Expression**		40 (60)	25 (35)
Part A: Choose a correct word or phrase	15		
Part B: Identify an incorrect word or phrase	25		
Section Three **Vocabulary and Reading Comprehension**		60 (90)	45 (65)
Part A: Synonyms	30		
Part B: Reading Comprehension	30		
Section Four **Essay** July 11, 1986 administration and after		1	30
Total		150 (200) + Essay	140 (170)

NOTE:
The TOEFL will have four sections on the July 11, 1986 administration and subsequent administrations. The fourth section will require the examinees to write a 250 to 300 word essay in 30 minutes. There will be no choice of topic.

THE TOEFL: WHO NEEDS IT?
Most American colleges and universities require evidence of a student's English language proficiency for admission. The TOEFL is one of the tests for this purpose. The TOEFL, however, is only one of the criteria for admission. A satisfactory score on the TOEFL does not guarantee admission to a university.

The following chart is only a guide. Admission requirements vary from institution to institution and from year to year.

Admissions Policy	Graduate Humanities	Graduate Sciences	Under-graduate	Technical School or 2-year College
Acceptable	550-600	500-600	500-600	450-600
Acceptable with supplementary language training and reduced course load	500-550	450-500	400-500	400-450
Further English training required	Below 500	Below 450	Below 400	Below 400

THE TOEFL: WHO TAKES IT?

Different language groups score differently on the TOEFL. You should recognize those areas which have statistically proven difficult for others in your language group and then focus on these areas during your preparation.

Language Groups	Listening Comprehension				Structure and Written Expression				Reading Comprehension and Vocabulary			
	45	50	55	60	45	50	55	60	45	50	55	60
Arabic												
Bengali												
Chinese												
Farsi												
French												
German												
Greek												
Hindi												
Ibo												
Indonesian												
Japanese												
Korean												
Malay												
Spanish												
Tagalog												
Thai												
Urdu												
Vietnamese												
Yoruba												

TOEFL INFORMATION

TOEFL BULLETIN

All candidates for the TOEFL will need the *TOEFL Bulletin of Information and Application Form*. This bulletin lists the TOEFL test centers around the world, provides information regarding the cost of the TOEFL, and includes an application form.

To receive a copy of the *Bulletin* outside the U.S.A., contact the Cultural Affairs Officer of the local U.S. Information Service or an AMIDEAST or IIE regional office. You may also write directly to the TOEFL office:

```
TOEFL
Box 899
Princeton, NJ 08541
U.S.A.
```

Letter of Request
The letter you write may be similar to this:

> Dear Sirs:
>
> Please send the latest edition of the <u>TOEFL Bulletin of Information and Application Form</u> to:
>
> > *Print your name*
> > *Print your street address*
> > *Print your city, state/province*
> > *Print your postal code*
> > *Print your country*
>
> Sincerely yours,
>
> *Sign your name*

TEST CENTERS

International, Special Center, and Institutional TOEFL
The International TOEFL and Special Center TOEFL are identical in question format, length, and difficulty. New exams are given on each test date.

Test	Frequency/yr	Countries	Day
International TOEFL	6 times/yr	135	Saturday
Special Center TOEFL	6 times/yr	50	Friday

The Institutional TOEFL is used by local institutions and businesses to measure their own students' language proficiency. The exam is scheduled at the convenience of the testing institution. Old exams are used for the Institutional TOEFL; consequently, the scores are not considered valid by university admission officers.

PRE-TOEFL

The Pre-TOEFL is the Preliminary Test of English as a Foreign Language. It was designed to measure the English proficiency of students at the beginning and intermediate levels of English language study. The Pre-TOEFL measures in the 200-500 TOEFL range.

The Pre-TOEFL includes the same types of questions as the TOEFL. However, the Pre-TOEFL is shorter and the questions are less difficult. There are 95 multiple-choice questions, and the test lasts approximately 70 minutes.

The Pre-TOEFL is part of the Institutional Testing Program and is administered by local institutions and businesses at their convenience.

Students studying for the Pre-TOEFL can still use the **Super TOEFL Book** to become familiar with the format of the Pre-TOEFL and develop test-taking strategies.

REGISTRATION

International and Special Center TOEFL

You should complete the application in the *TOEFL Bulletin of Information and Application Form*. After the Educational Testing Service (ETS) receives your completed application and money, it will process a Confirmation Ticket for you. You will receive this Confirmation Ticket approximately one month before the test date.

Institutional TOEFL and Pre-TOEFL

Registration for giving the Institutional TOEFL and Pre-TOEFL is handled by the particular institutions administering these tests. You should contact them for more information.

SCORES

Current TOEFL Scores

On the day of the exam, you will be asked to list on your answer sheet four institutions, colleges, or universities that you wish to receive your scores. The institutions, colleges, or universities that you designate will receive the scores approximately one month after the test date. You also will receive your score approximately one month after you take the test.

If you listed fewer than four institutions, the remaining score reports will be sent to you. You may send them yourself to other colleges; however, the college may require an official score report received directly from ETS in Princeton.

Previous TOEFL Scores

The TOEFL scores are kept for only two years. If you took the test more than two years ago, you will have to take the TOEFL again to receive a new score.

If you took the test more than once, it is possible to have only your highest score sent to the institution or college. You will have to complete the <u>Request Form for Official Score Reports</u> noting the test date on which you scored higher.

HINTS

Before the Test
-Take a diagnostic test in this book.
-Prepare your Personal Study Plan (PSP).
-Study the Targets indicated on your PSP.
-Read as much English as you can.
-Listen to as much English as you can.
-Relax the day before the exam.

On the Day of the Test

- -Arrive on time.
- -Bring only:
    - a) three or four No. 2 pencils with erasers
    - b) your Confirmation Ticket from ETS
    - c) your passport or photo identification
    - d) a watch.
- -Sit near the record player or tape recorder speakers.
- -Make sure you are comfortable and can hear well.

During the Test

- -Work rapidly but carefully.
- -Read all directions carefully.
- -Read all choices carefully.
- -Leave no question on your answer sheet blank.
- -Guess: if you have no idea which choice is correct, choose A (or your favorite letter). Leave no question unanswered.
- -Keep your mind and eyes on your own test.
- -Check to make sure that you have answered every question.
- -Match the question number with the number on the answer sheet.
- -Do the questions that seem easy to you first.

GUESSING

There is no penalty for guessing. If you don't know an answer, make a guess. If you guess, it is better statistically always to guess using the same letter (always A, always B, always C, or always D -- choose your favorite).

THE ANSWER SHEET

Your answer sheet is divided into columns with numbers followed by letters enclosed in ovals.

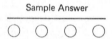

Each number stands for one question. There is only one answer per question. To mark an answer, completely fill in the corresponding oval. A soft lead (No. 2) pencil is best.

The day after Monday is
(A) Wednesday.
(B) Sunday.
(C) Tuesday.
(D) Thursday.

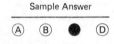

DO NOT mark two answers.
Both will be counted wrong.

DO NOT make any pencil marks elsewhere on the page.

YOU MAY erase, but do it <u>completely</u>.

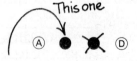

DO NOT draw arrows or make other marks. The test is scored by a machine that is not smart enough to read your messages. If it reads more than one answer per question, it marks the answers wrong.

DIAGNOSTIC TESTS

HOW TO TAKE THE DIAGNOSTIC TESTS

Diagnostic Tests

The diagnostic tests, when used with the Personal Study Plan, will give you an idea of your strengths and weaknesses in English. The results of the diagnostic tests will guide you in studying for the TOEFL. Before you begin to study any of the Target exercises in this book, you should take a diagnostic test. Take the test as if you were taking the real TOEFL. Find a room where you will be undisturbed and allow yourself 3 hours to take the exam.

The answer sheets for the diagnostic tests are found in the back of the book. You should tear it out before you begin. Mark the answers on the answer sheet just as if you were taking the TOEFL.

You will need the tapes that accompany the **Super TOEFL Book** and a tape recorder to do the listening comprehension sections. If you do not have the tapes or a tape recorder, the tapescripts are in the back of the book. You could have a friend read the tapescripts to you.

On July 11, 1986, an essay section will be added to the TOEFL. If you are preparing for a TOEFL on or after July 11, 1986, you should study the Essay Target section in this book.

Personal Study Plan

When you finish a diagnostic test, look at the *Diagnostic Tests Answer Key* at the end of the Diagnostic Test section. The answers are coded according to the type of structure and listening questions being tested. The code refers you to a particular Target Exercise to study. These Target exercises are listed on the *Personal Study Plan: Listening Targets* and the *Personal Study Plan: Structure Targets*. If you missed a question on a diagnostic test, note the corresponding Target on your Personal Study Plan. For example, if the explanatory answer code indicates

   23. (C) - Word Order: Subject-Verb

you should put a circle next to the Structure Target, *Word Order: Subject-Verb*, in the appropriate Diagnostic Test column.

STRUCTURE	1	2	3
Word Order: Subject-verb	O		

You should put a circle next to every Target you missed on the diagnostic test. When you begin to study for the TOEFL, you should first study those targets where you put a circle. This will make your study time more efficient.

After you have finished a particular Target exercise, put an X in the circle and go on to the next Target.

STRUCTURE	1	2	3
Word Order: Subject-Verb	⊗		

In the Personal Study Plan, there are four columns to record the results of four different diagnostic tests. After you study the Target exercises for a period of time, take another diagnostic test to see how much you have improved.

Section I
Listening Comprehension
Time: 40 minutes

Section I measures your ability to understand spoken English. There are three parts to the Listening Comprehension section. Each part has its own question types and its own directions.

Part A

Directions:
In this part of the test, you will hear a short statement which will NOT be repeated. You must pay careful attention to this statement.

In your test booklet, you will see four sentences. One of those written sentences means almost the same as the short statement you hear. You must choose the sentence which most closely matches the meaning of the oral statement. You must then mark your answer on the answer sheet.

Listen to an example.
You will hear:

In your test book, you will see:
(A) He will not eat beets.
(B) The candidate did not bet.
(C) They thought the dates sweet.
(D) His rival cannot beat him.

Sample Answer
Ⓐ Ⓑ Ⓒ ●

The correct answer is (D). "His rival cannot beat him" most closely matches the statement "The candidate will not be beat." The letter (D) should be blackened on your answer sheet.

Listen to another example.
You will hear:

In your text book, you will see:
(A) She is careless in her work.
(B) She always goes free on trains.
(C) She never has tension headaches.
(D) She never shops at sales.

Sample Answer
● Ⓑ Ⓒ Ⓓ

The correct answer is (A). "She is careless in her work" most closely matches the statement "She never pays attention to the details." The letter (A) should be blackened on your answer sheet.

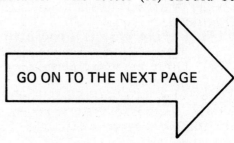
GO ON TO THE NEXT PAGE

1. (A) My son studies the sun.
   (B) My daughter has an excellent education.
   (C) My son has trouble with addition.
   (D) My daughter is not good to my son.

2. (A) Our flight leaves at 8:20.
   (B) Our flight leaves on the 20th at 8 o'clock.
   (C) Our flight leaves at 8:18 in the evening.
   (D) Our flight 818 departs on the 18th.

3. (A) George doesn't remember what I told him.
   (B) George told me he couldn't leave the house.
   (C) I gave George permission to leave.
   (D) I forget if I told George he couldn't leave.

4. (A) The flooded plain ruined the food crop.
   (B) Rice requires a lot of rain.
   (C) The drought raised the cost of food.
   (D) Eating on the train is expensive.

5. (A) The orchestra needed additional funds.
   (B) The project needs more money to continue.
   (C) The band of robbers raced further ahead.
   (D) For all his effort, he still failed.

6. (A) Twelve boys skipped history class.
   (B) Three boys had permission to miss class.
   (C) Four boys had to attend history class.
   (D) There were only two boys in the history class.

7. (A) Trainees must not overlook the fine points of the task.
   (B) The critics did not listen carefully.
   (C) The trainees were paid a great deal.
   (D) The end of the train stops by the sign.

8. (A) The guard returned the briefcase to the teacher.
   (B) The teacher gave her briefcase to the principal to keep.
   (C) The principal found the guard's suitcase.
   (D) The guard found the teacher's briefcase.

9. (A) Fewer book publishers attended last year.
   (B) Major publishers always display their books.
   (C) The fair was boycotted by all publishers.
   (D) More books were brought by fewer publishers.

10. (A) The police car crashed.
    (B) The police got to the car first.
    (C) I called for help after seeing the police.
    (D) The police raced me to the car.

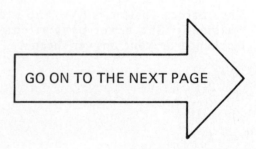

GO ON TO THE NEXT PAGE

11. (A) Bill gulped his drink.
    (B) Bill didn't enjoy his drink.
    (C) Bill enjoys his food a great deal.
    (D) Bill savored the taste of his drink.

12. (A) There were originally 14 in our crowd.
    (B) The original group had 12 members.
    (C) Six of us went to the movies.
    (D) Nine people went home before the movie.

13. (A) Labels were passed around to the participants.
    (B) They were eating and feeling jovial.
    (C) The group met around the table.
    (D) The round table had a few empty seats.

14. (A) The payments are $49.40 each month.
    (B) Payments for four months are due.
    (C) The payment is due on the 14th of the month.
    (D) The first payment is due on the 4th.

15. (A) He would change his mind.
    (B) He did not believe we would change our minds.
    (C) We changed his mind.
    (D) We thought that he would change his mind.

16. (A) The boy shattered the window.
    (B) The boy threw the ball through the window.
    (C) The boy didn't catch the ball.
    (D) The boy missed hitting the window.

17. (A) My brother visits us each summer.
    (B) My father and brother fixed the canoe.
    (C) My mother and father visited me last summer.
    (D) I saw my uncle last year.

18. (A) We plan to eat at a restaurant.
    (B) It rained so we ate inside.
    (C) The picnic will go on regardless of the weather.
    (D) We have alternate plans if it rains.

19. (A) The conductor waved from the train.
    (B) The conductor ran to the train and gave the signal.
    (C) The conductor signaled before he boarded.
    (D) The conductor remained on the platform.

20. (A) Education and defense budgets are greater than the health budget.
    (B) More money is spent on health than education.
    (C) The health budget is equal to the defense budget.
    (D) The most money is spent on education.

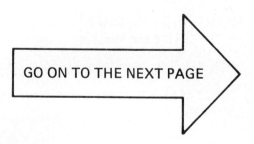
GO ON TO THE NEXT PAGE

Part B

Directions:

In this part there will be 15 short dialogues between two speakers. A third person will ask a question about the dialogue. This question will not be repeated.

Listen carefully to the dialogue and the question and then choose an answer from one of the four possible answers given in the test booklet. Mark the corresponding letter on your answer sheet.

Listen to an example.
You will hear this dialogue:

Sample Answer

Ⓐ ● Ⓒ Ⓓ

In your test booklet you will see:
(A) Finish the program, then study.
(B) Study rather than watch the program.
(C) See the show he saw last week.
(D) Watch the program while studying.

Listening to the dialogue, we learned that the man is going to study and not watch the TV program. Therefore, (B) is the most appropriate answer. The letter (B) should be blackened on your answer sheet.

21. (A) Buy a new light
    (B) Get new shoes
    (C) Eat a pear
    (D) Paint her walls blue

22. (A) 16
    (B) 15
    (C) 32
    (D) 33

23. (A) 16
    (B) 60
    (C) 6
    (D) 66

24. (A) Write the letter
    (B) Paint the shelves

    (C) Fix a shelf
    (D) Search for the pen

25. (A) She imagined the hotel exactly.
    (B) She agreed with the man.
    (C) She's been in worse hotels.
    (D) She had other expectations.

26. (A) Four
    (B) Two
    (C) Five
    (D) Six

27. (A) Traffic on the bridge
    (B) Ice on the bridge
    (C) Ice on the ridge
    (D) Slow pace

GO ON TO THE NEXT PAGE

28. (A) He goes to college.
    (B) He works for his father.
    (C) He takes another test.
    (D) He chooses another school.

29. (A) They are pests.
    (B) They are cute.
    (C) They are for children.
    (D) They are pets.

30. (A) The man's trip is shorter.
    (B) The man leaves after the woman.
    (C) The woman leaves tonight.
    (D) The woman's trip is shorter.

31. (A) The woman has a dog.
    (B) He sees a doghouse.
    (C) He might not have a place to stay.
    (D) The dog won't stay home.

32. (A) $1 million
    (B) $1/2 million
    (C) $1/4 million
    (D) $2 million

33. (A) In 11 minutes
    (B) In 15 minutes
    (C) In 50 minutes
    (D) In 5 minutes

34. (A) The woman likes the man's looks.
    (B) The man wants to be pitied.
    (C) The man rarely reads his books.
    (D) The man collects looms.

35. (A) They both will go back.
    (B) The man will not return.
    (C) The man promises to go back.
    (D) The man won't try to avoid the place.

Part C

Directions:
In Part C, you will hear several short talks on a variety of subjects. Each talk will be followed by several questions. Neither the talks nor the questions will be repeated. You will have to pay close attention to both.

After you hear the question, you will have to pick the most appropriate answer from the four choices in the test booklet. You will then mark the corresponding letter on your answer sheet.

Listen to the example.
You will hear:

Sample Answer
● Ⓑ Ⓒ Ⓓ

Here is the first question:

In your test booklet, you will see:
(A) Neptune
(B) Mars
(C) Venus
(D) Mercury

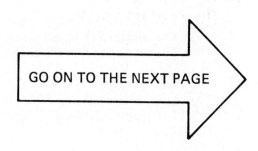
GO ON TO THE NEXT PAGE

The correct answer to the question "Which planet is fifth from the earth?" is (A) Neptune. You should blacken (A) on your answer sheet.

Here is the second question:

In your test booklet, you will see:
(A) Mars
(B) Venus
(C) Pluto
(D) Mercury

Sample Answer

Ⓐ Ⓑ Ⓒ ●

The correct answer to the question "Which planet resembles our moon?" is (D) Mercury. You should blacken (D) on your answer sheet.

36. (A) Large
    (B) Black
    (C) Male
    (D) Small

37. (A) In the zoo
    (B) At the office
    (C) In the park
    (D) On a bus

38. (A) The man threw soot at her.
    (B) She was chasing something.
    (C) She heard a loud noise.
    (D) The woman called to her.

39. (A) That he hold the leash firmly
    (B) That they look for the dog
    (C) That he change the dog's name
    (D) That he stay out of the park

40. (A) Small
    (B) Color
    (C) A name
    (D) Size

41. (A) The audience wants refunds.
    (B) The actors are sick.
    (C) The electricity won't work.
    (D) The stage crew is on strike.

42. (A) This evening
    (B) Next Tuesday
    (C) Tomorrow morning
    (D) Next week

43. (A) The stage electricians
    (B) The audience
    (C) The actors
    (D) The box office staff

44. (A) Washington
    (B) New York
    (C) San Francisco
    (D) Tokyo

45. (A) U.N. delegates
    (B) Earthquakes in the United States
    (C) A committee to study earthquakes
    (D) Experts on earthquakes

46. (A) Building methods
    (B) Government committees
    (C) The status of scientists
    (D) International experts

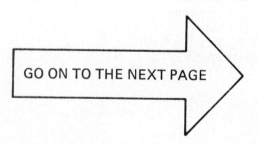

GO ON TO THE NEXT PAGE

1	1	1	1	1	1	1	1

47. (A) Noncommercial
    (B) Substandard
    (C) Efficient
    (D) Uniform

48. (A) King Charles II
    (B) The Germans
    (C) Charles I
    (D) Cromwell

49. (A) He retired.
    (B) He was killed.
    (C) He went into exile.
    (D) He gave up his title.

50. (A) German
    (B) English
    (C) Scottish
    (D) French

THIS IS THE END OF THE LISTENING COMPREHENSION SECTION.
LOOK AT THE TIME NOW BEFORE YOU BEGIN WORK ON SECTION II.
YOU WILL HAVE EXACTLY 25 MINUTES TO WORK ON SECTION II.

Section II
Structure and Written Expression
Time: 25 minutes

Section II measures your ability to recognize standard written English. There are two parts to this section. Each part has a different type of question and a different set of directions.

Directions for Questions 1-15:
You will see a sentence with a portion missing. Following the sentence will be four words or phrases. One of those words or phrases will best complete the sentence. Mark your choice on your answer sheet.

Look at this example:
The new instructor came _____ if the apartment was still available.

(A) seeing
(B) for to see
(C) to see
(D) and saw

Sample Answer

Ⓐ Ⓑ ● Ⓓ

The most appropriate standard English expression would be "The new instructor came <u>to see</u> if the apartment was still available." You should mark (C) on your answer sheet.

Look at the second example:
John and _____ are old friends.

Sample Answer

Ⓐ ● Ⓒ Ⓓ

(A) me
(B) I
(C) mine
(D) my

The most appropriate standard English expression would be "John and <u>I</u> are old friends." You should mark (B) on your answer sheet.

When you have read and understood the directions, answer questions 1-15.

1. The organizers of the convention have arranged accommodations for those participants _____ from out of town.

   (A) who comes
   (B) which will come
   (C) are coming
   (D) coming

GO ON TO THE NEXT PAGE

2. The farmers recruited to work in the paper mill complained that they were not accustomed _____ a timecard.

(A) to punching
(B) to punch
(C) by punching
(D) having punched

3. The playground supervisor reprimanded _____ for our shouting.

(A) ourselves
(B) us
(C) ours
(D) we

4. _____ the lawyer's opinion, the case should not go to trial.

(A) By
(B) On
(C) In
(D) With

5. The job applicant was worried about the interview _____ he was well prepared.

(A) because
(B) if
(C) unless
(D) even though

6. _____ the predicament and solving it are two different problems.

(A) Identification
(B) Identifying
(C) It is identifying
(D) To identify

7. The human rights activist considered it _____ honor to be nominated for the award.

(A) an
(B) a
(C) the
(D) this

8. The spectators breathed a sigh of relief when _____.

(A) the whistle has blown
(B) the referee blows the whistle
(C) they heard the final whistle
(D) the whistle blows

9. Although the members of the faculty seem inflexible, _____ to suggestions.

(A) they are always open
(B) always they are open
(C) open they are always
(D) they are open always

10. _____ rain now, the farmers will have to postpone the harvest.
(A) It should
(B) Will it
(C) Should it
(D) When it will

11. Some consider Las Vegas _____ city in the world to live in.

(A) the bad
(B) worse
(C) worst
(D) the worst

GO ON TO THE NEXT PAGE

2	2	2	2	2	2	2	2

12. The phonograph next door was so loud that we could _____ hear the television in our own room.

   (A) hard
   (B) harder
   (C) hardly
   (D) hardy

13. The parent scolded the child and made her promise _____ again.

   (A) never to do that
   (B) what to do never
   (C) that never to do that
   (D) so never to do that

14. The motivation of the workers _____ not a monetary reward, but the satisfaction of a job well done.

   (A) was
   (B) were
   (C) should be
   (D) could be

15. Highly motivated, ambitious people often _____ more hours in a day.

   (A) needing
   (B) need
   (C) needed
   (D) are needing

Directions for Questions 16-40

In this section you will be given a sentence with four words or phrases underlined. One of the underlined words or phrases is not standard English. You must choose the incorrect portion and blacken the corresponding letter on your answer sheet.

Look at this example:

    <u>Being organized</u> is one of <u>the</u> most important <u>aspect</u> of being a good <u>worker</u>.
       A   B   C   D

Sample Answer

(A) (B) ● (D)

The underlined word "aspect," letter (C), is not standard written English. You should blacken (C) on your answer sheet.

After you have read and understood the directions, begin questions 16-40.

16. The use <u>of videodisc</u> in the classroom, a <u>potentially powerful educational</u> tool,
             A   B

   <u>it will not</u> be widespread until <u>prices come down.</u>
     C   D

17. Recent <u>studies done by</u> the Department of Labor <u>have shown</u> that
            A   B

   <u>nonsmoking are</u> more productive than those who <u>smoke.</u>
     C   D

GO ON TO THE NEXT PAGE

18. The <u>new, more stringent</u> requirements <u>for obtaining</u> a driving license
            A   B

    <u>has resulted</u> in <u>a decrease</u> in traffic accidents.
        C   D

19. <u>We all</u> thought the office <u>manager had</u> gone <u>too far</u>, but his staff
    A   B   C

    <u>did supported him</u>.
        D

20. <u>Hearing</u> the <u>fire alarm sound</u>, the librarian requested <u>those reading</u> to leave
    A   B   C

    their books <u>headed for the nearest exit</u>.
                D

21. The scientific experiments <u>conducted</u> by the class <u>was</u> placed on <u>the</u>
                         A   B   C

    center table <u>for</u> the judges to evaluate.
           D

22. Ms. Amelia Earhart, <u>like</u> many of the world's <u>greatest heroes</u>, sacrificed
                        A   B

    <u>their</u> life for the sake <u>of adventure</u>, glory, and country.
    C   D

23. The anthropologists reviewed <u>its</u> findings and discovered that <u>a fossil</u>
                            A   B

    previously <u>thought to date</u> from the Mesozoic period <u>was</u> a current forgery.
                C   D

24. The organizers of the picnic thought <u>they</u> had put <u>enough</u> food <u>on</u> the
                                 A   B   C

    basket, but there obviously was not enough <u>for</u> six hungry people.
                                       D

25. <u>The general's</u> political judgment <u>or his ability</u> to analyze
    A   B

    <u>a situation accurately</u> were both <u>as remarkable as</u> his military skill.
         C   D

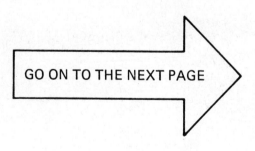
GO ON TO THE NEXT PAGE

26. Welcoming the astronaut <u>to the community</u> <u>and prepare</u> a big banquet <u>were</u>
                               A   B   C

    important responsibilities for the <u>newly formed</u> citizens group.
                                         D

27. The <u>freezing point and boiling</u> point of water <u>are standard</u> reference
                     A   B

    <u>points used</u> in <u>calibrating thermometer.</u>
     C   D

28. Sacajawea, <u>the woman Indian</u> <u>who accompanied</u> Lewis and Clark
                     A   B

    <u>on their journey,</u> has been the inspiration for <u>countless romantic</u> legends.
       C   D

29. <u>Ceramic materials</u> ,taken directly from the earth's crust <u>have used</u> <u>as building</u>
        A   B   C

    materials since <u>time immemorial.</u>
                   D

30. People who follow <u>the</u> pseudoscience astrology, <u>a false science,</u> <u>believe that</u>
                       A   B   C

    stars <u>govern</u> the fate of men.
         D

31. The force of <u>gravity becomes</u> <u>least</u> as one goes <u>farther from</u> the center
                  A   B   C

    <u>of the earth.</u>
       D

32. <u>Using</u> herbal medicines, <u>treat doctors</u> more <u>illness</u> for <u>less cost.</u>
    A   B   C   D

33. Elizabeth Charlotte <u>provisions</u> through her bawdy <u>outspoken</u> letters
                       A   B

    <u>an unparalleled</u> <u>contemporary</u> view of the court of Louis XIV.
       C   D

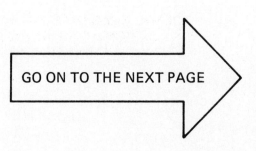

GO ON TO THE NEXT PAGE

34. <u>Child labor</u> laws <u>were instituted</u> to protect the <u>neglected long rights</u>
      A   B   C

    of <u>children</u>.
       D

35. <u>If</u> excess air <u>was pumped</u> into <u>an elastic</u> cylinder, <u>the cylinder</u> will explode.
    A   B   C   D

36. English, <u>is spoken</u> by <u>slightly more than</u> 8 percent of <u>the earth's population</u>,
              A   B   C

    is <u>the most common</u> language after Chinese.
       D

37. Many people, <u>physicians included,</u> <u>fail to appreciate</u> that <u>can bee stings</u>
                 A   B   C

    have <u>fatal results</u> in minutes.
         D

38. Today's <u>playing cards</u> <u>who are modeled</u> after 18th century English design, trace
            A   B

    <u>their roots</u> to <u>Turkey.</u>
    C   D

39. The brain's left <u>hemisphere controls</u> <u>logic and language</u>, while the
                     A   B

    <u>right controlling</u> intuitive talents and musical <u>ability</u>.
    C   D

40. <u>Upon immigrants</u> arriving in America <u>at the turn</u> of the century, <u>most</u>
    A   B   C

    immigrants <u>passed through</u> Ellis Island.
               D

DO NOT WORK ON ANY OTHER SECTION OF THE TEST

**IF YOU FINISH IN LESS THAN 25 MINUTES, GO OVER YOUR ANSWERS ON
SECTION II ONLY. AT THE END OF 25 MINUTES, GO TO SECTION III.
YOU WILL HAVE 45 MINUTES TO WORK ON SECTION III.**

Section III
Reading Comprehension and Vocabulary
Time: 45 minutes

In this section of the test, there are two types of questions. Each question type has its own directions.

Directions for Questions 1-30:
In each sentence a word or phrase has been underlined. There are four other words or phrases below each sentence. You must select the one word or phrase which most closely matches the meaning of the underlined word.

Example:
She always wore dresses made of <u>synthetic</u> cloth.

(A) artificial
(B) expensive
(C) fashionable
(D) new

Sample Answer

(A) is the correct answer. "She always wore dresses of artificial cloth" most closely matches the meaning of the original sentence. The letter (A) should be blackened on your answer sheet.

When you fully understand the directions, answer the following questions.

1. If one has an open mind, it is not difficult to <u>appreciate</u> another's point of view.

   (A) respect
   (B) agree with
   (C) contradict
   (D) understand

2. There are some people who <u>advocate</u> relaxation over work.

   (A) insist on
   (B) recommend
   (C) appreciate
   (D) deplore

3. An employer must verify that the applicants have the proper <u>qualifications</u>.

   (A) credentials
   (B) measurements
   (C) forms
   (D) attire

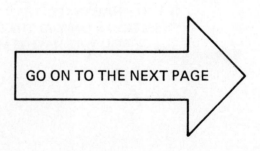

GO ON TO THE NEXT PAGE

4. Allowing books to be sold at the exhibition would <u>set a precedent</u> for future conventions.

   (A) start a fad
   (B) establish a pattern
   (C) upset the applecart
   (D) be a first

5. The lawyers obliged the newspaper to <u>retract</u> their allegations.

   (A) withdraw
   (B) deny
   (C) apologize for
   (D) correct

6. It is often difficult to <u>reveal</u> one's true feelings to others.

   (A) divulge
   (B) explain
   (C) discover
   (D) recognize

7. Since the beginning of time, there have been people who <u>predict</u> that the end of the world is near.

   (A) are sure that
   (B) agree
   (C) forecast
   (D) are afraid

8. The size of our staff was <u>reduced</u> to reflect the change in the budget.

   (A) implemented
   (B) augmented
   (C) decreased
   (D) reevaluated

9. Some people can eat large <u>quantities</u> of food, yet never gain any weight.

   (A) varieties
   (B) plates
   (C) items
   (D) amounts

10. The building is so well <u>constructed</u> that it will survive even the strongest earthquake.

    (A) guaranteed
    (B) built
    (C) located
    (D) insured

11. Jane looked at <u>an assortment of</u> necklaces before choosing one with green beads.

    (A) inexpensive
    (B) a few pieces of
    (C) multicolored
    (D) a variety of

12. The caterers must know <u>approximately</u> how many people are expected.

    (A) nearly
    (B) essentially
    (C) confidentially
    (D) truthfully

13. The chart showed the amount of money spent on food compared with the amount spent on <u>recreation</u>.

    (A) necessities
    (B) education
    (C) incidentals
    (D) amusement

14. The woman, who sponsored the civic art show, has not been seen <u>recently</u>.

    (A) anywhere
    (B) inside
    (C) lately
    (D) outside

GO ON TO THE NEXT PAGE

15. The man's brother <u>accompanied</u> him to the corner and then went in a different direction.

    (A) went with
    (B) sent
    (C) followed
    (D) helped

16. When I heard the alarm, I was <u>prepared</u> to run!

    (A) anxious
    (B) going
    (C) afraid
    (D) ready

17. History is best learned from <u>contemporary</u> sources.

    (A) ancient
    (B) concurrent
    (C) modern
    (D) several

18. This flag <u>symbolizes</u> what is important to our country.

    (A) summarizes
    (B) reveals
    (C) contains
    (D) represents

19. It is advisable to have <u>an alternative</u> plan.

    (A) a substitute
    (B) a better
    (C) an easier
    (D) an equal

20. One is not always able to choose one's <u>associates</u>.

    (A) colleagues
    (B) neighbors
    (C) superiors
    (D) students

21. Reports of the <u>discovery</u> were telegraphed to the waiting nation.

    (A) election
    (B) find
    (C) district
    (D) dance

22. **The film rights were <u>negotiated</u> by the author's lawyers.**

    (A) rejected
    (B) suggested
    (C) demanded
    (D) arranged

23. The results of experiments on the intelligence of monkeys have not been <u>conclusive</u>.

    (A) understood
    (B) final
    (C) valid
    (D) predicted

24. A recent <u>census</u> of home buying patterns shows that many people under 30 are still renting.

    (A) survey
    (B) group
    (C) number
    (D) newspaper

25. The use of the microcomputer is as <u>pedestrian</u> as the use of the telephone.

    (A) unusual
    (B) newsworthy
    (C) common
    (D) public

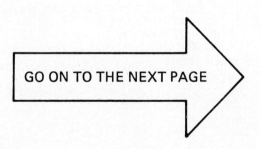
GO ON TO THE NEXT PAGE

26. The price of gold <u>fluctuated</u> and then plummeted on the world market last quarter.

    (A) varied
    (B) rose
    (C) stabilized
    (D) decreased

27. Congressional debate over the passage of this <u>controversial</u> bill was inevitable.

    (A) popular
    (B) personal
    (C) disputatious
    (D) biased

28. The picture illustrates the <u>compassion</u> the artist has for his native land.

(A) feeling
(B) distrust
(C) revulsion
(D) knowledge

29. The drought caused escalation of prices and <u>depletion</u> of supplies.

    (A) craving
    (B) exhaustion
    (C) hoarding
    (D) maintenance

30. The worker's <u>aggressive</u> personality kept him from having many friends.

    (A) assertive
    (B) depressed
    (C) unstable
    (D) insecure

Directions for Questions 31-56:
In this section, you will read passages on a variety of subjects and then answer several questions about the passages. Some of the answers will come directly from the passages; others may only be implied. Select the most appropriate answer and blacken the answer on your answer sheet.

Look at this example:

> According to scientists, 70 percent of the earth's surface is covered by water, and this watery wilderness is the habitat of four of every five living things. To aid oceanographers in their explorations of the seas and oceans of the world, scientists have been designing more and better types of undersea vessels to accomplish this task with greater safety and with more efficient tools and techniques.

Answer the first question:
1. What percentage of the earth's surface is covered by water?

    (A) 30 percent
    (B) 70 percent
    (C) 100 percent
    (D) 50 percent

The correct answer is (B) 70 percent.

Sample Answer

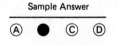

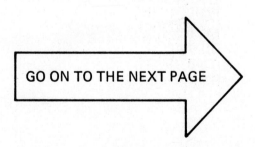

GO ON TO THE NEXT PAGE

3	3	3	3	3	3	3	3

Answer the second question:

2. What percentage of the earth's inhabitants live on land?

(A) 10 percent
(B) 20 percent
(C) 40 percent
(D) 50 percent

Sample Answer

The correct answer is (B) 20 percent. If four out of every five living things live in water, one of every five things, or 20 percent, must live on land.

After you have read and understood the examples, you may start to read.

Questions 31-35

EMERGENCY NUMBERS
Clarendon University

Accidents (on University Property)	6111
Ambulance or Rescue Squad	611 or 9911
Fire	9 - 911
University Hospital	0
Campus Security	6111
From phones not on the University telephone system	676-6111
Calls other than emergency	6110
To report a theft of University property	6110
Metropolitan Police	9 - 911

31. A student who burned his hands in the chemistry laboratory at the university should dial

(A) 9-9111
(B) 6111
(C) 6110
(D) 676-6111

32. A university student calling the campus police from his home should dial

(A) 0
(B) 9-911
(C) 6110
(D) 676-6111

33. A faculty member who wanted to report an arson incident in progress should dial

(A) 9-911
(B) 0
(C) 6110
(D) 6111

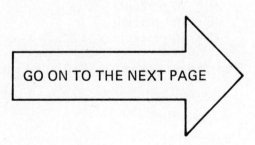

GO ON TO THE NEXT PAGE

34. A student who wanted to contact a friend recovering from surgery should dial

    (A) 9-911
    (B) 6111
    (C) 0
    (D) 6110

35. A professor returned to his office and found that the door lock had been broken and university equipment was missing. He should call

    (A) 0
    (B) 6110
    (C) 9-911
    (D) 6111

Questions 36-39

TAPE HEAD CLEANER/DEMAGNETIZER INSTRUCTIONS for the Thriftex BCD Cassette

This special cleaning/demagnetizing cassette was designed to prolong the life and promote the fidelity of your sound equipment. The cassette should be used after every ten hours of equipment operation to achieve maximum performance of your system. Before inserting the cassette, lower the volume. Rewind the tape completely and then press play. Play the tape until it stops. DO NOT REWIND AGAIN. Remove the cassette and store it in the provided case.

36. The head cleaner/demagnetizer should be used

    (A) after each tape play.
    (B) every time tape is rewound.
    (C) after a 10 hour period of use.
    (D) when the head is dirty.

37. The tape should be rewound

    (A) twice.
    (B) after cleaning.
    (C) before cleaning.
    (D) not at all.

38. Before rewinding the tape, you should

    (A) insert the cassette.
    (B) play the tape to the end.
    (C) use it for 10 hours.
    (D) demagnetize the tape.

39. Using the head cleaner will

    (A) weaken the cassettes.
    (B) improve the sound quality.
    (C) demagnetize the tape.
    (D) increase the volume.

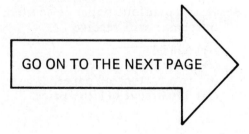

GO ON TO THE NEXT PAGE

Questions 40-43

SEND NO MONEY
TWILL CORPORATION SALE
Best Buys
Office and Microcomputer Products

Yes, I want to take advantage of TWILL's SPECIAL SALE. Please send me:

Quantity		Description	Price
_____	pks	SS/DD 50-disk Bulk-pack	$94.50/pack
_____	bxs	3M SS/DD 10-disk box	$21.90/box
_____	cts	Econo-pack printout paper	$28.94/ctn
_____	ea	Brown Steno Chair	$49.88/each
_____	ea	Black Steno Chair	$49.88/each

I may return the merchandise within 30 days and receive a full credit or refund if I am not 100% satisfied.

40. The advertisement is aimed at

   (A) the home consumer.
   (B) a student.
   (C) a business person.
   (D) an artist.

41. The total cost for 40 disks is

   (A) $21.90.
   (B) $87.60.
   (C) $94.50.
   (D) $18.90.

42. The chair will most likely be used

   (A) in front of a computer.
   (B) in a school classroom.
   (C) in a dining room.
   (D) in a mobile home.

43. If the printout paper is spotted, the purchaser will receive

   (A) $28.94.
   (B) some disks instead.
   (C) two cartons of paper.
   (D) 30 percent off the price.

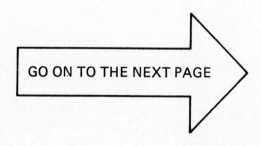
GO ON TO THE NEXT PAGE

Questions 44-47

Before the American Revolution, British policy as well as American preferences caused manufacturing workshops to remain in Europe while the colonists engaged chiefly in agriculture and commerce. The Revolution, however, drastically altered the realities of international trade. American foreign commerce suffered from the dissolution of ties with British firms, from the destruction of traditional lines of credit, and from the competition with and sometimes harassment by the businesses and government of Britain. Moreover, the Revolution stimulated the expansion of household manufacturing. The American Constitution, the policies of Alexander Hamilton, and most especially the Napoleonic Wars and the development of an interdependent relationship between the cotton and iron industries, contributed to the inception of what would become the industrial revolution in the United States and the origin of a distinctive "American system of manufacturing." Manufacturing replaced foreign trade as America's major business enterprise in the first half of the 19th century, adding a bold new dimension to the economic order and altering popular attitudes toward business enterprise.

44. The main idea of this passage concerns

  (A) British policy prior to the American Revolution.
  (B) the effects of the American Revolution.
  (C) the relationship between foreign trade and American business.
  (D) the realities of international trade.

45. Which of the following was not a factor in the industrial revolution?

  (A) The policies of Alexander Hamilton
  (B) The relationship between the cotton and iron industries
  (C) The American Constitution
  (D) The expansion of cottage industries

46. According to the passage, international commerce was affected most seriously by

  (A) the Napoleonic Wars.
  (B) the American Revolution.
  (C) the cotton and iron industries.
  (D) European manufacturers.

47. The initial effects of the Revolution

  (A) were useful to the colonists.
  (B) were troublesome to the colonists.
  (C) destroyed British firms.
  (D) caused the workshops to remain in Europe.

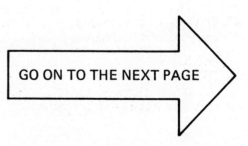
GO ON TO THE NEXT PAGE

Questions 48-52

When scientists are trying to understand a particular set of phenomena, they often make use of a "model." A model, in the scientists' sense, is a kind of analogy or mental image of the phenomena in terms of something we are familiar with. One example is the wave model of light. We cannot see light as if it were made up of waves because experiments on light indicate that it behaves in many respects as water waves do.

The purpose of a model is to give us a mental or visual picture -- something to hold onto -- when we cannot see what is actually happening. Models often give us a deeper understanding: the analogy to a known system (for instance, water waves in the above example) can suggest new experiments to perform and can provide ideas about what other related phenomena might occur.

48. The author is concerned with an explanation of the term

(A) wave.
(B) model.
(C) analogy.
(D) all of the above.

49. Another example of a scientific model would be

(A) a map.
(B) a paper airplane.
(C) an atom.
(D) a light bulb.

50. Why are models necessary?

(A) They connect invisible phenomena to those we are familiar with.
(B) Scientists could not experiment without them.
(C) They give the scientist a sense of security.
(D) They provide deeper insight into the workings of the human mind.

51. Models provide us with deeper understanding because

(A) they make us think about our universe.
(B) they were used to represent some other phenomenon.
(C) they are more precise than theories.
(D) they indicate further directions and help us make predictions.

52. An analogy is

(A) the study of the universe.
(B) a comparison.
(C) the study of light waves.
(D) the result of scientific investigation.

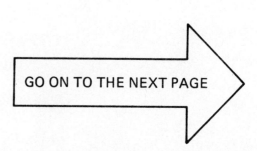

GO ON TO THE NEXT PAGE

Question 53-56

The blues is the root and foundation upon which all jazz has developed. Indeed, without the blues there would be no jazz as we know it today. Every style of jazz, even the avant-garde, has been found to have a heritage in the blues.

Work songs were structurally simple two-harmony songs that were sung by a leader and responded to by other workers. Another kind of song, the "country blues," was developed at the same time, however. The first blues songs were sung by itinerant male singers in the South and Southwest who went to bars and social gatherings singing songs full of earthy lyrics in exchange for liquor. Early blues singers drank, danced, and mingled freely with the patrons and guests, and their music was informal, unrestrained, and often improvised (composed on the spot). The themes of these songs concerned the basic human problems of sex and love, poverty and death.

53. Which of the following statements is true?

(A) Without jazz, the blues would not exist.
(B) The blues grew out of jazz.
(C) The blues underlies all forms of jazz.
(D) The blues and jazz are avant-garde musical forms.

54. Early country blues can best be characterized as

(A) itinerant.
(B) amusing.
(C) depressing.
(D) not rigid.

55. Which of the following would be the most appropriate topic for a country blues song?

(A) the birth of a child
(B) the death of one's lover
(C) the wedding of a relative
(D) the theft of one's guitar

56. The singers of the first blues songs

(A) stayed in one place.
(B) sang for alcohol.
(C) were immortal.
(D) were urban sophisticates.

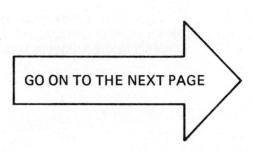

GO ON TO THE NEXT PAGE

Directions for Questions 57-60:
In this section, you must select the statement that most nearly matches the original statement. Many of the statements are true, but only one is a restatement of the original.

57. The best way to learn a foreign language is to study daily and never miss an opportunity to speak to native speakers.

   (A) Foreign language learning requires studying and speaking with native speakers.

   (B) The foreign language learner should study every day and capitalize on every chance to converse with native speakers.

   (C) Daily study with native speakers insures success in foreign language learning.

   (D) Do you want to learn a foreign language? Then study every day and talk to native speakers.

58. Everybody involved was convinced to take the early flight to Chicago.

   (A) Everybody took the early flight to Chicago.

   (B) Nobody decided to go to Chicago at night.

   (C) After some discussion, all of the involved parties decided to take the early flight to Chicago.

   (D) The flight to Chicago was what everyone wanted to take.

59. The reason some athletes live longer than others is that their conditioning program is more intensive.

   (A) If an athlete conditions himself intensively, he will live longer than other athletes.

   (B) The best athletes use intensive conditioning to prolong their lives.

   (C) Some athletes have longer careers than other athletes because they engage in intensive training programs.

   (D) Athletes who do not condition themselves properly run the risk of curtailing their careers.

60. He who laughs last, laughs best.

   (A) The best laugh is the last laugh.
   (B) It is better to laugh last.
   (C) The best laugher laughs last.
   (D) Laughing last is good.

DO NOT WORK ON ANY OTHER SECTION OF THE TEST

IF YOU FINISH IN LESS THAN 45 MINUTES, GO OVER YOUR ANSWERS ON SECTION III ONLY. AT THE END OF 45 MINUTES, STOP WORK AND CORRECT YOUR ANSWERS WITH THE ANSWER KEY WHICH FOLLOWS.

CODED ANSWER KEY DIAGNOSTIC TEST 1

Section I: Listening Comprehension

Part A - Statements

1. (C) - minimal pair
2. (D) - number discrimination
3. (D) - conditional
4. (C) - cause/effect
5. (B) - conditional
6. (C) - computation
7. (A) - synonym
8. (D) - contextual reference
9. (D) - contextual reference
10. (B) - chronological order
11. (D) - synonym
12. (A) - computation
13. (C) - minimal pair
14. (D) - number discrimination
15. (D) - negation
16. (C) - cause/effect
17. (D) - contextual reference
18. (D) - conditional
19. (C) - chronological order
20. (B) - comparison

Part B - Conversations

21. (B) - minimal pair
22. (A) - computation
23. (B) - number discrimination
24. (C) - chronological order
25. (D) - negation
26. (A) - computation
27. (B) - cause/effect
28. (A) - conditional
29. (A) - minimal pair
30. (D) - comparison
31. (C) - contextual reference
32. (B) - computation
33. (B) - number discrimination
34. (C) - minimal pair
35. (B) - negation

Part C - Mini Talks

36. (D)	41. (C)	46. (A)
37. (C)	42. (C)	47. (D)
38. (B)	43. (B)	48. (D)
39. (A)	44. (B)	49. (B)
40. (B)	45. (C)	50. (B)

Section II: Structure and Written Expression

Part A

1. (D) - subordinate clause: reduced adjective
2. (A) - verb: tense
3. (B) - pronoun: form
4. (C) - preposition
5. (D) - conjunction: form
6. (B) - conjunction: parallel structure
7. (A) - article
8. (C) - verb: tense
9. (A) - word order: adverb placement
10. (C) - word order: subject-verb
11. (D) - comparison
12. (C) - word family
13. (A) - subordinate clause: noun
14. (A) - verb: agreement
15. (B) - verb: tense

Part B

16. (C) - subject: repetition *use = it*
17. (C) - subject: omission *nonsmoking employees*
18. (C) - subject: agreement *requirements have*
19. (D) - verb: unnecessary form *staff supported*
20. (D) - conjunction: parallel structure *to leave their books and head*
21. (B) - verb: agreement *were placed*
22. (C) - pronoun: agreement *her life*
23. (A) - pronoun: agreement *anthropologists reviewed their findings*
24. (C) - preposition *found in the basket*
25. (B) - conjunction: form *judgment and ability both*
26. (B) - conjunction: parallel structure *Welcoming and preparing*
27. (D) - article *a thermometer (or the)*
28. (A) - word order: adjective *the Indian woman*
29. (B) - active-passive *have been used*
30. (B) - redundancy *omit*
31. (B) - comparison *less*
32. (B) - word order: subject/verb *doctors treat*
33. (A) - word family *provides*
34. (C) - word order: adjective/adverb *long neglected*
35. (B) - conditional *is pumped*
36. (A) - subordinate clause: reduced adjective *English, spoken*
37. (C) - subordinate clause: noun *that bee stings can*
38. (B) - subordinate clause: adjective *which are modeled*
39. (C) - subordinate clause: adverb *while the right controls*
40. (A) - subordinate clause: reduced adverb *upon arriving*

Section III: Reading Comprehension and Vocabulary

Vocabulary

1. (A)	16. (D)
2. (B)	17. (B)
3. (A)	18. (D)
4. (B)	19. (A)
5. (A)	20. (A)
6. (A)	21. (B)
7. (C)	22. (D)
8. (C)	23. (B)
9. (D)	24. (A)
10. (B)	25. (C)
11. (D)	26. (A)
12. (A)	27. (C)
13. (D)	28. (A)
14. (C)	29. (B)
15. (A)	30. (A)

Reading Comprehension

31. (B) - fact
32. (D) - fact
33. (A) - fact
34. (C) - fact
35. (B) - fact
36. (C) - fact
37. (C) - fact
38. (A) - fact
39. (B) - inference
40. (C) - inference
41. (B) - inference
42. (A) - inference
43. (A) - inference
44. (B) - main idea
45. (D) - fact
46. (B) - fact
47. (B) - fact
48. (B) - main idea
49. (C) - inference
50. (A) - paraphrase
51. (D) - paraphrase
52. (B) - definition
53. (C) - paraphrase
54. (D) - fact
55. (B) - inference
56. (B) - fact
57. (B) - paraphrase
58. (C) - paraphrase
59. (C) - paraphrase
60. (A) - paraphrase

Section I
Listening Comprehension
Time: 40 minutes

Section I measures your ability to understand spoken English. There are three parts to the Listening Comprehension section. Each part has its own question types and its own directions.

Part A

Directions:
In this part of the test, you will hear a short statement which will NOT be repeated. You must pay careful attention to this statement.

In your test booklet, you will see four sentences. One of those written sentences means almost the same as the short statement you hear. You must choose the sentence which most closely matches the meaning of the oral statement. You must then mark your answer on the answer sheet.

Listen to an example.
You will hear:

In your test book, you will see:

(A) He will not eat beets.
(B) The candidate did not bet.
(C) They thought the dates sweet.
(D) His rival cannot beat him.

Sample Answer

(A)   (B)   (C)   ●

The correct answer is (D). "His rival cannot beat him" most closely matches the statement "The candidate will not be beat." The letter (D) should be blackened on your answer sheet.

Listen to another example.
You will hear:

In your text book, you will see:

(A) She is careless in her work.
(B) She always goes free on trains.
(C) She never has tension headaches.
(D) She never shops at sales.

Sample Answer

●   (B)   (C)   (D)

The correct answer is (A). "She is careless in her work" most closely matches the statement "She never pays attention to the details." The letter (A) should be blackened on your answer sheet.

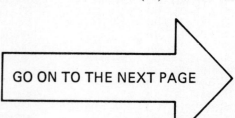

GO ON TO THE NEXT PAGE

1. (A) The accountant is poor.
   (B) There isn't enough money in the account.
   (C) I have no faith in the accountant's judgment.
   (D) The man cannot count.

2. (A) The team walked 13 miles.
   (B) The coach walked 15 miles.
   (C) The coach walked 30 miles.
   (D) Both walked 12 miles.

3. (A) The test starts at 9 o'clock.
   (B) 30 people are taking the exam.
   (C) 12 boys are in the group.
   (D) 13 boys are taking the test.

4. (A) The orphans were put in a home.
   (B) The windows were covered with dust.
   (C) Everyone remembers the feast we had.
   (D) Women honored their deceased husbands.

5. (A) The tenant wanted to rent the house.
   (B) The landlord didn't want to rent to the tenant anymore.
   (C) The landlord still cannot understand the tenant's decision.
   (D) The landlord and the tenant share a house.

6. (A) The engineer submitted the plans.
   (B) The city planner didn't agree with the engineer.
   (C) Only one person disagreed.
   (D) The builder needed the city's plans.

7. (A) The nurse turned over as she slept.
   (B) The nurse woke late because of her clock.
   (C) She always does her duty.
   (D) The nurse shouldn't sleep on duty.

8. (A) I married a prince.
   (B) The prince married the princess.
   (C) I like all your prints.
   (D) I could be a princess if I were married to a prince.

9. (A) The roommate ran after the athlete.
   (B) They ran before they ate dinner.
   (C) The roommate exercised before the athlete did.
   (D) The athlete ate after she exercised.

10. (A) Larger jets make less noise than old small ones.
    (B) The smaller the jet, the less noise it makes.
    (C) The most noisy aircraft are the newest.
    (D) The older jets are larger.

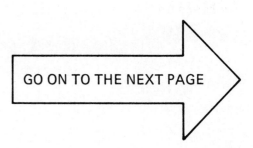
GO ON TO THE NEXT PAGE

11. (A) The highway department has enough men.
    (B) More laborers are required to finish the job.
    (C) The highways are wider than the roads.
    (D) More men are needed during the winter.

12. (A) Clothes must be put on in the dark.
    (B) Wear protective clothing at all times.
    (C) Do not turn on the electricity before the lid is off.
    (D) The electricity must be off before the cover is removed.

13. (A) She got an A without studying.
    (B) She didn't study and didn't get an A.
    (C) She changed her grade to an A.
    (D) She will get an A if she studies.

14. (A) The wind blew the door open.
    (B) The door smashed the vase.
    (C) The wind blew the table over.
    (D) The wind knocked the vase over.

15. (A) The Citizens Concert is a popular event.
    (B) The mayor is carefully supervised.
    (C) The consensus of the group may not count.
    (D) The citizens presented the mayor with a new watch.

16. (A) The man doesn't like to rake leaves.
    (B) The manager never closes the door.
    (C) The manager keeps the door closed against the wind.
    (D) The manager cancelled his bank drafts.

17. (A) It's difficult to walk after sitting.
    (B) We spoke with him for hours.
    (C) He talked to us with amusement.
    (D) We were silent after hearing him.

18. (A) Nine of us saw the show.
    (B) Four of us couldn't go.
    (C) Five of us were turned away.
    (D) Four of us went to the show.

19. (A) I was 50 minutes late.
    (B) I was 15 minutes late.
    (C) I slept until 8:13.
    (D) I slept until 8:03.

20. (A) The crowd fell asleep.
    (B) The speech was restful.
    (C) He spoke about the prime rate.
    (D) The crowd fidgeted.

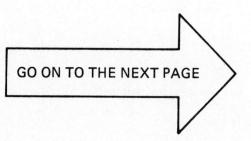

GO ON TO THE NEXT PAGE

Part B

Directions:
In this part there will be 15 short dialogues between two speakers. A third person will ask a question about the dialogue. This question will not be repeated.

Listen carefully to the dialogue and the question and then choose an answer from one of the four possible answers given in the test booklet. Mark the corresponding letter on your answer sheet.

Listen to an example.
You will hear this dialogue:

In your test booklet you will see:
(A) Finish the program, then study.
(B) Study rather than watch the program.
(C) See the show he saw last week.
(D) Watch the program while studying.

Listening to the dialogue, we learned that the man is going to study and not watch the TV program. Therefore, (B) is the most appropriate answer. The letter (B) should be blackened on your answer sheet.

21. (A) It's cool inside.
    (B) It's noisy outside.
    (C) The windows are bare.
    (D) The curtains need some care.

22. (A) 6 hours
    (B) 10 hours
    (C) 4 hours
    (D) 1 hour

23. (A) 25 cents each
    (B) 25 dollars
    (C) 5 dollars
    (D) 50 cents

24. (A) With zest
    (B) Delicately
    (C) Deliciously
    (D) Simply

25. (A) The prices
    (B) The menu
    (C) The restaurant
    (D) The desserts

26. (A) The man's
    (B) The woman's
    (C) The boss's
    (D) His own

27. (A) He practiced.
    (B) He ate a lot.
    (C) He rowed hard yesterday.
    (D) He didn't tire.

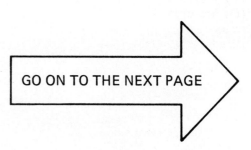
GO ON TO THE NEXT PAGE

28. (A) Go to Paris
    (B) Spend a weekend at home
    (C) Go to London
    (D) Visit her cousin

29. (A) Napped
    (B) Shopped
    (C) Walked
    (D) Dined

30. (A) Larger
    (B) Older
    (C) Useful
    (D) Efficient

31. (A) She knows the language well.
    (B) She has committed a crime.
    (C) She has given up.
    (D) She doesn't know all the words.

32. (A) Unfair
    (B) Hard of hearing
    (C) Near by
    (D) Complaining

33. (A) 9:13
    (B) 8:05
    (C) 9:30
    (D) 9:06

34. (A) 14
    (B) 5
    (C) 6
    (D) 7

35. (A) His hearing
    (B) His hair
    (C) Some weight
    (D) His overnight case

Part C

Directions:
In Part C, you will hear several short talks on a variety of subjects. Each talk will be followed by several questions. Neither the talks nor the questions will be repeated. You will have to pay close attention to both.

After you hear the question, you will have to pick the most appropriate answer from the four choices in the test booklet. You will then mark the corresponding letter on your answer sheet.

Listen to the example.
You will hear:

Sample Answer
● Ⓑ Ⓒ Ⓓ

Here is the first question:

In your test booklet, you will see:
(A) Neptune
(B) Mars
(C) Venus
(D) Mercury

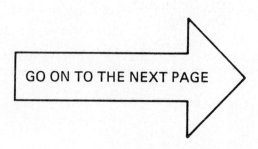

GO ON TO THE NEXT PAGE

The correct answer to the question "Which planet is fifth from the earth?" is (A) Neptune. You should blacken (A) on your answer sheet.

Here is the second question:

In your test booklet, you will see:
(A) Mars
(B) Venus
(C) Pluto
(D) Mercury

Sample Answer

(A) (B) (C) ●

The correct answer to the question "Which planet resembles our moon?" is (D) Mercury. You should blacken (D) on your answer sheet.

36. (A) With pen
    (B) With ink
    (C) With pencil
    (D) With magic marker

37. (A) 50 percent
    (B) 30 percent
    (C) 10 percent
    (D) 0

38. (A) Practice
    (B) Final
    (C) Essay
    (D) Oral

39. (A) Practice makes perfect.
    (B) Never make a mistake.
    (C) Do not use an eraser.
    (D) Everything is of equal importance.

40. (A) All colors are equal.
    (B) Colors change depending on their juxtaposition to other colors.
    (C) Purple is a cooler color than violet.
    (D) Colors continually change from orange to blue.

41. (A) Tony Orange
    (B) Violet White
    (C) Josef Albers
    (D) Will Alter

42. (A) The muted tone
    (B) The brilliant color
    (C) The adjacent color
    (D) The theory of hue

43. (A) 15 inches
    (B) 50 inches
    (C) Over 30 inches
    (D) Over 100 inches

44. (A) Man made phenomena
    (B) Industrialists
    (C) Politicians
    (D) Scientists

45. (A) Pollution
    (B) Volcanoes
    (C) Weapon tests
    (D) Corruption

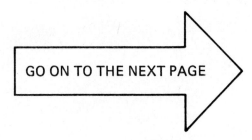

GO ON TO THE NEXT PAGE

46. (A) Over volcanoes
    (B) Near military bases
    (C) Worldwide
    (D) Near an industrial park

47. (A) To the lobby
    (B) To his room
    (C) To the company director
    (D) To the telephone company

48. (A) They are coin operated.
    (B) They are locked away.
    (C) They are for guests.
    (D) They are not in service.

49. (A) Mr. Hill's wife
    (B) Mr. Hill's secretary
    (C) The company director
    (D) The desk clerk

50. (A) Important
    (B) Lengthy
    (C) Delayed
    (D) Caustic

**THIS IS THE END OF THE LISTENING COMPREHENSION SECTION.
LOOK AT THE TIME NOW BEFORE YOU BEGIN WORK ON SECTION II.
YOU WILL HAVE EXACTLY 25 MINUTES TO WORK ON SECTION II.**

Section II
Structure and Written Expression
Time: 25 minutes

Section II measures your ability to recognize standard written English. There are two parts to this section. Each part has a different type of question and a different set of directions.

Directions for Questions 1-15:
You will see a sentence with a portion missing. Following the sentence will be four words or phrases. One of those words or phrases will best complete the sentence. Mark your choice on your answer sheet.

Look at this example:
The new instructor came _____ if the apartment was still available.

(A) seeing
(B) for to see
(C) to see
(D) and saw

Sample Answer
Ⓐ Ⓑ ● Ⓓ

The most appropriate standard English expression would be "The new instructor came <u>to see</u> if the apartment was still available." You should mark (C) on your answer sheet.

Look at the second example:
John and _____ are old friends.

Sample Answer
Ⓐ ● Ⓒ Ⓓ

(A) me
(B) I
(C) mine
(D) my

The most appropriate standard English expression would be "John and <u>I</u> are old friends." You should mark (B) on your answer sheet.

When you have read and understood the directions, answer questions 1-15.

1. An employment survey revealed today that demand for high-level executives _____ increased this year.

   (A) have
   (B) be
   (C) has
   (D) were

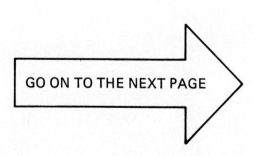

GO ON TO THE NEXT PAGE

2. Lawmakers are considering banning both beer _____ wine commercials from television.

   (A) also
   (B) than
   (C) or
   (D) and

3. Every fall geese _____ over the house located directly on the bay.

   (A) fly
   (B) flies
   (C) have flown
   (D) flown

4. Of the many opinions expressed to the council members by the various citizens' groups present, _____ was the only opinion that mattered.

   (A) their
   (B) their one
   (C) theirs
   (D) they

5. The Rosetta stone has provided scientists _____ a link to ancient civilizations.
   (A) of
   (B) to
   (C) by
   (D) with

6. If poisons like DDT _____ to control insects, there will be serious environmental repercussions.

   (A) use
   (B) uses
   (C) are used
   (D) used

7. Carnival sideshows often feature acrobats who juggle knives and balls _____ same time.

   (A) all at the
   (B) at all
   (C) all at a
   (D) all at some

8. Literature _____ provides only fragments of information about the Anglo Saxon period.

   (A) recorded in the century tenth
   (B) in the recorded tenth century
   (C) in the century tenth recorded
   (D) recorded in the tenth century

9. _____ the railroads were built, early settlers had organized an elaborate system of trails and canals.

   (A) After
   (B) During
   (C) When
   (D) Before

10. Technology has increased _____, or the amount of goods and services available.

    (A) produce
    (B) productivity
    (C) producers
    (D) products

11. National Park conservationists think _____ concession stands mar the natural beauty of the park.

    (A) of
    (B) about
    (C) that
    (D) a lot

GO ON TO THE NEXT PAGE

12. The receptionist, _____ job it was to answer the phone, had laryngitis.

    (A) whose
    (B) who
    (C) who's
    (D) that

13. The grasslands and deciduous forest climates are similar except that the former receives _____ rainfall.

    (A) least
    (B) few
    (C) less
    (D) fewer

14. The embezzler, _____ his actions, wanted to make restitution to the company.

    (A) were
    (B) regretful
    (C) was regretting
    (D) regretting

15. _____ lunch, the finance committee resumed the meeting.

    (A) Having to eat
    (B) Have to eat
    (C) Having eaten
    (D) Having eat

Directions for Questions 16-40

In this section you will be given a sentence with four words or phrases underlined. One of the underlined words or phrases is not standard English. You must choose the incorrect portion and blacken the corresponding letter on your answer sheet.

Look at this example:

    <u>Being organized</u> is one of <u>the</u> most important <u>aspect</u> of being a good <u>worker</u>.
       A   B   C   D

Sample Answer

Ⓐ Ⓑ ● Ⓓ

The underlined word "aspect," letter (C), is not standard written English. You should blacken (C) on your answer sheet.

After you have read and understood the directions, begin questions 16-40.

16. <u>The</u> system of <u>time measured</u> in 24-hour days is <u>based upon used</u>
   A   B   C
<u>in ancient Babylon</u>.
      D

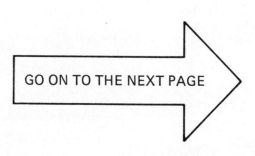

GO ON TO THE NEXT PAGE

17. Most <u>automobile engine</u> use <u>a liquid</u>, usually water, <u>to maintain the</u>
            A   B   C

    engine at a constant <u>operating temperature</u>.
                                      D

18. <u>Not able</u> to type accurately <u>would</u> hurt a graduate's chances of <u>finding</u> a
    A   B   C

    suitable job <u>as a secretary</u>.
                  D

19. <u>Roman law had</u> became <u>the foundation for</u> law codes that
           A   B

    <u>subsequently developed</u> in Europe <u>and in other</u> parts of the world.
              C   D

20. <u>When</u> the government <u>eliminated federal funds</u> for day care centers,
    A   B

    <u>many working</u> <u>parents are obliged</u> to take part-time jobs.
         C   D

21. The <u>group of spectators was</u> dispersed <u>by</u> the police <u>who was</u> at the scene
                 A   B   C

    of the accident <u>within minutes</u>.
                    D

22. Dame Judith Anderson, <u>an Australian</u> actress, <u>made his professional</u> theater
                             A   B

    <u>debut</u> in Sydney <u>in 1915</u>.
    C   D

23. Cities <u>that highly polluted air</u> show <u>the effects</u> of the <u>weathering</u> caused by
                 A   B   C

    acid rain <u>on buildings, statues, and parks</u>.
               D

24. Trade relationships <u>between</u> the two countries <u>have improved</u> if <u>their</u>
                    A   B   C

    respective leaders could agree on <u>the</u> proposed quotas.
                                    D

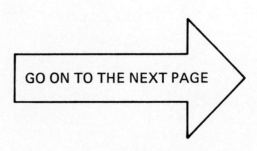

GO ON TO THE NEXT PAGE

25. The appropriate action <u>to take</u> could not <u>be decided</u> <u>on by</u> either the
                                     A   B   C

    president <u>nor</u> the vice president.
                 D

26. Aristotle, the ancient Greek Philosopher, believed <u>that any piece</u> <u>of matter</u>
                                                            A   B

    could be indefinitely cut into <u>smaller and smaller</u> pieces
                                       C

    <u>without limit</u>.
          D

27. Jack London's <u>tour</u> <u>of South Pacific</u> <u>was delayed by</u> his illness and
                 A   B   C

    the <u>San Francisco earthquake</u> of 1906.
                 D

28. <u>With</u> all accounts, the defendant was innocent <u>of</u> the heinous crimes <u>for which</u>
    A   B   C

    he <u>was being</u> tried.
          D

29. <u>By</u> the year 2010, the earth <u>will inhabit</u> <u>twice</u> as many people <u>as it is</u> today.
    A   B   C   D

30. High school <u>students need</u> to finish <u>and complete</u> courses in <u>history and</u>
                     A   B   C

    science <u>before graduating</u>.
                 D

31. <u>Working</u> together, scientists and genetic researchers <u>recently have made</u>
    A   B

    discoveries <u>that are</u> causing <u>philosophical</u> debates.
                 C   D

32. At <u>no time</u> a student's <u>cheating</u> on a <u>final</u> examination <u>can</u> be condoned.
       A   B   C   D

33. <u>A hush</u> fell <u>over the concert</u> hall when <u>the well-known</u> classical guitarist
    A   B   C

    in the world <u>stepped onto</u> the stage.
                 D

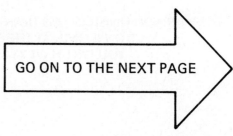
GO ON TO THE NEXT PAGE

2	2	2	2	2	2	2	2

34. In postindustrial <u>society factories</u> became <u>less</u> places of <u>hard physics</u>
            A   B   C
    labor and more places of <u>automated operation</u>.
                                         D

35. The honeysuckle bush, which smells <u>so sweetly</u> <u>when it blooms</u>, was
                                             A   B
    <u>originally brought</u> to the U.S. <u>from</u> Japan.
            C   D

36. The Forest Service <u>ascertains that</u> no <u>more timber cut</u> in one year
                              A   B
    <u>than a single</u> year's growth <u>can replace</u>.
            C   D

37. The <u>guests were</u> surprised by <u>their</u> host's <u>furniture was made</u> in Italy
            A   B   C
    <u>especially for</u> the new gallery.
            D

38. Fish flour must be proved <u>fit for</u> human <u>consumption</u> <u>although it</u> is
                                   A   B   C
    <u>allowed to be</u> distributed to the public.
            D

39. Were <u>banks increase</u> <u>their</u> loans to businesses, <u>which</u> would use these
            A   B   C
    funds to increase their inventories, <u>investment</u> would increase.
                                              D

40. Parents, before <u>they are</u> moving to another state, <u>should consider</u>
                         A   B
    the <u>effect the move</u> may have on <u>their children</u>.
            C   D

DO NOT WORK ON ANY OTHER SECTION OF THE TEST

**IF YOU FINISH IN LESS THAN 25 MINUTES, GO OVER YOUR ANSWERS ON
SECTION II ONLY. AT THE END OF 25 MINUTES, GO TO SECTION III.
YOU WILL HAVE 45 MINUTES TO WORK ON SECTION III.**

Section III
Reading Comprehension and Vocabulary
Time: 45 minutes

In this section of the test, there are two types of questions. Each question type has its own directions.

Directions for Questions 1-30:
In each sentence a word or phrase has been underlined. There are four other words or phrases below each sentence. You must select the one word or phrase which most closely matches the meaning of the underlined word.

Example:
She always wore dresses made of synthetic cloth.

(A) artificial
(B) expensive
(C) fashionable
(D) new

Sample Answer
● Ⓑ Ⓒ Ⓓ

(A) is the correct answer. "She always wore dresses of artificial cloth" most closely matches the meaning of the original sentence. The letter (A) should be blackened on your answer sheet.

When you fully understand the directions, answer the following questions.

1. In spite of his many faults, Paul is very dedicated to his mother.

(A) polite
(B) devoted
(C) agreeable
(D) considerable

2. Mrs. Smith will demonstrate how this computer works.

(A) guess
(B) unnecessary
(C) describe
(D) show

3. The columnist's remarks were inappropriate and rude.

(A) unsuitable
(B) unnecessary

(C) inconsistent
(D) inarticulate

4. The argument, although understandable, was not very convincing.

(A) persuasive
(B) realistic
(C) reliable
(D) clear

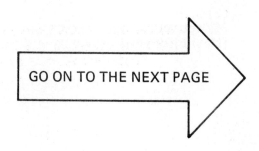

GO ON TO THE NEXT PAGE

5. The judge would not hear the case because the evidence was not underline{sufficient}.

   (A) proper
   (B) legal
   (C) adequate
   (D) positive

6. Being underline{meek}, the stranger had difficulty making friends.

   (A) lonely
   (B) lazy
   (C) loud
   (D) humble

7. The gem is so rare it could be underline{fake}.

   (A) expensive
   (B) stolen
   (C) simulated
   (D) sold

8. An inexperienced driver is a underline{potential} danger.

   (A) possible
   (B) certain
   (C) actual
   (D) definite

9. When the wind died, the sailboat underline{drifted} toward the beach.

   (A) headed
   (B) floated
   (C) hurried
   (D) returned

10. This course focuses underline{primarily} on the history of early civalizations.

   (A) objectively
   (B) mainly
   (C) actively
   (D) subjectively

11. Success is most deserved by underline{amiable} people.

   (A) efficient
   (B) prestigious
   (C) good-humored
   (D) essential

12. An underline{ulterior} motive is behind the question.

   (A) A concealed
   (B) A good
   (C) An important
   (D) An exceptional

13. There is no resolution to this underline{conflict}.

   (A) decision
   (B) condition
   (C) action
   (D) disagreement

14. There was a long underline{pause} before the music began.

   (A) interval
   (B) introduction
   (C) prayer
   (D) play

15. A underline{brisk} walk in cool weather is invigorating.

   (A) short
   (B) long
   (C) lively
   (D) solemn

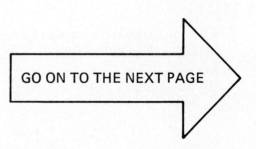

GO ON TO THE NEXT PAGE

16. Some tall people often feel <u>clumsy</u>.

    (A) superior
    (B) ignored
    (C) noticed
    (D) awkward

17. All typing errors must be <u>deleted</u> from this memo.

    (A) erased
    (B) corrected
    (C) circled
    (D) determined

18. The name of that <u>ferocious</u> looking animal is unforgettable.

    (A) hairy
    (B) fierce
    (C) silly
    (D) callous

19. The manager was found to be <u>harassing</u> his employees.

    (A) asking
    (B) bribing
    (C) coaxing
    (D) bothering

20. The government will <u>issue</u> a statement about tax increases soon.

    (A) invent
    (B) deny
    (C) give out
    (D) propose

21. The <u>garments</u> of colonial times, if in good condition, are highly prized.

    (A) homes
    (B) pictures
    (C) clothes
    (D) tools

22. The two personalities have few similarities and are basically <u>incompatible</u>.

    (A) dissimilar
    (B) antagonistic
    (C) different
    (D) incomparable

23. More responsibility and higher salaries are <u>incentives for</u> on-the-job training.

    (A) implicit in
    (B) integral part of
    (C) privileges of
    (D) inducements for

24. The product to use to <u>douse</u> a grease fire is salt or baking soda.

    (A) extinguish
    (B) create
    (C) prolong
    (D) deter

25. The <u>suspect</u> is being held for arraignment without bail.

    (A) nonbeliever
    (B) judge
    (C) robber
    (D) accused

26. The <u>quaint</u> style of the homes is typical of this region.

    (A) curious
    (B) ancient
    (C) elaborate
    (D) ultramodern

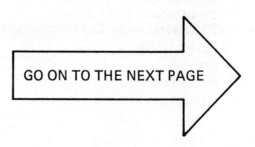
GO ON TO THE NEXT PAGE

27. Doctors discourage <u>massive</u> doses of drugs for infants.

(A) light
(B) huge
(C) repetitive
(D) infrequent

28. The <u>provisions</u> of the contract exclude any division of the property for 50 years.

(A) writers
(B) clauses
(C) readers
(D) lawyers

29. History has shown that rulers do not <u>relinquish</u> power easily.

(A) abandon
(B) hold
(C) control
(D) gain

30. Modern music is usually characterized by a remarkable <u>dissonance</u>.

(A) melody
(B) clarity
(C) discord
(D) volume

Directions for Questions 31-56:
In this section, you will read passages on a variety of subjects and then answer several questions about the passages. Some of the answers will come directly from the passages; others may only be implied. Select the most appropriate answer and blacken the answer on your answer sheet.

Look at this example:

> According to scientists, 70 percent of the earth's surface is covered by water, and this watery wilderness is the habitat of four of every five living things. To aid oceanographers in their explorations of the seas and oceans of the world, scientists have been designing more and better types of undersea vessels to accomplish this task with greater safety and with more efficient tools and techniques.

Answer the first question:
1. What percentage of the earth's surface is covered by water?

(A) 30 percent
(B) 70 percent
(C) 100 percent
(D) 50 percent

Sample Answer
Ⓐ ● Ⓒ Ⓓ

The correct answer is (B) 70 percent.

Answer the second question:
2. What percentage of the earth's inhabitants live on land?

(A) 10 percent
(B) 20 percent
(C) 40 percent
(D) 50 percent

Sample Answer
Ⓐ ● Ⓒ Ⓓ

GO ON TO THE NEXT PAGE

The correct answer is (B) 20 percent. If four out of every five living things live in water, one of every five things, or 20 percent, must live on land.

After you have read and understood the examples, you may start to read.

Questions 31-34

In health and human disease, the activities of microorganisms greatly affect human life. Whether in country or city, tropics, midlatitudes, or the arctic, human beings are continually influenced by microbes. The science that deals with the study of microorganisms is called "microbiology" and is a branch of biology parallel to "botany," the study of plants, and "zoology," the study of animals. However, the procedures and practices by which microorganisms are studied are quite different from those used to study plants and animals. It is for this reason that microbiology developed as a science independent of botany and zoology. The goal of the microbiologist is to understand the beneficial and harmful activities of microorganisms and through this understanding to devise ways in which benefits may be increased and damages curtailed. Microbiologists have been successful in achieving this goal, and microbiology has played a major role in the advancement of human health and welfare.

31. Microbes are

   (A) microorganisms.
   (B) goal oriented.
   (C) prevalent in specific areas.
   (D) types of diseases.

32. Microbiology, botany, and zoology are all

   (A) concerned with animal life.
   (B) branches of biology.
   (C) concerned with microorganisms.
   (D) parallel to biology.

33. The special contribution of microbiologists has been to

   (A) study microbes.
   (B) make our world a healthier place to live.
   (C) eliminate all diseases caused by microbes.
   (D) show how microbiology differs from botany and zoology.

34. The reason why microbiology has developed as a separate science is that

   (A) botany and zoology do not deal with microorganisms.
   (B) microorganisms are more numerous than plants and animals.
   (C) microbiologists deal with applied biology.
   (D) microorganisms cannot be studied like plants and animals.

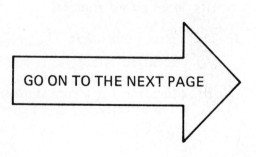
GO ON TO THE NEXT PAGE

Questions 35-39

It is clear today that education must become a matter of national policy. We are, indeed, in the midst of an educational revolution.

One may witness in today's society the concern for advanced technical training and the reorganization of curricula and technique in the secondary schools to provide for the gifted student. Within these concerns, we also see many advanced placement programs with provisions for individual progress and with emphasis upon the opportunity for creativity, primarily in the technical and related fields. At present there is a widespread feeling that we have been overlooking too much potential talent, but the concern for this loss is not entirely recent. Terman called our attention to the problem many years ago, especially in his "Genetic Studies of Genius." The renewed emphasis on this idea is part of the revolution.

35. Which best expresses the main idea of the passage?

(A) Because we are in the middle of an educational revolution, education must clearly become a matter of national policy.
(B) Since education is clearly a matter of national policy, we need an educational revolution.
(C) It is necessary that education become a matter of national policy.
(D) Although we are having an educational revolution, we still must make education a clear national policy.

36. Which of the following is not an example of the educational revolution mentioned in the passage?

(A) Concern for advanced technical training
(B) Reorganization of curricula and technique
(C) Advanced placement programs
(D) More gifted students

37. The writer thinks that

(A) education is not yet recognized to the extent it should be.
(B) education for gifted students is a top priority.
(C) we need an educational revolution.
(D) concern for the loss of potential talent is recent.

38. Which problem did Terman call our attention to many years ago?

(A) Genetic studies of children
(B) Opportunities for creativity
(C) Reorganization of curricula and technique
(D) Failure to develop the abilities of talented students

39. Which of the following would result if the writer's suggestions were adopted by government officials?

(A) Education for average students would be ignored.
(B) There would be more emphasis on the sciences than on the arts.
(C) The educational revolution would be successful.
(D) The federal government would increase its role in education policy.

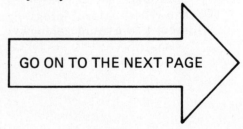
GO ON TO THE NEXT PAGE

Questions 40-44

Many of the domestic plants originated from obvious and well-known wild ancestors. Both wheat and barley, for example, come from wild grasses that still grow in parts of the Near East. There are still mysteries, however, about the origins of some domestic plants. Where corn came from has been a puzzle for generations, and the question still proves a battleground for botanical camps armed with research, and, sometimes, invectives. Corn has become so highly domesticated that it is even more a captive of man than the lap dog. Left alone, a field of maize would fail to produce new plants within a season or two; and, if we should ever lose our struggle for survival, corn will perish with us. The reason is that in becoming so well suited as a food plant, corn has lost the means to disperse its seeds and must depend on being sowed for its survival.

40. The primary focus of this passage is

(A) wheat and its relationship to corn.
(B) where corn comes from.
(C) types of corn.
(D) botany and the origins of plants.

41. Unless tended, a corn field would

(A) yield for years.
(B) perish in a year or two.
(C) reproduce itself.
(D) become overgrown.

42. The reason corn is compared to a lap dog is that it is

(A) totally dependent on man.
(B) domestic.
(C) useful.
(D) a good friend to man.

43. We can infer from the passage that

(A) there has not been much research into the origins of corn.
(B) there is considerable harmony among botanists regarding the origins of corn.

(C) we will never know where corn came from.
(D) rival botanists sometimes use insulting language in defending their theories about corn.

44. Which of the following is the primary reason corn would perish if mankind perished?

(A) Only man eats corn.
(B) Fertilization is important.
(C) Corn no longer spreads its seeds independently.
(D) Corn only grows in maize fields.

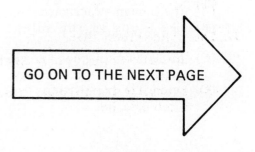
GO ON TO THE NEXT PAGE

Questions 45-47

Scientists give the title "law" to certain concise but general statements about how nature behaves (that momentum is conserved, for example); sometimes the statement takes the form of a relationship or equation between quantities (such as Newton's law of universal gravitation, $F=Gm_1m_2/r^2$).

To be called a law, a statement must be found experimentally valid over a wide range of observed phenomena; in a sense, the law brings a unity to many observations. For less general statements, the term principle is often used (such as Archimedes' principle). Where to draw the line between laws and principles is, of course, arbitrary, and there is not always complete consistency.

45. Which of the following does not characterize the term "law"?

(A) Concise
(B) General
(C) Valid
(D) Particular

46. We can infer that

(A) some principles might actually be laws.
(B) Newton's law is actually a principle.

(C) the briefer a law, the more valid it is.
(D) Archimedes was less important than Newton.

47. Archimedes's principle is

(A) not general.
(B) actually a law.
(C) precise.
(D) $F=Gm_1m_2/r^2$.

Questions 48-51

The outstanding approach to the problems of our modern age is our highly developed technique for gaining insight into all aspects of our experiences -- namely, the scientific method. Steps in the scientific method are (1) observing a chosen phenomenon; (2) accumulating the facts; (3) noting a pattern among the facts; (4) finding a plausible explanation of the pattern within these facts (hypothesis); (5) making a new prediction on the basis of the plausible explanation; and (6) checking the prediction experimentally -- hence increasing or decreasing the belief in the plausible explanation, depending upon whether the new findings agree or disagree with the prediction.

48. The main focus of this passage is

(A) the human experience.
(B) the steps in the scientific method.
(C) human techniques for gaining insight.
(D) scientific explanation.

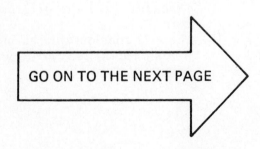
GO ON TO THE NEXT PAGE

49. In which of the six steps does it become necessary to do laboratory work?

    (A) Step 1
    (B) Step 3
    (C) Step 6
    (D) None of the above

50. After step 6, it might be necessary for a scientist to

    (A) be adamant about his prediction.
    (B) ignore the facts.
    (C) search for a less plausible reason.

    (D) design more precise experiments.

51. The author

    (A) limits the use of the scientific method to the hard sciences like physics.
    (B) thinks that all questions will eventually be answered by scientists.
    (C) does not confine the scientific method to any particular science.
    (D) wants the reader to become a scientist.

Questions 52-56

Riverdale Adult Ed

The following courses are offered at the Community center. They are open to all members of the Riverdale Community. Applicants over 60 years of age may register for any course for free.

SA-248 Advanced Parapsychology
Interested in the other world? Learn how to send your thoughts to another person; how to move objects with your mind; and how to communicate with the dead.

SA-252 Writer's Lab
For our graduates who took "Write Right!" Students will criticize each other's work and discuss the potential markets for their work.

SA-255 Easy Spanish Conversation
Speak Spanish like the natives. Shop and travel with ease in only 20 hours.

SA-258 Elementary Auto Mechanics
Learn where the engine is and how to fill up your gas tank. Other mysteries revealed.

SA-259 Auto Mechanics II
Tuning the engine. Must have taken SA-258 or have the instructor's permission to enroll.

SA-274 Handwriting Analysis
Read between your lines! Learn the history and the future of the art of handwriting analysis. Bring samples of your friends', and spouse's handwriting. Find out what they are really like.

SA-270 Income Tax Returns
Are those federal and state forms a big mystery to you? Simplify those returns with a few simple steps.

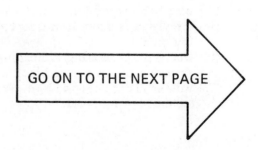

GO ON TO THE NEXT PAGE

52. How many hours does the Spanish class meet in total?

(A) 40
(B) 10
(C) 20
(D) 50

53. People interested in the hidden meanings in their signatures should sign up for

(A) SA-274.
(B) SA-252.
(C) SA-273.
(D) SA-248.

54. People interested in mysticism should enroll in

(A) Income Tax Returns.
(B) Easy Spanish Conversation.
(C) Handwriting Analysis.
(D) Advanced Parapsychology.

55. People with a basic understanding of automotive mechanics but in need of further training should enroll in

(A) SA-259.
(B) SA-258.
(C) SA-270.
(D) SA-255.

56. Permission of the instructor or previous training is required for

(A) Easy Spanish Conversation.
(B) Advanced Parapsychology.
(C) Income Tax Returns.
(D) Auto Mechanics II.

Directions for Questions 57-60

In this section, you must select the statement that most nearly matches the original statement. Many of the statements are true, but only one is a restatement of the original.

57. Color television has totally superseded black and white except in countries lacking color programming.

(A) Black and white television is inferior to color television except in countries lacking color programming.
(B) It is clear that color television is superior to black and white since color programming is in use in most countries.
(C) Except in those countries where color programming is not yet in use, the use of black and white television is subordinate to color television.
(D) Color programming is no longer in use in places where black and white television has been superseded by color.

58. The speaker urged members of the audience to enroll in computer classes if they were serious about earning more money.

(A) The audience was urged to sign up for computer courses in order to increase their income.
(B) Earning more income through computer science is what the speaker urged.

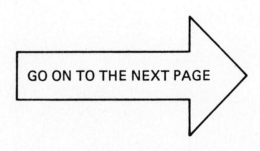

GO ON TO THE NEXT PAGE

3	3	3	3	3	3	3	3

(C) The audience was told that the speaker thought that they could earn more money by enrolling in computer classes.

(D) "Sign up for computer classes and earn while you learn" urged the speaker.

59. Even John could feel the seriousness of the moment.

(A) John, who is never serious, felt serious at that moment.

(B) The seriousness of the moment was perceived by all involved, even John.

(C) John could even feel the seriousness of the moment.

(D) Everybody was in a serious mood, even John.

60. The army marched all the way to the Des Moines River and stopped to spend the night.

(A) When they got as far as the Des Moines River the army stopped to spend the night.

(B) Once they got to the Des Moines River, the army stopped and rested.

(C) Stopping at the Des Moines River, the army rested for the night.

(D) The Des Moines River was the point at which stopping and resting seemed appropriate to the army.

DO NOT WORK ON ANY OTHER SECTION OF THE TEST

IF YOU FINISH IN LESS THAN 45 MINUTES, GO OVER YOUR ANSWERS ON SECTION III ONLY. AT THE END OF 45 MINUTES, STOP WORK AND CORRECT YOUR ANSWERS WITH THE ANSWER KEY WHICH FOLLOWS.

CODED ANSWER KEY DIAGNOSTIC TEST 2

SECTION I: LISTENING COMPREHENSION

Part A - Statements

1. (C) - synonym
2. (B) - computation
3. (A) - number discrimination
4. (D) - synonym
5. (C) - negation
6. (C) - contextual reference
7. (B) - cause/effect
8. (D) - conditional
9. (C) - chronological order
10. (A) - comparison
11. (B) - comparison
12. (D) - chronological order
13. (B) - conditional
14. (D) - cause/effect

15. (B) - synonym
16. (C) - negation
17. (D) - synonym
18. (C) - computation
19. (B) - number discrimination
20. (D) - synonym

Part B - Conversations

21. (B) - minimal pair
22. (C) - computation
23. (A) - number discrimination
24. (A) - synonym
25. (C) - negation
26. (C) - contextual reference
27. (A) - cause/effect

28. (C) - conditional
29. (C) - chronological order
30. (A) - comparison
31. (D) - negation
32. (A) - synonym
33. (C) - number discrimination
34. (C) - computation
35. (B) - minimal pair

Part C - Mini Talks

36. (C)   41. (C)   46. (C)
37. (D)   42. (C)   47. (A)
38. (A)   43. (C)   48. (C)
39. (A)   44. (D)   49. (C)
40. (B)   45. (D)   50. (A)

SECTION II: STRUCTURE AND WRITTEN EXPRESSION

Part A

1. (C) - verb: agreement
2. (D) - conjunction
3. (B) - verb: agreement
4. (C) - pronoun: form
5. (D) - preposition
6. (C) - conditional
7. (A) - article
8. (D) - word order: adjective placement
9. (D) - subordinate clause: adverb
10. (B) - word family
11. (C) - subordinate clause: noun
12. (A) - subordinate clause: adjective
13. (C) - comparision
14. (D) - subordinate clause: reduced adjective
15. (C) - subordinate clause: reduced adverb

Part B

16. (C) - subject: omission *upon the system (that was) used*
17. (A) - subject: agreement *engines*

18. (A) - verb: omission *not being able to*
19. (A) - verb: unnecessary form *omit had*
20. (D) - verb: tense *were obliged*
21. (C) - verb: agreement *who were*
22. (D) - pronoun: agreement *her*
23. (A) - subordinate clause: adjective *that have slightly*
24. (B) - conditional
25. (A) - conjunction: form *or the vice president*
26. (D) - redundancy *omit*
27. (B) - article *the South Pacific*
28. (A) - preposition *by all accounts*
29. (B) - active-passive *will be inhabited*
30. (B) - redundancy *omit*
31. (B) - word order: adjective/adverb *have recently made*
32. (D) - word order: subject/verb *can a student's cheating be*
33. (C) - comparison *the best known*
34. (C) - word family *physical*
35. (A) - word family *so sweet*
36. (B) - subordinate clause: noun *timber is cut*
37. (C) - subordinate clause: adjective *furniture which was*
38. (C) - subordinate clause: adverb *before*
39. (A) - subjunctive *were banks to increase*
40. (A) - subordinate clause: reduced adverb *omit they are*

SECTION III: READING COMPREHENSION AND VOCABULARY

Vocabulary

1. (B)   16. (D)
2. (D)   17. (A)
3. (A)   18. (B)
4. (A)   19. (D)
5. (C)   20. (C)
6. (D)   21. (C)
7. (C)   22. (B)
8. (A)   23. (D)
9. (B)   24. (A)
10. (B)   25. (D)
11. (C)   26. (A)
12. (A)   27. (B)
13. (D)   28. (B)
14. (A)   29. (A)
15. (C)   30. (C)

Reading Comprehension

31. (A) - definition
32. (B) - fact
33. (B) - inference
34. (D) - fact
35. (C) - main idea
36. (D) - fact
37. (A) - inference
38. (D) - paraphrase
39. (D) - inference
40. (B) - fact/main idea
41. (B) - inference
42. (A) - inference
43. (D) - inference
44. (C) - paraphrase
45. (D) - definition

46. (A) - inference
47. (A) - fact
48. (B) - main idea
49. (C) - inference
50. (D) - paraphrase
51. (C) - inference
52. (C) - fact
53. (A) - paraphrase
54. (D) - fact
55. (A) - inference
56. (D) - vocabulary
57. (C) - paraphrase
58. (A) - paraphrase
59. (B) - paraphrase
60. (A) - paraphrase

Section I
Listening Comprehension
Time: 40 minutes

Section I measures your ability to understand spoken English. There are three parts to the Listening Comprehension section. Each part has its own question types and its own directions.

Part A

Directions:
In this part of the test, you will hear a short statement which will NOT be repeated. You must pay careful attention to this statement.

In your test booklet, you will see four sentences. One of those written sentences means almost the same as the short statement you hear. You must choose the sentence which most closely matches the meaning of the oral statement. You must then mark your answer on the answer sheet.

Listen to an example.
You will hear:

Sample Answer

Ⓐ Ⓑ Ⓒ ●

In your test book, you will see:
(A) He will not eat beets.
(B) The candidate did not bet.
(C) They thought the dates sweet.
(D) His rival cannot beat him.

The correct answer is (D). "His rival cannot beat him" most closely matches the statement "The candidate will not be beat." The letter (D) should be blackened on your answer sheet.

Listen to another example.
You will hear:

Sample Answer

● Ⓑ Ⓒ Ⓓ

In your text book, you will see:
(A) She is careless in her work.
(B) She always goes free on trains.
(C) She never has tension headaches.
(D) She never shops at sales.

The correct answer is (A). "She is careless in her work" most closely matches the statement "She never pays attention to the details." The letter (A) should be blackened on your answer sheet.

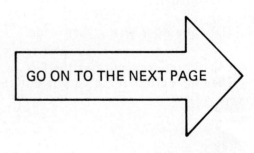

GO ON TO THE NEXT PAGE

1. (A) I couldn't hear well.
   (B) The bugs ran through the dust.
   (C) I got dusty beating the rug.
   (D) My hair is clean.

2. (A) Eleven boys finished.
   (B) Nine boys finished.
   (C) Thirteen boys finished.
   (D) Two boys finished.

3. (A) I got 15 cards.
   (B) I got 13 cards.
   (C) I got 30 cards.
   (D) I got 50 cards.

4. (A) I got a seat on the train.
   (B) The tension wire lay across the walk.
   (C) He got hurt when he didn't move.
   (D) His intentions were common.

5. (A) He has studied biology all his life.
   (B) He had never seen a cannon.
   (C) The canyon was not unique.
   (D) The geologist was impressed.

6. (A) The trainer must return all sports equipment.
   (B) The school no longer is in session.
   (C) All school equipment is used for sports.
   (D) The trainer is in charge of the school's equipment.

7. (A) The catastrophe was minor.
   (B) The door opened into the garden.
   (C) The cat got out.
   (D) The door was a yard wide.

8. (A) Three men put out the fire.
   (B) We called them to put out the fire.
   (C) You put out the fire when you were called.
   (D) The fire burned because no one was there to put it out.

9. (A) Jim saw the movie before I did.
   (B) I saw the movie before Jim.
   (C) I saw the movie, then ate.
   (D) Jim ate, then saw the movie.

10. (A) Plan C is the most comprehensive.
    (B) Plan A is better than Plan C.
    (C) Plan B is less complete than Plan A.
    (D) Plan A is less comprehensive than Plan C.

11. (A) The further the distance, the narrower the river.
    (B) Her wide smile is contagious.
    (C) You can see her smile from here.
    (D) The river is at its widest a few miles away.

12. (A) The bus started after the bags were loaded.
    (B) Two of us pulled the candy away from the boys.
    (C) The suitcases were left on the curb.
    (D) Those attending brought a bag lunch.

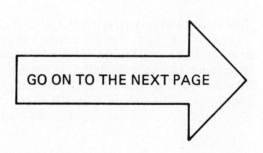

GO ON TO THE NEXT PAGE

13. (A) She always stayed away from hospitals.
    (B) The county erected a memorial to the wounded.
    (C) Many people were absent because they were sick.
    (D) All ballots should have been counted.

14. (A) The beds are in a long row in the room.
    (B) The batteries are dead.
    (C) Photographers work long hours.
    (D) Even bad cameras take good pictures.

15. (A) The technicians were reluctant to work.
    (B) We deserve more responsibility.
    (C) The technician did not earn our trust.
    (D) The technician worked without pay.

16. (A) They avoided the problem by obeying the rules.
    (B) The rules were not followed.
    (C) Ignoring the rules caused no problem.
    (D) The arrow was straight as a ruler.

17. (A) The program finished sooner than expected.
    (B) The serious program was too long.
    (C) The issue grew worse over time.
    (D) These problems are hardly serious.

18. (A) There were 11 tents.
    (B) There were 13 tents.
    (C) There were 10 tents.
    (D) There were 30 tents.

19. (A) We walked 40 miles.
    (B) We walked 23 miles.
    (C) We walked 10 miles.
    (D) We walked 13 miles.

20. (A) The sun shone after the rain.
    (B) Rye is a shiny grain.
    (C) I would have polished it.
    (D) The wood had a gray color.

Part B

Directions:
In this part there will be 15 short dialogues between two speakers. A third person will ask a question about the dialogue. This question will not be repeated.

Listen carefully to the dialogue and the question and then choose an answer from one of the four possible answers given in the test booklet. Mark the corresponding letter on your answer sheet.

Listen to an example.

You will hear this dialogue:

In your test booklet you will see:
(A) Finish the program, then study
(B) Study rather than watch the program
(C) See the show he saw last week
(D) Watch the program while studying

Sample Answer

Ⓐ ● Ⓒ Ⓓ

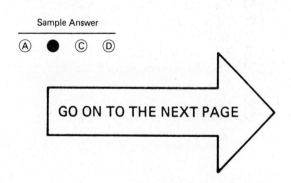

GO ON TO THE NEXT PAGE

Listening to the dialogue, we learned that the man is going to study and not watch the TV program. Therefore, (B) is the most appropriate answer. The letter (B) should be blackened on your answer sheet.

21. (A) The woman walks slowly.
    (B) The woman is a fast talker.
    (C) The woman couldn't walk.
    (D) The woman walks too quickly.

22. (A) Met friends
    (B) Saw a movie
    (C) Went for a walk
    (D) Made a phone call

23. (A) The man can't drive.
    (B) The party is over.
    (C) They can't turn around.
    (D) They're lost.

24. (A) A librarian
    (B) A laborer
    (C) A banker
    (D) A thief

25. (A) Her grandfather's
    (B) Her mother's
    (C) Her brother's
    (D) Her father's

26. (A) A hand
    (B) His briefcase
    (C) A typewriter
    (D) His papers

27. (A) Look for work
    (B) Take a lonely cruise
    (C) Buy a horse
    (D) Cut the grass

28. (A) 56
    (B) 80
    (C) 7
    (D) 8

29. (A) $2.00
    (B) $1.00
    (C) 50 cents
    (D) $1.50

30. (A) The shoes
    (B) The color
    (C) The tie
    (D) The suit

31. (A) Waited for his friends
    (B) Gone out
    (C) Stayed inside
    (D) Taken a train

32. (A) She started swimming.
    (B) She stopped reading.
    (C) She baked some bread.
    (D) She lost weight.

33. (A) Experience
    (B) Good looks
    (C) Degrees
    (D) Age

34. (A) It occurred before the war.
    (B) It caused the secession.
    (C) It was a success.
    (D) It came much later in the war.

35. (A) Cost of food
    (B) Skyscrapers
    (C) Price riots
    (D) Directions

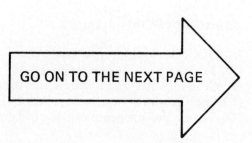
GO ON TO THE NEXT PAGE

1	1	1	1	1	1	1	1

Part C

Directions:
In Part C, you will hear several short talks on a variety of subjects. Each talk will be followed by several questions. Neither the talks nor the questions will be repeated. You will have to pay close attention to both.

After you hear the question, you will have to pick the most appropriate answer from the four choices in the test booklet. You will then mark the corresponding letter on your answer sheet.

Listen to the example.
You will hear:

Here is the first question:

In your test booklet, you will see:
(A) Neptune
(B) Mars
(C) Venus
(D) Mercury

Sample Answer
● Ⓑ Ⓒ Ⓓ

The correct answer to the question "Which planet is fifth from the earth?" is (A) Neptune. You should blacken (A) on your answer sheet.

Here is the second question:

In your test booklet, you will see:
(A) Mars
(B) Venus
(C) Pluto
(D) Mercury

Sample Answer
Ⓐ Ⓑ Ⓒ ●

The correct answer to the question "Which planet resembles our moon?" is (D) Mercury. You should blacken (D) on your answer sheet.

36. (A) It's loud.
    (B) It's quiet.
    (C) It's classical.
    (D) It's familiar.

37. (A) Often
    (B) Once before
    (C) Twice before
    (D) This one time

38. (A) Dislikes it
    (B) Likes it

    (C) Bored by it
    (D) Is undecided

39. (A) Morning
    (B) Evening
    (C) Afternoon
    (D) Weekend

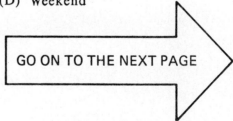
GO ON TO THE NEXT PAGE

40. (A) There's no net.
    (B) Because they don't stop.
    (C) They last all afternoon.
    (D) The crew does it.

41. (A) Greatest
    (B) Deadly
    (C) Precise
    (D) Long

42. (A) Spain
    (B) New York
    (C) Germany
    (D) Iowa

43. (A) A painting
    (B) An altar piece
    (C) A wall relief
    (D) A trophy cup

44. (A) It was German.
    (B) It was 15th century.
    (C) It was an original.
    (D) It was a fake.

45. (A) A Hapsburg prince
    (B) The board chairman

(C) The curators
(D) The clerics

46. (A) Clarity
    (B) Brilliance
    (C) Originality
    (D) Dullness

47. (A) Sunny
    (B) Cold
    (C) Rainy
    (D) Snowy

48. (A) Early morning
    (B) Midafternoon
    (C) Nightfall
    (D) Next week

49. (A) Canada
    (B) New England
    (C) Hartford
    (D) The South

50. (A) A month
    (B) One day
    (C) A week
    (D) Since nightfall

**THIS IS THE END OF THE LISTENING COMPREHENSION SECTION.
LOOK AT THE TIME NOW BEFORE YOU BEGIN WORK ON SECTION II.
YOU WILL HAVE EXACTLY 25 MINUTES TO WORK ON SECTION II.**

Section II
Structure and Written Expression
Time: 25 minutes

Section II measures your ability to recognize standard written English. There are two parts to this section. Each part has a different type of question and a different set of directions.

Part A

Directions for Questions 1-15:
You will see a sentence with a portion missing. Following the sentence will be four words or phrases. One of those words or phrases will best complete the sentence. Mark your choice on your answer sheet.

Look at this example:
The new instructor came _____ if the apartment was still available.

(A) seeing
(B) for to see
(C) to see
(D) and saw

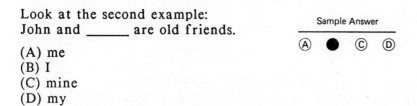

The most appropriate standard English expression would be "The new instructor came to see if the apartment was still available." You should mark (C) on your answer sheet.

Look at the second example:
John and _____ are old friends.

(A) me
(B) I
(C) mine
(D) my

The most appropriate standard English expression would be "John and I are old friends." You should mark (B) on your answer sheet.

When you have read and understood the directions, answer questions 1-15.

1. Powder when mixed with water _____.

   (A) dissolving
   (B) dissolves
   (C) it dissolve
   (D) dissolved

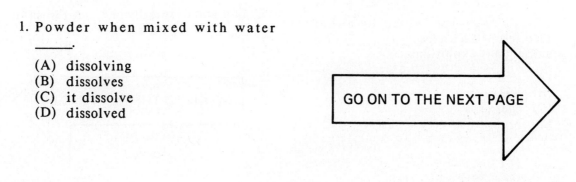

GO ON TO THE NEXT PAGE

2. _____ is thought to be one of the best investments of the decade.

(A) That the artist works
(B) That the artists work
(C) The work of that artist
(D) That the artist's work

3. Water boils _____ if there is a cover on the pan.

(A) faster
(B) more fast
(C) as fast as
(D) fast

4. In one year rats eat 40 to 50 times _____ weight.

(A) its
(B) and
(C) their
(D) of

5. If there were life on Mars, such life forms _____ unable to survive on earth.

(A) would be
(B) are
(C) will be
(D) should

6. Little is known about platinum _____ so little of it exists.

(A) but
(B) why
(C) because
(D) although

7. The damage was caused by either the earthquake _____ the subsequent explosions.

(A) and
(B) but
(C) then
(D) or

8. After _____ , the supernova hurls its mass into the black void of space.

(A) it exploding
(B) exploding
(C) explosive
(D) explodes

9. Fatal reactions to bee stings among adults _____ than once believed.

(A) more are probably common
(B) more common probably are
(C) are more probably common
(D) are probably more common

10. The vineyards are open all year except for August, which _____ .

(A) the best time to harvest is
(B) is the best time to harvest
(C) to harvest is the best time
(D) the best time is to harvest

11. Because of intermittent charging by the _____, the lights flickered.

(A) generation
(B) general
(C) generator
(D) generated

12. New research in geophysics disproved _____ had been a universally accepted truth.

(A) that
(B) which
(C) whom
(D) what

13. The static interference on the radio _____ an airplane.

GO ON TO THE NEXT PAGE

(A) was caused by
(B) was causing
(C) has caused
(D) caused by

14. Water vapor _____ on a window pane produces condensation.

   (A) which accumulating
   (B) accumulating

(C) accumulates
(D) is accumulating

15. The management requests that all personnel _____ their complaints to their immediate supervisor.

(A) will direct
(B) directs
(C) directing
(D) direct

Directions for Questions 16-40

In this section you will be given a sentence with four words or phrases underlined. One of the underlined words or phrases is not standard English. You must choose the incorrect portion and blacken the corresponding letter on your answer sheet.

Look at this example:

    Being organized is one of the most important aspect of being a good worker.
       A   B   C   D

The underlined word "aspect," letter (C), is not standard written English. You should blacken (C) on your answer sheet.

Sample Answer

Ⓐ Ⓑ ● Ⓓ

After you have read and understood the directions, you may begin questions 16-40.

16. Because of the rising cost of living, more families today they are
                 A   B
    discovering that both husband and wife must work.
                    C   D

17. A team of specialists concluded that the patient's blindness was
           A   B   C
    contemporary.
        D

18. After given the award, the recipient of the Peace Prize made
    A   B
    a short acceptance speech which was followed by a standing ovation.
                           C   D

GO ON TO THE NEXT PAGE

19. When <u>the Spanish</u> constructed <u>its missions</u> <u>in the New World</u>, they
           A   B   C

    incorporated <u>Moorish architectural features</u>.
                              D

20. Marcel Duchamp, <u>who died in 1969</u>, <u>is known</u> <u>as the artist</u> who
                                A   B   C

    <u>has abandoned</u> art for chess.
           D

21. <u>Although the country's</u> military <u>budget</u> is insufficient, the army
               A   B

    <u>be expected</u> <u>to perform well</u> in war.
        C   D

22. <u>After</u> two weeks of intensive computer training, the new recruits
    A

    <u>were allowed</u> to <u>write a program</u> <u>theirselves</u>.
        B   C   D

23. <u>The archeologist</u> believed <u>which the tomb</u> <u>discovered in</u> North Africa
        A   B   C

    <u>belonged to</u> one of Hannibal's generals.
      D

24. Meteorologists <u>have been using both computers</u> <u>or</u> satellites <u>to help make</u>
                           A   B   C

    weather forecasts <u>for two decades</u>.
                  D

25. <u>There is</u> a folk myth that <u>the horsehair</u> in a container of rainwater
      A   B

    <u>placed in the sunshine</u> <u>will develop into</u> a snake.
        C   D

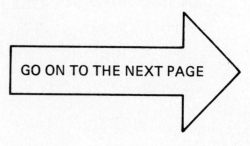

GO ON TO THE NEXT PAGE

26. The Arctic ice pack is 40 percent thin and 12 percent less in area
          A   B   C
than it was a half century ago.
 D

27. Crime prevention experts believe that if the possession of small firearms
                       A   B   C
were limited, crime and violence decreased.
                        D

28. For nesting and shelter, the sparrow seeks out the seclusion
          A   B
and being secure offered by tangled vines and thick bushes.
        C   D

29. The advent of calculators did fundamentally changed
        A   B
the teaching methods for mathematics.
        C   D

30. Aluminum, which making up about 8 percent of the earth's crust,
               A   B
is the most abundant metal available.
C   D

31. The screenwriter who provides the words for a film is acclaimed seldom,
                    A   B   C
unlike the director and the actors and actresses.
                           D

32. The cowboy epitomizes the belief held by many Americans for rugged
                               A   B
individualism and the frontier spirit.
        C   D

33. Most early immigrants are coming from an agricultural background find
        A   B   C
work on farms.
     D

GO ON TO THE NEXT PAGE

34. <u>Recently</u> gasoline manufacturers have begun to develop
    A

    <u>additives will reduce</u> the <u>harmful</u> emissions <u>from automobile engines</u>.
         B   C   D

35. <u>People, when</u> they sleep <u>less than</u> normal, <u>awake</u> more friendly
      A   B   C

    <u>and more aggression</u>.
        D

36. <u>As cooling</u> slows <u>the life</u> process, blood cells in the laboratory <u>is stored</u>
      A   B   C

    at <u>low temperatures</u>.
        D

37. The lawyers for <u>the administration</u> <u>met</u> with the representative of the
                A   B

    <u>students had been</u> occupying the building for <u>a week.</u>
        C   D

38. Restaurant patrons <u>who stay</u> after 11 o'clock will <u>have to drive, walk, or</u>
              A   B

    take a taxi home <u>unless the subway</u> stops <u>operating</u> then.
                C   D

39. The citizens, <u>who been</u> tolerant <u>of the mayor's</u> unsavory practices in
          A   B

    the past, <u>finally impeached</u> the <u>amoral politician</u>.
            C   D

40. <u>During</u> the industrial revolution, the <u>birth rate</u> in Europe <u>declined,</u>
    A   B   C

    <u>as the death rate.</u>
        D

DO NOT WORK ON ANY OTHER SECTION OF THE TEST

**IF YOU FINISH IN LESS THAN 25 MINUTES, GO OVER YOUR ANSWERS ON
SECTION II ONLY. AT THE END OF 25 MINUTES, GO TO SECTION III.
YOU WILL HAVE 45 MINUTES TO WORK ON SECTION III.**

Section III
Reading Comprehension and Vocabulary
Time: 45 minutes

In this section of the test, there are two types of questions. Each question type has its own directions.
Directions for Questions 1-30:
In each sentence a word or phrase has been underlined. There are four other words or phrases below each sentence. You must select the one word or phrase which most closely matches the meaning of the underlined word.

Example:
She always wore dresses made of
<u>synthetic</u> cloth.

(A) artificial
(B) expensive
(C) fashionable
(D) new

Sample Answer

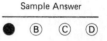

(A) is the correct answer. "She always wore dresses of artificial cloth" most closely matches the meaning of the original sentence. The letter (A) should be blackened on your answer sheet.

When you fully understand the directions, answer the following questions.

1. The <u>issue</u> we are discussing concerns everyone who has children.

    (A) subject
    (B) book
    (C) article
    (D) equation

2. The evaluation stated that the secretary's work has been <u>satisfactory</u>.

    (A) whimsical
    (B) adequate
    (C) audacious
    (D) comprehensive

3. The hospital is looking for people willing to <u>donate</u> their organs.

    (A) supply
    (B) offer
    (C) give
    (D) show

4. Most teenagers think their actions are <u>mature</u>.

    (A) grown-up
    (B) intelligent
    (C) serious
    (D) childlike

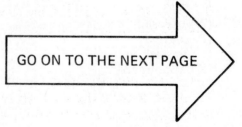

GO ON TO THE NEXT PAGE

Diagnostic Tests   69

5. The chorale wanted to <u>rehearse</u> the song before the performance.

(A) sing
(B) rewrite
(C) introduce
(D) practice

6. After an extended break, the class <u>resumed</u>.

(A) continued
(B) returned
(C) repeated
(D) receded

7. <u>Prejudice</u> towards minorities probably stems from fear of the unknown.

(A) anger
(B) bias
(C) rudeness
(D) action

8. The bank needed some <u>assurance</u> that the loan would be repaid.

(A) reliance
(B) approval
(C) guarantee
(D) presence

9. The sign requested that we <u>extinguish</u> all fires before leaving the camp ground.

(A) plug in
(B) put out
(C) remember
(D) destroy

10. Invitations were <u>extended</u> to everyone who had worked on the project.

(A) offered
(B) mailed
(C) passed on
(D) announced

11. The roof of the house was <u>practically</u> falling in and the front steps were rotting away.

(A) almost
(B) essentially
(C) always
(D) conveniently

12. Their <u>inept</u> handling of our account made us reevaluate our relationship with them.

(A) efficient
(B) clever
(C) inappropriate
(D) inferior

13. The article <u>alluded to</u> the devastation in the countryside, caused by the wind storms.

(A) misrepresented
(B) referred to
(C) forgot about
(D) recounted

14. The <u>zealous</u> demonstrators were ignored by the media.

(A) ardent
(B) colorful
(C) rude
(D) clever

15. No one ever knew the reason for the <u>enmity</u> between the two families.

(A) relationship
(B) hatred
(C) friendship
(D) closeness

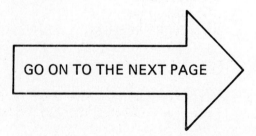

GO ON TO THE NEXT PAGE

16. The teacher thought the aspiring writer's essays were <u>verbose</u>.

    (A) interesting
    (B) concise
    (C) clever
    (D) redundant

17. The organizer's <u>intransigent</u> manner helped her get her way.

    (A) honest
    (B) stubborn
    (C) friendly
    (D) loud

18. The humidity made us more <u>lethargic</u> than usual.

    (A) thirsty
    (B) indifferent
    (C) warm
    (D) careless

19. People usually think cats are naturally <u>ferocious</u>, but it depends on the type of cat.

    (A) friendly
    (B) furry
    (C) savage
    (D) independent

20. Generosity is believed to be <u>an innate</u> quality of man.

    (A) hidden
    (B) a benevolent
    (C) natural
    (D) an unselfish

21. The greatest physical <u>distinction</u> between humans and apes is the hollow space humans have under their chins.

    (A) attraction
    (B) danger
    (C) comfort
    (D) difference

22. Physicists have made discoveries that challenge our most <u>fundamental</u> theories of the universe.

    (A) basic
    (B) permanent
    (C) interesting
    (D) ancient

23. The most recent research <u>indicates</u> that dinosaurs were warm blooded animals.

    (A) admits
    (B) insists
    (C) suggests
    (D) predicates

24. Contrary to popular belief, Cleopatra, the famous Egyptian queen, was Greek, spoke six languages, and was <u>a brilliant</u> military strategist.

    (A) an intelligent
    (B) a known
    (C) a professional
    (D) a popular

25. An archeologist must know <u>exactly</u> where and when an artifact was found.

    (A) intuitively
    (B) immediately
    (C) briefly
    (D) precisely

26. The budget director wanted to <u>be certain that</u> his officers were aware of the deadline.

    (A) ask if
    (B) pretend that
    (C) make sure that
    (D) know if

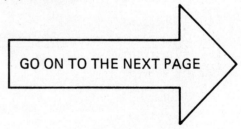
GO ON TO THE NEXT PAGE

27. The cab driver was <u>discourteous</u>.

   (A) handsome
   (B) rude
   (C) irritable
   (D) lost

28. The children in the neighborhood have a club that <u>excludes</u> everyone over eight.

   (A) laughs at
   (B) avoids
   (C) leaves out
   (D) invites

29. What is the <u>gist</u> of the article?

   (A) ending
   (B) length
   (C) title
   (D) point

30. A good magician can make an elephant <u>disappear</u>.

   (A) behave
   (B) forget
   (C) happy
   (D) vanish

Directions for Questions 31-56:
In this section, you will read passages on a variety of subjects and then answer several questions about the passages. Some of the answers will come directly from the passages; others may only be implied. Select the most appropriate answer and blacken the answer on your answer sheet.

Look at this example:

> According to scientists, 70 percent of the earth's surface is covered by water, and this watery wilderness is the habitat of four of every five living things. To aid oceanographers in their explorations of the seas and oceans of the world, scientists have been designing more and better types of undersea vessels to accomplish this task with greater safety and with more efficient tools and techniques.

Answer the first question:
1. What percentage of the earth's surface is covered by water?

   (A) 30 percent
   (B) 70 percent
   (C) 100 percent
   (D) 50 percent

   Sample Answer
   (A) ● (C) (D)

The correct answer is (B) 70 percent.

Answer the second question:
2. What percentage of the earth's inhabitants live on land?

   (A) 10 percent
   (B) 20 percent
   (C) 40 percent
   (D) 50 percent

   Sample Answer
   (A) ● (C) (D)

GO ON TO THE NEXT PAGE

The correct answer is (B) 20 percent. If four out of every five living things live in water, one of every five things, or 20 percent, must live on land.

After you have read and understood the examples, you may start to read.

Questions 31-34

LAND AND SEA ALMANAC
Sun, Moon, and Planets
June 14, 1986

Moon phases

New	First	Full	Last
June 26	July 2	July 11	June 19

	RISES	SETS
Sun	6:20 a.m.	8:04 p.m.
Moon	9:54 a.m.	8:58 p.m.
Mercury	8:17 a.m.	8:40 p.m.
Venus	7:42 a.m.	8:52 p.m.
Mars	2:31 p.m.	12:04 a.m.
Jupiter	5:09 p.m.	2:30 a.m.
Saturn	12:50 p.m.	11:30 p.m.
Uranus	3:19 p.m.	12:53 a.m.

Planets rise in the East and set in the West. Their highest points on the north-south meridian are reached halfway between their times of rising and setting.

31. The first full moon after June 14 will be

(A) June 19.
(B) July 2.
(C) July 11.
(D) June 26.

32. How long after the sun rises does the moon rise?

(A) 2 hours and 44 minutes
(B) 15 hours and 34 minutes
(C) 3 hours and 34 minutes
(D) 1 hour and 44 minutes

33. Which planet will appear first in the day?

(A) Mars
(B) Uranus
(C) Mercury
(D) Venus

34. Which planet is at its highest point at 6:10 p.m.?

(A) Saturn
(B) Uranus
(C) Venus
(D) Mercury

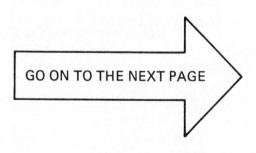
GO ON TO THE NEXT PAGE

Questions 35-38

Notice to Members:

Members' discounts on purchases of publications and reproductions were reduced 5 percent to 15 percent, effective August 27. This modest reduction is made necessary by financial difficulties that continue to effect the operations and programs of the Museum. We hope our members will understand the need for this action.

35. The members' discount was originally

(A) 5 percent.
(B) 15 percent.
(C) 20 percent.
(D) 27 percent.

36. The discount is applied to

(A) membership.
(B) admissions.
(C) programs.
(D) books.

37. Financial difficulties are being experienced by

(A) the members.
(B) the museum.
(C) the reproduction department.
(D) the publications department.

38. The notice was prepared by the

(A) membership.
(B) museum staff.
(C) book sellers.
(D) operation accountants.

Questions 39-43

Since World War II, advertising expenditures have made quantum leaps in terms of dollars allocated. As early as 1968, the United States was spending $3,775 per capita annually on advertising while the amount spent in other industrialized countries was much smaller. Per capita expenditures ranged from $2,004 in West Germany to $1,916 in Great Britain and $986 in Japan. More than half of the world's expenditures on advertising were made in this country. The volume of advertising continued to accelerate into the 1980's, paralleling the rise of discretionary spending power of American families. The results of this tremendous outlay of expenditures included further consumerism as a major factor in the national economy.

39. Which sentence is closest in meaning to the first sentence in the reading passage?

(A) The price of advertising has gone out of control since World War II.
(B) U.S. allocation of money for advertising has increased sharply since World War II.

(C) Since World War II, the U.S. has been advertising at a record rate.
(D) The quantity of dollars earned from advertising has increased in the U.S. since World War II.

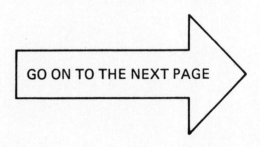
GO ON TO THE NEXT PAGE

40. The writer implies, but does not directly state, that

    (A) advertising was and is a factor in increasing American consumerism.
    (B) standardization is one of the negative effects of advertising.
    (C) too much money has been spent on advertising.
    (D) advertising is one of the most tremendous aspects of American society.

41. From the statistics cited by the author, it can be inferred that

    (A) West Germany, Great Britain, and Japan combined spent one-half as much as the United States on advertising.
    (B) The United States spent twice as much as West Germany, Great Britain, and Japan combined on advertising.
    (C) The United States spent more than twice as much per capita on advertising as did Great Britain.
    (D) West Germany, Great Britain, and Japan are less consumer oriented than the United States.

42. During the 1980's,

    (A) there has been more advertising in the United States than ever before.
    (B) American families have become more discrete in their spending habits.
    (C) the high volume of advertising resulted in the rise of the discretionary spending power of American families.
    (D) the volume of advertising and the rise of spending power are inversely proportional.

43. The author thinks that

    (A) advertising is beneficial for American business.
    (B) advertising is detrimental to American business.
    (C) advertising is a significant factor in American culture.
    (D) advertising is indispensable in a consumer-oriented society.

Question 44-47

Data collection aids the smooth functioning of government, business, and research. Personal data is used for tax assessment, job selection, credit rating assignment, and many other purposes. Aggregate data is useful for planning and formulating social

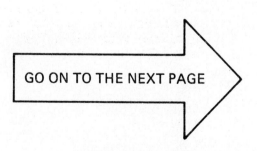

GO ON TO THE NEXT PAGE

policies. The general availability of data supports freedom of speech and freedom of the press.

Conversely, the gathering of data can erode personal privacy. Data can be used for blackmail, especially large-scale political blackmail by governments or police with too much power. Harassment of individuals by law enforcement agencies and monopolistic corporations (including utility companies) can also occur. Errors in data collection can lead to many unfair practices, such as denial of employment or denial of credit. Outdated or incomplete data can lead to personal trauma. Retention of information for long periods can result in excessive punishment of a person for a misdemeanor long since atoned for.

44. The attitude of the author can be characterized as

(A) favorable to data collection.
(B) unfavorable to data collection.
(C) fearful of the possible uses of the data collected.
(D) resigned to the inevitabilty of intrusions on privacy.

45. The reason that data supports freedom of speech and freedom of the press is that

(A) people need to discuss data freely.
(B) the more data we have, the freer people are to discuss it.
(C) it fits into a free enterprise system.
(D) it makes data available to the general public.

46. What kind of problem might be caused by incomplete data?

(A) Jail or imprisonment
(B) Loss of a job
(C) Waste of time
(D) Personal trauma

47. The author implies, but does not directly state, that

(A) some governments would blackmail their citizens.
(B) people with credit problems are victims of unfair data collection practices.
(C) data collection should be abolished.
(D) personal trauma victims should be compensated for their injuries.

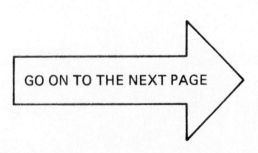

GO ON TO THE NEXT PAGE

Questions 48-51

There is still much question about the cause and effect relationship between the so-called psychologically induced ailments and the emotional problems of people suffering from these afflictions. Does the emotional state of an individual precipitate his illness, or does the illness itself bring about personality changes?

While the etiology (origins) of diseases may differ, some diseases are not to be approached exclusively through mind and others exclusively through treatment of the body. Ideally, all medicine should be psychosomatic, with the mind and the body treated as a unit.

48. Which of the following is true according to research?

(A) Psychological ailments cause emotional problems.
(B) Emotional problems cause psychological ailments.
(C) Emotional problems have no precise cause.
(D) The relationsip between emotional problems and psychological ailments is undetermined.

49. Psychosomatic medicine treats

(A) psychologically disturbed people.
(B) a variety of ailments.
(C) the mind as well as the body.
(D) the etiology of a disease.

50. A person who gets sick prior to examinations is suffering from

(A) a personality problem.
(B) a psychosomatic problem.
(C) a psychological problem.
(D) an emotional problem.

51. The author implies, but does not directly state, that

(A) the etiology of all psychosomatic illness will eventually be known.
(B) all medicine should be psychosomatic.
(C) more research needs to be done on the etiology of certain diseases.
(D) the mind and body are separate entities.

Questions 52-56

In 1905 Albert Einstein, a young European theorist and mathematician, swept many previous assumptions away with his "Special Theory of Relativity" (followed in 1916 by his "General Theory"). An international sensation occurred among scientists that by the 1920's spread to the general educated population, producing an outpouring of

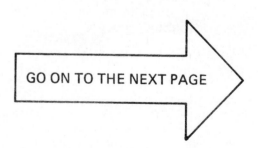
GO ON TO THE NEXT PAGE

startled and fascinated editorials, popular articles, and scholarly books. Einstein began first by making famous a hitherto little-noted experiment, conducted in Ohio in 1887 by Albert A. Michelson and Edward W. Morely, that proved that ether did not exist. Physicists were shocked, for they had built all their theories about light, energy, and other radiations on the assumption that they were transmitted through the universe by ether much as water transmits waves. Michelson and Morely proved something else as well: that the speed of light is a constant 186,000 miles per second whether the person measuring its speed is moving toward the light source or away from it. How could this be?

52. One of the assumptions swept away by Einstein was that

(A) ether did not exist.
(B) light was transmitted through the universe by ether.
(C) water transmits waves through the ocean.
(D) the speed of light is not constant.

53. Michelson and Morely's work

(A) contradicted Einstein's work.
(B) followed Einstein's work.
(C) stimulated Einstein to invalidate their results.
(D) was consistent with Einstein's work.

54. The reason that the author asks "How could this be?" is that

(A) it is difficult to measure the speed of light.
(B) the speed of light is incredibly fast.
(C) it isn't easy to understand how the speed of light can be constant given motion by the person measuring it.
(D) it is very difficult to understand how anyone could move fast enough to measure the speed of light.

55. Michelson and Morely's experiment was

(A) well known before 1905.
(B) not accepted until 1906.
(C) not generally appreciated until 1905.
(D) none of the above.

56. In the paragraph following this one, the author would probably

(A) explain how Einstein resolved the apparent contradiction regarding the measurement of the speed of light.
(B) go on to cite more of the work of Michelson and Morely which Einstein made famous.
(C) enumerate the editorials, articles, and books influenced by Einstein's work.
(D) begin a lengthy exposition of the differences between Einstein's special and general theories of relativity.

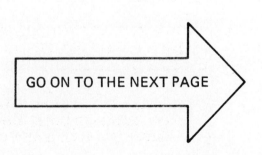

GO ON TO THE NEXT PAGE

Directions for Questions 57-60

In this section, you must select the statement that most nearly matches the original statement. Many of the statements are true, but only one is a restatement of the original.

57. Yellow legal pads come in two sizes: 81/2" by 11" and 81/2" by 14".

(A) There are two main sizes of legal pads: 81/2" by 11" and 81/2 by 14".

(B) 81/2" by 11" and 81/2" by 14" are the dimensions of the legal pads.

(C) Yellow legal pads are 81/2" wide and between 11" and 14" in length.

(D) Two legal types of yellow pads are 81/2" by 11" and 81/2" by 14".

58. Dinner was excellent except for the fried zucchini, which was a little bit on the mushy side.

(A) In general, dinner was good, but the mushy zucchini was not to my liking.

(B) Outside of the mushy fried zucchini, I enjoyed my dinner.

(C) If it hadn't been for the fried zucchini, dinner would have been excellent.

(D) Except for the mushy fried zucchini, dinner was excellent.

59. As far as the emperor was concerned, Trok was the Middle Kingdom; barbarian nations would continue to pay tribute.

(A) "Trok is the Middle Kingdom," thought the emperor. "Why should the barbarians not pay tribute?"

(B) The emperor's view was that the barbarian countries would be required to continue to pay tribute since Trok was, after all, the Middle Kingdom.

(C) The emperor regarded continuation of tribute to be the duty of the barbarian countries with respect to the Middle Kingdom.

(D) The emperor of the Middle Kingdom was adamant in his view that tribute would continue to be paid by the barbarian nations.

60. Who can say if the true value of a liberal education will ever be calculated?

(A) None will ever know the true worth of liberal studies.

(B) It is problematical that a liberal education's value will ever be correctly calculated.

(C) Can somebody tell me what a liberal education is worth?

(D) Who can say whether or not calculating a liberal education is worth it?

DO NOT WORK ON ANY OTHER SECTION OF THE TEST

IF YOU FINISH IN LESS THAN 45 MINUTES, GO OVER YOUR ANSWERS ON SECTION III ONLY. AT THE END OF 45 MINUTES, STOP WORK AND CORRECT YOUR ANSWERS WITH THE ANSWER KEY WHICH FOLLOWS.

CODED ANSWER KEY DIAGNOSTIC TEST 3

SECTION I: LISTENING COMPREHENSION

Part A - Statements

1. (C) - minimal pair
2. (B) - computation
3. (B) - number discrimination
4. (C) - negation
5. (D) - synonym
6. (D) - contextual reference
7. (C) - cause/effect
8. (D) - conditional
9. (A) - chronological order
10. (B) - comparison
11. (D) - comparison
12. (C) - chronological order
13. (D) - conditional
14. (B) - cause/effect
15. (C) - contextual reference
16. (B) - negation
17. (C) - synonym
18. (D) - number discrimination
19. (B) - computation
20. (D) - minimal pair

Part B - Conversations

21. (A) - comparison
22. (B) - chronological order
23. (D) - conditional
24. (B) - cause/effect
25. (D) - minimal pair
26. (D) - contextual reference
27. (A) - minimal pair
28. (A) - number discrimination
29. (D) - computation
30. (B) - contextual reference
31. (C) - contextual reference
32. (D) - cause/effect
33. (D) - conditional
34. (A) - chronological order
35. (A) - comparison

Part C - Mini Talks

36.	(A)	41.	(A)	46.	(B)
37.	(D)	42.	(D)	47.	(C)
38.	(D)	43.	(C)	48.	(B)
39.	(C)	44.	(D)	49.	(A)
40.	(A)	45.	(C)	50.	(C)

SECTION II: STRUCTURE AND WRITTEN EXPRESSION

Part A

1. (B) - verb: tense
2. (C) - subject: agreement/word order
3. (A) - comparison
4. (C) - pronoun: agreement
5. (A) - conditional
6. (C) - conjunction: form
7. (D) - conjunction: parallel structure
8. (B) - subordinate clause: reduced adverb
9. (D) - word order: adjective-adverb
10. (B) - word order: subject-verb
11. (C) - word family
12. (D) - subordinate clause: noun
13. (A) - active-passive
14. (B) - subordinate clause: reduced adjective
15. (D) - subjunctive

Part B

16. (B) - subject: repetition *omit they*
17. (D) - word family *temporary*
18. (A) - active-passive: verb omission *being*
19. (B) - pronoun: agreement *their missions*
20. (D) - verb tense *abandoned*
21. (C) - verb: is expected
22. (D) - pronoun: *themselves*
23. (B) - subordinate clause: noun *that*
24. (B) - conjunction: form *and*
25. (B) - article *a*
26. (B) - comparison *thinner*
27. (D) - conditional *would decrease*
28. (C) - conjunction: parallel structures *security*
29. (B) - verb: unnecessary verb omit *did*
30. (A) - subordinate clause: reduced adjective *omit which*
31. (C) - word order: adverb *is seldom acclaimed*
32. (B) - preposition: *in rugged*
33. (B) - subordinate clause: reduced adjective *omit are*
34. (B) - subordinate clause: adjective *additives which will*
35. (D) - conjunction: parallel structure *more aggressive*
36. (C) - verb: agreement *cells are stored*
37. (C) - subordinate clause: adjective *students who had*
38. (C) - subordination: adverb clause *because*
39. (A) - subordination: adjective clause *who had been*
40. (D) - verb: omission *as did the death rate*

SECTION III: READING COMPREHENSION AND VOCABULARY

Vocabulary

1.	(A)	16.	(D)
2.	(B)	17.	(B)
3.	(C)	18.	(B)
4.	(A)	19.	(C)
5.	(D)	20.	(C)
6.	(A)	21.	(D)
7.	(B)	22.	(A)
8.	(C)	23.	(C)
9.	(B)	24.	(A)
10.	(A)	25.	(D)
11.	(A)	26.	(C)
12.	(C)	27.	(B)
13.	(B)	28.	(C)
14.	(A)	29.	(D)
15.	(B)	30.	(D)

Reading Comprehension

31. (C) - fact
32. (C) - fact
33. (B) - fact
34. (A) - fact
35. (C) - inference
36. (D) - inference
37. (B) - main idea
38. (B) - inference
39. (B) - paraphrase
40. (A) - inference
41. (C) - fact
42. (A) - fact
43. (C) - inference
44. (C) - inference
45. (D) - fact
46. (D) - fact
47. (A) - inference
48. (D) - fact
49. (C) - fact
50. (B) - inference
51. (C) - inference
52. (B) - inference
53. (D) - inference
54. (C) - fact
55. (C) - inference
56. (A) - inference
57. (B) - paraphrase
58. (D) - paraphrase
59. (B) - paraphrase
60. (A) - paraphrase

Section I
Listening Comprehension
Time: 40 minutes

Section I measures your ability to understand spoken English. There are three parts to the Listening Comprehension section. Each part has its own question types and its own directions.

Part A

Directions:
In this part of the test, you will hear a short statement which will NOT be repeated. You must pay careful attention to this statement.

In your test booklet, you will see four sentences. One of those written sentences means almost the same as the short statement you hear. You must choose the sentence which most closely matches the meaning of the oral statement. You must then mark your answer on the answer sheet.

Listen to an example.
You will hear:

Sample Answer

Ⓐ Ⓑ Ⓒ ●

In your test book, you will see:
(A) He will not eat beets.
(B) The candidate did not bet.
(C) They thought the dates sweet.
(D) His rival cannot beat him.

The correct answer is (D). "His rival cannot beat him" most closely matches the statement "The candidate will not be beat." The letter (D) should be blackened on your answer sheet.

Listen to another example.
You will hear:

Sample Answer

● Ⓑ Ⓒ Ⓓ

In your text book, you will see:
(A) She is careless in her work.
(B) She always goes free on trains.
(C) She never has tension headaches.
(D) She never shops at sales.

The correct answer is (A). "She is careless in her work" most closely matches the statement "She never pays attention to the details." The letter (A) should be blackened on your answer sheet.

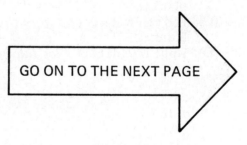

GO ON TO THE NEXT PAGE

1. (A) We owed him for the fish.
   (B) Fishing is best at night.
   (C) He kept the boat until evening
   (D) He did not return the boat.

2. (A) We got them 6 minutes later.
   (B) We got them 16 minutes later.
   (C) It was 11:30 when we called them.
   (D) It was 11:36 when we called.

3. (A) In distress she sat down.
   (B) Her dress was torn.
   (C) She gave her address downtown.
   (D) The store was close to town.

4. (A) We woke at 8:30.
   (B) We woke at 6:32
   (C) We had 9 hours of sleep.
   (D) We woke at 9:00.

5. (A) The Brazil flight was number 60.
   (B) The Brazil flight was due at 6:16.
   (C) The Brazil flight was due at 6:10.
   (D) The Brazil flight was number 16.

6. (A) The airport was 15 minutes away.
   (B) The plane left at 8:13.
   (C) I woke at half past 8.
   (D) The flight left at 8:30.

7. (A) I put the blanket into the car.
   (B) I dried the car with the blanket.
   (C) I drove the car over the blanket.
   (D) I put the blanket over the car.

8. (A) He offered me some raisins.
   (B) He was too angry for a rational discussion.
   (C) He showed me his new play.
   (D) He showed me his list of reasons.

9. (A) I never heard the phone.
   (B) They'll sweep the top story.
   (C) I always cry at stories about orphans.
   (D) I never listen to sad children.

10. (A) The best people were present.
    (B) Two people received prizes.
    (C) She was presented an address book.
    (D) The community leaders wanted a prestigious address.

11. (A) Farmers sent bills to the senator's attention.
    (B) Bill lived in the top floor apartment.
    (C) The rain was only one reason not to go.
    (D) There was a great deal of legislation.

12. (A) The lecture notes were almost blown by the wind.
    (B) The guests asked for some paper.
    (C) The newspaper reported the speech.
    (D) Strong opinions should not be repeated.

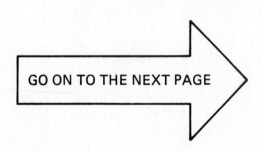
GO ON TO THE NEXT PAGE

13. (A) The printer approved the editor's magazine.
    (B) The magazine was not approved by the editor.
    (C) The magazine was not printed.
    (D) The editor approved the magazine before it was printed.

14. (A) Three power generators will be installed next year.
    (B) People must not use electricity for cooking.
    (C) Demand for power will exceed supply.
    (D) This generation must eat less and reduce.

15. (A) Buildings in earthquake zones need strong support.
    (B) The proof could not have been greater.
    (C) The motion was defeated.
    (D) The motion of the boat made it hard to stand on our feet.

16. (A) The men stood in a row.
    (B) Two soldiers received a promotion.
    (C) The commander stood higher than the others.
    (D) The men's names were on a list.

17. (A) The car ran out of gas during a long race.

    (B) This long sofa is not very functional.
    (C) A problem with the pump shortened the mission.
    (D) They jumped at the chance to stay longer.

18. (A) The cat chased the mouse after climbing the tree.
    (B) The cat chased the mouse before climbing the tree.
    (C) The bird left after the cat climbed the tree.
    (D) The cat left after the nest was abandoned.

19. (A) The gas for the new car is cheaper.
    (B) There is less gas in the new car's tank.
    (C) The gas for my old car was more expensive.
    (D) My new tank is bigger.

20. (A) I studied, but the exam was difficult.
    (B) The exam was easy because I studied.
    (C) I didn't study, but the exam was easy.
    (D) The exam was difficult because I didn't study.

Part B

Directions:
In this part there will be 15 short dialogues between two speakers. A third person will ask a question about the dialogue. This question will not be repeated.
Listen carefully to the dialogue and the question and then choose an answer from one of the four possible answers given in the test booklet. Mark the corresponding letter on your answer sheet.

GO ON TO THE NEXT PAGE

1	1	1	1	1	1	1	1

Listen to an example.
You will hear this dialogue:

In your test booklet you will see:
(A) Finish the program, then study
(B) Study rather than watch the program
(C) See the show he saw last week
(D) Watch the program while studying

Listening to the dialogue, we learned that the man is going to study and not watch the TV program. Therefore, (B) is the most appropriate answer. The letter (B) should be blackened on your answer sheet.

21. (A) An opthalmologist
    (B) A pediatrician
    (C) An intern
    (D) A neurosurgeon

22. (A) 6 p.m.
    (B) 7 p.m.
    (C) 10 p.m.
    (D) 11 p.m.

23. (A) 80
    (B) 18
    (C) 5:38
    (D) 5:18

24. (A) Retired
    (B) Withdrawn
    (C) Fatigued
    (D) Talkative

25. (A) Avoid them
    (B) Go home
    (C) Repeat himself
    (D) Attend a party

26. (A) Mrs. Smith
    (B) Her father's family
    (C) Her family
    (D) Mr. Smith

27. (A) The trash taken outside
    (B) Something for her rash
    (C) The man to fill the sack
    (D) Enough to fill out the bag

28. (A) They didn't like the other restaurant.
    (B) He generally eats more than she.
    (C) She eats more than he.
    (D) This is the most they've ever eaten.

29. (A) Go to the mechanic
    (B) Go to the office
    (C) Go home
    (D) Stop for groceries

30. (A) Thin socks
    (B) Too much walking
    (C) New shoes
    (D) Not enough exercise

31. (A) The woman
    (B) Too little sleep
    (C) A hat
    (D) The sun

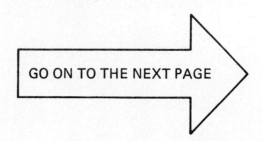

GO ON TO THE NEXT PAGE

32. (A) The man's
    (B) Annie's
    (C) Bill's
    (D) Joe's

33. (A) Tall
    (B) Short
    (C) Bald
    (D) Thin

34. (A) With a funny story
    (B) With a laugh
    (C) With a lecture
    (D) Easily

35. (A) It's the dullest.
    (B) It's ridiculous.
    (C) It's short.
    (D) It's plain.

Part C

Directions:

In Part C, you will hear several short talks on a variety of subjects. Each talk will be followed by several questions. Neither the talks nor the questions will be repeated. You will have to pay close attention to both.

After you hear the question, you will have to pick the most appropriate answer from the four choices in the test booklet. You will then mark the corresponding letter on your answer sheet.

Listen to the example.
You will hear:

Here is the first question:

In your test booklet, you will see:
(A) Neptune
(B) Mars
(C) Venus
(D) Mercury

Sample Answer
● Ⓑ Ⓒ Ⓓ

The correct answer to the question "Which planet is fifth from the earth?" is (A) Neptune. You should blacken (A) on your answer sheet.

Here is the second question:

In your test booklet, you will see:
(A) Mars
(B) Venus
(C) Pluto
(D) Mercury

Sample Answer
Ⓐ Ⓑ Ⓒ ●

The correct answer to the question "Which planet resembles our moon?" is (D) Mercury. You should blacken (D) on your answer sheet.

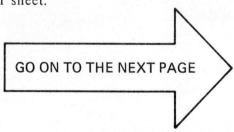
GO ON TO THE NEXT PAGE

36. (A) Balmy weather
    (B) Heavy rain
    (C) Drought
    (D) Heat waves

37. (A) New England
    (B) Texas
    (C) California
    (D) New York

38. (A) Unchanging
    (B) Inconsistent
    (C) Fluctuating
    (D) Volatile

39. (A) Tea room etiquette
    (B) Chinese exports
    (C) Design trends in history
    (D) Fine arts

40. (A) 16th century
    (B) 1600
    (C) 1685
    (D) 18th century

41. (A) Its shape
    (B) Its color
    (C) Its rarity
    (D) Its taste

42. (A) All have spouts.
    (B) All are silver.
    (C) All have covers.
    (D) All have handles.

43. (A) It was cheap.
    (B) It maintained heat.

(C) It could be decorated.
(D) It could be found anywhere.

44. (A) Expensive machines
    (B) Adequate protection from dust
    (C) Continuous maintenance
    (D) More delicate components

45. (A) 17 by 8
    (B) 7 by 5
    (C) 17 by 5
    (D) 70 by 17

46. (A) Their small size
    (B) Their lack of reliability
    (C) Their delicateness
    (D) Their maintenance problems

47. (A) One made especially for a drive
    (B) One passed by customs
    (C) One designed by computer
    (D) One made for each customer

48. (A) Geometry
    (B) Cooking
    (C) English
    (D) Medicine

49. (A) He likes the teacher.
    (B) He likes the subject.
    (C) It's required to graduate.
    (D) He needs English.

50. (A) Freshman
    (B) Junior
    (C) Sophomore
    (D) Senior

**THIS IS THE END OF THE LISTENING COMPREHENSION SECTION.
LOOK AT THE TIME NOW BEFORE YOU BEGIN WORK ON SECTION II.
YOU WILL HAVE EXACTLY 25 MINUTES TO WORK ON SECTION II.**

Section II
Structure and Written Expression
Time: 25 minutes

Section II measures your ability to recognize standard written English. There are two parts to this section. Each part has a different type of question and a different set of directions.

Directions for Questions 1-15:
You will see a sentence with a portion missing. Following the sentence will be four words or phrases. One of those words or phrases will best complete the sentence. Mark your choice on your answer sheet.

Look at this example:
The new instructor came _____ if the apartment was still available.

(A) seeing
(B) for to see
(C) to see
(D) and saw

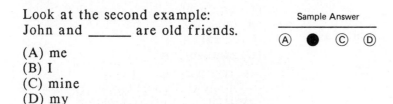

Sample Answer
Ⓐ Ⓑ ● Ⓓ

The most appropriate standard English expression would be "The new instructor came <u>to see</u> if the apartment was still available." You should mark (C) on your answer sheet.

Look at the second example:
John and _____ are old friends.

Sample Answer
Ⓐ ● Ⓒ Ⓓ

(A) me
(B) I
(C) mine
(D) my

The most appropriate standard English expression would be "John and <u>I</u> are old friends." You should mark (B) on your answer sheet.

When you have read and understood the directions, answer questions 1-15.

1. Although we sent out invitations, we have no idea _____ coming to the party.

   (A) who are
   (B) whom are
   (C) who is
   (D) whom is

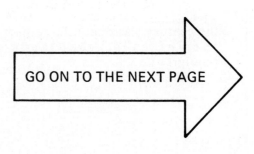

GO ON TO THE NEXT PAGE

2. The mayor felt that the police, in spite of the reports, had done _____ best in a difficult situation.

   (A) its
   (B) their
   (C) his
   (D) our

3. The pioneers _____ the frontier had a difficult life with few comforts.

   (A) on
   (B) in
   (C) inside
   (D) over

4. _____ there is a snowstorm or some other bad weather, the mail always comes on time.

   (A) because
   (B) if
   (C) so
   (D) unless

5. The typist was fast _____, and was hired immediately.

   (A) but efficient
   (B) and efficiently
   (C) so efficient
   (D) and efficient

6. Since calculators were introduced, they _____ to be useful tools for people weak in math.

   (A) proved
   (B) will prove
   (C) have proved
   (D) are proving

7. The _____ economy at the turn of the century was due in large part to the influx of thousands of immigrants.

   (A) rapid expanding
   (B) rapid expand
   (C) expand rapidly
   (D) rapidly expanding

8. Not being able to determine what _____ is the biggest obstacle for new managers.

   (A) the priority should be
   (B) it should be the priority
   (C) should the priority be
   (D) should be it the priority

9. Mr. Kwok cooks continental cuisine _____ as the best cooks in Europe.

   (A) as good
   (B) as better
   (C) better
   (D) as well

10. The nation was founded on the principle that all men are created _____.

    (A) equitable
    (B) equality
    (C) equal
    (D) equilibrium

11. Some doctors involved in brain research _____ that violence has its roots in certain sections of the brain.

    (A) are believing
    (B) believe
    (C) believing
    (D) believes

GO ON TO THE NEXT PAGE

12. That woman _____ speaking softly can barely be understood.

(A) whose
(B) whom is
(C) who is
(D) who

13. Even _____ to believe otherwise, the central Arctic is not a solid sheet of ice.

(A) though many do not want
(B) many do want not
(C) though not many do want
(D) many do not want

14. The language of the Sumerians, _____ , is unrelated to any known language.

(A) which remains obscure origin
(B) whose origin remains obscure
(C) whose remains obscure origin
(D) who is origin obscure remain

15. After _____ the angry mob shouting for his resignation, the President summoned his loyal aides to his office.

(A) their hearing
(B) they hearing
(C) heard
(D) hearing

Directions for Questions 16-40:
In this section you will be given a sentence with four words or phrases underlined. One of the underlined words or phrases is not standard English. You must choose the incorrect portion and blacken the corresponding letter on your answer sheet.

Look at this example:

Being organized is certainly one of the most important aspect of being a good
       A   B   C   D

worker.

The underlined word "aspect," letter (D), is not standard written English. You should blacken (D) on your answer sheet.

Sample Answer

Ⓐ   Ⓑ   Ⓒ   ●

After you have read and understood the directions, you may begin questions 16-40.

16. Physics is probably being the most highly organized branch of science today.
                A   B   C   D

GO ON TO THE NEXT PAGE

2	2	2	2	2	2	2	2

17. Psychologists <u>who study</u> sleep <u>habits believe</u> day dreaming is <u>an intrinsic and</u>
                A   B   C
essential part of <u>daily</u> life.
                D

18. People who <u>always</u> on time cannot understand the <u>seemingly</u> intentional
                A   B
<u>tardiness</u> of people <u>who</u> are always late.
   C   D

19. Elizabeth I <u>of England</u> had <u>more wigs</u> in her wardrobe <u>than</u> hairs <u>in her head</u>.
               A   B   C   D

20. Man can <u>control changes</u> in nature by <u>imitating them</u>, by using them,
             A   B   C
<u>and also man can inhibit them</u>, too.
                D

21. Greek <u>science preserved</u> for <u>posterity by the</u> Arabs, <u>who introduced</u> to science
             A   B   C
<u>the Arabic system of numbers</u>.
                D

22. If <u>a</u> <u>hydrogen-filled</u> balloon is brought <u>near a flame</u>, <u>it exploded</u>.
    A   B   C   D

23. Hormones are chemical <u>substances are produced</u> in the body by
                             A
<u>structures known</u> <u>as glands, such as</u> sweat <u>glands and</u> salivary glands.
      B   C   D

24. <u>Outside of Japan</u> <u>seldom potters are</u> regarded <u>as</u> anything
        A   B   C
<u>more than craftsmen</u>.
   D

GO ON TO THE NEXT PAGE

25. Tourists like <u>to travel</u> to <u>the</u> Eastern Shore <u>so the food is good</u>, the people
              A   B   C

    are <u>friendly</u>, and the prices are reasonable.
         D

26. <u>Getting used</u> to eating fast food <u>and traffic</u> jams are problems newcomers
        A   B

    <u>have to</u> face <u>after arriving</u> in Los Angeles.
     C   D

27. <u>Today it is</u> almost impossible <u>to imagination</u> the <u>boredom and constrictions</u>
      A   B   C

    of the <u>average middle-class woman's life</u> before World War II.
              D

28. <u>A</u> World Health Organization survey <u>showed that</u> <u>incidence of eye</u> disease
    A   B   C

    along <u>the Nile three times</u> that along the Amazon.
          D

29. <u>In a recent ranking</u> of American cities, Rand McNally rated Pittsburgh,
         A

    Pennsylvania, as the most <u>livable</u> city <u>and</u> Yuba City, California, <u>as the less</u>.
                         B   C   D

30. The <u>hippopotamus kills</u> <u>more men</u> each year <u>than lion</u> and the
          A   B   C

    <u>elephant combined</u>.
       D

31. The Federal Art Project of 1935 supported some 5000 <u>artists, enabling</u>
                                              A

    <u>their to work</u> all over America <u>rather than come</u> to New York
     B   C

    <u>in search of a market</u>.
       D

GO ON TO THE NEXT PAGE

32. The first sound at Groton is the great bell <u>in the school house tower</u>
                                                          A

    <u>tolling six times</u> over <u>the lawn</u> that is the center <u>at the school</u>.
           B   C   D

33. <u>Sophisticated</u> <u>communications have</u> taken the challenge <u>out of travel</u> in remote
         A   B   C

    places <u>which are far away</u>.
                  D

34. Since first <u>it being</u> performed <u>on a bare stage</u> <u>in the fifties</u>, Wagner's Ring
                    A   B   C

    Cycle <u>has usually been</u> done in minimalist conceptual decor.
               D

35. <u>Because</u> the African tsetse is <u>a serious threat</u> to human health, <u>it helps</u>
        A   B   C

    maintain <u>the delicate balance</u> of nature.
                    D

36. <u>Serious bird watchers</u> must know not only the <u>appearance nor the sounds</u>
              A   B

    of the 840-odd <u>species that can be</u> counted <u>in North America</u>.
                          C   D

37. Rhodes Tavern, a quaint building over 200 years old <u>which it will</u> be torn
                                                              A

    down <u>soon</u>, <u>was considered</u> a historical monument <u>until</u> investors
            B   C   D

    wanted it.

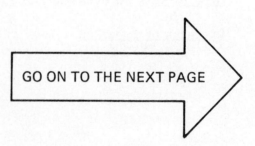

GO ON TO THE NEXT PAGE

2	2	2	2	2	2	2	2

38. Many sociologists <u>believe</u> <u>that sports organized</u> serve <u>both a recreational and</u>
                          A   B   C

    a social function <u>by reflecting</u> the values of society.
                           D

39. Critics of television <u>commercials</u> would prefer <u>that advertisers conform</u>
                          A   B

    to a stricter code of ethics <u>than was</u> currently <u>in effect</u>.
                             C   D

40. <u>Education on</u> enviromental issues <u>it should include</u> not only physical
          A   B

    <u>problems like pollution</u> but also social <u>problems caused by</u> pollution.
          C   D

DO NOT WORK ON ANY OTHER SECTION OF THE TEST

**IF YOU FINISH IN LESS THAN 25 MINUTES, GO OVER YOUR ANSWERS ON
SECTION II ONLY. AT THE END OF 25 MINUTES, GO TO SECTION III.
YOU WILL HAVE 45 MINUTES TO WORK ON SECTION III.**

Section III
Reading Comprehension and Vocabulary
Time: 45 minutes

In this section of the test, there are two types of questions. Each question type has its own directions.

Directions for Questions 1-30:
In each sentence a word or phrase has been underlined. There are four other words or phrases below each sentence. You must select the one word or phrase which most closely matches the meaning of the underlined word.

Example: She always wore dresses made of underlined{synthetic} cloth.

(A) artificial
(B) expensive
(C) fashionable
(D) new

Sample Answer

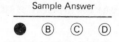

(A) is the correct answer. "She always wore dresses of artificial cloth" most closely matches the meaning of the original sentence. The letter (A) should be blackened on your answer sheet.

When you fully understand the directions, answer the following questions.

1. The icy roads made driving very underlined{hazardous}.

   (A) challenging
   (B) dangerous
   (C) slippery
   (D) exciting

2. After watching the sunset, I was left with a very underlined{tranquil} feeling.

   (A) queasy
   (B) sad
   (C) peaceful
   (D) sleepy

3. People with underlined{introverted} personalities find it difficult to make friends.

   (A) obnoxious
   (B) forward
   (C) reserved
   (D) cautious

4. The last mayor was underlined{assassinated} when he was fifty years old.

   (A) honored
   (B) murdered
   (C) elected
   (D) impeached

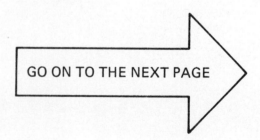

GO ON TO THE NEXT PAGE

5. As a result of the <u>expansion</u> of the public transit system, the university will disband its shuttle bus service.

   (A) problems
   (B) painting
   (C) decrease
   (D) enlargement

6. The child <u>charged</u> down the steps.

   (A) ran
   (B) fell
   (C) came
   (D) loped

7. The cry was barely <u>audible</u>.

   (A) able to be heard
   (B) able to be seen
   (C) able to be felt
   (D) able to be ignored

8. Self-confidence is <u>an essential</u> factor for a successful person.

   (A) a possible
   (B) an integral
   (C) a minor
   (D) a negative

9. The theater critics thought the movie was <u>horrendous</u>, and the audience agreed with them.

   (A) delightful
   (B) dreadful
   (C) spectacular
   (D) obscene

10. The politician's manner was <u>blatantly</u> dishonest, so the election results were not a surprise.

    (A) openly
    (B) hardly
    (C) offensively
    (D) extremely

11. The dog's <u>furtive</u> actions made me worry about him.

    (A) unusual
    (B) sleepy
    (C) secretive
    (D) sickly

12. Mark is a <u>kindred</u> soul, so my friends will like him.

    (A) related
    (B) kindly
    (C) polite
    (D) humorous

13. The popular singer was as <u>ludicrous</u> in his dress as he was in his speech.

    (A) comical
    (B) loud
    (C) somber
    (D) common

14. The teacher explained the <u>nuances</u> in Frost's poetry to the class.

    (A) images
    (B) subtleties
    (C) rhythm
    (D) rhymes

15. The <u>opportune</u> moment had arrived, but few took advantage of it.

    (A) awaited
    (B) lucky
    (C) appropriate
    (D) anticipated

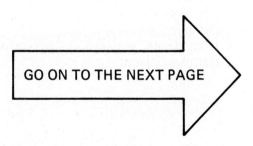

GO ON TO THE NEXT PAGE

16. The travel agent tried to <u>tantalize</u> me with details of a proposed trip to the islands.

    (A) tempt
    (B) dissuade
    (C) inform
    (D) fool

17. The natural elements <u>obliterated</u> the writing from the walls of the monument.

    (A) outlined
    (B) erased
    (C) covered
    (D) produced

18. The <u>sealed</u> chambers of the ancient pharaohs were the goal of the expedition.

    (A) hidden
    (B) unreachable
    (C) ancient
    (D) closed

19. Many of the pictures were <u>reproduced</u> and enlarged.

    (A) taken again
    (B) printed again
    (C) renewed
    (D) restored

20. The valley, wild and <u>inaccessible</u>, had been the haunt of bandits.

    (A) impenetrable
    (B) desolate
    (C) high
    (D) dry

21. Children often <u>imitate</u> their parents.

    (A) copy
    (B) criticize
    (C) admire
    (D) remember

22. The administration <u>took for granted</u> that we would agree.

    (A) hoped
    (B) assumed
    (C) guaranteed
    (D) were convinced

23. The tenor's singing <u>captivated</u> the audience.

    (A) frightened
    (B) bored
    (C) disgusted
    (D) enchanted

24. A review of the history of economics shows a recession may <u>precede</u> a depression.

    (A) point to
    (B) come before
    (C) indicate
    (D) cause

25. The punishment should reflect the <u>severity</u> of the crime.

    (A) seriousness
    (B) purpose
    (C) location
    (D) perpetrator

26. Many animals <u>collect a supply of</u> food for the winter.

    (A) bury
    (B) desire
    (C) accumulate
    (D) require

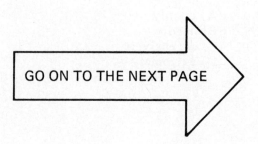
GO ON TO THE NEXT PAGE

27. The robot, although <u>reliable</u>, has limited use.

 (A) dependable
 (B) automatic
 (C) versatile
 (D) fast

28. In the United States a <u>typical</u> work day is eight hours long.

 (A) characteristic
 (B) complete
 (C) total
 (D) hard

29. If you are visiting a foreign country, you may be <u>unaccustomed to</u> eating unfamiliar foods.

 (A) surprised at
 (B) unused to
 (C) disappointed in
 (D) afraid of

30. Because the teenager was <u>ashamed</u> that she failed her driving test, she would not come home.

 (A) disappointed
 (B) unhappy
 (C) humiliated
 (D) disgusted

Directions for Questions 31-56:
In this section, you will read passages on a variety of subjects and then answer several questions about the passages. Some of the answers will come directly from the passages; others may only be implied. Select the most appropriate answer and blacken the answer on your answer sheet.

Look at this example:

> According to scientists, 70 percent of the earth's surface is covered by water, and this watery wilderness is the habitat of four of every five living things. To aid oceanographers in their explorations of the seas and oceans of the world, scientists have been designing more and better types of undersea vessels to accomplish this task with greater safety and with more efficient tools and techniques.

Answer the first question:
1. What percentage of the earth's surface is covered by water?

(A) 30 percent
(B) 70 percent
(C) 100 percent
(D) 50 percent

Sample Answer

Ⓐ ● Ⓒ Ⓓ

The correct answer is (B) 70 percent.

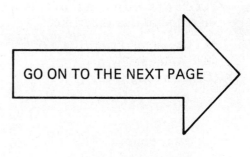
GO ON TO THE NEXT PAGE

3	3	3	3	3	3	3	3

Answer the second question:
2. What percentage of the earth's inhabitants live on land?

(A) 10 percent
(B) 20 percent
(C) 40 percent
(D) 50 percent

Sample Answer

Ⓐ ● Ⓒ Ⓓ

The correct answer is (B) 20 percent. If four out of every five living things live in water, one of every five things, or 20 percent, must live on land.

After you have read and understood the examples, you may start to read.

Questions 31-33

Courses for Children Grades 7-12

Roots of Primitive Art
For grades 7-9. This five-session course includes discussions of 18th and 19th century art, related studio workshops, and special visits to the Primitives and Masters exhibition at the Academy of Fine Arts. First class Fri. Oct. 23, 3:30-5:30. For information/registration, call 879-5550, ext. 3735.

Ancient Egypt: Lights, Camera, Action!
For grades 7-12. First program Tombs, Sat. Oct. 27, 2:00-2:45. City Center Auditorium. Free. Minimum age 11.

Drawing Class for Students
For grades 7-9. Sat. Oct. 13-Jan. 26, 1:00-2:30. Students may come once or every Saturday. Meet in the Calnon Center.

After School and Saturday Art Classes
For grades 9-12. Free classes include gallery talks, slide presentations, sketching projects. For further information call 879-5550, ext. 3961.

31. Which course accommodates both the youngest and the oldest students?

   (A) Roots of Primitive Art
   (B) Ancient Egypt
   (C) Drawing Class
   (D) After School and Saturday Classes

32. During which 10-week course may students come as often or as infrequently as they like?

   (A) Roots of Primitive Art
   (B) Ancient Egypt
   (C) Drawing Class

   (D) After School and Saturday Art Classes

33. These courses are probably offered by

   (A) a sports center
   (B) a church
   (C) a museum
   (D) a science center

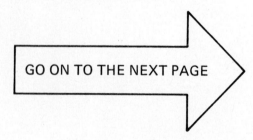
GO ON TO THE NEXT PAGE

3	3	3	3	3	3	3	3

Questions 34-36

Following are the top 10 network prime-time shows last week, ranked according to the percentage of the nation's 83.8 million TV households that watched between 7 and 10 o'clock. The statistics were compiled by the Ozzie Company. A share represents the percentage of actual sets in use tuned to a particular program when that program was being broadcast.

RATING		SHARE	NETWORK
1. 24.8	Dallas	44	CBS
2. 22.3	Love Boat	39	ABC
3. 17.5	Fantasy Island	30	ABC
4. 16.7	Riptide	36	NBC
5. 15.9	Remington Steele	28	NBC
6. 15.6	A-Team	29	CBS
7. 15.2	Webster	32	ABC
8. 15.1	Trapper John	27	CBS
9. 14.6	Alice	27	CBS
10. 13.8	Hill Street Blues	25	NBC

34. Between 7 and 10 o'clock in the evening

(A) most people are home.
(B) 83.8 million people watch TV.
(C) the show Dallas is on.
(D) is called prime time.

35. Which show had a greater number of shares but received a lower rating than the show above it?

(A) Hill Street Blues

(B) Riptide
(C) Fantasy Island
(D) Alice

36. Which network has the most shows in the top 10?

(A) ABC
(B) CBS
(C) NBC
(D) Not enough information

Questions 37-41

The system of training through apprenticeship was firmly established in England for a considerable period before the migration to North America began. At the time of the American Revolution it was still strong and was to continue so for a long time thereafter.

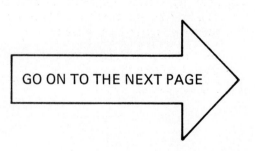
GO ON TO THE NEXT PAGE

In the apprenticeship system, a youth was bound to a master for a specific term of years, usually seven, the period ending when the boy was 21 or the girl 18. This generally meant that a boy began his period of service at age 14, although there were some variations for different occupations. The apprentice served without wages in the home of his master, learning the trade or craft and performing all the duties of a household servant in many cases. The youth was completely responsible to his master, who was obligated to furnish him with board and clothing and to give him such training in the trade as would make him a competent and an independent workman when his period of service was completed.

37. Apprenticeship, according to the passage, was

  (A) a type of slavery.
  (B) a purely British institution.
  (C) very useful during the American Revolution.
  (D) a system of training.

38. If a girl began her apprenticeship when she was 12, she was usually finished when she was

  (A) 15.
  (B) 18.
  (C) 21.
  (D) 20.

39. The male apprentice earned

  (A) very little money.
  (B) no money at all.
  (C) enough money to pay room and board.
  (D) more than the female apprentice.

40. The writer implies, but does not directly state, that

  (A) the apprenticeship system is old-fashioned.

  (B) the duties of the apprentice were greater than those of the master.
  (C) the apprentice system expected more of boys than girls.
  (D) the American Revolution stopped the apprentice system.

41. At the end of the apprenticeship, the apprentice

  (A) was obligated to repay the master.
  (B) no longer had to do household chores.
  (C) was supposed to work on his own.
  (D) become a partner with the master.

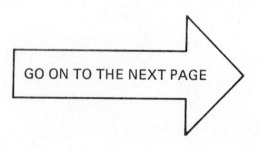

GO ON TO THE NEXT PAGE

Questions 42-45

Population increase and economic change heightened many of the old internal problems of American cities. Efforts to alleviate these pressures not only transformed cities but swept city dwellers into a whirlwind of complex social and political issues. Take, for example, the problem of securing adequate supplies of pure water. By the beginning of the 19th century, fear of fire and disease had induced city officials to think more seriously about providing water for their citizens. In the 1790's yellow fever ravaged the Northeast -- particularly Philadelphia -- causing several cities to become passionately convinced that cleanliness was the only way to prevent or minimize disease. This need for sanitation meant a more liberal use of water. Most urbanites drew their water from public or private wells, but the springs that fed these wells simply could not supply tens of thousands of people, and they were often polluted with seepage from privies and graves. Attention focused on nearby rivers and streams as sources of larger, cleaner supplies of water. Who should undertake projects to tap these sources -- the municipality or private companies?

42. The main idea of the passage is

(A) water wheels in America.
(B) American internal problems.
(C) growth in American cities and their problems.
(D) diseases spread by water.

43. Water supplies were increased to combat yellow fever because

(A) victims of the disease must drink a great deal of water.
(B) yellow fever thrives in a sanitary environment.
(C) people believed that uncleanliness reduced the threat of yellow fever.
(D) proper hygiene decreased the risk of all disease.

44. Which of the following is not part of the water problem referred to in the passage?

(A) The water supply in urban areas
(B) The threat of fire
(C) The possibility of war
(D) The best means for securing water

45. The author implies, but does not directly state, that

(A) private corporations were best equipped to tap water sources.
(B) cities were best equipped to supply clean water.
(C) cities wanted corporations to supply water.
(D) the question of who should tap nearby rivers and streams was problematical.

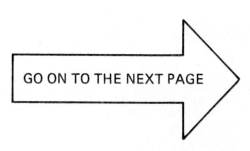
GO ON TO THE NEXT PAGE

Questions 46-48

It is interesting to consider the characteristics which make humans so much more successful than computers for tasks requiring "intelligence." Unfortunately, our current knowledge of the human brain is either too detailed or too vague to answer this question. Neurophysiology studies the workings and interconnections of individual nerve cells in the brain, producing a mass of detailed facts. In contrast, psychology studies the behavior of the brain from largely external observations, yielding only vague conclusions. It is a challenge to computer science to understand the architecture of the brain from a computational viewpoint. What are the major computational structures in the brain? Which functions do they compute? How are they interconnected? What is the form of the computation inside the human brain?

46. How does the author answer his own question why humans are better at tasks requiring intelligence?

(A) They have brains.
(B) Machines aren't properly programmed.
(C) Computer science is a young science.
(D) Not enough information on the brain is known.

47. Which of the following is not true?

(A) Neurophysiology is the study of nerve cells in the brain.
(B) Psychology does not offer precise conclusions.
(C) We do not know much about the workings of the human brain.
(D) Computers will teach us everything we need to know about the human brain.

48. In order to answer the questions posed by the author, we must assume that

(A) there are structures in the brain which involve computation.
(B) people's brains are like computers.
(C) human thinking operates like a mathematical calculus .
(D) psychologists will become experts in computer science.

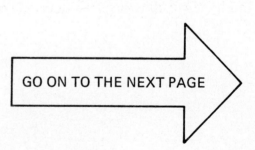
GO ON TO THE NEXT PAGE

3	3	3	3	3	3	3	3

Questions 49-52

The intellectual independence of the art historian, the serious remoteness of the aesthete, the fierce unconventionality of the artist do not appear to the public gaze, but the scandals that regularly crop up in the art world invariably occasion excitement, even hilarity, in the newspapers and among the public. There is perhaps natural pleasure in the sight of an expert being, or appearing to be, confounded. The complexity of the observer's emotions, from envy to a sense of inferiority, usually expresses itself in thoughtless glee.

49. According to the passage, the public is

    (A) aware of fraud but unaware of art history.
    (B) quick to recognize artistic genius.
    (C) amused at the unconventionality of artists.
    (D) quick to condemn art scandals.

50. The writer's attitude toward the art observer seems to be

    (A) indifferent.
    (B) callous.
    (C) negative.
    (D) empathetic

51. The term "occasion" in this passage means

    (A) time
    (B) cause
    (C) event
    (B) environment

52. The writer's main message seems to be that art scandals are

    (A) frequent.
    (B) natural.
    (C) confounding.
    (D) serious matters.

Questions 53-56

People from the 1870's would be astonished and embarrassed by the sexual revolution and surprised by the transformed position of women in society. To a degree unimagined in the 1870's, women work outside the home in gainful employment. The vote, styles of dress, public visibility -- these and other aspects of women's lives would come as a shock. They would note, however, that despite all the changes, the authority structure in modern society is still dominated by men. Though the high divorce rate would be far beyound their experience -- a phenomenon caused in good part by rising expectations -- people from the 1870's would find Americans to be a child- and family-centered people, as they had been a century before. Indeed, there is today a stronger awareness of the importance of the family constellation in the development of personality.

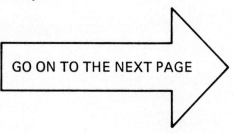

GO ON TO THE NEXT PAGE

53. This passage is comparing

   (A) the roles of men and women in 1870.
   (B) differences between today's sex roles and those of the 1870's.
   (C) men today and those of the 1870's.
   (D) the family system today with the family system of 1870.

54. The author implies, but does not directly state, that

   (A) women today are too free.
   (B) women of 1870 had few rights.
   (C) the people of 1870 cared more about the family.
   (D) women of 1870 would approve of the role of women today.

55. Which of the following statements is true?

   (A) People today are more aware of the psychological aspects of family living.
   (B) People today do not think the family is important to child development.
   (C) People in 1870 cared more about the family.
   (D) Women of 1870 would be shocked by the role of women today.

56. The author implies, but does not directly state, that

   (A) women in 1870 were trying to get the right to vote.
   (B) women in 1870 did not have the right to vote.
   (C) men in 1870 were fighting against female suffrage.
   (D) men today are still opposed to female suffrage.

Directions for Questions 57-60:
In this section, you must select the statement that most nearly matches the original statement. Many of the statements are true, but only one is a restatement of the original.

57. Physics is a hard science, unlike sociology, which does not lend itself to fixed laws.

   (A) Unlike sociology, physics has strict laws.
   (B) Physics and sociology are alike except for the fixedness of their laws.
   (C) The laws of physics, a hard science, and sociology differ in terms of their fixedness.
   (D) Sociology is a soft science, unlike physics, which lends itself to fixed laws.

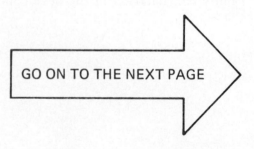
GO ON TO THE NEXT PAGE

58. As the soldiers marched through the valley, the terrorists were lurking in the trenches waiting for their leader's signal.

    (A) The soldiers were marching through the valley while the terrorists lurked in the trenches awaiting a sign from their leader.
    (B) The leader's signal was awaited by the lurking terrorists, who were prepared to attack the soldiers in their trenches.
    (C) The trenches were filled with terrorists who were waiting for the leader of the marching soldiers to give them the signal to enter the valley.
    (D) Through the valley marched the soldiers while terrorists hid in the trenches according to their leader's signal.

59. The scope of applied linguistics, although narrower than it once was, is, in certain respects, more pragmatic.

    (A) Applied linguistics once had a broad, impractical scope, but this has changed.
    (B) Even though applied linguistics is not as comprehensive as it once was, it is more pragmatic in some ways.
    (C) Linguistics is now applied, in certain respects, to a narrower, more pragmatic scope.
    (D) Applying linguistics is more pragmatic but less widespread than in the past.

60. What we need is a few good men.

    (A) Few good men are what is needed.
    (B) We require only a few good men.
    (C) Few good men are needed.
    (D) Our specifications are such that only a few stalwarts are anticipated.

DO NOT WORK ON ANY OTHER SECTION OF THE TEST

IF YOU FINISH IN LESS THAN 45 MINUTES, GO OVER YOUR ANSWERS ON SECTION III ONLY. AT THE END OF 45 MINUTES, STOP WORK AND CORRECT YOUR ANSWERS WITH THE ANSWER KEY WHICH FOLLOWS.

CODED ANSWER KEY DIAGNOSTIC TEST 4

SECTION 1: LISTENING COMPREHENSION

Part A - Statements

1. (D) - minimal pair
2. (C) - computation
3. (B) - minimal pair
4. (A) - computation
5. (C) - number discrimination
6. (C) - number discrimination
7. (D) - contextual reference
8. (B) - synonym
9. (C) - negation
10. (B) - comparison
11. (D) - contextual reference
12. (A) - cause/effect
13. (B) - chronological order
14. (C) - cause/effect
15. (C) - conditional
16. (B) - contextual reference
17. (C) - conditional
18. (B) - chronological order
19. (D) - comparison
20. (B) - negation

Part B - Conversations

21. (A) - contextual reference
22. (C) - computation
23. (C) - number discrimination
24. (C) - synonym
25. (D) - negation
26. (B) - contextual reference
27. (A) - conditional
28. (C) - comparison
29. (A) - chronological order
30. (C) - cause/effect
31. (D) - cause/effect
32. (C) - contextual reference
33. (B) - synonym
34. (A) - chronological order
35. (B) - comparison

Part C - Mini Talks

36. (B)
37. (D)
38. (A)
39. (C)
40. (A)
41. (C)
42. (B)
43. (B)
44. (B)
45. (B)
46. (A)
47. (A)
48. (C)
49. (C)
50. (D)

SECTION II: STRUCTURE AND WRITTEN EXPRESSION

Part A

1. (C) - subject-verb: agreement
2. (B) - pronoun: agreement
3. (A) - preposition
4. (D) - conjunction: form
5. (D) - conjunction: parallel structure
6. (C) - verb: tense
7. (D) - word order: adjective/adverb
8. (A) - word order: subject/verb
9. (D) - comparison
10. (C) - word family
11. (B) - verb: tense
12. (C) - subordinate clause: adjective
13. (A) - subordinate clause: adverb
14. (B) - subordinate clause: adjective
15. (D) - subordinate clause: reduced adverb

Part B

16. (A) - verb: unnecessary verb *omit being*
17. (C) - redundancy *omit intrinsic*
18. (A) - verb: omission: *who are always on time*
19. (D) - preposition *on her head*
20. (D) - conjunction: parallel structure *and by inhibiting them*
21. (A) - active-passive *was preserved*
22. (D) - conditional *will explode*
23. (A) - subordinate clause: reduced adjective *omit are*
24. (B) - word order: adverb *potters are seldom regarded*
25. (C) - conjunction: form *because*
26. (B) - conjunction: parallel structure *dealing/coping with traffic*
27. (B) - word family *to imagine*
28. (D) - subordinate clause: noun *is three times*
29. (D) - comparison: *as the least*
30. (C) - article *the lion*
31. (B) - pronouns: form *them*
32. (D) - preposition *of the school*
33. (D) - redundancy *omit*
34. (A) - subordinate clause: reduced adverb *first being*
35. (A) - subordinate claused: adverb *although*
36. (B) - conjunction: form *and*
37. (A) - subordinate clause: adjective *which will be*
38. (B) - word order: adjective noun *that organized sports*
39. (C) - verb: tense *that is currently*
40. (B) - subject: repetition *omit it*

SECTION III: READING COMPREHENSION AND VOCABULARY

Vocabulary

1. (B)
2. (C)
3. (C)
4. (B)
5. (D)
6. (A)
7. (A)
8. (B)
9. (B)
10. (A)
11. (C)
12. (A)
13. (A)
14. (B)
15. (C)
16. (A)
17. (B)
18. (D)
19. (B)
20. (A)
21. (A)
22. (B)
23. (D)
24. (B)
25. (A)
26. (C)
27. (A)
28. (A)
29. (B)
30. (C)

Reading Comprehension

31. (B) - fact
32. (C) - fact
33. (C) - inference
34. (D) - inference
35. (B) - fact
36. (B) - fact
37. (D) - fact
38. (B) - fact
39. (B) - fact
40. (C) - inference
41. (C) - fact
42. (C) - inference
43. (D) - fact
44. (C) - fact
45. (D) - inference
46. (D) - fact
47. (D) - fact
48. (A) - inference
49. (C) - fact
50. (D) - inference
51. (B) - fact
52. (A) - fact
53. (B) - fact
54. (B) - inference
55. (D) - fact
56. (B) - inference
57. (A) - paraphrase
58. (A) - paraphrase
59. (B) - paraphrase
60. (B) - paraphrase

LISTENING TARGETS

INTRODUCTION

The Listening Comprehension section tests your ability to understand spoken English. It measures your ability to discriminate among sounds and words as well as to understand the grammar of spoken English.

There are three parts to the Listening Comprehension section. You will have approximately 40 minutes for this section.

Part A	Statements	20 Questions
Part B	Conversations	15 Questions
Pârt C	Mini-Talks	15 Questions

Part A

In Part A, Statements, you must match a written statement with an oral statement. You will hear a sentence and must choose a sentence with a similar meaning from the four written sentences in the test booklet. This section will test your ability to distinguish between discrete sounds (minimal pairs, numbers); your ability to recognize grammatical markers (*contextual reference, negation, conditional, comparisons*); your ability to recognize discourse markers (*cause and effect, chronological order*); and your ability to recognize synonyms.

The statements in the test booklet often have sounds, words, or phrases that are similar to the oral statement. Pay careful attention to the *meaning* of the oral statement.

Part B

In Part B, Conversations, you must answer a question about a conversation between two people. The question, which is asked by a third person, tests your ability in the same areas as Part A. Again, there may be words in the answer choices that are similar to the words in the conversation. You must pay attention to the *meaning* of the conversation.

Part C

In Part C, Mini-Talks, you will answer three to five questions about a lengthy conversation or a short lecture. The subjects discussed may be in a variety of areas. The topics used in this section are representative of the kind of subjects that might be on the TOEFL: *overheard conversations; announcements; advertisements; news reports; weather reports; academic lectures; informative talks; and class discussions.*

Listening Tips
Before the TOEFL
1. Listen to English as much as possible: radio, television, and movies.
2. Listen to native English speaking conversations in hotels, buses, or wherever you find native English speakers conversing. Try to guess what they are talking about.
3. Do all the listening exercises in this book.

During the TOEFL
1. Sit close to the speakers, if possible.
2. Try to read through the answer choices to guess the question.
3. Do not be fooled by similar sounds or words. Pay close attention to the meaning of the utterance.

STATEMENTS

MINIMAL PAIRS

Minimal pairs are words that sound almost alike, such as *bit* and *beat; beet* and *bet; candidate* and *cannot eat; car* and *cart; tin* and *ten.*

In the following questions, you will hear a statement. You must choose the sentence that most closely restates the original.

1. (A) I looked like a teen.
   (B) The ten carts looked alike.
   (C) Ten people were in the car.
   (D) The car was made of tin.

2. (A) He looked at the seat near us.
   (B) We sat in the nook near the door.
   (C) We left the books by the door.
   (D) We took a seat on the floor.

3. (A) He goes to sleep early.
   (B) He is surly at bedtime.
   (C) It is better that he have a hobby.
   (D) His rabbit is in the flower garden.

4. (A) He is giving up his work.
   (B) His health prevents long hours at work.
   (C) He helps his fellow workers.
   (D) He ruined his health working with lime.

5. (A) He kept her clothes for her.
   (B) They were close to the pier.
   (C) She couldn't hear the convocation.
   (D) Near her, he overheard them talking.

6. (A) The icing on the cake is almost melted.

   (B) The heat will melt the ice.
   (C) We met the nicest people on our walk.
   (D) This sleet will turn to ice.

7. (A) We praise the dog and cat all the time.
   (B) We might get a long-tailed cat.
   (C) The dog and cat play with leather.
   (D) Dogs and cats raised together may not fight.

8. (A) Restaurants in Rome were excellent.
   (B) He didn't mean to steal.
   (C) I feel the house was quite dim.
   (D) We ate well in our house.

9. (A) They are involved in a lot of trouble.
   (B) We took two of everything.
   (C) They are similar in their looks.
   (D) There is not likely to be much there.

10. (A) We needed our boots on the farm.
    (B) The boat fared well during the storm.
    (C) She bought the boots from the store.
    (D) The storm sank the boat fast.

STATEMENTS

COMPUTATION

You may be asked to do simple arithmetic requiring you to add, subtract, multiply, or divide.

In the following questions, you will hear a statement. You must choose the sentence that most closely restates the original. These examples are difficult. They will train your short-term memory.

1. (A) Twelve of us went to the party.
   (B) Five people saw the show.
   (C) There were seventeen of us at the reception.
   (D) Seven people decided not to attend the reception.

2. (A) He arrived at 4:20.
   (B) It was 3:25 when we met.
   (C) I met him at 3:45.
   (D) We met at 4:05.

3. (A) There were 39 people in the group.
   (B) There were 66 people in the group.
   (C) The group contained 52 adults.
   (D) There were 40 children in the group.

4. (A) We drove 15 miles in the wrong direction.
   (B) We drove 22 miles before asking for help.
   (C) John drove 56 miles before we arrived.
   (D) We drove 21 miles before getting help.

5. (A) It takes 45 minutes to get home.
   (B) We need 1 hour and 20 minutes to get home.
   (C) Our home is 15 minutes away.
   (D) We must allow an hour and a half to get home.

6. (A) She came at 10 minutes after 8.
   (B) She arrived at 10 minutes before 8.
   (C) She arrived at 10:00.
   (D) She was 2 hours late.

7. (A) We drove for 60 miles.
   (B) The car was 5 miles over the limit.
   (C) We traveled at a speed of 55 miles.
   (D) We were 15 miles under the limit.

8. (A) The show usually begins at 8:30.
   (B) The show starts at 9:30.
   (C) The show lasts an hour.
   (D) We will be home before 9:30.

9. (A) The drive took 2 hours and 15 minutes.
   (B) We only drove 45 minutes.
   (C) It took 3 3/4 hours to get there.
   (D) We counted 3 hours.

10. (A) The original group was 96.
    (B) There were 25 in the team.
    (C) Three times as many went as stayed.
    (D) There were 150 in the entire team.

STATEMENTS

NUMBER DISCRIMINATION

Many numbers sound alike. Be careful to listen for the differences between numbers, such as *13* and *30* or *15* and *50*.

In the following questions, you will hear a statement. You must choose the sentence that most closely restates the original. These are difficult. They will test your understanding as well as your short-term memory. Read the answer choices before you listen to the statement.

1. (A) Books should be opened to page 16.
   (B) There were six pages in the book.
   (C) 16 books were opened.
   (D) The books were on page 60.

2. (A) The flight leaves at 8:13.
   (B) There are 13 flights at 8:30.
   (C) Flight 30 departs at half past 8.
   (D) The Madrid flight leaves at 8:30.

3. (A) There are 80 graduates in our class.
   (B) The eighth is graduation day for 18 of us.
   (C) Eight of us will graduate.
   (D) The graduation is on the 18th.

4. (A) There are 14 columns on page 90.
   (B) The class reread page 4.
   (C) The book has nine pages of four columns.
   (D) We reread the fourth column on page 19.

5. (A) The teenager gets up at 7:15.
   (B) He gets up 10 minutes before 8.
   (C) The old man gets up at 7:15.
   (D) He gets up at 7:17.

6. (A) John was born on the 15th.
   (B) John was born on the 30th.
   (C) John was born on the 13th.
   (D) John was born in 1930.

7. (A) The teams appear at 9:20.
   (B) Nineteen teams appear on the field.
   (C) Twenty teams of nine each appear.
   (D) The teams arrive before 9.

8. (A) Only half of us understood all 60 questions.
   (B) Five percent of us understood all the questions.
   (C) Fifteen percent understood all 60 questions.
   (D) Fifteen percent of us understood six questions.

9. (A) Sixteen of us are travelling to New York.
   (B) The train leaves at 6:16.
   (C) The train leaves at 6:50.
   (D) The train to New York should take 60 of us.

10. (A) There were 19 steps to the top.
    (B) There were 19 steps, then an extra 13.
    (C) There are 13 steps after the first 90.
    (D) There were 90 steps followed by 30.

STATEMENTS

SYNONYMS

You may be asked to identify words that have a similar meaning, such as: *careless* and *inattentive; rational* and *reasonable; goad* and *taunt.*

In the following questions, you will hear a statement. You must choose the sentence that most closely restates the original.

1. (A) She put the empty box in the elevator.
   (B) The package was empty.
   (C) She was too young to dress herself.
   (D) She had difficulty moving the package.

2. (A) Her excuses were invalid, but John listened politely.
   (B) She was explaining milestones to John.
   (C) Her explanation had no effect on John's aloofness.
   (D) John had his bad marks explained.

3. (A) Cages make practical homes for all bears.
   (B) Bears are kept in outdoor cages.
   (C) The forest is the only habitat for bears.
   (D) Most bears taken from the wild live in cages.

4. (A) The game appeals to logical thinkers.
   (B) Enjoyment is one of the reasons everyone plays.
   (C) Reasonable people expect to win this game.
   (D) People go to extremes when they play this game.

5. (A) We dropped the envelope in the fog.
   (B) We missed the mailbox off to the side.
   (C) The fog made it impossible to see our companions.
   (D) She missed the envelope, although it was in sight.

6. (A) We'd also planned a raft trip.
   (B) Conditions forced us to cancel the expedition.
   (C) We tripped over the height of the raft.
   (D) We'd carefully planed the surface of the raft.

7. (A) We've put clocks in each case.
   (B) Our journey depends on weather conditions.
   (C) We've spent time on the case.
   (D) Time is the most important factor in the decision.

8. (A) She had little time to recover before having to travel again.
   (B) She had to fly on her business trip.
   (C) She had no choice between taking a boat and a plane.
   (D) She was about over her illness.

9. (A) The fine tread on his tires has worn out.
   (B) He's paid close attention to her health.
   (C) She has no problem keeping up with him.
   (D) He's noticed her difficulties with fatigue.

10. (A) He threw the ball at the window.
    (B) You could count on his support.
    (C) He was the "king" of pitchers.
    (D) The boy was persistent.

STATEMENTS

Negation

Words like *not*, *no*, and *any* are sometimes difficult to distinguish. Be aware of these potential problems.

In the following questions, you will hear a statement. You must choose the sentence that most closely restates the original.

1. (A) She wanted the table to have books on it.
   (B) She wanted fewer books on the table.
   (C) I thought she wanted books.
   (D) She didn't want books on the table.

2. (A) We doubt they invited the boys.
   (B) All the boys got an invitation.
   (C) We think the boys went away.
   (D) They asked the boys but not us.

3. (A) She amuses herself easily.
   (B) She is never left alone.
   (C) She is left without any problems.
   (D) She has a problem staying amused.

4. (A) At no time are there mosquitoes.
   (B) There are never mosquitoes at this time of year.
   (C) Mosquitoes are not around now.
   (D) At the same time a year ago, one didn't find mosquitoes.

5. (A) There are more people than chairs.
   (B) There are too many empty seats.
   (C) There are never enough people.
   (D) There are more than enough seats.

6. (A) I would not want to fall asleep here.
   (B) Nobody would sleep during this performance.

(C) Not many people fall asleep during the show.

(D) I would expect people to fall asleep watching this.

7. (A) Larry and Bill did nothing deserving attention.

(B) Larry and Bill are modest about their accomplishments.

(C) Larry and Bill do not want to look at their feet.

(D) No one recognizes Larry and Bill.

8. (A) He can call me any time he wants.

(B) I am never here when he calls.

(C) I pretend I'm not home each time he calls.

(D) I am never out when he calls.

9. (A) We have to sell bananas.

(B) They told us there were no bananas.

(C) They told us we couldn't sell bananas.

(D) We can have any bananas we want to sell.

10. (A) Marjorie had no books about reasoning.

(B) Marjorie bought the book without thinking.

(C) The book was not for sale.

(D) There was no need for her to buy it.

STATEMENTS

CONTEXTUAL REFERENCE

To answer some of the questions, you will have to identify appropriate antecedents or referents. A pronoun refers to some noun in the sentence. Don't confuse the pronoun related to the subject with one related to the object.

NOTE: Watch for differences in:

1. Gender (*John...his, Sally...hers*)
2. Number (*children...they, the boy...his*).

In the following questions, you will hear a statement. You must choose the sentence that most closely restates the original.

1. (A) I used Frank's car with his permission.

(B) Louise lent Frank's car to me without his knowledge.

(C) Louise lent her car to me and I gave it to Frank.

(D) I lent Louise Frank's car.

2. (A) They thought my route was quicker.

(B) I found their route faster.

(C) Anne found Claire's route more direct.

(D) They thought their route was faster.

3. (A) Their families are wearing our clothes.

(B) We gave clothes to their family.

(C) The charity gave its clothing to us.

(D) The members and their families gave us clothes.

4. (A) Richard cut my sister's roses.

(B) I cut roses for Richard with my sister's knife.

(C) I used Richard's knife to cut roses for my sister.

(D) My sister cut roses for me and Richard.

5. (A) Laurie was playing with Ronald's ball.

(B) Ronald and I played ball with Laurie.

(C) Ronald gave me his ball.

(D) I gave my ball to Laurie.

6. (A) Bill's brother was Jim's best friend.
   (B) Bill was closer to his brother.
   (C) Paul and Jim were brothers.
   (D) Jim is no relation to Paul.

7. (A) Chris told us about his sister.
   (B) Our sister told us about Chris' lying.
   (C) Had Chris not lied, his sister would have been able to warn us.
   (D) We would have told Chris if our sister had not lied.

8. (A) I lent my car to George's mother.
   (B) George lent my mother his car.
   (C) My mother is picking up George's laundry.
   (D) I lent my mother his car for the weekend.

9. (A) My father and my brother visited my sister.
   (B) My father visited my brother at camp.
   (C) My father and his brother saw their sister.
   (D) My father and my uncle saw my sister.

10. (A) Karen gives me her answers.
    (B) John gives Karen the answers.
    (C) I give John her answers.
    (D) John wants both our answers.

STATEMENTS

CAUSE AND EFFECT

Cause and effect statements show the result of a particular action. One part of the sentence will state a situation which is followed by its effect.
NOTE: Pay attention to:

1. Verb tense
2. Subject of each sentence
3. Words like *any* or *not*
4. Words that sound alike.

In the following questions, you will hear a statement. You must choose the the sentence that most closely restates the original.

1. (A) The heavy traffic made me arrive late at the airport.
   (B) The plane was late, so I didn't catch a taxi.
   (C) I caught a taxi on a side lane.
   (D) The taxes on the plane ticket were high.

2. (A) I did not have to enough money to eat.
   (B) The food only cost a dime.
   (C) I was able to save a dime towards my food.
   (D) I had a meal without paying for it.

3. (A) It rained on the birds.
   (B) The birds sang until it rained.
   (C) The rain made the birds sing with joy.
   (D) Birds like what the rain brings.

4. (A) My compass led me to the path.
   (B) I passed by the correct path.
   (C) I used the compass to find my way.
   (D) Without the compass, I was lost.

5. (A) She missed Sam so much it made her sick.
   (B) It was a bad day to take an exam.
   (C) She could not take the test because she was sick.
   (D) She felt bad about missing the exam.

6. (A) While traveling, he was as hungry as four people.
   (B) He traveled for a week with us.
   (C) With him gone, there were just four of us to feed.
   (D) He planned to travel for four weeks.

7. (A) She didn't agree with his choice of names.
   (B) She called his name without success.
   (C) They called out the names of people receiving degrees.
   (D) In her anger she called him names.

8. (A) My smiling won his confidence.
   (B) He smiled warmly at me.
   (C) He can talk openly about me.

   (D) He walked a mile in the open.

9. (A) At present, he has no plans for the program.
   (B) He was new in the program, unlike her.
   (C) The change in the program astonished him.
   (D) His being on the program made her rearrange her schedule.

10. (A) Before we moved, Loren came to say goodbye.
    (B) Loren left without saying goodbye to us.
    (C) Loren spoke well about our leaving.
    (D) Before he left, he told us he was going.

STATEMENTS

CONDITIONALS

A conditional statement is one of the most difficult English structures. It consists of two clauses and can express the following conditions:
   (A) Factual condition:
      If you turn the key, the motor starts.
   (B) Future condition:
      If he comes after six, we'll be gone.
   (C) Imaginative condition:
      If my mother could see me now, she'd be very proud.

In the following questions, you will hear a statement. You must choose the sentence that most closely restates the original.

1. (A) Sailors should not drink milk.
   (B) Milk would have made their bones stronger.
   (C) Drinking milk made their bones strong.
   (D) It was wrong for them to drink milk.

2. (A) We left before it rained.
   (B) The rain prevented us from leaving.
   (C) They bet the rain would stop soon.
   (D) She hated the rain as much as we did.

3. (A) The economy is dependent on imported goods.

   (B) They analyzed why important foods affected the economy.
   (C) In case the economy suffers, food can be imported.
   (D) The handicapped require quality goods.

4. (A) The computer turns the system off.
   (B) Memory failure necessitates switching the power off.
   (C) My memory failed me for a moment.
   (D) They turned off the computer for a while.

5. (A) Their arrival would make my departure possible.

(B) They leave when I go to work.
(C) I left the television with them.
(D) They wish I would leave so they could repair the TV.

6. (A) Noise is on the increase these days.
(B) The door closed and it was quiet.
(C) Closing the door will muffle the sound.
(D) The noisy door needs grease.

7. (A) I would repeat the same mistakes.
(B) It's a mistake to want to be younger.
(C) I make mistakes because I am young.
(D) I would do things differently if I were young again.

8. (A) People will disobey the regulations.

(B) Only recent rules apply.
(C) Overweight people must stick to their diets.
(D) Regal attitudes will not inspire civic pride.

9. (A) Voters must register by calling the polling office.
(B) The telephone office received the most complaints.
(C) No one asked about the quality of the produce.
(D) The defective product will be reclaimed.

10. (A) Her arrival means she longs for a walk.
(B) Where we're walking, it will be dusty.
(C) The dust makes the walk seem longer.
(D) If she comes before twilight, we'll go walking.

STATEMENTS

CHRONOLOGICAL ORDER

The questions below require you to determine the order of events: what happened *first, second, third*, and so forth.
NOTE: Pay attention to :

1. Words that modify actions, such as *second...two, third...three*, and so forth,
2. Words that indicate order, such as *before*, *after*, and so forth.

In the following questions, you will hear a statement. You must choose the sentence that most closely restates the original.

1. (A) The stars came out before sunset.
(B) We saw stars as the sun set.
(C) The stars appeared after the sun went down.
(D) The stars came out before the sun.

2. (A) The waitress told the diners to finish their trays first.
(B) They finished their trays after the waitress tried to take them away.
(C) The waitress finished their trays for them.

(D) The waitress removed the trays when the diners were done.

3. (A) I had seen him once before.
(B) I saw him the second the show ended.
(C) It was after the second performance that I met him.
(D) He saw me twice after the performance.

4. (A) The children went home before finishing their game.
(B) One child left earlier than the others.

Listening Targets   115

(C) Two children went home before the third stopped playing.

(D) Two children stopped playing before the third one left.

5. (A) We built the fire before we went skiing.

(B) They went skiing as we built the fire.

(C) We relaxed by the fire before going skiing.

(D) After we skied, we relaxed by the fire they started for us.

6. (A) They got married after the reception.

(B) It was their second marriage.

(C) They arranged to get married after going to the hall.

(D) They planned the reception before they got married.

7. (A) While dinner was cooking, we went to the store.

(B) We cooked dinner, visited the store, and slept.

(C) We ate and then were too tired to shop.

(D) After shopping, we had dinner and slept.

8. (A) The guest room was painted for his visit.

(B) He came because the guest room was painted.

(C) He painted the guest room when he came.

(D) We painted the room, then went to see him.

9. (A) She went to the concert, then the party.

(B) The party ended before the concert.

(C) The party stopped her from going to the concert.

(D) She went to the party, then the concert.

10. (A) She cried as he fell down.

(B) He couldn't remember if he fell.

(C) He remembered her crying before he fell.

(D) He heard her crying after he fell.

STATEMENTS

COMPARISONS

A comparison shows how two things are similar or different.

NOUN:
Different: Bill has fewer *cavities* than Jack.
Similar: Jack has as many *cavities* as Rosalind.

VERB:
Different: John *studies* more than Bill.
Similar: Bob *talks* as much as George.

ADVERB:
Different: We speak more *quickly* than they.
Similar: She drives as *slowly* as my mother.

ADJECTIVE:
Different: Betty is *shorter* than Raymond.
Similar: This car is as *expensive* as a house.

In the following questions, you will hear a statement. You must choose the sentence that most closely restates the original.

1. (A) The bridge was too narrow.
   (B) The engineer thought the bridge too wide.
   (C) At the engineer's insistence, they leveled the bridge.
   (D) All agreed the bridge was too high.

2. (A) I think Joe used to be better than Cliff.
   (B) I do better than Joe and Cliff.
   (C) Cliff seems to test better than Joe.
   (D) Joe does better than Cliff on the exams.

3. (A) Urban malls are growing larger.
   (B) Shops in the city are not doing well.
   (C) Suburban trains contribute to the growth.
   (D) Stores make more money downtown.

4. (A) Kate writes as well as George.
   (B) I write better than Kate.
   (C) My writing is not as nice as George's.
   (D) Kate writes better than us both.

5. (A) There are longer runways in the Western Hemisphere.
   (B) The new runway is not the longest.
   (C) The long runway runs toward the land.
   (D) The runway is long but in need of repair.

6. (A) Lynn is a faster thinker than us.
   (B) We think like Lynn.
   (C) We think faster than she does.
   (D) There is no difference between her and us.

7. (A) Winter has longer days.
   (B) Days are longer in the summer.
   (C) Winter days are longer than summer days.
   (D) Summer days are shorter than winter days.

8. (A) There were fewer people than plants.
   (B) The balcony was too narrow for plants.
   (C) A lot of crows were among the rows of corn.
   (D) No one could carry any more plants.

9. (A) I eat more than the old man.
   (B) He eats as much as his wife.
   (C) His wife eats less than her husband.
   (D) He eats more than I give him.

10. (A) Christine has more money than I do.
    (B) Christine gave Rob more money than I did.
    (C) I gave Christine more money than I did Rob.
    (D) Rob has as much as Christine does.

CONVERSATIONS

MINIMAL PAIRS

In the following questions, you will hear a short conversation followed by a question about the conversation. You must choose the most appropriate answer.

1. (A) Spread a rumor
   (B) Miss someone
   (C) Herd some cattle
   (D) Tell a joke

2. (A) He's become hoarse.
   (B) Someone beat the horse.
   (C) He doesn't eat beets.

(D) He wouldn't gamble on the horse.

3. (A) He relax a while.
   (B) She keep him from harm.
   (C) He take the test.
   (D) He smile for the camera.

4. (A) Who is better
   (B) Who wrote the letter
   (C) Where is the ladder
   (D) Who the batter is

5. (A) Crying
   (B) Looking for her brother
   (C) Frying with lard
   (D) Trying to tear the card

6. (A) He lies.
   (B) He tells the truth.
   (C) His eyes are blue.
   (D) He is leaving.

7. (A) Clapping
   (B) The curtain

(C) The toys
(D) The boys

8. (A) His home
   (B) The bakery
   (C) Rome
   (D) The lake

9. (A) To be rich
   (B) A light
   (C) His sight
   (D) To be liked

10. (A) Potted plants
    (B) A song
    (C) Ants
    (D) Planets

CONVERSATIONS

COMPUTATION

In the following questions, you will hear a short conversation followed by a question about the conversation. You must choose the most appropriate answer.

1. (A) 90 minutes
   (B) 60 minutes
   (C) 30 minutes
   (D) 9 minutes

2. (A) 3
   (B) 6
   (C) 4
   (D) 10

3. (A) $16
   (B) $8
   (C) $32
   (D) $64

4. (A) 6:15
   (B) 6:40
   (C) 5:35
   (D) 6:01

5. (A) 15 minutes
   (B) 20 minutes
   (C) 41 minutes
   (D) 35 minutes

6. (A) 20 feet
   (B) 24 feet
   (C) 32 feet
   (D) 42 feet

7. (A) $40
   (B) $80
   (C) $14
   (D) $28

8. (A) 6
   (B) 2
   (C) 4
   (D) 10

9. (A) 9:20
   (B) 9:14
   (C) 9:26
   (D) 9:06

10. (A) $46
    (B) $86
    (C) $56
    (D) $130

CONVERSATIONS

NUMBER DISCRIMINATION

In the following questions, you will hear a short conversation followed by a question about the conversation. You must choose the most appropriate answer.

1. (A) 8:30
   (B) 8:13
   (C) 8:33
   (D) 3:30

2. (A) 30
   (B) 14
   (C) 13
   (D) 40

3. (A) 4:00
   (B) 4:22
   (C) 4:15
   (D) 4:20

4. (A) 60
   (B) 16
   (C) 15
   (D) 6

5. (A) 8:50
   (B) 8:15
   (C) 8th
   (D) 18th

6. (A) 16
   (B) 18
   (C) 68
   (D) 8

7. (A) 9
   (B) 90
   (C) 50
   (D) 15

8. (A) 2
   (B) 50
   (C) 22
   (D) 15

9. (A) 16
   (B) 20
   (C) 88
   (D) 60

10. (A) 13 cents
    (B) 30 cents
    (C) 33 cents
    (D) 3 cents

CONVERSATIONS

SYNONYMS

In the following questions, you will hear a short conversation followed by a question about the conversation. You must choose the most appropriate answer.

1. (A) Careless
   (B) Conscientious
   (C) Attentive
   (D) Horselike

2. (A) Ice storm
   (B) Hard bed
   (C) Tornado
   (D) Thunderstorm

3. (A) Coarse sand
   (B) Being sad
   (C) Calm water
   (D) A stormy ocean

4. (A) Have her heart checked
   (B) Purchase bread
   (C) Try harder
   (D) Laugh at her problems

5. (A) Dinner on shore
   (B) Lunch in port
   (C) Port wine with dinner
   (D) Dinner on board

6. (A) Alternate jobs
   (B) Go to bed
   (C) Run a factory
   (D) Quit work

7. (A) The man is disinterested.
   (B) She shares his fear.
   (C) The woman is not scared.
   (D) The woman is cowardly.

8. (A) Apologetic
   (B) Disappointed
   (C) Apathetic
   (D) Angry

9. (A) Objective
   (B) Timid
   (C) Hostile
   (D) Sympathetic

10. (A) She was losing her voice.
    (B) She forgot the words.
    (C) She was getting sleepy.
    (D) She needed to warm up.

CONVERSATIONS

NEGATION

In the following questions, you will hear a short conversation followed by a question about the conversation. You must choose the most appropriate answer.

1. (A) The man is unobservant.
   (B) She doesn't know the man.
   (C) He can have the book later.
   (D) The book is new.

2. (A) Cloistered
   (B) Well-traveled
   (C) Provincial
   (D) Inexperienced

3. (A) The man did not study.
   (B) The man is not nervous.
   (C) The woman did not study.
   (D) The woman is as nervous as the man.

4. (A) Contrary
   (B) Malicious
   (C) Angry
   (D) Apologetic

5. (A) Don't use ice cubes.
   (B) Be nice.
   (C) Boil the water first.
   (D) Lose some weight.

6. (A) Go to work
   (B) Read awhile
   (C) Go lie down
   (D) Stay awake

7. (A) Watching television
   (B) In a furniture store
   (C) At a gymnasium
   (D) At a theatre

8. (A) A pessimist
   (B) A loser
   (C) An optimist
   (D) A misanthrope

9. (A) They've met before.
   (B) The man remembers her.
   (C) The woman agrees with the man.
   (D) They have never met before.

10. (A) At the beach
    (B) Near the refrigerator
    (C) On the ski slopes
    (D) At the show

CONVERSATIONS

CONTEXTUAL REFERENCE

In the following questions, you will hear a short conversation followed by a question about the conversation. You must choose the most appropriate answer.

1. (A) Kate
   (B) The man's brother
   (C) Kate's brother
   (D) The woman's brother

2. (A) The man
   (B) The woman
   (C) Sam's sister
   (D) Sam

3. (A) On the weekend
   (B) Within 2 days
   (C) Tomorrow
   (D) Yesterday

4. (A) Laura
   (B) The woman
   (C) Joan
   (D) Himself

5. (A) Two men
   (B) Robin and Joan
   (C) Four dogs
   (D) The woman

6. (A) To tie her shoes
   (B) Through the gate
   (C) To the lake
   (D) Under the hedge

7. (A) Carol's
   (B) The man's
   (C) The woman's
   (D) The college's

8. (A) George and his sister
   (B) George's family
   (C) The man's family
   (D) The man's grandfather

9. (A) Susan's
   (B) Sidney's
   (C) The man's
   (D) The woman's

10. (A) George
    (B) The children
    (C) The charity
    (D) Dolores

CONVERSATIONS

CAUSE AND EFFECT

In the following questions, you will hear a short conversation followed by a question about the conversation. You must choose the most appropriate answer.

1. (A) He couldn't take the test.
   (B) He lost his job.
   (C) The rest left without him.
   (D) He had to rest.

2. (A) The dry spell
   (B) The rain
   (C) The growers
   (D) The tree

3. (A) They hate to travel.
   (B) A tour bus left without them.
   (C) The highway is covered with water.
   (D) The woman forgot her songs.

4. (A) She prefers apples.
   (B) There was nothing else to eat.
   (C) She's on a diet.
   (D) It's only a snack.

5. (A) She angered the models.
   (B) People thought she was a designer.
   (C) She got a purple dress.
   (D) People thought she was a model.

6. (A) Be ill
   (B) Eat
   (C) Drink buttermilk
   (D) Stand up

7. (A) Feet
   (B) Shoes
   (C) Solvent
   (D) Work

8. (A) She clean her refrigerator
   (B) She eat the ice cream
   (C) She let it melt
   (D) She put it in the cooler

9. (A) Everything
   (B) Grapefruit
   (C) Running
   (D) Quick eating

10. (A) Fall
    (B) Spring
    (C) Winter
    (D) Summer

CONVERSATIONS

CONDITIONALS

In the following questions, you will hear a short conversation followed by a question about the conversation. You must choose the most appropriate answer.

1. (A) The woman will cook.
   (B) He won't buy enough.
   (C) He'll get in a bad mood.
   (D) He will make dinner.

2. (A) A driving permit
   (B) A new watch
   (C) A new car
   (D) An empty road

3. (A) Overseas
   (B) Czechoslovakia
   (C) To the bank
   (D) Anywhere

4. (A) Farm yield
   (B) Summer vacations
   (C) Phonograph records
   (D) Starvation

5. (A) Vengeful
   (B) Dishonest
   (C) Fair
   (D) Unreasonable

6. (A) Go biking
   (B) Pay the bills
   (C) Dress warmly
   (D) Have more candy

7. (A) Get a raise
   (B) Be home for the boss
   (C) Leave when he comes
   (D) Sleep in the afternoon

8. (A) Bald
   (B) Overweight
   (C) Thin
   (D) Sallow

9. (A) The man will come with her.
   (B) She has too much work.
   (C) She promised herself.
   (D) No work is due the next day.

10. (A) Borrow some money
    (B) Ask if he's forgotten borrowing money
    (C) Ask if he needs a loan
    (D) Repay him

CONVERSATIONS

CHRONOLOGICAL ORDER

In the following questions, you will hear a short conversation followed by a question about the conversation. You must choose the most appropriate answer.

1. (A) Before the man came home
   (B) After the man came home
   (C) After the woman left
   (D) When both were home

2. (A) Paula
   (B) The woman
   (C) The man
   (D) No one

3. (A) Before putting out the lights
   (B) After taking a walk
   (C) After putting out the lights
   (D) Before taking a walk

4. (A) In an hour
   (B) After Sally arrives
   (C) Before Sally arrives
   (D) When they return

5. (A) Canoeing, eating, hiking, sailing
   (B) Canoeing, sailing, eating
   (C) Eating, hiking, canoeing, sailing
   (D) Hiking canoeing, sailing

6. (A) Go to bed
   (B) Walk through town
   (C) Tour museums
   (D) Rest

7. (A) They left with the man.
 (B) The man arrived too early.
 (C) They didn't wait for the man.
 (D) The man waited for them.

8. (A) Next year
 (B) Soon
 (C) When he finishes writing
 (D) After he visits her

9. (A) In the house
 (B) On a boat
 (C) In the hotel
 (D) In a tent

10. (A) Elephants
 (B) Walruses
 (C) Lions
 (D) The man

CONVERSATIONS

COMPARISONS

In the following questions, you will hear a short conversation followed by a
question about the conversation. You must choose the most appropriate answer.

1. (A) Smaller
 (B) Larger
 (C) Same size
 (D) Slight

2. (A) The man
 (B) The woman
 (C) Mary
 (D) John

3. (A) The light bulb
 (B) The shade
 (C) The wattage
 (D) The power

4. (A) The mountain's height
 (B) The woman's height
 (C) The view
 (D) Their ages

5. (A) A big country
 (B) Increasing deafness
 (C) A growing debt
 (D) Escalating rents

6. (A) It's just fine.
 (B) It's too dark.
 (C) It's lighter than Gill's.
 (D) It's too light.

7. (A) Shopping for clothes
 (B) Taking a trip
 (C) Exercising
 (D) Studying

8. (A) Blue company
 (B) Grey Express
 (C) Shore Line
 (D) Eastern Sea

9. (A) Closer to the people
 (B) Farther away from people
 (C) Equidistant from the people
 (D) Behind them

10. (A) This play is shorter.
 (B) Last year's play is shorter.
 (C) The plays are of equal length.
 (D) Last year's play was longer.

MINI-TALKS

OVERHEARD CONVERSATIONS

In the following questions, you will hear a short conversation followed by questions
about the conversation. You must choose the most appropriate answers.

1. (A) He doesn't like museums.
 (B) He is lost.
 (C) He doesn't want to be late.
 (D) He has to stay home.

2. (A) Stay home
 (B) Accompany her
 (C) Be late for dinner
 (D) Drop her off at the museum

3. (A) The restaurant
   (B) The car
   (C) The museum
   (D) Home

4. (A) Always
   (B) Frequently
   (C) Every other night
   (D) Never

5. (A) They are not sweet.
   (B) They come from the wrong market.
   (C) They are cooked.
   (D) They make the woman sick.

6. (A) Compliant
   (B) Poor
   (C) Complaining
   (D) Easy to please

7. (A) He robbed something.
   (B) He needs to get in somewhere.
   (C) He telephoned someone.
   (D) He misplaced something.

8. (A) Helpful
   (B) Cheerful
   (C) Angry
   (D) Unconcerned

9. (A) To take out money
   (B) To enter checks already written
   (C) To give to the woman
   (D) To put it away

10. (A) In the city
    (B) In the stable
    (C) In the country
    (D) In a car

11. (A) In spring
    (B) In summer
    (C) In the rain
    (D) In autumn

12. (A) Walking
    (B) Driving
    (C) Riding
    (D) Hiking

13. (A) Happy
    (B) Sad
    (C) Angry
    (D) Apologetic

14. (A) In the trunk
    (B) On the front seat
    (C) Behind the door
    (D) On the back seat

15. (A) Lock the car door
    (B) Open the car door
    (C) Take the briefcase with her
    (D) Leave the man in the car

16. (A) In the front seat
    (B) In the trunk
    (C) In the back seat
    (D) By the door

17. (A) The man's
    (B) The woman's
    (C) The children's
    (D) The neighbor's

18. (A) He is joking.
    (B) He is mean.
    (C) He is frightened.
    (D) He is repulsive.

19. (A) Bringing home their friends
    (B) Hiding their father
    (C) Asking their parents to join them
    (D) Avoiding being seen

20. (A) Sleep
    (B) Laugh
    (C) Study
    (D) Sing

MINI-TALKS

ANNOUNCEMENTS

In the following questions, you will hear a short announcement followed by questions about the announcement. You must choose the most appropriate answers.

1. (A) Madrid
   (B) The United States
   (C) England
   (D) Panama

2. (A) The passengers
   (B) The crew
   (C) The pilot
   (D) The ticket clerks

3. (A) The gate
   (B) The number of passengers
   (C) The flight
   (D) The time

4. (A) In a theater
   (B) On the street
   (C) At a concert
   (D) At a school

5. (A) Macbeth
   (B) Macduff
   (C) Douglas Cole
   (D) Harold

6. (A) Macbeth
   (B) Harold Zimmer
   (C) The management
   (D) Macduff

7. (A) Macduff
   (B) Harold Zimmer
   (C) Douglas Cole
   (D) Macbeth

8. (A) His wallet
   (B) His coat
   (C) His cart
   (D) His groceries

9. (A) Blue
   (B) Green
   (C) Orange
   (D) Red

10. (A) To the cart
    (B) To the manager's office
    (C) To the corridor
    (D) To the left

11. (A) A library
    (B) A hotel
    (C) A school
    (D) A store

12. (A) Impertinent
    (B) Emotional
    (C) Businesslike
    (D) Temperamental

13. (A) He lost a book.
    (B) He has a package.
    (C) He cashed a check.
    (D) No reason was given.

14. (A) Sportsmen
    (B) Panelists
    (C) Commentators
    (D) Sportswriters

15. (A) Other players
    (B) Writers and commentators
    (C) The public
    (D) Other winners

16. (A) Every month
    (B) Every year
    (C) Every 2 years
    (D) Every 6 months

17. (A) The cast is sick.
    (B) The film did not arrive.
    (C) The station cannot transmit in color.
    (D) The television is broken.

18. (A) Turn off the television.
    (B) Watch another show.
    (C) Add color to the show.
    (D) Not to adjust the set.

19. (A) Up to 24 hours
    (B) That night
    (C) That hour
    (D) Through next week

20. (A) In the evening
    (B) In the morning
    (C) Daily
    (D) In the afternoon

MINI-TALKS

ADVERTISEMENTS

In the following questions, you will hear a short advertisement followed by questions about the advertisment. You must choose the most appropriate answers.

1. (A) Coats
   (B) Stocks
   (C) Barns
   (D) Factories

2. (A) In a factory
   (B) In a barn
   (C) In a store
   (D) In a bank

3. (A) Give away coats
   (B) Double the customer's money
   (C) Sell coats cheaply
   (D) Open savings accounts

4. (A) A film
   (B) A television program
   (C) A musical
   (D) An opera

5. (A) Soon
   (B) Now
   (C) Next year
   (D) Next season

6. (A) Repose
   (B) Adventure
   (C) Battle scenes
   (D) Horse races

7. (A) In Britain
   (B) In Africa
   (C) In the drawing room
   (D) In a theater

8. (A) Contemporary
   (B) 18th century
   (C) 19th century
   (D) Italian

9. (A) By machine
   (B) By skilled craftsmen
   (C) By assembly line
   (D) On commission

10. (A) $100 to $200
    (B) $50 to $200
    (C) $150 to $200
    (D) $50 to $200

11. (A) 25 percent
    (B) 100 percent
    (C) 50 percent
    (D) 200 percent

12. (A) A few
    (B) Hundreds
    (C) Fifty
    (D) None

13. (A) Fall
    (B) Winter
    (C) Spring
    (D) Summer

14. (A) Trucks
    (B) Cars
    (C) Loans
    (D) Homes

15. (A) 18 percent
    (B) 8.8 percent
    (C) 8 percent
    (D) 88 percent

16. (A) $88
    (B) $1,986
    (C) $8,800
    (D) $0

17. (A) Next year
    (B) In 4 years
    (C) Immediately
    (D) In eight weeks

18. (A) 29 cents a dozen
    (B) 15 cents a dozen
    (C) 50 cents a dozen
    (D) Free

19. (A) Corn
    (B) Squash
    (C) Tomatoes
    (D) Green beans

20. (A) Trucker's strike
    (B) Low inventory
    (C) Farm surplus
    (D) Summer sales

MINI-TALKS

NEWS REPORTS

In the following questions, you will hear short news reports followed by questions about the report. You must choose the most appropriate answers.

1. (A) Five
   (B) Three
   (C) Two
   (D) Seven

2. (A) Following the car
   (B) Tapping the phone
   (C) Knocking on hotel doors
   (D) Using trained dogs

3. (A) In the countryside
   (B) In the White House
   (C) Near the White House
   (D) In the hospital

4. (A) The climate appeals to him.
   (B) He's lived there before.
   (C) He wants to be a cowboy.
   (D) He likes the television show.

5. (A) In a high rise
   (B) On a ranch
   (C) In the city
   (D) In a townhouse

6. (A) Texas
   (B) Manhattan
   (C) Washington
   (D) California

7. (A) The school board
   (B) Supervisor McLean
   (C) The mayor
   (D) Supervisor Walsh

8. (A) At next month's meeting
   (B) Next week
   (C) At the November elections
   (D) Tomorrow

9. (A) Too noisy
   (B) Too dangerous
   (C) Too expensive
   (D) Too dull

10. (A) August
    (B) September
    (C) July
    (D) October

11. (A) The mayor
    (B) His press aide
    (C) Paul Morrisey
    (D) The City Council

12. (A) Belief
    (B) Sympathy
    (C) Skepticism
    (D) Bitterness

13. (A) Firing city employees
    (B) Eliminating pay raises
    (C) Disbanding the Council
    (D) Cutting hospital programs

14. (A) Loss of job
    (B) Loss of votes
    (C) Loss of influence
    (D) Loss of confidence

15. (A) Last spring
    (B) Last fall
    (C) Last week
    (D) Last winter

16. (A) A rock
    (B) A screen
    (C) A branch
    (D) A chair

17. (A) 5
    (B) 4
    (C) 15
    (D) 1

18. (A) 6 hours
    (B) 12 hours
    (C) 3 hours
    (D) 9 hours

19. (A) Mortgage
    (B) Car
    (C) Consolidation
    (D) Home improvement

20. (A) The loan officer
    (B) The branch manager
    (C) The press officer
    (D) The president

MINI-TALKS

WEATHER REPORTS

In the following questions, you will hear short weather reports followed by
questions about the report. You must choose the most appropriate answers. The
questions will require you to pay close attention to small details. This will train
your short-term memory.

1. (A) Evening
   (B) Morning
   (C) Afternoon
   (D) Late night

2. (A) Low 40's
   (B) High 60's
   (C) High 40's
   (D) Low 60's

3. (A) Rain
   (B) Wind
   (C) Cold
   (D) Snow

4. (A) 32 degrees
   (B) 42 degrees
   (C) 10 degrees
   (D) 0 degrees

5. (A) 10 degrees
   (B) 42 degrees
   (C) 32 degrees
   (D) 0 degrees

6. (A) Blizzard
   (B) Freezing rain
   (C) Snow
   (D) High winds

7. (A) Snowing
   (B) Raining
   (C) Cloudy
   (D) Warming

8. (A) 3 weeks ago
   (B) 7 years ago
   (C) 10 years go
   (D) 5 days ago

9. (A) 3 inches around
   (B) 5 inches around
   (C) 3 inches across
   (D) 7 inches across

10. (A) $3 million
    (B) $13 million
    (C) $30 million
    (D) $3.3 million

11. (A) Thursday
    (B) Friday
    (C) Saturday
    (D) Sunday

12. (A) 10 percent
    (B) 20 percent
    (C) 30 percent
    (D) 40 percent

13. (A) A traffic jam
    (B) Low temperatures
    (C) Showers
    (D) Hail storms

14. (A) A plateau region
    (B) The desert
    (C) Canada
    (D) Northern New England

15. (A) 70
    (B) 80
    (C) 100
    (D) 60

16. (A) Warm
    (B) Cold
    (C) Snowing
    (D) Dry

17. (A) Arizona
    (B) Wyoming
    (C) Wisconsin
    (D) Kansas

18. (A) Power failures
    (B) Heavy winds
    (C) Hail stones
    (D) Floods

19. (A) Missouri
    (B) Arizona
    (C) Wisconsin
    (D) Kansas

20. (A) 15 degrees
    (B) 20 degrees
    (C) 59 degrees
    (D) 19 degrees

MINI-TALKS

ACADEMIC LECTURES

In the following questions, you will hear a short academic lecture followed by questions about the lecture. You must choose the most appropriate answers.

1. (A) Stones
   (B) Handles
   (C) Cotton pads
   (D) Rollers

2. (A) Leather
   (B) Paper
   (C) Earth
   (D) Stone

3. (A) On the ground
   (B) On the stone
   (C) On the ink ball
   (D) On the type

4. (A) Real
   (B) Fabulous
   (C) Adventurous
   (D) Depressing

5. (A) History
   (B) Morality
   (C) Spirituality
   (D) Comedy

6. (A) Private authors
   (B) Small publishers
   (C) Literary critics
   (D) Major publishing houses

7. (A) Early 20th century

   (B) Late 20th century
   (C) 11th century
   (D) Late 18th century

8. (A) The Romantics
   (B) The Classicists
   (C) The Enlightenment
   (D) The famous

9. (A) Cost
   (B) Length
   (C) Hyperbole
   (D) Naturalness

10. (A) Regulated them
    (B) Gave them an example
    (C) Hindered them
    (D) Imprisoned them

11. (A) An Indian
    (B) A couple in the woods
    (C) An older painting
    (D) The most recent painting

12. (A) A war dance
    (B) A battle
    (C) A picnic
    (D) A walk in the woods

13. (A) At preparatory school
    (B) In a museum

(C) At home
(D) At the painter's house

14. (A) Sculpture
    (B) Painting
    (C) Ceramics
    (D) Textiles

15. (A) Cubists
    (B) Impressionists
    (C) Expressionists
    (D) Transcendentalists

16. (A) Euphoria
    (B) Patriotism
    (C) Disillusion
    (D) Disinterest

17. (A) Realist

(B) Abstract
(C) Symbolist
(D) Pointillist

18. (A) No
    (B) Yes
    (C) Doesn't know
    (D) Doesn't say

19. (A) Casual preparation
    (B) High fats
    (C) Large portions
    (D) Lower calories

20. (A) West Coast
    (B) East Coast
    (C) South
    (D) Midwest

MINI-TALKS

INFORMATIVE TALKS

In the following questions, you will hear a short informative talk followed by questions about the talk. You must choose the most appropriate answers.

1. (A) Aries
   (B) Leo
   (C) Virgo
   (D) Cancer

2. (A) Gemini
   (B) Taurus
   (C) Virgo
   (D) Scorpio

3. (A) Aquarius
   (B) Pisces
   (C) Scorpio
   (D) Sagittarius

4. (A) Ivy
   (B) Cabbage rose
   (C) Tansy
   (D) Anemone

5. (A) Lotus
   (B) Wild tansy
   (C) Anemone
   (D) Birch

6. (A) Extensively
   (B) Hardly at all

(C) In classrooms
(D) In foreign countries

7. (A) Along the river
   (B) On the coast
   (C) In the mountains
   (D) On the main highway

8. (A) Griswold Inn
   (B) Bee and Thistle
   (C) Old Lyme
   (D) Essex

9. (A) Since 1900
   (B) Since early 1800s
   (C) Since late 1800s
   (D) Since 1918

10. (A) Characters
    (B) A single detective
    (C) Complex plots
    (D) Simplicity

11. (A) A false clue
    (B) A kind of fish
    (C) A detective
    (D) A difficult murder

12. (A) French
    (B) English
    (C) Belgian
    (D) American

13. (A) Pluto
    (B) Jupiter
    (C) Venus
    (D) Mercury

14. (A) 265
    (B) 365
    (C) 180
    (D) 88

15. (A) Mars
    (B) Venus
    (C) Pluto
    (D) Mercury

MINI-TALKS

CLASS DISCUSSIONS

In the following exercise you will hear a short class discussion followed by questions about the discussion. You must choose the most appropriate answers.

1. (A) Never
   (B) Not
   (C) Ever
   (D) None

2. (A) Agrees
   (B) Contradicts
   (C) Supports
   (D) Negates

3. (A) English
   (B) Mathematics
   (C) Photography
   (D) Geography

4. (A) A painter
   (B) An engineer
   (C) A writer
   (D) A teacher

5. (A) Worked in an office
   (B) Sailed on whaling ships
   (C) Reviewed others' books
   (D) Gone into retreat

6. (A) He had a broken hand.
   (B) He went back to sea.
   (C) Critics didn't like his books.
   (D) He was bored with writing.

7. (A) An engineer
   (B) An astronomer
   (C) A teacher
   (D) A student

8. (A) The teacher
   (B) The student
   (C) The father
   (D) All three

9. (A) In his head
   (B) On his fingers
   (C) With a calculator
   (D) On the blackboard

10. (A) Zoo
    (B) Museum
    (C) School
    (D) Restaurant

11. (A) Pencils
    (B) Tape recorders
    (C) Lunches
    (D) Papers

12. (A) He wasn't in class Friday.
    (B) He wasn't hungry.
    (C) He would eat at the zoo.
    (D) He only eats dinner.

13. (A) Music
    (B) Grammar
    (C) Math
    (D) Sports

14. (A) He's afraid of the woman.
    (B) He'll make mistakes.
    (C) He knows no languages.
    (D) He only talks about math.

15. (A) She encourages it.
    (B) It makes her cry.
    (C) It makes her angry.
    (D) She thinks it's silly.

LISTENING TARGET ANSWER KEY

STATEMENTS

Minimal Pairs		Computation		Number Discrimination		Synonyms		Negation	
1. C	6. B	1. D	6. A	1. A	6. B	1. D	6. B	1. D	6. D
2. C	7. D	2. D	7. B	2. D	7. D	2. C	7. D	2. A	7. B
3. A	8. D	3. C	8. A	3. B	8. A	3. D	8. A	3. A	8. C
4. B	9. C	4. D	9. C	4. D	9. D	4. A	9. D	4. D	9. C
5. D	10. D	5. A	10. B	5. C	10. C	5. C	10. B	5. A	10. D

Contextual Reference		Cause and Effect		Conditionals		Chronological Order		Comparisons	
1. B	6. B	1. A	6. C	1. B	6. C	1. C	6. D	1. A	6. A
2. D	7. C	2. A	7. D	2. B	7. D	2. D	7. D	2. C	7. B
3. A	8. C	3. B	8. A	3. A	8. A	3. A	8. A	3. B	8. A
4. C	9. D	4. D	9. D	4. B	9. D	4. B	9. D	4. D	9. C
5. D	10. D	5. C	10. D	5. A	10. D	5. D	10. D	5. A	10. C

CONVERSATIONS

Minimal Pairs		Computation		Number Discrimination		Synonyms		Negation	
1. D	6. B	1. A	6. C	1. B	6. C	1. C	6. D	1. A	6. C
2. D	7. B	2. D	7. B	2. C	7. C	2. A	7. C	2. B	7. D
3. A	8. B	3. B	8. B	3. A	8. A	3. D	8. A	3. A	8. C
4. A	9. B	4. C	9. C	4. B	9. D	4. B	9. B	4. D	9. A
5. A	10. A	5. D	10. A	5. C	10. B	5. A	10. A	5. A	10. C

Contextual Reference		Cause and Effect		Conditionals		Chronological Order		Comparisons	
1. C	6. C	1. A	6. C	1. A	6. C	1. A	6. C	1. A	6. A
2. B	7. B	2. B	7. A	2. D	7. B	2. C	7. C	2. D	7. C
3. C	8. A	3. C	8. B	3. C	8. B	3. C	8. C	3. B	8. C
4. A	9. A	4. B	9. B	4. A	9. D	4. C	9. B	4. D	9. A
5. C	10. C	5. D	10. A	5. C	10. B	5. B	10. C	5. C	10. A

MINI-TALKS

Overheard Conversations		Announcements		Advertisements		News Reports	
1. C	11. D	1. A	11. B	1. A	11. C	1. B	11. B
2. A	12. C	2. A	12. C	2. C	12. D	2. B	12. C
3. C	13. A	3. C	13. D	3. C	13. D	3. C	13. D
4. D	14. D	4. A	14. A	4. A	14. A	4. D	14. C
5. A	15. A	5. B	15. B	5. A	15. B	5. B	15. B
6. C	16. B	6. C	16. B	6. B	16. D	6. B	16. C
7. D	17. C	7. C	17. C	7. D	17. C	7. D	17. B
8. C	18. A	8. A	18. D	8. C	18. A	8. A	18. B
9. B	19. A	9. D	19. A	9. B	19. D	9. C	19. A
10. C	20. B	10. B	20. A	10. A	20. A	10. A	20. D

Weather Reports		Academic Lectures		Informative Talks		Class Discussions	
1. A	11. C	1. D	11. C	1. A	11. A	1. C	11. C
2. D	12. B	2. A	12. B	2. A	12. C	2. D	12. A
3. D	13. C	3. B	13. A	3. C	13. A	3. A	13. B
4. C	14. A	4. B	14. B	4. B	14. D	4. C	14. B
5. A	15. C	5. C	15. C	5. D	15. D	5. B	15. D
6. A	16. A	6. D	16. C	6. B		6. C	
7. C	17. C	7. D	17. B	7. B		7. A	
8. B	18. B	8. A	18. A	8. A		8. C	
9. A	19. B	9. D	19. D	9. B		9. C	
10. A	20. C	10. B	20. A	10. C		10. A	

STRUCTURE TARGETS

INTRODUCTION

The Structure and Written Expression section tests your understanding of basic English grammar as used in written English.

There are two parts to the Structure and Written Expression section:

PART A	Incomplete Sentences	15 questions
PART B	Incorrect Sentence Part	25 questions

Part A
In Part A, a sentence will have a blank space. You are to choose a word or phrase from the four possible answer options to complete the sentence. The choices represent the most common errors made by students.

> This is _____.
> (A) an example of one
> (B) of one an example
> (C) a example of one
> (D) of one example

The most appropriate word order is (A) *an example of one*. You would have blackened (A) on your answer sheet.

Part B
In Part B, a sentence will have four words or groups of words underlined. You are to choose the underlined part that should be changed to make the sentence grammatically correct.

> This is <u>a example</u> <u>of a sentence</u> <u>with</u> an error <u>underlined</u>.
>   A   B   C   D

Choice (A) should be changed to read *an example*. You would have blackened (A) on your answer sheet.

STRUCTURE TIPS

Before the TOEFL
The exercises in this book focus on the most common errors made by students learning English.

Although it is easy to make mistakes, it is not easy to categorize them. An error in a subordinate clause could be a misplaced modifier, a subject reversed with a verb, the addition of an extra word (subject or verb), or the wrong subordinate marker. Consequently, when you review the mistakes you made on a diagnostic test, you should try to determine *why* you made a mistake. For example, did you make a mistake because you did not remember to use the passive mode, or did you use a passive verb but place it incorrectly in the sentence?

When you itemize your errors on your Personal Study Plan, you should mark for further study not only the general problem (e.g. passive voice) but also the specific problem (e.g. word order). The Personal Study Plan will help you focus your attention on one of many potential grammatical problems. Only you will be able to determine everything you should study.

The exercises that follow will help you with the many different parts of English grammar. The exercises are meant to help you *review* what you already know. The exercises define grammatical terms and remind you of important patterns and rules. They are designed to focus your attention on test strategies. If you need additional practice or explanation of a grammar concept itself, you should refer to one of the Prentice-Hall grammar texts listed at the end of the book.

During the TOEFL
1. Concentrate on what you know.
2. Be aware of common mistakes.
3. Try to avoid these mistakes.
4. Guess if you don't know the answer.

ACTIVE-PASSIVE VERBS

Sentences are either in the active voice (or mode) or passive voice. The subject is the **doer** of the action in an active voice sentence. The subject is the **receiver** in a passive construction. The passive construction consists of *be + ed/en.*

Potential problems with active and passive voice are:
1. One voice form may be substituted for the other.
2. The auxiliary may not agree in tense or number.

Study the following potential problems:

INCORRECT VOICE
Incorrect
She couldn't consult the map because it was packing away.
Correct
She couldn't consult the map because it was packed away.

INAPPROPRIATE AUXILIARY: NUMBER
Incorrect
The people was given small party favors.
Correct
The people were given small party favors.

ACTIVE-PASSIVE I
Choose the one answer that best completes the sentence.

1. Although the mission was to be kept a secret, it _____ to the press.

   (A) reveals
   (B) revealed
   (C) was revealed
   (D) reveal

2. The secretary opened the mail which _____ that morning.

   (A) had delivered
   (B) delivered
   (C) had been delivered
   (D) is delivered

3. Foreign aid funds _____ by the committee at the President's recommendation.

   (A) were cut
   (B) will cut
   (C) cut
   (D) cut it

4. In spite of popular support, the radio program _____ off the air very soon.

   (A) had been taken
   (B) will be taken

(C) takes
(D) were taken

(C) will take
(D) will be taken

5. The questions to the Board _____ in a belligerent tone by the stockholder.

(A) poses
(B) was posed
(C) were posed
(D) posed

6. Strange things _____ by seemingly reasonable people under stress.

(A) have done
(B) does
(C) is done
(D) are done

7. The commissioners assured the crowd that the problem _____ care of as soon as possible.

(A) has been taken
(B) had been taken

8. Some people believe that giving gifts is one way _____ by others.

(A) to love
(B) love
(C) to be loved
(D) is loved

9. When the facade needed to be renovated, the building committee voted to _____ .

(A) have done it
(B) have it done
(C) be done
(D) have been done

10. Government control of the press _____ by every concerned citizen.

(A) has been opposed
(B) has opposed
(C) has been opposing
(D) opposed

ACTIVE-PASSIVE II

In the sentences below, identify the one underlined phrase that is incorrect.

1. Although some <u>difficulty was expected</u>, the extent of the problem
   A

   <u>was not known</u> until the <u>project completed</u> and the final report was
   B   C

   <u>distributed</u>.
   D

2. Metal <u>must be hammered</u>, worked, <u>and cooled rapidly</u> <u>to relieve</u> internal
   A   B   C

   <u>stresses causing</u> by heating.
   D

3. To add <u>distilled</u> water, a large-gauge <u>hollow</u> needle <u>inserted</u> through a
   A   B   C

   cork in the base <u>made of</u> opaque material.
   D

4. Theories and <u>laws applied to</u> phenomena to <u>increase understanding</u> of them
   A   B

   and to <u>adapt them</u> <u>in creating</u> products for man's use.
   C   D

5. A stain which <u>has first been</u> soaked in solvent can then easily <u>removed</u> by
               A   B *(be)*

   <u>adding water</u> which has <u>been distilled</u>.
       C   D

6. Spacecraft <u>destined</u> for orbit will <u>be boosting</u> from low earth <u>orbit by</u> *(boosted)*
                 A   B   C

   <u>rockets developed</u> by a west coast engineering firm.
       D

7. The <u>well-known</u>, well-advertised <u>products developed</u> by major corporations
            A   B

   <u>have become</u> an industry standard <u>to emulated</u> rather than improved upon. *(be) (copy)*
       C   D

8. The store front <u>being painted</u>, so the customers <u>were required</u> *(was)*
                        A   B

   <u>to enter through</u> the alley <u>that ran behind</u> the building.
       C   D

9. Risks which <u>are taking</u> by today's entrepreneurs <u>are considerable</u> and, <u>while</u> *(taken)*
                A   B   C

   <u>stimulating, pose threats</u> to their financial security.
           D

10. Oil and gold, both of which <u>had an unparalleled</u> price increase in the 70's,
                                   A

    <u>have not been</u> popular recently and <u>not placed</u> on the <u>most favored</u> *(have) (be)*
        B   C   D
    stock lists.

ARTICLES

There are **definite** and **indefinite** articles. The definite article *(the)* can be used before a singular or plural countable noun. Sometimes the article is omitted before a plural countable noun. The indefinite article *(a* or *an)* is used only before singular countable nouns or adjectives. *An* precedes nouns beginning with a vowel sound.

Potential problems with articles are:
    1. Addition of an article,
    2. Omission of an article, and
    3. Inappropriate use of an article.

Study the following potential problems:

ADDITION
Incorrect
The New York City is the largest city in New York.
Correct
New York City is the largest city in New York.

OMISSION
Incorrect
The newspaper is on table.
Correct
The newspaper is on the table.

INAPPROPRIATE USE
Incorrect
A sugar spilled on the floor.
Correct
The sugar spilled on the floor.

ARTICLES I

Choose the one answer that best completes the sentence. If no article is appropriate (or required), select (D) 0.

1. _____ eagle is the national bird of the U.S.A.

   (A) A
   (B) An
   (C) The
   (D) 0

2. _____ Nantucket Island is a superb spot for watching the eclipse.

   (A) A
   (B) An
   (C) The
   (D) 0

3. The cat is _____ beautiful animal, but its intelligence leaves much to be desired.

   (A) a
   (B) an
   (C) the
   (D) 0

4. We loved _____ Lake Geneva especially in the fall.

   (A) a
   (B) an
   (C) the
   (D) 0

5. Families like _____ Rockefellers have become synonymous with wealth.

   (A) a
   (B) an
   (C) the
   (D) 0

6. Mrs. James did not arrive until sometime in _____ late afternoon.

   (A) a
   (B) an
   (C) the
   (D) 0

7. _____ University of Chicago has an excellent law school.

   (A) A
   (B) An
   (C) The
   (D) 0

8. Western art of the 19th century shows the influence of _____ Far East.

   (A) a
   (B) an
   (C) the
   (D) 0

9. _____ Finland is known for its beautiful forests and seacoasts.

   (A) A
   (B) An
   (C) The
   (D) 0

10. _____ Air and Space Museum has the highest attendance record of all the museums in the world.

    (A) A
    (B) An
    (C) The
    (D) 0

ARTICLES II

In the sentences below, identify the one underlined phrase that is incorrect.

1. The sugar the cook left on shelf was eaten by a mouse as large as a rat.
   A   B   C   D

2. To design a house the architect needs only a ruler, a pencil, piece of paper
                  A   B   C
   and an eraser.
       D

3. Some people prefer hotels to apartment buildings, but most like the houses the
                      A   B   C
   best of the three.
          D

4. There are 103 universities in the Tokyo with more than
             A   B
   one-half million students from all parts of Japan.
   C   D

5. People who dislike concerts prefer listening to records, but musicians insist
                                                    A
   that an orchestra must be heard in person to appreciate the strength
        B   C
   and subtleties of a music.
                     D

6. Television replaced radio as the most widely enjoyed form of
   A   B   C
   the broadcasting in the United States.
   D

7. The biology teacher suggested class collect sea shells, rocks, wildflowers, or
   A   B   C
   fossils.
   D

8. The new doorman has the problem remembering the names of the people with
   A   B   C
   offices in the building.
           D

9. All travelers should carry change of clothes, extra money, and their
   A   B
   passport in a small bag that can be carried on the plane.
              C   D

10. A computer with a terminal, monitor, and printer is often referred to as
    A   B   C
    work station.
    D

COMPARISONS

ADJECTIVES
The comparative and superlative forms of adjectives are used to compare two or more nouns. Adjectives describe or modify nouns. Adjectives usually precede nouns or follow linking verbs. They answer the question *What kind?*

Adjective Comparisons:
Equal: Ping pong is as boring as tennis.
Comparative: Tennis is more (less) boring than football.
Superlative: Golf is the most (least) boring game.

Equal: Jack is as happy as a clown.
Comparative: Jack is happier (less happy) than he was last year.
Superlative: He is the happiest (least happy) person I know.

ADVERBS
The comparative and superlative forms of adverbs are used to compare two verbs or adjectives. Adverbs modify action verbs, adjectives, or other adverbs. Many adverbs end with the suffix *ly*. Adverbs answer the question *How?*

Adverb Comparison:
Equal: Lawrence eats *as* more slowly *as* than his wife.
Comparative: Lawrence eats more (less) slowly than his son.
Superlative: Lawrence eats the most (least) slowly of all his friends.

Equal: His boat sails as fast as mine.
Comparative: My boat sails faster than yours.
Superlative: Hers sails the fastest.

Potential problems with adjectives and adverbs are:
  1. The comparative and superlative forms may be incorrect.
  2. The modifiers may be replaced by other words of the same word family.

Study the following potential problems:

MORE/MOST ADDITION
Incorrect
The deck is more longer than the couch.
Correct
The deck is longer than the couch.

INCORRECT COMPARATIVE OR SUPERLATIVE FORM
Incorrect
Today's lecture was most stimulating than ever before.
Correct
Today's lecture was more stimulating than ever before.

COMPARISONS I

Choose the one answer that best completes the sentence.

1. It took five men to carry the tree,   (B) as tall
   which was _____ than a three-story   (C) more taller
   building.   (D) the tallest

   (A) taller

2. One of the _____ inventions of the century was the holograph.

(A) cleverest than
(B) cleverer
(C) more clever
(D) most clever

3. The plan to use existing resources was considered the _____ solution.

(A) good
(B) most better
(C) best
(D) more better

4. Language policy has been a subject of _____ debate in multilingual nations.

(A) sharp
(B) sharper
(C) sharpest
(D) more sharp

5. The weather is _____ at this time of year than in the spring.

(A) calm
(B) calmest
(C) calmer
(D) more calmer

6. The plan calls for a _____ defense than the one we currently have.

(A) stronger
(B) most strongest
(C) stronger than
(D) as stronger

7. The appreciation of platinum is _____ subject than that of gold to the vagaries of international circumstances.

(A) less
(B) few
(C) fewer
(D) least

8. The water temperature surrounding the kelp beds is _____ than that around reefs.

(A) cool
(B) coolest
(C) more cool
(D) cooler

9. Of all the amplifiers, this product with its wide range provides _____ stability within the audible spectrum.

(A) the greatest
(B) the greater
(C) greater
(D) greatest

10. When allowed to sleep, volunteers who were kept awake as many as 100 hours dreamed _____ than usual.

(A) more considerably
(B) considerably more
(C) most
(D) most considerably

COMPARISONS II

In the sentences below, identify the one underlined phrase that is incorrect.

1. The days become <u>more long</u> <u>as</u> the sun moves into a <u>wider</u> orbit <u>farther</u>
                A   B   C   D
from the earth.

2. The competition was <u>the easy</u> the swimmer could remember, although
                         A

<u>the other contestants</u>, who were <u>younger</u>, thought it was <u>hard</u>.
     B   C   D

3. The <u>strange</u> sound that came through <u>the thick</u> walls separating <u>the two</u>
    A   B   C
buildings seemed to be as close <u>than</u> next door.
                                  D

4. The <u>lengthy</u> report was given <u>more directly</u> to the <u>responsible</u> supervisor, who
      A   B   C

read it <u>without haste</u>.
        D

5. <u>The brave man</u> the city has ever seen was that <u>strong</u> fireman who worked
   as
      A   B

<u>most of the night</u> saving lives from <u>the big fire</u> at the Ballingall Hotel.
       C   D

6. The <u>more rapid changes</u> in <u>modern</u> technology have left <u>many computer owners</u>
           A   B   C

with <u>obsolete</u> equipment.
       D

7. A <u>greater</u> number of doctors in <u>fewest</u> hospitals indicates another
                               fewer
   A   B

<u>significant</u> change in the status of health care for the <u>low</u>-income family.
   C   D

8. The industrial community should be <u>closer enough</u> to the <u>crowded</u> centers,
                                 close
                                      A   B

but <u>distant</u> enough to reduce <u>potential</u> hazards.
     C   D

9. Before dental care became <u>more widespread</u>, people looked <u>older</u> before their
                                                      old
                                     A   B

time since so <u>many</u> lost their teeth at <u>an early</u> age.
           C   D

10. The plane's instrument console, <u>one</u> of its <u>more</u> intricate design features,
                                   A   B
      lower
is <u>lowest</u> in the compartment than usual, especially for those
     C

crew members <u>as tall as</u> those doing the testing of the plane.
              D

CONDITIONALS

Conditional sentences have two parts: **the condition** and **the result.** The condition is usually introduced by *if* although it may be introduced by other structures. The form of the verb in both parts depends on the type of condition.

Conditional sentences are used to indicate **contrary to fact** or **real** conditions in the present or past tenses.

Potential problems with conditionals are:
  1. Inappropriate sequence of tenses,   *mach*
  2. Inappropriate introductory marker, and
  3. The incorrect form of *to be* in first and third persons singular.

Study the following potential problems:

INAPPROPRIATE TENSE

Incorrect
If I know his number, I'd call him now.
Correct
If I knew his number, I'd call him now.

Incorrect
If she helped, we would have finished.
Correct
If she had helped, we would have finished.

INTRODUCTORY MARKER

Incorrect
We had known, we would have brought a gift.
Correct
Had we known, we would have brought a gift.

Incorrect
We would have enjoyed ourselves more you had been there.
Correct
We would have enjoyed ourselves more if you had been there.

INCORRECT TO BE FORM:

Incorrect
I would answer truthfully if I was you.
Correct
I would answer truthfully if I were you.

Incorrect
If he was younger, he would join.
Correct
If he were younger, he would join.

CONDITIONALS I

Choose the one answer that best completes the sentence.

1. If they _____ overworked in the beginning, the volunteers would have helped finish the project.

   (A) were not
   (B) was not
   (C) had not been
   (D) have not been

2. If Marie _____ , tell her I will call her back as soon as I return.

   (A) calls
   (B) called
   (C) will call
   (D) is going to call

3. The supervisors could have prevented this problem _____ it beforehand.

   (A) if they knew
   (B) had they known
   (C) if had they known
   (D) whether

4. The boy's parents knew he _____ if he had passed the final exam.

   (A) graduated
   (B) would graduate
   (C) could have graduated
   (D) will graduate

5. Because Mr. Gleason worked only a month, the personnel director would not write a recommendation for him even if he _____ .

   (A) could ask
   (B) asks

(C) asked
(D) will ask

6. If _____ enough interest, the proposed flexible work schedule will be implemented.

(A) there be
(B) there will be
(C) there are
(D) there is

7. The teaching assistant's explanations to the class will be more understandable if he _____ more clearly next time.

(A) speaks
(B) spoke
(C) will speak
(D) has spoken

8. If it _____ rain, the band's members will have to cover their instruments.

(A) will start
(B) starts to
(C) started
(D) had started

9. Had the damage been worse, the insurance company _____.

(A) would pay
(B) paid
(C) would have paid
(D) had paid

10. If the art dealer _____ the money, he would have bought the painting.

(A) had had
(B) has
(C) had
(D) would have

CONDITIONALS II

In the sentences below, identify the one underlined phrase that is incorrect.

1. If the terms <u>had been</u> better, the borrower <u>would accept</u> the bank's proposal
   A   B
   <u>even though</u> he <u>disagreed</u> with some of the conditions.
   C   D

2. <u>It</u> is not impossible to overcome the difficulties <u>of learning</u> a new language
   A   B
   <u>if</u> one <u>will have</u> the right attitude.
   C   D

3. <u>Had they known</u> the snowstorm <u>would</u> be so treacherous, the hikers
   A   B
   <u>did not venture</u> into <u>it</u> without proper equipment.
   C   D

4. <u>Realizing</u> the extent of the skier's <u>injuries</u>, his companions <u>would have felt</u>
   A   B   C
   more comfortable <u>if a doctor were</u> present.
   D

5. <u>If going</u> to that restaurant is Jeff's choice, <u>then</u> we automatically <u>vetoed</u>
   A   B   C
   it because <u>he is consistently</u> too extravagant for our tastes.
   D

6. If the resources of forest and water power were more fully developed, the
      A   B

   economy would not have been so dependent on imports.
                     C   D

   be (handwritten above "have been")

7. If the new student followed the rules as they were explained to him, he
                      A   B   C

   had (handwritten above "followed")

   would not have been in such a predicament.
      D

8. I think I would enjoy the movie we went to last night even more if I had read
     A   B   C

   had enjoyed (handwritten above "would enjoy")

   the book before seeing it.
                     D

9. If the library is closed over the holidays, it would be very difficult
   A   B   C

   w (handwritten above "If")   *will* (handwritten above "would be")

   to finish the research project.
      D

10. If all the members of the committee who are present would agree, the proposal
    A   B   C

    will go into effect immediately.
                        D

CONJUNCTIONS

A conjunction connects identical grammatical structures. There are **coordinating conjunctions** *(and, but, or, nor)*, **paired conjunctions** *(both...and; not only...but also; either...or; neither...nor)*, and **comparative conjunctions** *(than; and so; and...too; and... either; and...neither)*.

Potential problems with conjunctions are:
   1. The forms may connect nonparallel structures.
   2. The meaning of the forms may be confused.

Study the following potential problems:

NONPARALLEL STRUCTURE
   Incorrect
   The suggestion was to skim and then scanning for information.
   Correct
   The suggestion was to skim and then to scan for information.

INAPPROPRIATE FORM
   Incorrect
   It didn't matter whether the report was typed and handwritten.
   Correct
   It didn't matter whether the report was typed or handwritten.

FORM I

Choose the one answer that best completes the sentence.

1. _____ the classroom needs to be cleaned.

   (A) The offices and
   (B) Either the offices or
   (C) Both the offices
   (D) The offices nor

2. Relief organizations have contributed _____ money to famine in Africa.

   (A) both time and
   (B) neither and
   (C) time but
   (D) time nor

3. The baby _____ cries if he cannot get his way.

   (A) screams but
   (B) screams and
   (C) screams neither
   (D) either screams nor

4. The politician acted _____ about minority rights.

   (A) as if she cared
   (B) and if she cared
   (C) if she cared
   (D) either she cared

5. The group of students touring on bicycles went _____ to the mountains, but to the coast as well.

   (A) either
   (B) also
   (C) neither
   (D) not only

6. The Olympic judges thought the contestant ran the race _____ .

   (A) easily and well
   (B) easy but good
   (C) easily nor well
   (D) easily and good

7. The statesman gave us his reasons for acting and _____ as he did.

   (A) speaking
   (B) speak
   (C) his speaking
   (D) to speak

8. Not only the workers _____ the management are going to the union meeting.

   (A) or
   (B) also
   (C) but also
   (D) and

9. Since their organization has not followed the budgetary reforms we did, their gross revenues were less this year _____ .

   (A) than us
   (B) as ours
   (C) than ours
   (D) but also ours

10. This particular comet, which comes every 10 years, does not move _____ light.

    (A) as quicker than
    (B) as quickly as
    (C) but quickly than
    (D) as quickly

FORM II

In the sentences below, identify the one underlined phrase that is incorrect.

1. Mosquitos, which have a voracious appetite <u>and explosive</u> breeding rate, are
                                                          A

   <u>controlled neither</u> by the draining of <u>forest and swamp</u> areas
           B   C

   <u>by the spraying</u> of pesticides.
           D

2. Project Orbis, a flying eye <u>hospital on a</u> DC-8 jet that is both a classroom

   A

   and

   <u>or a clinic,</u> has visited 37 <u>countries, performed</u> 3,000 operations,

   B   C

   <u>and updated</u> the skills of at least 2,500 eye doctors.

   D

3. The cowboy turned <u>and rode</u> towards the sun, <u>but</u> neither the horse

                        A   B

   nor

   <u>or he</u> knew the exact path home, <u>and</u> soon both were lost.

   C   D

4. The job requires that the <u>applicant not only</u> speak <u>both Spanish and</u>

                               A   B

                            and

   English <u>but also be able</u> to type <u>but take</u> shorthand.

   C   D

5. Neither the photographer <u>and the reporter</u> witnessed <u>the event, but</u>

                        nor

                             A   B

   they <u>and their</u> editors prepared <u>both articles and</u> photos as if they

        C   D

   had been there.

6. The musician could play neither modern melodies <u>nor</u> classical <u>works, but</u>

                                                      A   B

                                                   both

   his performance of traditional folk tunes captivated <u>either</u> the parents

                                                          C

   and <u>the children</u>.

       D

7. Rodney asked that we come <u>and help</u> him, <u>but</u> when we arrived, he

                             A   B

                         and

   had already finished <u>but left</u>, with neither a note <u>nor an apology</u> for us.

                          C   D

8. Keeping awake was not as hard as <u>sitting</u> still, <u>or</u> it was still difficult to

                                      but

                                     A   B

   see how people could have called this movie <u>better than</u> the one we saw

                                                 C

   and <u>enjoyed</u> last week.

       D

9. A study <u>released last week indicates</u> that college <u>students, particularly</u> men,

            A   B

   regard female teachers <u>as less</u> worthy <u>of male</u> teachers.

                            C   D

10. <u>Both</u> Mr. Parkinson <u>or</u> Ms. Stewart have <u>run and lost</u> that race

     A   *and*

                        B   C

    <u>more than</u> anyone.

     D

PARALLEL STRUCTURES I

Choose the one answer that best completes the sentence.

1. The fruit delivered directly from the orchard was _____ also delicious.

   (A) not only ripe and
   (B) not only ripe but
   (C) only ripe
   (D) as ripe as but

2. In the future, the discovery which will most change the lives of people, most affect the health of the world, and _____ the drug industry is the cure for the common cold.

   (A) most change
   (B) most changing
   (C) with most change on
   (D) most change of

3. When I stop to consider my ambitions, I realize my main goals consist of doing well in school, graduating, and _____.

   (A) to make money
   (B) making money
   (C) be making money
   (D) make money

4. The physician considers going to bed early to be more sensible _____.

   (A) but staying up late
   (B) than to stay up late
   (C) than staying up lately
   (D) than staying up late

5. The risk the financial commission is taking is _____ .

   (A) greater than the bank
   (B) as greater than the bank's

   (C) greater than the bank's
   (D) as greater as the bank's

6. Although we have reason to believe otherwise, the editors believe they can write _____ .

   (A) as well as we do
   (B) as well we do
   (C) well as we do
   (D) as well than we do

7. The main sports at the college were _____, and baseball.

   (A) archery, to ride
   (B) archery, ride
   (C) to archery, ride
   (D) archery, riding

8. _____nor the faculty appreciated her negative remarks.

   (A) The administration
   (B) Both the administration
   (C) Neither the administration
   (D) Either the administration

9. The diplomat found the situation of being caught on the border during the fighting _____ exhilarating.

   (A) both terrifying but also
   (B) both terrifying and
   (C) as terrifying as also
   (D) not only terrifying and

10. The Empire State Building is quite tall, _____ the World Trade Center.

    (A) and so is
    (B) and as is
    (C) as
    (D) than so is

PARALLEL STRUCTURES II

In the sentences below, identify the one underlined phrase that is incorrect.

1. An <u>element</u> cannot be formed from simpler <u>substances</u>, nor can
           A   B

   <u>it be decompose</u> with <u>simpler</u> varieties of matter.
           C   D

2. Electric eels <u>use</u> charges to detect prey and also *stunned* <u>stunning</u> them <u>before</u>
              A   B   C

   <u>they</u> eat them.
    D

3. <u>Without</u> entering the body and *causing* <u>cause</u> damage, the CT is <u>far</u> superior to
       A   B   C

   the x-ray or <u>exploratory</u> surgery.
               D

4. <u>Prison reform</u>, *child abusing* <u>abusing children</u>, and toxic <u>wastes are</u> three
     A   B   C

   <u>issues which concern</u> citizens today.
         D

5. In our <u>society, where</u> peer recognition <u>is prized</u>, those who join everything
            A   *who*   B

   often <u>take spaces</u> from those <u>wanting to join</u>.
         C   D

6. Catching crabs in the bay is <u>profitable</u>, but <u>to fish</u> for bass <u>in</u> the river is
                       A   B   C

   more <u>relaxing.</u>
      D

7. I know that lying <u>is bad</u> and <u>to cheat</u> is too, but <u>no one</u> seems
                  A   B   C

   to have told <u>them</u>.
           D

8. The stockholders <u>expect the</u> chairman of the board whom <u>they elected</u> to
                A   B

   organize, direct, <u>controlling and</u> <u>supervise the operations</u> of
                 control C   D

   the company.

9. We need to know the hour <u>of your departure</u> and the time you are arriving,
                       A

   not <u>where</u> you have <u>been</u> or where you are <u>going</u>.
       B   C   D

10. <u>Telecommunication,</u> a phenomenon of this decade, <u>is insignificant</u> compared
     A   B

   to telepathic communication, <u>which is</u> a phenomenon <u>of the future</u>.
                         C   D

PREPOSITIONS

A preposition connects the object of a preposition to other structures in the sentence or clause. There are prepositions of **place, time, direction, cause,** and **location.**

A few of these prepositions are listed below.

Place	Time	Direction	Cause	Location
on	on	at	of	next to
in	for	from	in	opposite
among	until	into	to	on
between	during	up	due to	across
on top of	within	down	because of	behind
opposite	since	out(of)	for	near

As prepositions have different meanings in different contexts, it is important to pay attention to how they are used when you see and hear them.

Potential problems with prepositions are:
1. An inappropriate preposition may be used.
2. They may be omitted wholly or in part.
3. They may be used unnecessarily.

Study the following potential problems:

INAPPROPRIATE CHOICE
Incorrect
The books were left in the table.
Correct
The books were left on the table.

PREPOSITION OMISSION
Incorrect
I run into him time to time.
Correct
I run into him from time to time.

UNNECESSARY PREPOSITION
Incorrect
The audience came from out of the auditorium.
Correct
The audience came out of the auditorium.

Exercises illustrating these three problems are grouped together under *Structure Target Exercises* **Prepositions I and II.**

PREPOSITIONS I
Choose the one answer that best completes the sentence.

1. The chemist placed the bowl _____ the two test tubes.

   (A) among
   (B) between
   (C) in
   (D) through

2. The doctor sat _____ to the exit in case he had to leave early.

   (A) next
   (B) through
   (C) out
   (D) to

3. _____ the symphony, no one in the audience spoke.

   (A) By
   (B) For
   (C) During
   (D) From

4. The bird flew _____ the treetops.

   (A) opposite
   (B) with
   (C) up
   (D) over

5. The rain fell so heavily that it leaked _____ the ceiling.

   (A) at
   (B) over
   (C) since
   (D) through

6. The moment the curtain fell, the audience rushed _____ the steps.

   (A) on
   (B) through
   (C) up
   (D) out

7. In the Eastern Hemisphere, the eclipse of the sun occurred _____ mid-June.

   (A) on
   (B) in
   (C) from
   (D) until

8. The politician's constituency was very upset _____ his announcement.

   (A) out of
   (B) from
   (C) by
   (D) behind

9. The irate citizen kept a record of all the unauthorized buses that came _____ the residential street.

   (A) at
   (B) for
   (C) above
   (D) down

10. The parking lot _____ the restaurant was full.

   (A) across from
   (B) out of
   (C) between
   (D) from

PREPOSITIONS II

In the sentences below, identify the one underlined phrase that is incorrect.

1. The instructions <u>in</u> the manual state that the equipment must be placed <u>in</u> a
            A   B

   flat surface and <u>in</u> a climate-controlled room free <u>of</u> dust .
                  C   D

2. The hall was hung with flags draped <u>above</u> the ceiling, <u>from</u> the fireplaces,
                                        A   B

   <u>around</u> the moldings, and even <u>along</u> the window ledges.
     C   D

3. The young politician brings to her work <u>on</u> the city council the expertise that
                                                A

   makes her stand out <u>in</u> a crowd, puts her <u>above</u> the competition, and places
                       B   C

   her <u>under</u> her rivals.
      D

150   **Structure Targets**

4. My efforts to change the <u>procedures of the council</u> were not <u>met enthusiasm</u> *with*
                                        A   B

    <u>by</u> my colleagues <u>on</u> the board.
    C   D

5. The students looking <u>through</u> their binoculars <u>saw to the</u> birds sitting
                          A   B

    <u>on</u> the branch <u>of</u> the cherry tree.
    C   D

6. The music professor <u>from</u> the small midwestern school thought that
                        A

    <u>during</u> the concert the violin opposite <u>from</u> her seat <u>in</u> the first row
    B   C   D
    was not tuned properly.

7. All <u>since</u> the night, the bandleader hoped for a clear sky <u>at</u> dawn, as his plans *though*
        A   B
    <u>for</u> the parade depended <u>on</u> it.
    C   D

8. My best student <u>of</u> my grammar class speaks <u>with</u> an accent, but she will *in*
                       A   B

    have no <u>trouble getting</u> a job <u>with</u> her strong references.
               C   D

9. Recent studies show that <u>during</u> a volcanic eruption, ash spreads <u>by</u> the sky, *across*
                               A   B

    lava flows <u>down</u>, and hot winds travel <u>for</u> miles disturbing weather patterns.
               C   D

10. <u>In spite</u> <u>of the weather,</u> the <u>picnic on</u> the beach was <u>held the</u> usual spot. *at*
     A   B   C   D

PRONOUNS

There are five types of pronouns: **subject, object, possessive, possessive adjectives,** and **reflexive.**
Subject pronouns act as subjects or predicate nominatives (*I, we, she*).
Object pronouns are used as direct or indirect objects or objects of prepositions (*me, us, her*).
Possessive pronouns replace a noun understood from context (*mine, ours, hers*).
Possessive adjectives modify nouns by showing ownership (*my, our, her*).
Reflexive pronouns are used when the subject and object are the same, or are used to show emphasis (*myself, ourselves, herself*).

Potential problems with pronouns are:
1. The pronoun may not refer to the appropriate noun.
2. One type of pronoun may be substituted for another.
3. The pronoun may be omitted.
4. The pronoun may be repeated.

Study the following potential problems:

INAPPROPRIATE REFERENT
Incorrect
Since it was their vacation, it should be their decision how to spend them.
Correct
Since it was their vacation, it should be their decision how to spend it.

FORM
Incorrect
Compared to you and I, Maureen is extremely studious.
Correct
Compared to you and me, Maureen is extremely studious.

PRONOUN OMISSION
Incorrect
The problem was a complex one, so we needed ample time to discuss.
Correct
The problem was a complex one, so we needed ample time to discuss it.

PRONOUN REPETITION
Incorrect
John and his roommate, they have to get up early to get to class on time.
Correct
John and his roommate have to get up early to get to class on time.

Exercises illustrating pronoun omission and repetition are included in *Structure Target Exercises* on **Pronouns: Agreement, Form, and Extra Exercises.**

AGREEMENT

Choose the one answer that best completes the sentence.

1. The more students understand the concepts of geometry, the easier it is for _____ to appreciate the scientific achievements built on these formulas.

   (A) one
   (B) them
   (C) him
   (D) her

2. Working with computers is the best way to learn _____ capabilities.

   (A) our
   (B) its
   (C) their
   (D) his

3. When the contest was over and the results were posted, the team members were so exhausted they couldn't even read _____.

   (A) it
   (B) them
   (C) themselves
   (D) us

4. The way he talked, you would have thought the prize was his, although it was obviously _____, since I won it in front of them all.

   (A) yours
   (B) theirs
   (C) ours
   (D) mine

5. The child to _____ she was kind grew up to be one of our most distinguished teachers in this area.

   (A) whom
   (B) which
   (C) us
   (D) them

6. If you ask me for _____ next week, I will have time to find one.

   (A) it
   (B) our
   (C) whom
   (D) you

7. Have you ever caught us giving _____ an undeserved congratulations for doing well on a project?

   (A) yourself
   (B) themselves
   (C) ourselves
   (D) itself

8. The Secretary's peers did not approve of his decision to leave Congress since _____ feared a replacement would be hard to find.

   (A) they
   (B) it
   (C) we
   (D) you

9. The clients have only _____ to blame if the paper does not include the advertisement, because they submitted it too late for the advertising agency to use.

   (A) themselves
   (B) ourselves
   (C) itself
   (D) yourself

10. The jaws of the shark were so huge that we estimated a small craft could be damaged if _____ had the misfortune to encounter the beast in the ocean.

    (A) he
    (B) it
    (C) you
    (D) they

FORM

Choose the one answer that best completes the sentence.

1. We hoped _____ being there would give our cause credibility.

   (A) he
   (B) his
   (C) him
   (D) himself

2. The senator collects facts for his memoirs by writing notes to _____.

   (A) his own
   (B) his
   (C) himself
   (D) he

3. _____ arrival made it easier for us.

   (A) Him
   (B) He
   (C) Himself
   (D) His

4. One of _____ has to take responsibility for the act.

   (A) our
   (B) us
   (C) we
   (D) ourselves

5. In her notebook, _____ has written herself a short note.

   (A) her
   (B) her one
   (C) hers
   (D) she

6. They taught _____ to read Latin from the old grammar book.

   (A) themselves
   (B) they
   (C) their
   (D) there

7. We don't like to think of _____ in that way.

    (A) us
    (B) we
    (C) ourselves
    (D) our

8. Knowing one's score on the first test, _____ is apt to do better the second time.

    (A) one
    (B) it
    (C) she
    (D) he

9. _____ ears could not believe what I was hearing.

    (A) Mine
    (B) My
    (C) Myself
    (D) Me

10. Giving credit where _____ was deserved, the principal handed over the award.

    (A) it
    (B) itself
    (C) it's
    (D) its

EXTRA EXERCISES

In the sentences below, identify the one underlined phrase that is incorrect.

1. Management and Data Systems, a course for business executives and their
                                                                              A
   employees, offers their own approach to financial planning that class
                   B
   members can learn what they need to know for their jobs.
                  C   D

2. The district council and its lawyers, who met with the mayor, they discussed
                          A   B
   the issue of pay increases for themselves but did not resolve it.
                          C   D

3. Outdoing himself came in first in the marathon, beating the favorite whom we
               A   B   C
   all hoped would win.
             D

4. The computer case, designed it by two engineers for use in outer space,
                        A
   satisfies their requirements that it have strength and be light.
              B   C   D

5. We agreed that hers way was probably the easiest trail to our cabin
   A   B   C
   for them to follow.
        D

6. The geologists used their new instrument to determine how deep the well
                        A
   was, but its meter proved unreliable and they could not measure.
              B   C   D

7. He told me that I would have to speak to herself.
   A   B   C   D

8. If you thought about, you would see that I am right and he is wrong.
     A   B   C   D

9. Each time I caught sight of he was standing with his back to me.
              A   B   C   D

10. One's reputation is entirely based on your ability to meet the expectations
     A   B

of your colleagues and your family.
   C   D

REDUNDANCY

Redundant words or phrases express the same meaning within the same sentence.

Potential problems with redundancy are:
1. Duplication of meaning of nouns,
2. Duplication of meaning of adjectives,
3. Duplication of meaning of adverbs, or
4. Duplication of meaning of verbs.

Study the following potential problems:

NOUNS
Incorrect
Children and youngsters should enjoy the holidays.
Correct
Children should enjoy the holidays.
  or
Youngsters should enjoy the holidays.

ADJECTIVES
Incorrect
The book is free gratis.
Correct
The book is free.
  or
The book is gratis.

ADVERBS
Incorrect
He did it perfectly without a mistake.
Correct
He did it perfectly.
  or
He did it without a mistake.

VERBS
Incorrect
The squirrel stored the food and put it away.

Correct
The squirrel stored the food.
   or
The squirrel put the food away.

REDUNDANCY I

Choose the one answer that best completes the sentence.

1. The realtor sent the homeowner several inquiries _____ his property.

   (A) asking about
   (B) questioning him on
   (C) concerning
   (D) with questions on

2. The student's stipend gave him more than enough _____ his needs.

   (A) for
   (B) oversupplying
   (C) in excess of
   (D) that was too much for

3. Cups, plates, and _____ were replaced on the shelf.

   (A) saucers
   (B) tableware
   (C) dishes
   (D) pottery

4. The hot day was remarkable for its _____ .

   (A) heat
   (B) humidity
   (C) scorching temperature
   (D) warmth

5. Even though I was afraid before I began speaking, my voice was hearty and _____ .

   (A) vigorous
   (B) dynamic
   (C) energetic
   (D) clear

6. The class started _____ the book.

   (A) to begin
   (B) at the beginning of
   (C) commencing with
   (D) to set about

7. The editorial staff _____ and finished the first draft.

   (A) terminated
   (B) ended
   (C) completed
   (D) corrected

8. The doorman admitted him by _____ .

   (A) letting him in
   (B) unlocking the door
   (C) allowing him to enter
   (D) permitting his entry

9. The investigator extracted the necessary information from the witness by _____ it.

   (A) withdrawing
   (B) asking for
   (C) pulling
   (D) removing

10. Peter borrows from and _____ his friends.

   (A) then repays
   (B) uses the credit of
   (C) takes loans from
   (D) is in debt to

REDUNDANCY II

In the sentences below, identify the one underlined phrase that is incorrect.

1. The <u>biannual</u> review was <u>published</u> every six months by the <u>pen and pencil</u>
       A   B   C

committee of the <u>Principals and Teachers</u> Association.
                              D

2. Louise was <u>unhappy to hear</u> about <u>the childless couple without children</u> who
                    A   B
   were still <u>upset and angry</u> over their treatment at the clinic where she
                    C
   worked as an <u>aide and part-time translator</u>.
                         D

3. Each boy I <u>speak</u> with <u>tells</u> me about <u>his mother, father, and parents</u> and
                    A   B   C
   wishes <u>they</u> could visit him at summer camp.
            D

4. George asked <u>us</u> to copy <u>all of everything</u> in the book, but we thought
                    A   B
   it would be <u>better</u> if he <u>waited and got</u> permission.
                    C   D

5. It was the <u>morning</u> dawn that convinced us we had stayed up <u>too late</u>
                    A   B
   and talked <u>too much</u>, and would now get no sleep until the <u>evening</u> hours.
                    C   D

6. I kept at the job <u>persistently</u> until I felt that I <u>finally</u> understood the
                         A   B
   <u>format and content</u> required by the <u>two</u> people who were my bosses.
            C   D

7. <u>Chickens and poultry</u> furnish a large <u>portion</u> of the <u>critical</u> protein
            A   B   C
   the body requires to maintain its many <u>functions</u>.
                                              D

8. Generally, Mr. Jones <u>usually</u> goes to the store on <u>Wednesday</u>, as he has found
                         A   B
   that on <u>weekdays</u> it is far <u>less crowded</u> and less frantic than on weekends.
                C   D

9. Even in Ms. Wilson's <u>poverty-stricken</u> days she was always <u>generous and giving,</u>
                         A   B
   helping the <u>needy</u> as if they were <u>worse off</u> than she was.
                    C   D

10. The <u>quarterly</u> payments on the loan are due every three months at the
            A
    <u>Savings and Loan</u> located on the <u>corner</u> of <u>North and Main.</u>
            B   C   D

SUBJECT

The subject of a sentence or clause is a noun which can be in the form of a *word*, *phrase* or *clause*. The subject usually precedes the verb and answers the question *Who?* or *What?* It agrees in number with the verb.

Potential problems with subjects are:
1. The subject may be omitted.
2. The subject may be repeated.
3. The subject may not agree with the verb.

Study the following potential problems:

SUBJECT OMISSION
Incorrect
I'll meet him when comes.
Correct
I'll meet him when he comes.

SUBJECT REPEATED
Incorrect
Telling their professor the truth, this made them feel better.
Correct
Telling their professor the truth made them feel better.

SUBJECT AGREEMENT
Incorrect
The paper are on the floor.
Correct
The papers are on the floor.

AGREEMENT

In the sentences below, identify the one underlined phrase that is incorrect.

1. The boys is thought to be one of the most gifted children in the class.
    A   B   C   D

2. The advent of low-cost, high-speed data processing facilities have provided
                              A   B   C
   school administrators with resources not available a few years ago.
                                          D

3. Splashing water from the shower produces negative charges in the room's
                   A   B
   air, which promotes a feeling of well-being.
           C   D

4. The law, which is in effect in 20 of the 50 states, safeguard against
                   A   B   C
   tax abuse by small corporations.
              D

5. Professor Janes has <u>told the class</u> repeatedly that <u>we has</u> no <u>business</u> in that room
   　　　　　　　　　　　　A　　　　　　　　　　　　　　B　　　　C

   <u>and should never</u> use it to study.
   　　　D

6. Banks in economically <u>depressed areas</u> <u>has demonstrated</u> their reluctance
   　　　　　　　　　　　　　A　　　　　　　　　B

   to <u>extend the loans</u> of <u>borrowers who have</u> not met their monthly payments.
   　　　C　　　　　　　　　　　D

7. The <u>appearance</u> of fresh <u>molten</u> rock on a volcano's lava <u>dome indicates</u>
   　　　A　　　　　　　　B　　　　　　　　　　　　　　　C

   that eruptions of new lava <u>flow is imminent</u>.
   　　　　　　　　　　　　　　D

8. Medical researchers <u>have discovered</u> a <u>way</u> in which the nervous systems of
   　　　　　　　　　　A　　　　　　B

   <u>primates appears</u> <u>to communicate</u> with their immune systems.
   　　C　　　　　　　D

9. <u>Arms control</u> is a major <u>issue</u> of this decade since all of mankind <u>live</u> under
   　　A　　　　　　　　B　　　　　　　　　　　　　　　　C

   the shadow of nuclear <u>war</u>.
   　　　　　　　　　　　D

10. This is an <u>idea</u> <u>researchers hope</u> will bring to them the <u>financial and moral</u>
    　　　　　A　　　　B　　　　　　　　　　　　　　　C

    support <u>he deserves</u>.
    　　　D

OMISSION

In the sentences below, identify the one underlined phrase that is incorrect.

1. <u>Carrying</u> the equipment easily, <u>rounded</u> the corner and <u>entered</u> the
   　A　　　　　　　　　　　　　　　B　　　　　　　　C

   <u>restricted-access</u> laboratory.
   　D

2. Since <u>the 1830's have trekked</u> to Hot Springs and its 4,000-acre
   　　　　　A

   <u>park to bathe in</u> 143-degree mineral water, <u>enjoy the view</u> from
   　　B　　　　　　　　　　　　　　　　　　　　C

   the 216-foot observation <u>towers, and sail</u> the nearby Diamond Lake.
   　　　　　　　　　　　D

3. The Communications Commission, usually in the news because of airwave

   <u>arguments, has issued</u> a <u>proposal could have</u> a <u>devastating</u> effect
   　A　　　　　　　　　　　B　　　　　　　　　C

   on <u>some landmark</u> districts.
   　　D

4. <u>Children who like</u> to read <u>usually read more</u> in the summer, and
        A   B

   <u>those only read</u> for school assignments <u>can be persuaded</u> to read for fun
        C   D

   in the summer because there is no school pressure.

5. Captain John Smith <u>found the</u> Potomac River <u>sparkling clean</u> and full of
                 A   B

   <u>fish when sailed</u> upriver <u>to what is now</u> Washington, D.C., at the beginning
          C   D

   of the 17th century.

6. <u>Moved</u> lightly up the steps that <u>curved</u> around the sides of the garden wall
     A   B

   <u>topped</u> by clusters of <u>climbing</u> roses.
     C   D

7. <u>Eating and drinking</u>, the tourists <u>worked</u> their way through the historic inns
        A   B

   <u>had read</u> about before <u>taking</u> the trip.
     C   D

8. Given the circumstances, <u>does</u> not seem strange that the caller would
                      A

   <u>have left</u> us this message without giving us her phone number
     B

   or <u>telling us</u> where she <u>could be reached</u>.
       C   D

9. Aaron <u>complained</u> that his colleague <u>was always correcting</u> his work without
        A   B

   <u>paying attention</u> to the work <u>did herself</u>.
     C   D

10. This is the last time the Harrisons plan <u>to go</u> to the country <u>since grows</u>
                             A   B

    cold in the fall, and <u>heating</u> the house <u>becomes</u> difficult.
               C   D

REPETITION

In the sentences below, identify the one underlined phrase that is incorrect.

1. The book of formulas <u>it</u> was kept a <u>secret</u> for many years, and <u>no one</u>, not
                   A   B   C

   even the chemist in charge of the project, knew where <u>it</u> was hidden.
                                        D

2. The computer, <u>it is</u> a 20th century <u>invention, has</u> created startling
             A   B

   technological <u>changes</u> in the way <u>we</u> organize and produce information.
            C   D

3. The <u>escalating</u> inflation <u>rate, which it has been</u> fodder for political
          A   B

   <u>speeches,</u> has shown <u>no sign</u> of stabilizing.
     C   D

4. Agreeing to the treaties, <u>which they were signed</u> early this morning, the two
                           A

   <u>superpowers</u> pledged not to reveal <u>their</u> contents to the
     B   C

   <u>press, who had been</u> waiting at the door.
       D

5. <u>New computerized</u> technologies <u>have given</u> doctors diagnostic and surgical tools
        A   B

   <u>offering a</u> precision which until recently <u>it was</u> only a tantalizing dream.
     C   D

6. A square dance <u>it is</u> merely the act of going <u>round and round</u> in
            A   B

   a <u>circle of dancers</u> <u>composed of four couples.</u>
       C   D

7. <u>Originally designed</u> to carry only cargo, the *Alexandria*, a 125-foot
     A

   three-masted <u>trading</u> <u>schooner built in</u> Sweden in 1929,
           B   C

   <u>it has been refitted</u> for passengers.
       D

8. <u>Economics,</u> a subject <u>which it has caused</u> many college students problems
     A   B

   in the <u>past, continues</u> to be one of the <u>least attended courses.</u>
          C   D

9. The <u>visiting delegation</u> <u>which inspected</u> the new <u>facilities was</u>
         A   B   C

   surprised to find the <u>building it was so large.</u>
                 D

10. The <u>typewriter, which it is</u> one of the world's great <u>inventions, has</u>
      A   B   C

   not yet been <u>replaced by the word</u> processor.
           D

EXTRA EXERCISES

Choose the one answer that best completes the sentence.

1. _____ question was not relevant to the research.

   (A) That it
   (B) That
   (C) Which it is
   (D) That is the

2. The foot and the ankle are the parts of the body system _____ .

   (A) that aid in walking

(B) aid in walking
(C) that walking
(D) walking

3. The struggle of entrepreneurs _____ to be financially independent.

   (A) which is
   (B) are
   (C) is
   (D) are being

4. ___ , the windy city, is the home of the skyscraper.

   (A) Chicago which is
   (B) Chicago it
   (C) This is Chicago
   (D) Chicago

5. When the crowd returned to their seats, _____ started his speech again.

   (A) this is the speaker
   (B) the speaker who
   (C) the speaker
   (D) the speakers

6. _____ ,which is a difficult task, requires balance.

   (A) Crossing the footbridge
   (B) The footbridge
   (C) Across the footbridge
   (D) The footbridge that is

7. As _____ leave, the security guard counts the number of visitors to the monument.

   (A) the groups
   (B) them
   (C) the group
   (D) their

8. When all the trainees reassembled, the foreman _____ showed them how to work the new drill.

   (A) who had been practicing
   (B) who practicing
   (C) he who had practiced
   (D) what had practiced

9. The *New York Times* _____ a prestigious paper.

   (A) it is considered
   (B) is considered
   (C) which is
   (D) which is considered

10. The _____ decided to return to their hotel for a rest after a day of sightseeing.

    (A) tourists were
    (B) tourist
    (C) tourists had been
    (D) tourists

SUBJUNCTIVE

The subjunctive verb form is used in noun or clauses that express **suggestion, possibility, or requirement**. The clause is always introduced by *that* and the verb is in the simple form regardless of the tense of the verb in the main clause.

Potential problems with the subjunctive are:
  1. The subjunctive may not be used after verbs or nouns that require it.
  2. The incorrect tense may be used.

Study the following potential problems:

SUBJUNCTIVE REQUIRED
Incorrect
It was necessary that he knew the formula.
Correct
It was necessary that he know the formula.

INCORRECT TENSE
Incorrect
It will be recommended that she will get the job.

Correct
It will be recommended that she get the job.

SUBJUNCTIVE I

Choose the one answer that best completes the sentence.

1. The woman being charged with tax evasion has insisted that her lawyer and accountant _____ present.

   (A) have been
   (B) be
   (C) were
   (D) are

2. Before a member can make a motion, it is necessary that he _____the presiding officer.

   (A) rise and address
   (B) will rise and address
   (C) rises and addresses
   (D) rise and addresses

3. The final recommendation was that the employee on probation _____ a special night class for one semester.

   (A) has attended
   (B) attended
   (C) attends
   (D) attend

4. The committee voted that all its members _____ a raise next year.

   (A) will be given
   (B) are going to be given
   (C) be given
   (D) have been given

5. The building contractors have asked that the unfinished project _____.

   (A) is extended
   (B) will be extended
   (C) has been extended
   (D) be extended

6. It is important that someone searching for a job _____ all the prospects.

   (A) consider
   (B) be considering
   (C) considers
   (D) will be considering

7. The politician urged that all citizens _____ to the polls on election day.

   (A) goes
   (B) went
   (C) must go
   (D) go

8. The U.S. Immigration Service requires that all passengers _____ a passport.

   (A) will have
   (B) have
   (C) must have
   (D) should have

9. The fire department ordered that the elevator _____.

   (A) be turned off
   (B) turn off
   (C) was turned off
   (D) turned off

10. The ad hoc committee proposed that the chairman _____.

    (A) promote
    (B) was promoted
    (C) be promoted
    (D) be promoting

SUBJUNCTIVE II

In the sentences below, identify the one underlined phrase that is incorrect.

1. School counselors <u>are convinced</u> that <u>it</u> will be obligatory that all applicants
                          A   B

   <u>must have</u> computer training to <u>enter</u> the job market in the future.
       C   D

2. The suggestion that taxes were cut   was vetoed by the mayor, who foresaw
                    A   B   C

a deficit that was not yet public knowledge.
              D

3. Educators are now recommending that reasoning skills are emphasized in the
                       A   B

classroom since recent tests indicate that many teachers in the past
                             C

have ignored these skills.
     D

4. After the man looking for work completed the application, he was told
                                 A   B

that it was necessary that he included a resume.
        C   D

5. The requirement that all students must pay an activities fee was met with
                                       A   B

protests from the students who would not benefit because they only
                               C

attended classes at night.
D

6. The stubborn young man did not follow the advice that he reflected on his
                         A   B

behavior since he refused to believe he had done anything wrong.
                   C   D

7. The lawyers for the defense made the recommendation to the judge that the
                        A

trial will be delayed until the missing witness was found.
      B   C   D

8. Before renovation could continue, it was imperative that the owner
                          A   B

approve the work and will suggest additional improvements.
C   D

9. It is the requirement of the personnel director that the applicant is a
                                                                A

college graduate, even though the director has never felt the
                              B   C

need to go to college herself.
     D

10. The federal government recommends that local civic groups will accept the
                A   B

responsibility of welfare disbursement to the needy.
                  C   D

164   Structure Targets

SUBORDINATE CLAUSES

Subordinate (or dependent) clauses cannot stand alone. There are **noun, adjective,** and **adverb clauses.** Noun clauses are used as subjects, objects, and objects of prepositions. Adjective clauses modify nouns, and adverb clauses modify verbs.

Potential problems with subordination are:
1. Word order: the subject may be preceded by the verb.
2. The marker may be omitted.
3. The subject or verb may be omitted.
4. The subject may be repeated.
5. An inappropriate marker may be used.
6. There may be no independent clause.
7. A *To Be* form may be added in reduced clauses.

Study the following potential problems:

WORD ORDER
Incorrect
He asked his tutor what is the right way to solve a problem.
Correct
He asked his tutor what the right way to solve a problem is.

MARKER OMISSION
Incorrect
Classes were cancelled there was so much snow.
Correct
Classes were cancelled because there was so much snow.

SUBJECT OR VERB OMISSION
Incorrect
Although witnessed the theft, no one would testify.
Correct
Although some passers-by witnessed the theft, no one would testify.

SUBJECT REPETITION
Incorrect
The orchestra which it had cancelled all performances has disbanded.
Correct
The orchestra which had cancelled all performances has disbanded.

INAPPROPRIATE MARKER
Incorrect
We will be ready to start while he comes.
Correct
We will be ready to start when he comes.

NO INDEPENDENT CLAUSE
Incorrect
The campus, which had become desolate and deserted during the holidays.
Correct
The campus, which had become desolate and deserted during the holidays, was teeming with activity during registration.

TO BE ADDITION
Incorrect
The winner was ecstatic about the results, jumped up and down.
Correct
The winner, ecstatic about the results, jumped up and down.

These general problems are examined in more detail below under specific types of subordination.

NOUN CLAUSES

A noun clause is used in the same way as a noun: **a subject, object,** or **object of preposition.** It may be introduced by these words: *when, where, why, who(m), how, what, which, whose, whether, if, that.* Used as a subject, the noun clause takes a singular verb.

Potential problems with noun clauses are:
1. The verb may come before the subject.
2. A subject noun clause may lack an introductory word.
3. A plural verb may be used after a single noun clause.

Study the following potential problems:

WORD ORDER
Incorrect
He asked what time was it.
Correct
He asked what time it was.

INTRODUCTORY WORD OMITTED
Incorrect
The research had been easy astounded him.
Correct
That the research had been easy astounded him.

VERB AGREEMENT
Incorrect
Whose essays were missing were on everyone's mind.
Correct
Whose essays were missing was on everyone's mind.

NOUN CLAUSES I

Choose the one answer that best completes the sentence.

1. _____ was not the way the event happened.

   (A) What the press reported
   (B) What reported the press
   (C) What reported
   (D) The press reported

2. No announcement has been made concerning _____ on the next shuttle flight.

   (A) who go
   (B) who is going
   (C) is who going
   (D) who gone

3. It is a fact _____.

   (A) that we all have to eat
   (B) that all we have to eat
   (C) that we all have ate
   (D) all we have to eat

4. Regarding our current Director of Finance, _____ is of no consequence to me.

   (A) he goes or stays
   (B) whether he goes or stays
   (C) whether he go or stays
   (D) he goes whether he stays

5. _____ is his own decision.

   (A) When leaving
   (B) When does he leave
   (C) When he leaves
   (D) He leaves

6. The prosecutor questioned the witness about _____ .

   (A) what knew he
   (B) what did he know
   (C) he knew
   (D) what he knew

7. The reporter was unable to make an appointment with the celebrity _____.

   (A) she had hoped to interview
   (B) to interview she had hoped
   (C) she to interview had hoped
   (D) had hoped she to interview

8. _____ the election is the question both political parties are asking.

   (A) Who's candidate will win
   (B) Whose candidate will win
   (C) Whose will win the candidate
   (D) Candidate will win

9. How the _____ fascinated the reader of the mystery.

   (A) crime solved the detective
   (B) detective solved the crime
   (C) crime
   (D) crime solved

10. The reasons given for postponing the meeting until next week suggested _____ unprepared.

    (A) the managers
    (B) to the managers
    (C) how the managers were
    (D) that the managers were

NOUN CLAUSES II

In the sentences below, identify the one underlined phrase that is incorrect.

1. The home video market increased so rapidly was a surprise to market
      A   B
   analysts who had found it difficult to get new investors.
      C   D

2. Who the President sees at what place and time what is a subject that inspires
   A   B   C   D
   much gossip.

3. What needs the community and is actively looking for is a source of income
             A   B   C
   not generated by local taxes.
      D

4. Whether the concert hall has adequate acoustics are, essentially,
        A   B   C
   the question the engineers ask themselves.
        D

5. How much of the $96 billion advertising expenditures will be aimed at the
          A   B

new teen and university <u>markets are</u> an advertising
C [*is* handwritten above "are"]

executive's chief concern.
D

6. Medical economists question <u>whether outweigh the benefits</u> of improved
A

<u>medical care</u>   <u>the high cost</u> of developing <u>new treatments</u>.
B   C   D

7. Most urban professionals <u>talk about how</u> much <u>they did exercise</u> <u>rather than</u>
A   B   C

<u>how much money</u> they earned.
D

8. <u>That the mayor's</u> commission <u>has done an admirable job</u> of <u>protecting the city's</u>
A   B   C

architectural <u>features are not</u> denied by the preservationists.
D [*is* handwritten above "are"]

9. <u>Started out</u> to be an easy <u>project has turned into</u> a very long <u>time consuming</u>
A   B   C [*What is* handwritten to the left]

<u>one</u>.
D

10. Where the <u>children play</u> is where <u>intend they</u> to put a food store, <u>but I</u>
A   B   C

don't know <u>when or</u> how soon.
D

ADJECTIVE CLAUSES

An adjective clause is a dependent clause which modifies a noun. It may be introduced by these words: *who(m), which, that, whose, where, why, after, before, when, and so forth.*

Potential problems with adjective clauses are:
1. The subject or verb may be omitted.
2. The subject may be repeated.
3. The clause marker may be omitted.
4. There may be no independent clause.
5. The marker may be inappropriate.

Study the following potential problems:

SUBJECT OMISSION
Incorrect
His name, which had known before, escaped me.
Correct
His name, which I had known before, escaped me.

VERB OMISSION
Incorrect
They took the steps because of the elevator, which broken.

Correct
They took the steps because of the elevator, which was broken.

SUBJECT REPETITION
Incorrect
We beckoned to the waitress who she was so busy.
Correct
We beckoned to the waitress who was so busy.

MARKER OMISSION
Incorrect
The book was required reading was being held at the reference desk.
Correct
The book which was required reading was being held at the reference desk.

NO INDEPENDENT CLAUSE
Incorrect
The campus, which had become desolate and deserted during the holidays.
Correct
The campus, which had become desolate and deserted during the holidays, suddenly came to life again.

INAPPROPRIATE MARKER
Incorrect
The girls which won were honored by their friends.
Correct
The girls who won were honored by their friends.

ADJECTIVE CLAUSES I

Choose the one answer that best completes the sentence.

1. Buildings _____ of brick last longer than those made of mud.

   (A) which
   (B) which they are made
   (C) which are made
   (D) are made

2. The team _____ waiting for finally arrived.

   (A) who been
   (B) whom we had
   (C) who we
   (D) we had been

3. The mouse _____ comes out at night to nibble at the cheese we leave as bait.

   (A) whom lives in the wall
   (B) whom the wall lives in
   (C) that lives in the wall
   (D) that live in the wall

4. Statistics _____ substantiated by research are considered valid.

   (A) are
   (B) which
   (C) which are
   (D) that be

5. The corporation _____ first will host the delegation for lunch.

   (A) whose plant we visit
   (B) whose visit
   (C) whose visit we plant
   (D) whose we plant

6. The president refused to accept the decision _____ .

   (A) which the committee proposed
   (B) proposed the committee
   (C) which proposed the committee
   (D) who the committee proposed

7. Malcolm wanted to take the exam _____ .

   (A) we fail
   (B) us failed
   (C) that failed
   (D) that we failed

8. The author eagerly anticipates the time _____ finished, and she can start a new one.

   (A) when her book
   (B) when her book is
   (C) her book be
   (D) her will be

9. Trade relations among the states, _____ improving, are currently at an ebb.

   (A) constantly are
   (B) which are constant
   (C) which constantly
   (D) which are constantly

10. The economic recession was the focus of the debate, _____ .

    (A) surprises to no one
    (B) no one was surprised
    (C) which surprised no one
    (D) to no one was surprised

ADJECTIVE CLAUSES II

In the sentences below, identify the one underlined phrase that is incorrect.

1. Mr. Jacobs, who immigrated to a country which was known for its business
        A   B

   opportunities, always wanted his partners, of whom my father was one,
                                        C

   to continue the firm which started.
                  D

2. Miami, which is known for its temperate winters, has become the home of many
    A   B

   retired citizens which left their homes in the North, where winters were
            C   D

   too severe.

3. The exhibition, toured in major cities, has returned to the Boston
              A

   Museum, where it originated and where it will be on view for
       B   C   D

   another month.

4. The metric system, which introduced in England where it met strong
                    A   B

   resistance, is a system of measurement which uses the unit 10 as a standard.
                                   C   D

5. A new running shoe monitors the runner's motion and calculates time, average
            A   B

   speed, distance, and caloric expenditures is currently on the market.
               C   D

6. The officers who were from the corporation that it sponsored the golf
        A   B

tournament felt that <u>announcing the name</u> of a <u>rival as the next</u> sponsor
              C   D

of the tournament was inappropriate.

7. Restaurants <u>where</u> people smoke, parks where <u>people</u> play loud radios,
            A   B

   that

   <u>pools</u> that are too crowded, and grass <u>is</u> mowed annoy many people.
    C   D

   has

8. The gardeners <u>who the grounds have maintained</u> <u>which</u> surround the
                        A   B

   <u>hospital have</u> gone on a <u>strike that</u> threatens to last through the summer.
        C   D

   whose no

9. The <u>accountant is known</u> for his <u>honesty was</u> troubled by the
            A   B

   <u>discrepancy which he</u> discovered in the <u>ledgers that he</u> examined.
                C   D

   whose that ?

10. Rome is a <u>city where</u> the streets are crowded with <u>sights attract</u>
                    A   B

    <u>tourists, where</u> churches are magnificently decorated, and where
            C

    the <u>language has its own music</u>.
                    D

ADVERB CLAUSES

An adverb clause is a dependent clause which modifies a verb. It can express **time**, **cause and effect**, **opposition**, or **condition**. An adverb clause is introduced by subordinating conjunctions (*after, before, because, whereas, and so forth).*

Potential problems with adverb clauses are:
   1. The subject or verb may be omitted.
   2. The clause marker may be omitted.
   3. There may be no independent clause.
   4. An inappropriate marker may be used.

Study the following potential problems:

SUBJECT OMISSION
Incorrect
Although witnessed the theft, no one would testify.
Correct
Although some witnessed the theft, no one would testify.

VERB OMISSION
Incorrect
They took a small gift in case she depressed.
Correct
They took a small gift in case she was depressed.

MARKER OMISSION

Incorrect
Classes were cancelled there was so much snow.
Correct
Classes were cancelled because there was so much snow.

NO INDEPENDENT CLAUSE

Incorrect
After driving for days across the desert without seeing another living thing.
Correct
After driving for days across the desert without seeing another living thing, we ran out of gas.

INAPPROPRIATE MARKER

Incorrect
We will be ready to start while he comes.
Correct
We will be ready to start when he comes.

Adverb Clauses I

Choose the one answer that best completes the sentence.

1. While tomatoes are in season, _____ .

   (A) and inexpensive
   (B) they are inexpensive
   (C) inexpensive
   (D) besides inexpensive

2. The applicant was turned down by the college _____ were too low.

   (A) his test scores
   (B) because
   (C) because his test scores
   (D) if test scores

3. The governess agreed to teach the temperamental child _____ she was given complete authority.

   (A) whether
   (B) for
   (C) that
   (D) provided

4. _____ the rain has stopped, the field will dry out.

   (A) Though
   (B) While
   (C) Even if
   (D) Now that

5. _____ , the graduate student who was late every day will still take the test.

   (A) You think it wise
   (B) You think it wise that
   (C) Whether or not you think it wise
   (D) Whether it wise

6. The service attendant filled the tires _____ could ride our bikes.

   (A) as we
   (B) so that we
   (C) even if we
   (D) so that

7. _____ , the chorus should have learned the music by heart.

   (A) By the time they rehearse
   (B) By the time rehearse
   (C) By the time they will rehearse
   (D) They rehearse by the time

8. The meeting was postponed _____ .

   (A) although no reason was given
   (B) no reason given
   (C) why no reason was given
   (D) although given no reason

9. _____ there will be a change in administrations.

   (A) In she wins,
   (B) She wins,
   (C) In the event she wins,
   (D) She wins the event,

10. _____ my brother , I don't have to believe everything he says.

   (A) Even though he is
   (B) So he is
   (C) As
   (D) Where he is

ADVERB CLAUSES II

In the sentences below, identify the one underlined phrase that is incorrect.

1. The doctor, who came soon after the family called, could tell she saw
         A   B   C

   their expressions that she was too late.
             D

2. Before the motion was approved and while it was being debated, the
       A   B

   opposition tried to influence the chairman although he had refused
                                       C

   to hear arguments the motion was made.
          D

3. Although a time saving device, the computer is difficult to operate
         A   B

   and, when it not functioning properly, is impossible to use.
         C   D

4. The merchandise arrived before was expected, and since no one was home,
                           A   B

   the postman left it in front of the door.
        C   D

5. When the electricity came back on, the power surge blew the fuses, so the
         A   B

   hospital continued to rely on the emergency generator until the electrician.
             C   D

6. Even though maintained a united front, the migrant workers quarreled among
           A   B

   themselves until the strike ended and they returned to work.
            C   D

7. The rain had not stopped the roads would have been inundated
          A

   and no travelers, unless they rode in amphibious vehicles,
        B   C

   would be able to pass.
        D

8. As the foreman of the jury the verdict, the defendant could not
        A   B

   look at his mother, who had promised never to leave his side.
      C   D

9. The first English settlers in the New World quickly established living patterns
                                                       A

   based on their various backgrounds, the conditions they had left,
      B   C

   and those in which they found themselves when arrived.
                                               D

10. When the noise died down and when order restored to the lecture hall, the
                       A   B

    controversial speaker began where he had left off.
       C   D

REDUCED ADJECTIVE CLAUSES

An adjective clause can be reduced in two ways: the subject pronoun and the verb *to be* can be omitted; or the subject pronoun can be omitted and the verb changed to a present participle.

Adjective Clause
The man who is walking in the rain will get sick.

Reduced Adjective Clause
The man walking in the rain will get sick.

Potential problems with reduced adjective clauses are:
1. The subject may be added.
2. A *to be* form may be added.
3. The clause marker may be added.
4. The incorrect participle may be used.

Study the following potential problems:

SUBJECT ADDITION
Incorrect
He having quit school, the student found a job.
Correct
Having quit school, the student found a job.

"TO BE" ADDITION
Incorrect
The winner was ecstatic about the results, jumped up and down.
Correct
The winner, ecstatic about the results, jumped up and down.

MARKER ADDITION
Incorrect
He was proud to see his grades which posted on the bulletin board.
Correct
He was proud to see his grades posted on the bulletin board.

INCORRECT PARTICIPLE

Incorrect
The teacher, reviewed for the test, asked if there were questions.
Correct
The teacher, reviewing for the test, asked if there were questions.

REDUCED ADJECTIVE CLAUSES I

Choose the one answer that best completes the sentence.

1. The phone _____ started ringing.

   (A) which next door
   (B) was next door
   ✓ (C) next door
   (D) it was next door

2. The chessmen, _____, are displayed in a glass case.

   (A) which from ivory
   (B) which carved from ivory
   ✓ (C) carved from ivory
   (D) carving from ivory

3. The sympathetic audience understood the man's speech, no matter how _____.

   (A) it slurs
   ✓ (B) slurred   *not speak clear*
   (C) it was slur
   (D) slurs

4. The noise of the trains _____ into the station was deafening.

   (A) that come
   (B) which was coming
   (C) coming
   (D) that coming

5. The letter _____ our guests' intention to visit came after their arrival.

   (A) it announcing
   ✓ (B) announcing
   (C) had announced
   (D) having announced

6. A political campaign _____ will be costly.

   (A) which for months last
   (B) lasts for months
   ✓ (C) lasting for months
   (D) will last for months

7. My best friend, _____ quickly, told the teacher I was home sick.

   (A) who thinking
   (B) be thinking
   ✓ (C) think
   (D) thinking

8. The barn, _____, went up in flames.

   ✓ (A) loaded with hay
   (B) it was loading hay
   (C) it loaded hay
   (D) which loaded with hay

9. The man _____ the wheelbarrow ignored our calls.

   (A) who pushing
   ✓ (B) pushing
   (C) was pushing
   (D) be who pushed

10. The stock _____ in value should be sold.

    ✓ (A) which has not increased
    (B) has not increased
    (C) not been increasing
    (D) who has not increased

REDUCED ADJECTIVE CLAUSES II

In the sentences below, identify the one underlined phrase that is incorrect.

1. Cape Cod <u>Canal, is said</u> <u>to be</u> the widest sea level <u>canal anywhere,</u>
           A   B   C

is cluttered during the summer season with as many as 300 or

more pleasure craft a day, <u>most coming</u> from Boston.
                                    D

donated

2. The boys <u>who were</u> first in line <u>were given</u> the T-shirts <u>donating</u> by
          A   B   C

   the philanthropist <u>who has</u> always supported our charity.
                          D

3. The physical matter in a "black hole" in the galaxy is so <u>dense that it creates</u>
                                                                      A

   a gravitational <u>pull which strong</u> enough <u>to prevent anything</u>, even
                          B   C

   <u>light, from escaping</u>.
          D

4. The <u>crowd, anxiously await</u> the arrival of the soccer <u>team, pressed</u> against
          A   B

   the fence <u>separating them</u> from <u>the playing field</u>.
                    C   D

5. The <u>flights were not being</u> allowed to take off until the control tower
          A

   <u>which monitoring</u> <u>the changing weather</u> felt <u>it was safe</u>.
          B   C   D

promoting

6. The <u>talks promote</u> the expansion of trade between the two neighboring
          A

   <u>countries</u> were <u>discontinued</u> after certain protocol agreements <u>were violated</u>.
          B   C   D

7. The <u>delays are caused</u> by the <u>striking longshoremen</u> <u>cost the steamship</u>
          A   B   C

   companies millions every <u>day their ships were</u> not allowed to dock.
                                    D

8. <u>Muttering</u> to herself, the woman, being hot and <u>was weary</u>, <u>sat down</u> on a
       A   B   C

   stump <u>next to</u> the road.
             D

9. The <u>freezing rain</u> made <u>driving</u> dangerous, <u>was obliging many motorists</u> to
          A   B   C

   <u>use public transportation</u>.
          D

10. The statement made by the press <u>was implying</u> that the <u>Senator was</u> a fool was
                                          A   B

    <u>retracted the</u> <u>following morning</u> with an apology.
          C   D

An adverb clause can be reduced if the subject of the adverb clause and the subject of the independent clause are the same. These reduced adverb clauses are also called participial phrases.

Adverb Clause
While I was visiting New York, I met many people.

Reduced Adverb Clause
While visiting New York, I met many people.

Potential problems with reduced adverb clauses are:
1. The subject may be added.
2. A *to be* form may be added.
3. The subjects may not be the same.
4. The marker may be omitted.
5. The incorrect participle may not be used.

Study the following potential problems:

SUBJECT ADDITION
Incorrect
While she singing the anthem, she had tears in her eyes.
Correct
While singing the anthem, she had tears in her eyes.

"TO BE" ADDITION
Incorrect
Daniel waited, was getting more and more nervous until the moment arrived.
Correct
Daniel waited, getting more and more nervous until the moment arrived.

MIXED SUBJECTS
Incorrect
The alarm going off, Victor got out of bed.
Correct
Hearing the alarm go off, Victor got out of bed.

MARKER OMISSION
Incorrect
Reading, she keeps her headphones on.
Correct
While reading, she keeps her headphones on.

INCORRECT PARTICIPLE
Incorrect
After talked to the counselor, the student enrolled in the course.
Correct
After talking to the counselor, the student enrolled in the course.

REDUCED ADVERB CLAUSES I

Choose the one answer that best completes the sentence.

1. _____, flowers need a lot of sun and water.

    (A) When growth
    (B) When they growing
    (C) They are growing
    (D) When growing

2. Pedestrians should look to the left and right _____ the street.

    ✓ (A) when crossing
    (B) when they be crossing
    (C) they cross
    (D) when to cross

3. The sailor, home at last, is happy _____.

    (A) he be sitting in the garden
    (B) whenever sitting in the garden
    (C) in the garden sitting
    (D) whenever sit in the garden

4. _____, the nurse checked the patient's temperature.

    (A) Called the doctor
    ✓ (B) Before calling the doctor
    (C) The doctor calling
    (D) Before the doctor calling

5. _____, the commissioners like to take a walk.

    (A) After they eating
    (B) Eating
    ✓ (C) After eating
    (D) After to be eaten

6. _____ asleep, the young child was really awake and listening.

    (A) Although pretending to be
    (B) Being
    (C) To be
    (D) Although pretended to be

7. _____, the mind lets suppressed thoughts surface.

    ✓ (A) While we dream
    (B) While dreaming
    (C) While we dreaming
    (D) While the mind it dreams

8. _____, the candidate checked his facts.

    ✓ (A) Before making the speech
    (B) Before he is making the speech
    (C) Before the speech is making
    (D) Making their speech

9. The fireman ran into the burning building _____ would not collapse.

    (A) to be hoping
    (B) hoping
    (C) him hoping
    ✓ (D) hoping it

10. The deadline, _____, had been extended to accommodate our schedule.

    (A) passing
    ✓ (B) although past
    (C) while being passed
    (D) passed

REDUCED ADVERB CLAUSES II

In the sentences below, identify the one underlined phrase that is incorrect.

1. Although <u>they frequently misinterpreted</u>, <u>these laws</u> apply, in part, to groups
          A   B

   <u>seeking</u> redress for wrongs <u>without their having</u> to hire a lawyer.
      C   D

2. The extension services of the university, while <u>it is</u> providing an opportunity
                                                      A

   for the community <u>to take</u> courses, <u>offer</u> full-time students greater
                         B   C

   flexibility <u>in arranging</u> their schedules.
                    D

3. <u>After signing it</u>, the insurance policy covers illness <u>on or off</u> the company
A   B

    grounds, <u>where</u> most accidents are likely <u>to occur.</u>
C   D

[handwritten: being signed]

4. After <u>you testifying</u>, your statement and <u>that of</u> the officer will be sent
A   B

    to the court, <u>which</u> will hold both documents <u>until</u> the hearing.
C   D

[handwritten: testified]

5. While <u>be covered</u> by warranty <u>for</u> the next two years, the <u>product</u> is
A   B   C

    guaranteed <u>to be</u> free of defects.
D

[handwritten: being]

6. When <u>coming</u> to school, the children need <u>to think</u> before <u>they crossing</u> the
A   B   C

    streets <u>where</u> there is no crossing guard.
D

[handwritten: cross]

7. <u>Before design</u> the building, the architect <u>studied</u> the <u>plans of</u> other buildings
A   B   C

    <u>built near</u> the site.
D

[handwritten: designing]

8. <u>Conserving</u> heat in the winter and <u>reduce heat in</u> the summer, deciduous trees
A   B

    <u>planted at the west</u> and south parts of a house <u>are natural</u> energy savers.
C   D

[handwritten: reducing]

9. <u>When they traveling</u> long distances, <u>tourists should</u> <u>reduce</u> caloric intake and
A   B   C

    and <u>limit consumption</u> of alchohol.
D

10. Since <u>they moving</u> to the east coast, the Parsons have not <u>been able</u> <u>to find</u>
A   B   C

    a home <u>large enough</u> for their family.
D

VERB

The verb in a sentence or a clause shows **action, being,** or **state of being** of the subject. It usually follows the subject. It also agrees in number with the subject.

Potential problems with verbs are:
1. Verbs may be omitted wholly or in part.
2. There may be an additional, unnecessary auxiliary with the verb.
3. Verbs may not agree with the subject.
4. Verbs may be in the wrong tense.

Study the following potential problems:

VERB OMISSION
Incorrect
The students will completed the essay by the end of the class.
Correct
The students will have completed the essay by the end of the class.

UNNECESSARY WORD
Incorrect
The messenger did delivered the package.
Correct
The messenger delivered the package.

VERB AGREEMENT
Incorrect
The news of their successes were met with cheers.
Correct
The news of their successes was met with cheers.

INAPPROPRIATE TENSE
Incorrect
I'm going to eat as soon as the cafeteria will open.
Correct
I'm going to eat as soon as the cafeteria opens.

OMISSION
In the sentences below, identify the one underlined phrase that is incorrect.

1. Local transit <u>officials that</u> bus and rail <u>patronage</u> appears <u>to have</u> reached
   A   B   C

   a <u>level last</u> recorded 10 years ago.
   D

2. The <u>administration urged</u> the lawmakers to adopt <u>legislation requiring</u> all
   A   B

   passengers of motor vehicles <u>which driven</u> in the city <u>to wear</u> seat belts.
   C   D

3. Whenever John <u>thinks</u> <u>about quitting work</u> and going back to school, he becomes
   A   B

   <u>worried that</u> he <u>won't able</u> to pay the rent.
   C   D

4. Cairo University, the Arab <u>world's first secular</u> university, <u>founded in 1925</u>
   A   B

   <u>with seven main</u> faculties <u>and colleges</u>.
   C   D

5. <u>Keeping to a routine</u> <u>by establishing</u> <u>patterns useful</u> in <u>meeting deadlines</u>.
   A   B   C   D

6. The assistant manager <u>asked</u> the clerk <u>to help him</u> <u>move the supplies</u>, but the
   A   B   C

   clerk <u>claimed he too</u> busy.
   D

7. The new head of the <u>Park Service promised</u> <u>to protect and expand</u> the park
                              A   B
system even <u>if it raising fees</u> and <u>sometimes closing</u> the gates because
                    C   D
of overcrowding.

8. <u>To catch</u> our colleague at home, you <u>must early</u> in the morning because he
       A   B
<u>leaves</u> at 7 a.m. <u>to go to</u> work.
    C   D

9. The <u>county school</u> board learned last night that local 10th graders
           A
<u>continuing</u> to score <u>higher than</u> the national <u>average on reading</u> tests.
    B   C   D

10. Even though the guest did not like <u>sleeping</u> on a hard bed, she <u>managed</u>
                                          A   B
to fall <u>asleep</u> because <u>she so tired</u>.
          C   D

UNNECESSARY FORM

In the sentences below, identify the one underlined phrase that is incorrect.

1. During the fire, most of the injured <u>were been</u> trampled <u>or crushed</u>
                                              A   B
when the <u>spectators raced</u> for <u>the exits</u>.
              C   D

2. <u>Thinking</u> through their plan thoroughly <u>did convinced</u> the committee they
       A   B
<u>were wrong</u> to believe that no one else <u>would find</u> fault with their logic.
      C   D

3. The journalist, who <u>had not slept</u> for 36 hours, <u>was obliged</u> <u>to must drive</u>
                          A   B   C
through the <u>fog to interview</u> the union leader.
                D

4. Some <u>mammals that live</u> in the <u>wild have thick skins</u> or <u>hides which</u> <u>are protect</u>
            A   B   C   D
them from the weather and their enemies.

5. <u>Music is</u> an international language and a way for <u>newly arrived immigrants</u>
       A   B
<u>to be assimilate</u> themselves into the <u>cultural activities</u> of the community.
        C   D

6. In spite of recent <u>advances in</u> modern medicine, the <u>long-sought</u> cure for
                          A   B

cancer <u>has not been</u> found, and the incidence of the <u>disease is being increasing</u>.
          C   D

7. Many service personnel <u>like being</u> plumbers and <u>repairmen charge</u> high
                        A   B

prices <u>and do</u> an inadequate <u>job unworthy</u> of their qualifications.
      C   D

8. Working hard <u>may have been</u> good for the new recruit, but <u>it tired him</u>
                A   B

out <u>so much</u> that <u>he was collapsed</u>.
   C   D

9. <u>Tokyo, founded in</u> the 16th century, <u>is older</u> than New York, but because of
       A   B

fires, earthquakes, and war destruction, much less <u>is remains</u> of old
                                             C

Tokyo <u>than of old New York</u>.
        D

10. Each of the owners of the building <u>had took</u> a look at the terrain
                                 A

<u>before they agreed</u> <u>to landscape</u> it and <u>put in</u> a road.
     B   C   D

AGREEMENT

In the sentences below, identify the one underlined phrase that is incorrect.

1. My English grade, which for many <u>reasons was</u> not deserved, <u>were sent</u>
                                       A   B

to my <u>parents, who chose</u> not to <u>comment on it</u>.
              C   D

2. The monuments in <u>Washington was built</u> through the years and
                            A

consequently <u>do not share</u> a common theme like those <u>built</u> and
                B   C

<u>designed</u> during one period.
   D

3. There <u>were</u> no clear-cut sides in the Civil War unless the local
       A

<u>stories which tend</u> to <u>propagate partition</u> <u>is considered</u>.
      B   C   D

4. The counselors from <u>the college feels</u> <u>it is unwise</u> for students to select a major
                            A   B

before <u>they have</u> <u>the opportunity to experience</u> different academic subjects.
             C   D

5. <u>Telling</u> ghost stories <u>is</u> one of my grandfather's favorite hobbies, and
     A   B

                                        sends
   when he <u>begins</u> to whisper, it <u>send</u> chills up and down my spine.
            C   D

6. Several authors <u>whose publishers rejected</u> their finished manuscripts
                         A

   <u>and demanded</u> <u>they return</u> their advances <u>has prevailed</u> in court in recent years.
       B   C   D

                                     nods
7. The camel, <u>which shuffles</u> its feet and <u>nod its head</u>, <u>has been</u>,
             A   B   C

   as the desert <u>tribes know</u>, a true beast of burden.
                D

8. The <u>pedestrian passing</u> the construction site <u>fell</u> in the hole where the
           A   B

                                         s
   crew <u>has been</u> working to replace the cover <u>that protect</u> the spot.
         C   D

9. Violence at recent soccer matches <u>is causing</u> city officials <u>to reevaluate</u>
                                  A   B

                             have
   security <u>measures which</u> <u>has proven</u> ineffectual.
              C   D

                                                    is
10. The political power at <u>stake in</u> the upcoming <u>elections are</u> small, <u>considering</u>
                        A   B   C

   that none of the three opposition <u>parties is</u> supporting a candidate.
                                   D

Tense

In the sentences below, identify the one underlined phrase that is incorrect.

                  has
1. My book <u>is having</u> three torn pages, which I <u>tried</u> <u>to tape</u> before I
            A   B   C

   <u>left</u> home.
    D

                        experiences
2. This area <u>seldom</u> <u>is experiencing</u> rain in summer, when the <u>heat breaks all</u>
             A   B   C

   <u>maintained</u> records.
       D

                                                   settled
3. Knowing how long the test <u>would run</u>, the students who finished <u>settle</u> back
                        A   B

   and <u>opened</u> their books to read while time <u>passed</u>.
        C   D

4. The astronauts who <u>were not allowed</u> <u>to join</u> the shuttle mission for medical
                      A   B

reasons monitored <u>the orbits</u> of the *Columbia* from Houston after
                              C
it <u>is launched</u>.
         D

(handwritten: was)

5. A labor <u>survey revealed</u> that <u>less than</u> 4 or 5 percent of the labor
                  A   B
force <u>is doing</u> its <u>work at</u> home last year.
          C   D

(handwritten: was)

6. The chairman <u>will speak</u> to the crowd, which <u>did</u> not appear <u>to hear</u>
                     A   B   C
him even when he <u>raised</u> his voice.
                      D

(handwritten: spoke)

7. Businesses <u>are looking</u> for software that they <u>can adapt</u> and
                   A   B
<u>applied immediately</u> to their own <u>accounting procedures</u>.
        C   D

(handwritten: apply)

8. The nurse's <u>aides will have learned</u> during their training last month that
                       A
color blindness <u>is</u> a condition <u>affecting</u> thousands with <u>varying</u>
                    B   C   D
degrees of severity.

(handwritten: learned)

9. <u>Since</u> last fall, the young researcher <u>watched</u> the flowers
       A   B
she <u>grows</u> <u>respond</u> to the sun.
        C   D

(handwritten: has) (handwritten: grew)

10. <u>Workman clear brush</u> away from the cave entrance <u>when they suddenly saw</u>
             A   B
what turned out to be <u>the first unspoiled Indian</u> burial
                              C
<u>chamber to be unearthed</u> in Utah.
             D

(handwritten: were clearing)

EXTRA EXERCISES

Choose the one answer that best completes the sentence.

1. Most universities _____ only people
   entering the freshman class.

   (A) will be accepted
   (B) accept *(checkmark)*
   (C) although it accepts
   (D) accepting

2. _____ , the examinees knew it was
   time to stop.

   (A) Hearing the bell

   (B) Heard the bell
   (C) To have been heard the bell
   (D) To hear the bell

3. The debate _____ by the partisan
   review drew a large crowd.

   (A) sponsored *(checkmark)*
   (B) was sponsored
   (C) has sponsored
   (D) sponsoring

4. Although the subscription department claims _____ our order, we are still getting the magazine.

   (A) having received
   (B) not receiving
   (C) not to have received
   (D) was receiving

5. The permission that was needed to build the roads _____.

   (A) it will be granted
   (B) was granted
   (C) was being granted
   (D) have been granted

6. The pilots _____ the most direct route to save fuel.

   (A) although choosing
   (B) when they chose
   (C) was to choose
   (D) chose

7. The song had a melody that _____ like this.

   (A) was gone

(B) went
(C) is to go
(D) had went

8. One's success cannot always _____ in terms of money.

   (A) be measured
   (B) being measured
   (C) to measure
   (D) measure

9. The reasons _____ the proposal were numerous.

   (A) although to reject
   (B) for to reject
   (C) for rejected
   (D) for rejecting

10. If the superintendent does not _____ his mind, there is nothing more to be done.

    (A) changes
    (B) have changed
    (C) change
    (D) to change

WORD FAMILIES

Many **nouns, verbs, adjectives,** and **adverbs** are related. They come from the same *root* word; that is, they are from the same word family.

VERB	NOUN	ADJECTIVE	ADVERB
repeat	repetition	repeated	repeatedly
persuade	persuasion	persuasive	persuasively
destruct	destruction	destructive	destructively
beautify	beauty	beautiful	beautifully

The potential problem with word families is:
   The appropriate word may be replaced by another word in the same family.

Study the following potential problems:

NOUN SUBSTITUTION
Incorrect
The ocean was two miles depth at that point.
Correct
The ocean was two miles deep at that point.

ADVERB SUBSTITUTION
Incorrect
The fruit tasted bitterly.
Correct
The fruit tasted bitter.

WORD FAMILIES I

Choose the one answer that best completes the sentence.

1. The naive man _____ believed what he read in the papers.

   (A) foolish
   ✓(B) foolishly
   (C) fool
   (D) fooled

2. After _____ attempts, the police were able to enter the building.

   (A) repeating
   (B) repetition
   (C) repeatedly
   · (D) repeated

3. The gardens which were planted this spring should _____ the roadway.

   (A) beautifully
   (B) beautiful
   ﹨(C) beauty
   (D) beautify

4. The values of a society are reflected in its _____.

   (A) traditional
   (B) traditions
   (C) traditionally
   (D) traditionalize

5. The major _____ were reported by the press without bias.

   (A) eventual
   (B) eventfully
   (C) eventful
   ✓(D) events

6. Although the couch looks _____, it is extremely hard.

   (A) comfortable
   (B) comfortably
   ✓(C) comfortableness
   (D) comfort

7. The bodybuilder _____ tossed the child into the air.

   (A) easily
   (B) easy
   (C) ease
   (D) eased

8. The _____ of landing men on the moon is unsurpassed in modern technology.

   (A) achieve
   (B) achiever
   (C) achievement
   (D) achievable

9. The first in _____ was the general who served his country only during peacetime.

   (A) commander
   (B) commandment
   (C) commanding
   (D) command

10. A family with 10 children in a small restaurant is easily _____.

    (A) noticed
    (B) notice
    (C) notify
    (D) notification

WORD FAMILIES II

In the sentences below, identify the one underlined phrase that is incorrect.

1. Our partner, being business <u>oriented</u>, <u>provided</u> us with the <u>information</u> we
                        A   B   C

   needed to start our own <u>commerce</u> venture.
                   D

2. The accountant <u>careful</u> looked over the <u>monthly</u> accounts, trying to
                 A   B

   find the <u>terrible</u> error we had made <u>inadvertently</u>.
          C   D

3. The agent asked <u>politely</u> for the <u>wooded</u> case, but the clerk <u>adamantly</u>
                    A   B   C

    refused to give it to her until she brought the <u>proper</u> authorization.
                                                              D

4. To give <u>credit</u> where it is due, the assistant <u>loyal</u> supported his
           A   B

    <u>superior</u> even when all seemed <u>hopeless</u>.
    C   D

5. The lecturer <u>smilingly</u> addressed the <u>massively</u> audience in the <u>city</u> auditorium
                   A   B   C

    without using her <u>numerous</u> notes.
                       D

6. <u>Given</u> the foul weather, the Coast Guard <u>strongly</u> urges all sailors to think
    A   B

    <u>careful</u> about taking out <u>small</u> boats.
    C   D

7. The major <u>investors</u> decided <u>without warn</u> to withdraw their large
              A   B

    contribution and <u>refused</u> to <u>elaborate</u> on the decision.
                            C   D

8. The journalist asked the <u>elected</u> official <u>presently</u> to make a statement, but he
                                A   B

    <u>refused</u> to <u>comment</u>.
    C   D

9. The government's <u>obligation</u> to its <u>constituency</u> prompted it to
                  A   B

    <u>resume</u> local food distribution <u>immediate</u>.
    C   D

10. For the <u>first time</u> the <u>unpopular</u> regulations were <u>temporarily</u> <u>suspension</u>
         A   B   C   D

    during the week-long celebration.

WORD ORDER

There are three forms of word order that are often difficult: **subject - verb;
adjective - noun;** and **adverb - adjective.** Generally, in affirmative statements the
subject precedes the verb, the adjective precedes the noun, and the adverb precedes
the adjective it modifies.

Many of the problems associated with word order have been discussed in other
sections. As English sentences derive most of their meaning from word order, it is
important to have extra practice in this area.

Potential problems with word order are:
  1. The subject and verb may be reversed.

2. An adjective may follow a noun.
3. An adverb may be placed after the adjective it modifies.
4. Adjectives may be in the wrong order.

Study the following potential problems:

SUBJECT - VERB ORDER

Subject precedes verb
When wh or yes/no questions are added to an independent clause
    Incorrect
    They wondered where was he.
    Correct
    They wondered where he was.

Verb precedes subject
With expletive there or it
    Incorrect
    There the door is.
    Correct
    There is the door.

With an initial prepositional phrase of place and an intransitive verb
    Incorrect
    Around the table the directors sat.
    Correct
    Around the table sat the directors.

Auxiliary precedes subject
With only and a time phrase or word
    Incorrect
    Only if he comes, I will come, too.
    Correct
    Only if he comes, will I come, too.

In certain conditional sentences
    Incorrect
    He had come, we would have finished.
    Correct
    Had he come, we would have finished.

Following a negative adverb
    Incorrect
    Never he has done that.
    Correct
    Never has he done that.

ADJECTIVES FOLLOW NOUNS/PRONOUNS

When the pronoun ends in -one, -body, -thing
    Incorrect
    Intelligent anyone could do it.

Correct
Anyone intelligent could do it.

When the modifier is a prepositional phrase
  Incorrect
  In the short dress, the girl looked ridiculous.
  Correct
  The girl in the short dress looked ridiculous.

ADVERBS PRECEDE ADJECTIVES

Incorrect
The event was well-planned extremely.
Correct
The event was extremely well-planned.

ADJECTIVES IN WRONG ORDER

Incorrect
He used a Japanese, new, lightweight, black, compact camera.
Correct
He used a compact, lightweight, new, black, Japanese camera.

SUBJECT AND VERB PLACEMENT

Choose the one answer that best completes the sentence.

1. Never_____ such a night.

   (A) I did see
   (B) have I seen
   (C) have seen I
   (D) I saw

2. There _____ the proofreader overlooked on this page.

   (A) a mistake is
   (B) is a mistake
   (C) a mistake be
   (D) be mistake

3. It_____ that the days seem to be getting shorter.

   (A) not my imagination
   (B) is not my imagination
   (C) not is my imagination
   (D) that is not my imagination

4. So little known_____ that the explorers had to proceed without maps.

   (A) was the terrain
   (B) the terrain was
   (C) the terrain
   (D) terrain was

5. Among the rafters overhead _____.

   (A) hung the bats
   (B) the bats hanging
   (C) bats was hung
   (D) hang bats

6. Close by the door _____ .

   (A) the spy listen
   (B) listening the spy
   (C) listened the spy
   (D) the listening spy

7. He was told under no circumstances _____ the computer.

   (A) he may use
   (B) he use may
   (C) may he use
   (D) may use

8. Only when it rains _____ .

   (A) does the river overflow

(B) the river does overflow
(C) overflows does the river
(D) overflow the river

9. Only once before _____ .

(A) has happened this
(B) happened this
(C) this has happened
(D) has this happened

10. So little _____ that the neighbors could not settle their differences.

(A) they agreed
(B) agreed did they
(C) did they agree
(D) they did agree

ADJECTIVE AND ADVERB PLACEMENT

Choose the one answer that best completes the sentence.

1. _____ are often used for laboratory experiments.

(A) Gray small mice
(B) That gray small mice
(C) They are small gray mice
(D) Small gray mice

2. The cost of _____ of both scientific and commercial interest may be prohibitive.

(A) large-scale projects research
(B) research large-scale projects
(C) projects research large-scale
(D) large-scale research projects

3. The young artist creates _____ .

(A) translucent marble sculptures
(B) marble translucent sculptures
(C) marble sculptures translucent
(D) translucent sculptures marble

4. The biological factor in food design requires _____ .

(A) safe food and nutritious
(B) safe and nutritious food
(C) food safe and nutritious
(D) safe and food nutritious

5. My father, the _____ person, managed to fix the toaster.

(A) world's least mechanical
(B) least mechanical in the world
(C) least world's mechanical
(D) least mechanical world's

6. _____ would have known the answer.

(A) Anyone is clever
(B) Clever anyone
(C) Anyone clever
(D) Clever is anyone

7. The woman who lost the key hoped the finder would turn it over to _____ .

(A) anyone official
(B) official anyone
(C) official
(D) anyone officially

8. Nuclear power _____ is a risk to civilization.

(A) as a system total
(B) as a total system
(C) total system
(D) system total

9. The trash can behind the juice stand was full of _____ .

(A) ripe banana skins
(B) banana ripe skins
(C) ripe skins banana
(D) skins banana ripe

10. The shore is the home of the new rich and is dotted with _____ .

(A) big great houses
(B) great big houses
(C) houses big great
(D) houses great big

ADJECTIVE PLACEMENT

In the sentences below, identify the one underlined phrase that is incorrect.

1. The <u>new company</u> <u>develops and markets</u> a series of high-quality, inexpensive
        A   B
   <u>products peripheral</u> for both <u>micro- and mini-computers</u>.
       C   D

2. <u>Strong winds</u> <u>flow naturally</u> from areas of <u>greater energy</u> concentration
     A   B   C
   to areas of <u>concentration less</u>.
              D

3. A <u>particular natural event</u> <u>called a phenomenon</u> is used by scientists
            A   B
   in <u>making guesses intelligent</u> <u>called hypotheses</u>.
            C   D

4. <u>Vanilla ice cream</u> was one of the <u>treats special</u> on the <u>Skylab menu</u>
      A   B   C
   provided for the <u>hardy astronauts</u>.
              D

5. The <u>brilliant star</u> that shone <u>that first night</u> was <u>barely visible</u> on the
        A   B   C
   <u>clear evening next</u>.
       D

6. The <u>recently renovated</u> home is located in a <u>beautiful natural</u>
          A   B
   <u>wooded setting</u> just minutes from a <u>local center shopping</u>.
       C   D

7. Even <u>granted extenuating circumstances</u>, the gardener <u>still might have</u>
             A   B
   managed to bring in the <u>fragile tree palm</u> and rose bush <u>before</u> the storm.
                   C   D

8. <u>The simple charity</u> organized by the <u>patron wealthy</u> is now the <u>biggest</u> in the
      A   B   C
   state with hundreds of <u>loyal volunteers</u>.
                 D

9. <u>A shrill horn</u> sounding by <u>my left ear</u> announced <u>the return triumphant</u>
     A   B   C
   of the <u>exhausted football</u> team to the rain-soaked field.
          D

10. The doctor, <u>unprepared for</u> the <u>difficult operation</u>, brought in <u>two special</u>
             A   B   C
   assistants to help <u>in areas dangerous</u> where he was not an expert.
                D

In the sentences below, identify the one underlined phrase that is incorrect.

1. <u>Upon further examination</u> it was discovered that your shipment, which
           A

   <u>late arrived,</u> was <u>incomplete</u> and <u>incorrectly</u> labeled.
      B   C   D

2. The <u>fast food trays</u> on the Space Shuttle <u>held not only</u> the food <u>in place,</u>
         A   B   C

   but also served as <u>warming devices.</u>
                    D

3. Laboratory studies <u>have long shown</u> that <u>stimulate violent films</u> aggressive
                      A   B

   impulses and action <u>among youthful subjects</u> <u>who view the films.</u>
                     C   D

4. <u>Long after sewing</u> machines were ubiquitous <u>in American life,</u> <u>quilts continued</u>
       A   B   C

   to be <u>by hand made.</u>
         D

5. <u>Porcelain is distinguished</u> from other clays in that <u>white it is,</u> <u>extremely creamy</u>
         A   B   C

   in consistency, and <u>virtually free</u> of impurities.
                      D

6. <u>Greatly the hotel strike</u> inconvenienced the <u>extremely</u> <u>elderly</u> patrons who
         A   B   C

   <u>unwillingly and ungraciously made</u> their own beds.
                 D

7. <u>Prices agricultural</u> are <u>determined daily</u> in <u>large central markets</u> by the
         A   B   C

   <u>laws of supply</u> and demand.
        D

8. <u>Presumably</u> the espionage agent has <u>quietly</u> and <u>without delay</u> left the
      A   B   C

   country after his accomplices <u>forcibly were</u> apprehended.
                            D

9. <u>Illegally cars parked</u> will be towed <u>at the owner's expense</u> and
         A   B

   <u>may not be retrieved</u> until the <u>following week.</u>
        C   D

10. <u>Early man</u>, to blunt the wind and conserve <u>body heat</u>, no doubt added the

      A   B

protective, <u>insulating, hairy skins</u> of other animals to his own

                             C

<u>thin one relatively</u>.

     D

Structure Target Answer Key

ACTIVE PASSIVE VERBS

Active-Passive I
1. C	6. D
2. C	7. B
3. A	8. C
4. B	9. B
5. C	10. A

Active-Passive II
1. C	6. B
2. D	7. D
3. C	8. A
4. A	9. A
5. B	10. C

ARTICLES

Articles I
1. C	6. C
2. D	7. C
3. A	8. C
4. D	9. D
5. C	10. C

Articles II
1. B	6. D
2. C	7. B
3. C	8. B
4. B	9. B
5. D	10. D

COMPARISONS

Comparisons I
1. A	6. A
2. D	7. A
3. C	8. D
4. A	9. A
5. C	10. B

Comparisons II
1. A	6. A
2. A	7. B
3. D	8. A
4. B	9. B
5. A	10. C

CONDITIONALS

Conditionals I
1. C	6. D
2. A	7. A
3. B	8. B
4. C	9. C
5. C	10. A

Conditionals II
1. B	6. C
2. D	7. A
3. C	8. B
4. D	9. C
5. C	10. C

CONJUNCTIONS

Form I
1. B	6. A
2. A	7. A
3. B	8. C
4. A	9. C
5. D	10. B

Form II
1. B	6. C
2. B	7. C
3. C	8. C
4. D	9. D
5. A	10. B

Parallel Structures I
1. B	6. A
2. A	7. D
3. B	8. C
4. D	9. B
5. C	10. A

Parallel Structures II
1. C	6. B
2. B	7. B
3. B	8. B
4. B	9. A
5. D	10. C

PREPOSITIONS

Prepositions I
1. B	6. C
2. A	7. B
3. C	8. C
4. D	9. D
5. D	10. A

Prepositions II
1. B	6. C
2. A	7. A
3. D	8. A
4. B	9. B
5. B	10. D

PRONOUNS

Agreement
1. B	6. A
2. C	7. C
3. B	8. A
4. D	9. A
5. A	10. B

Form
1. B	6. A
2. C	7. C
3. D	8. A
4. B	9. B
5. D	10. A

Extra Exercises
1. B	6. D
2. B	7. D
3. A	8. B
4. A	9. B
5. B	10. A

REDUNDANCY

Redundancy I
1. C	6. B
2. A	7. D
3. A	8. B
4. B	9. B
5. D	10. A

Redundancy II
1. A	6. A
2. B	7. A
3. C	8. A
4. B	9. B
5. A	10. A

SUBJECT

Agreement
1. A	6. B
2. C	7. D
3. C	8. C
4. C	9. C
5. B	10. D

Omission
1. B	6. A
2. A	7. C
3. B	8. A
4. C	9. D
5. C	10. B

Repetition
1. A	6. A
2. A	7. D
3. B	8. B
4. A	9. D
5. D	10. B

Extra Exercises
1. B	6. A
2. A	7. A
3. C	8. A
4. D	9. B
5. C	10. D

SUBJUNCTIVE

Subjunctive I
1. B	6. A
2. A	7. D
3. D	8. B
4. C	9. A
5. D	10. C

Subjunctive II
1. C	6. B
2. A	7. B
3. B	8. D
4. D	9. A
5. A	10. B

Subordinate Clauses

Noun Clauses I				Noun Clauses II				Adjective Clauses I				Adjective Clauses II				Adverb Clauses I			
1.	A	6.	D	1.	A	6.	A	1.	C	6.	A	1.	D	6.	B	1.	B	6.	B
2.	B	7.	A	2.	C	7.	B	2.	D	7.	D	2.	C	7.	D	2.	C	7.	A
3.	A	8.	B	3.	A	8.	D	3.	C	8.	B	3.	A	8.	A	3.	D	8.	A
4.	B	9.	B	4.	C	9.	A	4.	C	9.	D	4.	A	9.	A	4.	D	9.	C
5.	C	10.	D	5.	C	10.	B	5.	A	10.	C	5.	A	10.	B	5.	C	10.	A

Adverb Clauses II				Reduced Adjective Clauses I				Reduced Adjective Clauses II				Reduced Adverb Clauses I				Reduced Adverb Clauses II			
1.	A	6.	A	1.	C	6.	C	1.	A	6.	A	1.	D	6.	A	1.	A	6.	C
2.	D	7.	A	2.	C	7.	D	2.	C	7.	A	2.	A	7.	A	2.	A	7.	A
3.	C	8.	A	3.	B	8.	A	3.	B	8.	B	3.	B	8.	A	3.	A	8.	B
4.	A	9.	D	4.	C	9.	B	4.	A	9.	C	4.	B	9.	D	4.	A	9.	A
5.	D	10.	B	5.	B	10.	A	5.	B	10.	A	5.	C	10.	B	5.	A	10.	A

Verb

Omission				Unnecessary Form				Agreement				Tense				Extra Exercises			
1.	A	6.	D	1.	A	6.	D	1.	B	6.	D	1.	A	6.	A	1.	B	6.	D
2.	C	7.	C	2.	B	7.	A	2.	A	7.	B	2.	B	7.	C	2.	A	7.	B
3.	D	8.	B	3.	C	8.	D	3.	D	8.	D	3.	B	8.	A	3.	A	8.	A
4.	B	9.	B	4.	D	9.	C	4.	A	9.	D	4.	D	9.	C	4.	C	9.	D
5.	C	10.	D	5.	C	10.	A	5.	D	10.	B	5.	C	10.	A	5.	B	10.	C

Word Families

Word Families I				Word Families II			
1.	B	6.	A	1.	D	6.	C
2.	D	7.	A	2.	A	7.	B
3.	D	8.	C	3.	B	8.	B
4.	B	9.	D	4.	B	9.	D
5.	D	10.	A	5.	B	10.	D

Word Order

Subject-Verb Placement				Adjective and Adverb Placement				Adjective Placement				Adverb Placement			
1.	B	6.	C	1.	D	6.	C	1.	C	6.	D	1.	B	6.	A
2.	B	7.	C	2.	D	7.	A	2.	D	7.	C	2.	B	7.	A
3.	B	8.	A	3.	A	8.	B	3.	C	8.	B	3.	B	8.	D
4.	A	9.	D	4.	B	9.	A	4.	B	9.	C	4.	D	9.	A
5.	A	10.	C	5.	A	10.	B	5.	D	10.	D	5.	B	10.	D

VOCABULARY TARGETS

INTRODUCTION

You learn a word because you have a need to express yourself or to understand something. When you learned words in your own language, you did not sit down with huge lists. You heard words in context; you used them in context. You read words in context; you understood them in context. Learning words in context is the best way to increase your vocabulary.

On the TOEFL, however, the words in the Vocabulary section are not in context. They are in a sentence, but the sentence is isolated. The possible answers (the distractors) *All fit* the sentence grammatically and semantically, but only one is a synonym.

We gave the <u>errant</u> child what he deserved.

      (A) roving
      (B) good
      (C) handsome
      (D) late

In the above example, *roving* is a synonym for *errant*, but the other possible answers, if placed in the sentence, also describe the word *child* and also make sense in the sentence as a whole, but they are not synonyms for *errant*.

VOCABULARY TIPS

Before the TOEFL
Before you take the TOEFL, there are some techniques and exercises you can use to increase your vocabulary. Remember that only using a word will help you remember it.

1. **READ! READ! READ!**
   There is no substitute for a systematic approach to reading. The more you read, the more words you will discover. The more often you read, the more frequently you will see these words. You should read in a variety of subject matter areas. You should read books, magazines, newspapers, time schedules, letters, and so forth. You will find new words each time you pick up something to read.

2. **KEEP A NOTEBOOK**
   Once you find a new word, write it down in a notebook. Later look the word up in the dictionary and write synonyms for the word in your notebook next to the word. You must train yourself to recognize synonyms, not translations. Any time you have a spare moment, pull out your Word Notebook and study a few words and their synonyms.

3. **MAKE FLASH CARDS**
   Find a block of heavy paper (index or file) cards that are a convenient size (1"x 2" or 3"x 5"). Write a new word on one side and the English synonym or synonyms on the reverse. Carry these flash cards with you and give yourself mini-tests whenever you have spare time. Show yourself the word and guess the synonyms. Show yourself the synonyms and guess the word.

4. STUDY WORD LISTS

Some word lists are included in this section. Each day transfer some words and their synonyms from these lists into your Word Notebook or onto your flash cards.

It is difficult to memorize words on a word list. These lists, however, draw your attention to a word. You will soon begin to notice words which you saw on the list as you read. As you increase the amount you read, you will see the new words more frequently. The more you practice, the larger your vocabulary will become.

5. USE CONTEXT CLUES

Context clues will not help you in the Vocabulary section of the TOEFL; only your ability to recognize synonyms will help you. Context clues will help you in the Reading Comprehension section, and they will help you guess the meanings of words you encounter while practicing your reading skills before the TOEFL.

6. STUDY THIS SECTION

In the Vocabulary Target section are lists of words and prefixes that will help you prepare for the TOEFL. Study the following lists; then do the Vocabulary Target exercises that follow the lists.

> Synonyms
> Roots
> Common Prefixes
> Negative Prefixes
> Usage

During the TOEFL

When you take the Vocabulary section of the TOEFL:
1. Look mainly at the *underlined word*.
2. Look for the synonym.
3. Be aware of *false* clues (word families, grammar markers, and so forth).
4. If you do not know a word, do not waste time. GUESS.

WORD LISTS

SYNONYMS

Word	Synonym	Synonym
abandon	discard	vacate
accord	agree	grant
adversity	difficulty	misfortune
affluent	plentiful	rich
aggravate	annoy	infuriate
alleviate	lighten	mitigate
amenable	agreeable	favorable
anguish	distress	sorrow
apathetic	dispirited	lifeless
arrogant	disdainful	imperious
astonish	confound	overwhelm
atrocious	appalling	detestable
augment	add	enlarge

avoid v 逃避	ignore v	shun v
awkward a	graceless a opside dancing	inept a not good
baffle v	confuse v	deceive v
banal a	common a	plain a
barren a nothing woman can't have child	desolate a deaser	sterile a
berate v	criticize v	disapprove v
betray v	deceive v	fool v
bias n	inclination n	predisposition n
bitter a	acrid a	sour a
blend v	combine v	mix v
bliss n	happiness n	joy n
bluff v 诈唬	boast v 以于 说大活	feign v
bold a	daring a	fearless a
bonus n	award n	gift n
bother v	annoy v	irritate v
brief a	concise a	short a
brilliant a	clever a	intelligent a
brisk a	fast a	swift a
budget v	allot v	plan v
candid a	honest a	truthful a
caricature n	cartoon n	imitation n
casual a	informal a	natural a
category n	classification n	division n
cease v	desist	stop
chaotic a	disordered	messy
cherish v prash	esteem higher respect love	love
circumvent v	avoid v	go around
commemorate nothing remember	celebrate	honor
compensate v pay by money	balance	recompense
competent a quilify	able	capable
conceive v in your main	design	plan
confirmation n	acknowledgement	proof
contradict v	deny	oppose
contribution n giving	donation	grant
courteous a	polite	well-mannered
craving n	desire	longing
credulous a	confident	trustful
damp a	moist	wet
dare v	challenge	defy
decay v/n gobed	decline condition	rot
decent a	honorable	pure
dense a high wight like golden packed	filled	packed
designate v chose to name	name	select
detain v	hold	keep
disclose v	announce	reveal
dogma v very basic religen	belief apointe	view opinion idea
durable ad last long time	constant	lasting
dwindle v	abate hunger	diminish
eager a	earnest	keen apointed
eccentric a something a lude stronge	abnormal people do different	idiosyncratic
elaborate v	embellish	enhance make something look better
emanate v spornt out	arise	radiate

embezzle n — purloin — steal
eminent a — distinguished — prominent
encourage v — foster — induce
endure v — last — persist
erudite a — cultured — learned
essential a — basic — necessary
estimate v — guess — predict
evaluate v — appraise — judge
exhaust v — deplete — empty
exhilarated a — cheerful — zestful
explicit a — definite — specific

fastidious a — exacting — particular
federation n — alliance — band
feeble a — helpless — infirm
fervor n *succesion* — intensity — passion
feud n — argument — dispute
filth n — dirt — squalor *dirty very unclear*
flatter v — compliment — praise *something nice. good job*
fleet *fast* — nimble — swift
frivolous a *not important* — inconsequential — trivial
frugal a — prudent — saving *spend money careful*
furious a — angry — outraged *very angry*

generous a — benevolent — unselfish
genuine a — actual — real
glare v — gleam *shin too strong can't see* — glisten *all mean give out light.*
gloomy a *sad* — cheerless *dark* — dim
goad v — provoke — badger *try to produce someone angry.*
grasp v — grab — hold
greed n — avarice — longing
guarantee v — assure — pledge *promise*
guile n — cunning — deceit *a bility. fool a lie person.*
gullible a — credulous — unsuspicious

habitual a — accustomed — regular
handicap n — disability — disadvantage
harass v *be careful* — annoy — disturb
harmless a — innocuous — unoffensive
harsh a *rush 粗糙 unkind* — hard — coarse *ruff*
hasty a *rush (bad mean)* — abrupt *suddly* — hurried *too quick*
haughty a *feel (be done)* — arrogant — pretentious *just show your money*
humiliate v *making somebody feel lower* — humble — shame
hygiene n *cleaners* — cleanliness — sanitation *public*
hypocrisy n — duplicity *lying* — falseness

ideal n — goal — perfection
idle a *not doing anything* — lazy — unoccupied
ignorant a *never opticrite* — stupid — unintelligent
illogical *not logical* — incongruent *doesn't past together* — rambling *going on and on*
illustrious a — eminent — famous
imitate v — copy — reflect
immense a *very big* — huge — mammoth
impartial a — candid *be true* — impersonal
impatient a — anxious — eager
implicate v — accuse — insinuate *say something it not exactly*

importune	beg	solicit
inadvertent *a*	accidental	unintentional
indifferent *a* *I don't care*	apathetic	disinterested
isolate *v* *separat*	detach	quarantine
jargon *n* *special speech vocabulary*	argot	slang
jovial *a* *happy people great*	genial	merry
judge *n*	estimate	referee
justification *n*	excuse	reason
juvenile *a*	adolescent *teenagers*	immature
keen *h* *sharp inteligen*	clever	observant
label *v*	brand	classify
labor *v/n*	toil	work
lead *v*	direct *for people*	proceed
lean *a* *for animal*	slim	thin
leave *v*	abandon	desert
liberal	copious	unrestrained
liberal *a*	lenient	open-minded
limitation *n*	boundary	constraint
lucid *a*	clear	understandable
lucky *a*	auspicious	fortunate
mad *a*	furious	irate
manage *v*	administer	control
manipulate *v*	control	shape
marginal *a*	borderline	limited
match *v*	agree	correspond
maze *h*	complexity	labyrinth
meditate *v*	ponder	think
memorial *n*	commemoration	monument
mention *v*	allude	refer to
merge *v* *enjoy togeter*	blend	fuse
narrow *a*	confined	restricted
nature *n*	aspect	character
necessary *a*	mandatory	requisite
negate *v* *speak against*	contradict	refute *to prove a wrong*
negligent *a*	careless	remiss
negotiate *v*	bargain	deal
nice *a*	affable *friendly*	benign *honest*
noble *a*	aristocratic	distinguished
novice *a*	beginner	nonprofessional
stronger nuisance *something bother you*	annoyance	offense
obedient *a*	faithful	loyal
objection *n*	disapproval	protest
obligatory *a*	compulsory	required
observe *v*	notice	watch
obvious *a*	conspicious	definite
offend *v*	anger	irritate
offer *n*	bid	proposal
omen *n*	premonition	sign
omit *v*	exclude	remove
opportune *a*	advantageous	auspicious

pacify v *make peace*	appease	placate
pain n	ache	discomfort
paramont n	chief	leading
partisan a	biased	dogmatic
passive a	inactive	lethargic
pause v	break	cease
permeate v	diffuse	disseminate
perpetuate v	endure	preserve
perplex v *surprise*	astonish	baffle
strong persecute v *high right trusty*	afflict	harass

radiate v.	effuse	emanate
radical	basic	fundamental
range n	anger	furor
rank v	arrange	classify
realize v	accomplish	fulfill
recalcitrant a	obstinate	stubborn
receptacle n *put something inside*	container	repository
reconcile v *bring together*	atone	conciliate
regret v	deplore	grieve
reliable a	dependable	trustworthy

sanction n	approval	permit
scope n	aim	extent
section n	division	portion
settle v	adjust	compromise
shallow a *un important*	superficial	trivial
shrewd a *very careful to do*	careful	calculating
significant a	distinctive	important
slight a	delicate	slender
spontaneous a	impromptu	unplanned
spread v	announce	broadcast
stabilize v.	balance	steady

tame v *tame an animal awhile*	domesticate	subdue
tangle v	intertwine	twist
temper n	mood	nature
tendency n	inclination	trend *style*
term n	cycle	duration
thrift n	conservation	prudence
tough a	aggressive	unyielding
transfer v	convey	exchange
tumult n	agitation	commotion *a lot of action uncontrol*
turbulent a	disordered	violent

vain a	boastful *general*	inflated
valid a *good*	authorized	legitimate
variety n	assortment	diversity
verify v	authenticate	substantiate

Roots

A Root

A word is often formed from a *root*. This root can be traced back to the days when the root was borrowed from another language and adopted into English. Many English words have Greek or Latin roots. If you learn one Greek or Latin root, you will be able to recognize up to 35 English words. If you memorize 40 Latin or Greek roots, you will be able to recognize 1,400 English words.

Below are only a few examples of the thousands of roots found in English. When you look up a new word in the dictionary, look for the meaning of the root and add it to this list. As an exercise to increase your vocabulary, try to find other words with these roots.

Root	Meaning	Examples
annus enn	year	biennial, annual
anthropos	mankind	anthropology, misanthropic, philanthropic
biblio	book	bibliography
cedo	go	precede, succeed, intercede
chronos	time	chronology, synchronize
claudo	shut	include, preclude, exclusive, cloister, recluse
cura	care	curator, sinecure
ego	I / self	egotist, egocentric
fero	to carry	transfer, refer, differ
fid fidel	faith	fidelity, confidence, faith, diffident, perfidious
fluo	flow	fluent, fluid, influence
gnostos	know	agnostic, recognizance
haero	to stick	cohere, adhere
jacio	throw	reject, interject
later	side	bilateral
lingua	tongue	bilingual, linguistic
mania	madness	maniac, egomania
metron	measure	meter, speedometer
murus	wall	muralist, intramural
nihil	nothing	annihilate, nihilist
optikos	vision	optician, optical

ped	foot	pedestrial, pedal, impede
pend	hang	pendant, dependent
phobia	fear	claustrophobia, phobia
phone	sound	stereophonic, phoneme, telephone
pliao	fold	pleat, application, pliable, imply
ped	foot	octopus
press	push	repress, depress
scend	climb	transcend, ascend, descend
seco	cut	sector, section, insect
sed	sit	sediment, sedate, supersede, residence
sentio	feel	sentimental, presentiment, resent, consent
sophos	wise	sophistication
spectus	look	retrospective, inspect, spectacles
tactus	touch	tactile, contact
therme	heat	thermometer, thermos
urbo	city	suburban
verto	turn	inversion, revert, convert

COMMON PREFIXES

A Prefix

Pre in Latin means *before*. *Fix* is a Latin root meaning *to fix* (position). Prefix means *placed before*. The prefixes below were borrowed into the English language from either the Latin or Greek language. Knowing one Latin or Greek prefix will help you recognize up to 50 English words. Knowing 40 Latin or Greek prefixes will help you recognize up to 2,000 English words.

Prefix	Meaning	Examples
a, an	without or not	asexual, amoral, anarchy, antonym
a	to, toward	aloud, ameliorate, akin, aground

ab, abs	off, away from	abstain, absence, abnormal
ad (ac, ag, al, an, as, at)	to	adhere, account, aggregate, allocate, anchor, assure, attach
ambi/amphi	on both sides	ambivalent, amphibious, ambidextrous
ante	before	antecedent, anteroom, antebellum
ante	against, opposite	antidote, antibody, anticipate
apo	from, off	apology, apostrophe
bi	twice, two	bicycle, bilateral, bilingual
cata	down, against, back	catapult, category
circum	around, about	circumspect, circumvent
com (con, co, cog col, cor)	together or with	compare, constant, cohabitate, cognate, collect, correlate
contra (contro, counter	against opposing	contradiction controversial counterproductive
de	from, off down	deter, descend, decimate
di	twice, two	divide, dilemma
dis, dif, di	apart, away, not (see above)	disappear, different, digest
en, em	cause to be, put into	encircle, empower, entrust
ex, e	from, out of	except, egress, exit
extra, extro in, im, it, ir	outside, beyond not	extraterritorial, extravagant insufferable, impotent, illogical, irrefutable
in, im	in	ingest, imbibe
inter, intro	between, together	intermingle, introduction
intra	within	intrastate
mal	bad, wrong	malcontent, malevolent

mis	ill, wrong	misdeed, miserable
mono	one	monolingual, monocle *one eye*
multi	many	multiply, multilingual
non	non	nonsense, nondescript
ob (oc, of, op)	toward, against, to	obtuse, occur, offer, oppress
para	near, beyond, beside	paragraph, paradox, paralegal
per	throughout, completely	persuade, perversion
poly	many	polygamy, polyglot
post	after, behind	postpone, posterior, posthumous
pre (pro)	before	preclude, predate, prevent, proceed
pro	for	production
re	again, back	reverse, return
retro	backward	retrospective, retrograde
sub (suc, suf, sug, sup, sur)	under	substantial, succinct, suffocate, suggest, suppress, surrender
super, sur	over	superman, supervisor, surprise
syn (sym, syl, sys)	together	synchronize, symbolic, syllable, system
trans	across	transoceanic, transport, transcontinental
ultra	excessive	ultrafine, untrasensitive
un	not	undone, unhappy

Word Lists

NEGATIVE PREFIXES

Negative Prefix
A negative prefix added to a word implies the opposite of the word.

unsolicited - not solicited
disabled - not able/handicapped

incompatible - not compatible
impatient - not patient
irrelevant - not relevant
nonviolent - not violent
misspelled - not spelled correctly

Examples of words with these prefixes are listed below:

		never can come together	
unaware	imbecile	irreconcilable	nonalcoholic
unbearable	immaterial	irredeemable *so bad*	nonconformist
uncomplicated	immature *young*	irrefutable *prove wrong*	noneffective
undecided	immortal *for ever*	irreligious	nonpolitical
unfit	impatient	irremovable	nonpoisonous
ungrammatical	impolite	irreparable	nonproductive
uninteresting	impossible	irresistible	nonrestricitve
unpleasant	improbable	irrational	nonsense
unreliable	improper	irregular	nonstop
unsolicited	impure	irresponsible	nonviolent
disadvantage	inapplicable	misbehave	
disburse	incapable	miscalculate	
discharge	indecent *no good*	misconduct	
disembark	inexact	misfire	
disfavor	infallible	misfortune	
dishonest	inhuman	misgiving	
disinfect	inimitable *no copy*	misinterpret	
disjointed	inoffensive	mislay	
dislocate	insatiable	misplace	
displeasure	invalid	mispronounce	

USAGE

The following words are often confused and misused in English. Note their correct usage. The following abbreviations are used:

v.	= verb	*adj.*	= adjective	*prep.*	= preposition
n.	= noun	*adv.*	= adverb	*conj.*	= conjunction

1. accept: *v.* to receive or to answer affirmatively
   except: *prep.* excluding

                    Everyone accepted our invitation.
                    Everyone came except John.

2. advice: *n.* recommendation regarding a course of action.
   advise: *v.* to counsel or offer advice to

                    His advice to us was to stay home.
                    He advised us to stay home.

3. affect: *v.* to influence
   effect: *n.* the result
                    v. to cause to happen

                    We were all affected by the drought.

The effect of the drought was an increase in food prices.
The drought effected an increase in price.

4. already: *adv.* before or by a specified time
   all ready: *adv.* all prepared

   Is it 6 o'clock already?
   She was all ready to go.

5. amount: *n.* refers to noncount nouns
   number: *n.* refers to count nouns

   A huge amount of grain is stored in the silo.
   Though few in number, the students had power.

6. complimentary: *adj.* given free, or giving praise
   complementary: *adj.* supplying needs

   The boss was very complimentary about my work.
   The complementary relationship of the gene structure
   promotes cell growth.

7. different from: *prep.* precedes a noun phrase
   different than: *prep.* precedes a noun clause

   He is different from your average soldier.
   She is different than we had thought.

8. enough: *adv.* precedes a noun and follows an adjective

   He knows enough English to study chemistry.
   She is fast enough to win without trying.

9. every so often: *adv.* occasionally
   ever so often: *adv.* frequently

   He comes every so often. I wish he would come more.
   He comes ever so often. I wish he would stay home.

10. first: *adj.* refers to three or more items
    former: *adj.* refers to two or fewer items

    The first five runners collapsed.
    The former officers, the president and vice president, were
    present.

11. from/since/for

   FROM is a preposition followed by a noun or noun phrase.
   As a time marker, it requires *to* or another preposition.

      From now on, I am the boss.
      From Monday to Friday, you will be my slave.

   SINCE is a preposition followed by a noun or noun phrase.

It expresses the exact time something began.

> Since Wednesday, I have walked 6 miles a day.

SINCE is also a subordinate conjunction followed by a clause.
It expresses the time something began.

> Since I began walking 6 miles a day, I feel stronger.

FOR is a preposition followed by a noun or noun phrase.
It expresses the exact length of time something lasted.

> For 2 weeks I have walked every day.

12. healthful: *adj.* promotes health
    healthy: *adj.* have health

> Fruit and nuts are healthful.
> The boy is a very healthy youngster.

13. imply: *v.* a writer or speaker suggests
    infer: *v.* the reader or listener makes a conclusion

> The witness implied that Mr. Gibbons was the murderer.
> We inferred from his remarks that Mr. Gibbons did it.

14. irregardless: incorrect. Use regardless.

15. its: *adj.*
    it's: contraction of *it is*

> Its mane was long and black
> It's one of the seven wonders of the world.

16. lie: *v. (intransitive)* to recline (complement)
    lay: *v. (transitive)* to put or place (No complement)

> He lies down for a rest after lunch.
> He lay the book on the chair.

17. little: not much
    a little: some

> We think very little of her work.
> He gave me a little cheese.

18. on/in/at: These prepositions are frequently confused.

Prepositions of Place:
The circle is on the square.
The circle is in the square.

Prepositions of Time:
Be here at 6 o'clock so you will not miss the beginning.
He came on time.
He came in time to see the beginning.

19. passed: *v. (transitive)* past participle of the verb *pass*
    past: *adj.* preposition

                               She barely passed the exam.
                               We will keep school open past June.

20. quiet: *adj.* not noisy
    quite: *adv.* entirely, truly

                               A librarian is quiet by nature.
                               That piano player is quite a loud person.

21. raise: *v. (transitive)* to move to a higher place.
    rise: *v. (intransitive)* to rest on something.

                               The farmers raise chickens and children.
                               The sun rises at 6 a.m.

22. respectfully: *adv.* showing respect
    respectively: *adv.* in the order stated

                               She signed the letter "Respectfully yours."
                               Mary, Jane, and Alice wore pink, yellow, and green respectively.

23. say: *v. (transitive)* to express in words
    tell: *v. (transitive)* also to express in words

                               I said that he should stay home.
                               I told him to stay home.
                               (NEVER *told <u>to</u> him*)

24. sit: *v. (intransitive)* to rest on something.
    set: *v. (transitive)* to place something.

                               He is sitting on the beach.
                               She set the food on the table.

25. speak: *v.* to say aloud
    speech: *n.* what is said aloud

                               "Speak louder. I can't hear you!"
                               We slept through the politician's boring speech.

26. than: *conj.* for comparisons
    then: *adj.* or *adv. conj.* relates to time

                               She is later than her sister.
                               First we will eat; then we will watch TV.

27. their: possessive pronoun
    there: adverb or expletive
    they're: contraction of *they are*

                               Their chauffeur is waiting outside.

There are three jets on the runway.
They're the last to leave.

28. to: preposition
    too: adverb
    two: number

The two of us should go to the library if it is not too late.

29. to:

An infinitive is sometimes confused with prepositional phrases beginning with *to*.

An infinitive is formed with *to* plus the simple form of the *verb*.

to be   to have
to dance   to get

A preposition is followed by a noun or noun phrase.

to my house   to us
to this town   to the window

To is not used after modals except *ought*.

He must study.
He ought to work harder.

For to is incorrect. Use *to* or *in order to*.

He went to see the game.

30. watch: v. *(transitive)* to look or observe carefully
    see: v. *(transitive)* to perceive with the eye

He watched the ship for a long time.
He saw the ship as he passed the harbor.

Vocabulary Target Exercises

Select the one answer that is appropriate in the context.

1. The prisoner _____ on his bunk all day long.

   (A) lies
   (B) lays
   (C) laid
   (D) lazy

2. At the awards banquet, the recipients _____ their prizes with humility.

   (A) excepted
   (B) is excepting

   (C) accepted
   (D) accepting

3. What kind of _____ did the professor give his students?

   (A) advising
   (B) advice
   (C) advise
   (D) advised

4. Yesterday's rain had no _____ on the water level in the reservoir.

(A) affecting
(B) effecting
(C) affect
(D) effect

5. An enormous _____ of feathers is needed for each down pillow.

(A) amount
(B) number
(C) amounts
(D) numbers

6. The stern music master rarely _____ his students performances.

(A) complimenting
(B) complementary
(C) complements
(D) compliments

7. _____ , she will appear on my doorstep with new plans for working with me.

(A) Every so often
(B) So often
(C) Ever often
(D) Ever so often

8. Nutritionists advise their patients to eat _____ foods.

(A) healthful
(B) healthy
(C) health
(D) healthiest

9. The reporters _____ from the congressman's speech that he intends to resign.

(A) implied
(B) are inferred
(C) are implied
(D) inferred

10. _____ of the current rate of inflation, it is advisable to buy real estate.

(A) Irregardless
(B) Regarding
(C) Regardless
(D) Without regard

11. The soldier _____ the flag before sunrise.

(A) rises
(B) raises
(C) raising
(D) rised

12. The children's ages are 10, 12, and 14, _____.

(A) respectively
(B) respective
(C) respectably
(D) respectfully

13. The old man _____ stories to school children.

(A) says
(B) tells
(C) saying
(D) telling

14. The bus driver asked the passengers to _____ down.

(A) sit
(B) be set
(C) set
(D) be sitting

15. The school principal prepared _____ to the group of administrators.

(A) speeches
(B) speak
(C) speech
(D) to speak

16. The width of the counter is longer _____ its depth.

(A) then
(B) that
(C) than
(D) the

17. _____ five principal colors.

(A) There are
(B) They are
(C) Their
(D) They're

18. To learn how to program a computer is _____ difficult to do in a week.

(A) two
(B) too
(C) to
(D) as

19. The captain of the cargo ship told the mate to _____ for sudden squalls.

(A) see
(B) be seeing
(C) look
(D) have looked

20. The monument looks _____ what the tourists expected.

(A) different than
(B) different with
(C) different from
(D) different that

21. The army was _____ to begin the assault.

(A) already
(B) all ready
(C) to readied
(D) readily

22. Youngsters often remember vividly their _____ trip to camp.

(A) first

(B) former
(C) passing
(D) passed

23. The students were _____ slow to understand the message of the film.

(A) quiet
(B) quietly
(C) quite
(D) quit

24. The fashion for clothes from the _____ is spurred by our generation's nostalgia.

(A) passed
(B) past
(C) passing
(D) been past

25. The Skylab and _____ crew suffered no ill effects during the 10-day orbit.

(A) it's
(B) is it
(C) its
(D) it

PREFIX EXERCISE

Select the one word or phrase that most closely matches the meaning of the underlined word.

1. People said that the personalities of the young married couple were underline{incompatible}.

(A) discordant
(B) harmonious
(C) loveable
(D) blissful

2. The newspaper described the underline{amoral} activities of the terrorist group in detail.

(A) erotic
(B) unproductive
(C) philanthropic
(D) unethical

3. The debate team found their opponents' arguments illogical and consequently underline{irrefutable}.

(A) interesting

(B) challenging
(C) irritating
(D) incontrovertible

4. The underline{hostile} manner of the woman caused the committee to reconsider the issue.

(A) stubborn
(B) angry
(C) forthright
(D) charming

5. The fundraisers claim their motives are underline{apolitical}.

(A) pure
(B) laudable
(C) unbiased
(D) nonpartisan

6. The underline{antidote} was not where the doctor had left it.

(A) prescription
(B) medicine
(C) anecdote
(D) remedy

7. The house, although not unusually small, made us feel <u>uncomfortable</u>.

(A) dirty
(B) immobile
(C) uneasy
(D) impractical

8. The <u>disadvantage</u> of winning is the notoriety one receives.

(A) pleasure of
(B) thrill of
(C) drawback to
(D) inconvenience of

9. The students' actions toward the substitute teacher were <u>distasteful</u>.

(A) inappropriate
(B) unpleasant
(C) inconsiderate
(D) inhuman

10. The <u>insufficient</u> supply of food did not worry the villagers.

(A) increased
(B) abundant
(C) inadequate
(D) diminishing

11. The manager does not tolerate <u>imperfections</u> in himself or in others.

(A) shyness
(B) stupidity
(C) misbehavior
(D) defects

12. The recluse's <u>mistreatment of</u> animals did not go unnoticed.

(A) cruelty to
(B) protection of
(C) hatred of
(D) distrust of

13. The reporter wondered how <u>impartial</u> the decision really was.

(A) unprejudiced
(B) bigoted

(C) one-sided
(D) insensitive

14. The directions to the museum were not what most people would call <u>uncomplicated</u>.

(A) difficult
(B) simple
(C) illegible
(D) impractical

15. The soldiers' <u>disobedience</u> made them subject to disciplinary action.

(A) habit
(B) tardiness
(C) dishonor
(D) insubordination

16. The speech, contrary to what we all expected, was <u>inoffensive</u>.

(A) incomprehensible
(B) interminable
(C) ridiculous
(D) harmless

17. We all, at times, wish we were <u>invisible</u>.

(A) wealthy
(B) more powerful
(C) nonviolent
(D) inconspicuous

18. <u>Inorganic</u> items are catalogued by their Latin names.

(A) Nonmusical
(B) Inanimate
(C) Animated
(D) Chemical

19. We saw he was <u>displeased</u>, but there was not enough time to do anything about it.

(A) undressed
(B) far away
(C) unhappy
(D) annoyed

20. My aunt's reasoning was clever but <u>invalid</u>.

(A) unjust
(B) unsubstantiated
(C) twisted
(D) evasive

GENERAL VOCABULARY EXERCISE

Select the one word or phrase that most closely matches the meaning of the underlined word.

1. Parents should <u>establish</u> certain rules for their children.

   (A) increase
   (B) offer
   (C) determine
   (D) justify

2. There are <u>numerous</u> customs that dictate one's diet.

   (A) popular
   (B) many
   (C) religious
   (D) special

3. The teacher wanted to <u>provide</u> the class with enough work to keep them busy.

   (A) supply
   (B) irritate
   (C) overwhelm
   (D) exhaust

4. A botanist can identify a flower by its shape and its <u>scent</u>.

   (A) name
   (B) size
   (C) color
   (D) smell

5. Since an amoeba's old cell will divide into two new cells, it may be called <u>immortal</u>.

   (A) duplicitous
   (B) powerful
   (C) biological
   (D) undying

6. As instructed, the pilot <u>precisely</u> followed the control tower's directions.

   (A) exactly
   (B) purposefully
   (C) only
   (D) always

7. Eating and drinking too much increases the size of the <u>abdomen</u>.

   (A) headache
   (B) gathering
   (C) belly
   (D) hangover

8. In times of war, the army will draft all <u>able-bodied</u> men.

   (A) strong
   (B) single
   (C) young
   (D) eligible

9. <u>Notification</u> of taxes due will be sent in the near future.

   (A) Announcement
   (B) Annotation
   (C) Clarification
   (D) Amplification

10. The comedian has a tendency to be more <u>absurd</u> than funny.

    (A) late
    (B) greedy
    (C) ridiculous
    (D) proud

11. Few <u>bachelors</u> live in this family neighborhood.

    (A) intelligent people
    (B) unmarried men
    (C) strangers
    (D) peers

12. Regular <u>maintenance</u> of an auto will improve its efficiency.

    (A) washing
    (B) upkeep
    (C) protection
    (D) driving

13. Children may <u>ridicule</u> other children new to a neighborhood.

    (A) become tired of

(B) play with
(C) make fun of
(D) be shy around

14. <u>Instead of</u> raising taxes, the administration looked for different sources of revenue.

(A) rather than
(B) before
(C) after
(D) in addition to

15. My grandmother always had <u>kind</u> words to say about everyone she knew.

(A) good
(B) simple
(C) similar
(D) clever

16. The terrier was <u>kind of</u> short with long, black hair.

(A) considered
(B) described as
(C) somewhat
(D) captured

17. Twins usually wear the same <u>kind</u> of clothing.

(A) size
(B) color
(C) type
(D) outfit

18. The <u>probability</u> of the strike ending before the tourist season is not high.

(A) likelihood
(B) idea
(C) result
(D) controversy

19. Violators who <u>are ignorant of</u> the parking laws must still pay their fines.

(A) am tired of
(B) respectful of
(C) know nothing of
(D) want to change

20. The court <u>nullified</u> the agreement after months of debate.

(A) heard
(B) annulled
(C) ratified
(D) dismissed

VOCABULARY TARGET ANSWER KEY

READING TARGETS

INTRODUCTION

The Reading Target introduction is written like a TOEFL reading practice passage. As you study the passages, you will not only familiarize yourself with the test format, but also learn some reading strategies. More practice reading passages follow the introduction.

Questions 1 - 4

MAKING READING A HABIT

The only way you can become a good reader is through practice. You cannot read a few paragraphs in your English book once a week and become a fluent reader. You need to read constantly. You should carry something to read with you wherever you go. Tear out pages of English magazines, for example, and carry them in your pocket. Whenever you have the chance, pull out a page and read a paragraph or two.

You should read in as many different subject areas as you can. You should try to find English books on different subjects and read a few paragraphs in each chapter in each book. Your eyes and mind need to practice. Your eyes need to practice moving quickly across the page from left to right, and your mind needs to practice making quick associations between the printed word and meaning.

READING WITH A PURPOSE

When you begin to read you should ask yourself a basic question:

Why am I reading this?

If you are reading to practice your English, you will read in a certain way. You will read slowly and concentrate on the relationship between the words and the grammatical structures. If you are reading for information about a particular subject, you will read in another way. You will focus on main parts and supporting facts. You use the grammar of the passage as a means, not an end.

READING TO PRACTICE ENGLISH

Reading to practice English is the way most foreign students read English. In school you do not read English to learn about a particular subject; for example, you do not read English to learn history. You read English to learn how a sentence was put together, how the verbs agree with the subject, what the clause is, etc. This is the way you have to read for the Structure and Written Expression section of the TOEFL, but it is not the way you should read for the Reading Comprehension section.

1. The author believes that to become a good reader you need to

   (A) have a large vocabulary.
   (B) understand grammar.
   (C) practice.
   (D) move your eyes across the page.

2. Which of the following can be inferred from the paragraph?

   (A) You should always have some English reading material close to you.
   (B) You should buy more English books.
   (C) Most foreign students read English.
   (D) Reading a few paragraphs a week is sufficient.

3. With which statement would the author agree?

    (A) The Structure and Written Expression section and the Reading Comprehension section test the same skills.

    (B) You read a newspaper differently than you do a text-book.

    (C) Reading right to left is an important skill.

    (D) Read only the material that interests you.

4. Most foreign students read English by

    (A) reading every word.

    (B) only reading the important words.

    (C) asking themselves "Why am I reading this?"

    (D) tearing out pages.

Questions 5 - 8

READING FOR INFORMATION

Reading for Information is the kind of reading you do in your own language. You do not stop to analyze tenses and clauses when you pick up a book written in your native language. You understand structure without thinking about it. It is second nature to you.

Now you must develop this skill in English. You must be able to read beyond the clause markers and prepositions and other structure clues. You must learn to read for meaning.

A reading comprehension test measures how well you understand the meaning of a passage. It measures your ability to understand the author's main idea and the facts used to support the main idea. It measures your ability to read "between the lines" and use contextual clues to infer what the author implied. It measures your ability to do this as quickly as a native speaker of English.

To improve your reading comprehension, you have to develop certain skills. These skills include skimming or scanning a reading passage; identifying the main idea and supporting statements; making inferences; and using context clues to help you guess.

SCANNING AND SKIMMING

Scanning means looking over a passage very quickly to find specific information such as a date, a name, or a particular word. Skimming means getting a quick, general overview of the passage. Both are techniques you will begin to use today and continue to use each time you read something in English or your own language. Every time you read you should use a technique called SQ3R: Survey, Question, Read, Review, and Recall.

5. According to the passage, a reading comprehension test measures all but

    (A) understanding the main idea.

    (B) reading "between the lines."

    (C) using "contextual clues."

    (D) your reading speed.

6. Developing reading skills will

    (A) measure your comprehension.

    (B) improve your comprehension.

    (C) improve your grammar.

    (D) increase your vocabulary.

7. The author believes you should

   (A) ignore grammar.
   (B) read only the first and the last lines.
   (C) get an overview of the passage.
   (D) look for clause markers.

8. *S* in *SQ3R* stands for

   (A) skim.
   (B) scan.
   (C) survey.
   (D) skill.

Questions 9 - 12

Survey

A good survey of a reading passage is very important. When you walk into a strange house at night, you may have no idea how large it is until you go through all the rooms, opening doors that lead into other rooms. Starting to read line by line is like exploring a house in the dark. You won't know what it's all about until you get to the end. Most people would feel more comfortable if they had some idea of how large the house was without walking through every room. Similarly, most people would feel more comfortable knowing what a book is about before they begin to read.

To survey a reading passage, you read the first and last lines and let your eye pick up as many words as it can in a few seconds. A survey should take no more than 5 or 10 seconds.

This survey will give you a *general idea* of the passage you are reading. You are preparing your brain for *specific information.* You can generally tell from your survey the main subject and the time of the passage.

Question

When you finish your survey, you know something, but not very much. You do not know *Who, When, What, Where,* and *Why.* So you begin to formulate some questions, questions that are of interest to you. For example, if in your survey you noticed the words *invention, 19th century,* and *Atlantic Ocean,* your questions might be:

> *Who invented something?*
> *Did they invent it in the 19th century?*
> *What did they invent?*
> *Where did they live?*
> *Did the invention cross over/above/ under the ocean?*
> *Why was this important?*

The reading passage may or may not answer those questions. That is not important. What is important is that you have a specific goal for reading and that you read towards that goal. Knowing that the answers are *not* in the passage is as important as finding the answers in the passage.

Read

Once you have made your survey and asked yourself questions to give yourself a goal for reading, you read. You read to find specific information that will answer your questions or that will create new questions. You have become an active reader with a purpose. You now read quickly and efficiently.

9. The author compares the first look at a reading passage with

    (A) your brain.
    (B) an invention.
    (C) a strange house.
    (D) the ocean.

10. A survey is important because

    (A) it takes only a few seconds.
    (B) it prepares you for details.
    (C) it answers questions.
    (D) everyone does it.

11. The author suggests you should first

    (A) read, question, then survey.
    (B) question, read, then survey.
    (C) question, survey, then read.
    (D) survey, question, then read.

12. With which line would the author agree?

    (A) To try is as important as to succeed.
    (B) All good things come to those who wait.
    (C) Do not work too hard.
    (D) A little knowledge is dangerous.

Questions 13 - 16

Review and Recall
If a text is important enough to read once, it is important enough to read again. So skim the passage again to pick up missing details and remind yourself of what was important. Tomorrow or later try to recall what you read. You should learn to test your own reading comprehension. What did the author want to say?

> *What generalizations did he make?*
> *With what facts did he support them?*
> *What did he imply?*

SQ3R AND THE TOEFL
In the TOEFL, there will be reading passages on a variety of topics. Some will interest you more than others. But you have to treat them as if they were equally important.

First, survey the reading passage. Do it in less than 5 seconds and try to formulate *who, what, when, where,* and *why* questions. Then survey the comprehension questions and answer choices.

> *What do they expect of you?*
> *Do they ask for the main idea?*
> *Do they ask for details?*
> *Do they ask for a definition?*
> *Do they ask for the author's opinion?*
> *Do they ask for your opinion?*

After you have surveyed the passage and formulated some questions, begin to read. **BUT READ QUICKLY! DO NOT READ WORD BY WORD.** Read phrase by phrase, idea by idea. Finish quickly and try to answer the questions.

If you cannot remember the answers, SCAN for the particular information. **DON'T READ EVERY WORD! SCAN THE PASSAGE!** Keep your eyes moving quickly, looking for specific information. Use contextual clues to help you locate that information.

13. According to the passage, the TOEFL has

    (A) surveys at the beginning of each section.
    (B) passages on a variety of topics.
    (C) listening comprehension questions.
    (D) SQ3R.

14. The author suggests you survey the reading passage

    (A) in 5 seconds.
    (B) as fast as you can.
    (C) tomorrow.
    (D) after you survey the questions.

15. The comprehension questions test all but your knowledge of

    (A) the main idea.
    (B) the author's arguments.
    (C) your ability to scan.
    (D) specific information.

16. The author believes it is important to

    (A) do things twice.
    (B) read word by word.
    (C) read every word.
    (D) have a large vocabulary.

Questions 17 - 20

CONTEXTUAL CLUES

Contextual Clues are clues that you take for granted in your own language and that you need to recognize instantly in English. They include punctuation marks, grammar markers, transition words, and discourse markers. These clues will help you locate specific answers for the comprehension questions you asked yourself. An explanation of these clues along with the kinds of questions you should ask yourself (subconsciously) when you see them is given below.

PUNCTUATION MARKS

How does the punctuation affect the meaning in a sentence?

Look for the punctuation mark that ends a sentence. Is it a period, a semicolon, a question mark, or an exclamation mark? A period separates thoughts; a semicolon shows a relationship between the two sentences. What is that relationship?

Look for an apostrophe. Does it show possession? If so, who possesses what? Or does the apostrophe contract two words (e.g., *I'll*)? If so, which words?

Look for a comma. Does it separate a series of adjectives or does it set off an initial adverbial clause that might give you a time reference? What is the purpose of that comma?

STRUCTURE MARKERS

What structure markers are available to determine a word's meaning in a sentence?

Here are some examples or structure markers: a noun follows *a, an* and *the*; adverbs often end in *-ly*; *-ness* is noun suffix; verb markers include modals, auxiliaries, and participle forms. What do these structure markers mean to you? How can they help you when you scan for specific information?

TRANSITION WORDS

Time
What is the time frame of the passage?

First, they did this. *Then* they did that. *Finally*, they did something else. *When* did they do something?

Look for the markers: *first, second, third....before, after, later, then, as soon as, when, while, at the same time*, etc. What time relationships do they imply?

Comparison and Contrast
How does the author use comparison and contrast markers to stress or shift the point he is making?

On the other hand, look at this. *However*, you should also look at that. *Similarly*, look at this other thing.

Contrast and comparison markers give you an idea of how the author shifts his argument to make his point. They include the following:

similarly	likewise
in like manner	for the comparison
and for contrast	but
yet	and yet
however	still
nevertheless	on the other hand
on the contrary	after all
at the same time	otherwise

17. Context clues are found in

    (A) the comprehension questions.
    (B) your own experience.
    (C) the listening section.
    - (D) your own language.

18. An apostrophe is

    - (A) a context clue.
    (B) a transition word.
    (C) a time reference.
    (D) found in every language.

19. All but one are time markers.

    (A) January
    (B) Second
    (C) Last
    - (D) Clockwise

20. Comparison and contrast markers are used to

    - (A) show similarities and differences.
    (B) summarize.
    (C) provide additional information.
    (D) confuse the reader.

QUESTIONS 21 - 24

Addition
How does the author add additional supporting statements to his arguments?

The author makes one point. Then, *in addition*, he makes another, using such appropriate contextual clues as the following:

moreover	further
furthermore	besides
likewise	also
nor	too
again	equally important

Place
To what location, if any, does the reading relate?

The author locates the passage using such contextual clues as:

here	opposite
beyond	on the other side of
nearby	adjacent to

Purpose
Why all this discussion?

The author highlights his purpose by using such contextual clues as the following:

well	to this end
for this purpose	with this objective

Result
What happens in the end?

Having detailed his arguments, the author draws a conclusion, using such contextual clues as these:

hence	therefore
accordingly	consequently
thus	as a result
then	as can be seen

Summary
When will this passage ever end?

Before the author finishes, he sums up by using such contextual clues as these:

in brief	on the whole
in sum	in short
as I have said	in other words
that is	to be sure
as has been noted	in any event

DISCOURSE MARKERS

Comparison and Contrast
How does the author describe an object, person, or emotion?

An author may want to explain a particular thing (or thought) by describing how it is like or how it is different from other things or thoughts. Look for contextual clues such as these:

both...and	whereas
as...as	although
like	while
-er	however
-est	but

Cause and Effect
How does the behavior of one element affect another element?

The author may want to show you how the behavior of one element causes a certain behavior in another or several other elements. The contextual clues commonly associated with this style of discourse follow.

the consequence	why
consequently	as a result
therefore	the cause
the effect	for this reason
thus	because
result in	engendered
accordingly	when
if	by
as	the...-er, the...-er
so	due to
through	bring about
hence	for
cause	procedure

Process
How was something done?

The author may want to explain how something is done or how something is made. Contextual clues such as these can be used to explain a process:

first	second	third
then	next	before
when	during	while
as soon as	at the same time as	

Generalizations and Specifics
What facts support the main idea?

A writer may make several specific statements and then summarize them with one general statement. This generalization may be followed with specific facts. Some of these contextual clues or discourse markers follow.

in general	for example (e.g.)
that is (i.e.)	in summary
one, two	a case in point

Chronological Order
When did the events occur?

You saw some of these contextual clues above in the section *Transition Words*. Here an author uses the same markers to tell you the sequence in which events occurred:

after	while	before
first	next	eventually
second	then	subsequently
third	as	finally
prior to	when	simultaneously

PRACTICE

Now you have been given the tools that will help you read efficiently. You know how to skim, read for general information, and scan for specific ideas. You know how to use contextual clues to help you locate both general and specific information. You know how to recognize discourse markers. It is up to you now. Reading is a very private skill. You are in control of your actions.

21. Discourse means

   (A) the style of a passage.
   (B) the author's summary.
   (C) the effect of the passage.
   (D) the markers.

22. The author believes

   (A) recognizing clues makes you an efficient reader.
   (B) the process provides the explanation.
   (C) generalizations always follow facts.
   (D) comparing is more interesting than contrasting.

23. *On the other side* and *beyond* are what kind of markers?

   (A) addition
   (B) cause
   (C) place
   (D) contrast

24. Now that you have the tools, you must

   (A) summarize.
   (B) skim.
   (C) practice.
   (D) look for specific ideas.

GENERAL READING

ANNOUNCEMENTS

Questions 1 -3

The School of Education is responsible for professional courses and certification recommendations for students desiring to complete requirements for the Mid-Atlantic Teaching Certificate. All students from the School of Education and those from other state-approved training courses responsible for training teachers, administrators, counselors, and related instructional personnel must meet the requirements established by the School of Education. Prior to certification, a student's scores on the National Teacher Examination must be submitted in duplicate to the Office of the Dean. Information on this examination is available from the Teacher Certification Specialists in the Administrative Office.

1. The Certificate program is primarily for

   (A) experienced administrators.
   (B) specialists.
   (C) teachers in training.
   (D) the Dean's Office.

2. The Office of the Dean requires

   (A) two copies of the test scores.
   (B) a Teacher's Certificate.

   (C) Certification Specialists.
   (D) professional courses.

3. Students who take the National Teacher Examinations do not want to

   (A) teach chemistry.
   (B) counsel students.
   (C) work in the Dean's Office.
   (D) administer science programs.

Questions 4 - 7

THE SOUNDOFF JACKET

A brilliant combination in style and sound. This zip-off sleeve polyester jacket serves as either a jacket or -- zip off the sleeves -- a vest! There are outside compartments to hold your pocket tape player and cassette tapes. Slip on your jacket, adjust your headphones, and swing to the rhythm. Walk, jog, bike in comfort and style...in stereo sound. Men's XS-S-M-L $24.90 (reg. $34.99). Sale thru Saturday.

4. What article is for sale?

(A) Clothing
(B) A tape player
(C) A bike
(D) Headphones

5. Where is the tape player kept?

(A) In the hand
(B) On the bike
(C) In pockets
(D) At home

6. Which of the following is true?

(A) The vest is sold separately from the jacket.
(B) The jacket is available only for men.
(C) The jacket is not made of synthetic fiber.
(D) The stereo is part of the jacket.

7. On Saturday the jacket will

(A) cost $24.90.
(B) cost $34.99.
(C) be sold out.
(D) be marked up.

Questions 8 - 10

PREPARATION FOR VISION TESTING

Place the instrument on a table of conventional height, with sufficient surface area to permit the person conducting the tests to record results and manipulate the various controls. The subject should be able to get his knees comfortably under the table as the subject is seated at the instrument. Avoid positioning the instrument where strong, glaring light, such as sunlight, shines directly into the instrument or on the subject's face. The vision tests can be administered under normal room illumination (daylight or artificial) as the instrument is sufficiently hooded and protected so that outside illumination does not affect the results.

8. The instrument should be placed

(A) in a dark room.
(B) close to the subject's knees.
(C) in direct sunlight.
(D) on a table with ample room for the tester.

9. For the test, the room must

(A) be darkened.
(B) be brightly lit.
(C) have average lighting.
(D) be free of dust.

10. The result of the vision test could be made invalid by

(A) the person recording the results.
(B) outside light.
(C) a low table.
(D) the various controls.

HUMANITIES

Questions 1 - 4

Architecture and the applied and decorative arts have an essentially practical base: they serve the physical needs of society before they supply anything in enjoyment, inspiration, and aesthetic satisfaction. Buildings are made to shelter and protect and to provide a range of solutions to desired uses (temples, tombs, churches, palaces, stadia, factories, storage for a variety of products or materials, and, in great variety of scale and need, homes). They are made to be used, are justified by their use, and their effectiveness in use is a part measure of their quality. In the same way, the artifacts of society (furniture, ceramics, textiles, metalwork, and, more recently, plasticware, etc.) are made to be used and justified in use. The forms of such artifacts are not always, or even usually, determined by their simple use (a chair for sitting on) any more than the forms of building are.

1. From the passage, we can infer that the visual arts are

   (A) practical in many respects.
   (B) impractical in most respects.
   (C) theoretical in design.
   (D) unjustified.

2. What do the applied arts have in common with the artifacts of society?

   (A) They are made and justified by their use.
   (B) They are pleasing to the eye.
   (C) They satisfy our aesthetic sensibilities.
   (D) They are created by artisans, not by artists.

3. The author implies, but does not directly state, that

   (A) the best art is applied art.
   (B) art that cannot be used is worthless.
   (C) artifacts have more than just simple uses.
   (D) the world could use more architects.

4. The phrase "their effectiveness in use is a measure of their quality" refers to

   (A) products or materials.
   (B) buildings.
   (C) solutions.
   (D) artifacts.

Questions 5 - 7

The importance of architecture in the effective working of a complex civilization gives it a special position between the applied and decorative arts and the fine arts of painting and sculpture. For this reason, architecture is sometimes called "Mother of the Arts." The practical opportunities and limitations of architectural creativity make it peculiarly difficult to analyze, but, its specific technology apart, it is subject to the same processes as the fine arts of painting and sculpture. Painting and sculpture, on the other hand, have very little if any practical use. Their value depends on the emotive or intellectual effectiveness of their imagery and has almost nothing to do with their small cost in materials, in contrast to architecture and the materials employed in the applied arts.

5. Architecture is sometimes referred to as the "Mother of the Arts" because

   (A) it is the most important art.

   (B) it has much in common with the other arts.
   (C) it is essential to all societies.
   (D) it is more important than most other arts.

6. Which of the following terms does not characterize architecture?

  (A) Practical
  (B) Limited
  (C) Resistant to analysis
  (D) Peculiar

7. In which of the following aspects are sculpture and architecture related?

  (A) Practicality
  (B) Cost
  (C) The creative process
  (D) Limitations

HISTORY

Questions 1 - 3

The popular mind was excited by these new developments. So far as Einstein could be understood, he was saying that it was no longer possible for ordinary people to comprehend the universe, and that what scientists actually did understand was strange and unsettling. Time, space, matter, energy -- all these dissolved, shifted, blurred. Everything depended on where the observer was located; relativity replaced fixity; ultimate things were hidden.

1. Another way to say what Einstein was saying is that

  (A) nobody would ever be able to study the nature of the universe.
  (B) nonscientists would no longer be able to comprehend the universe, but scientists would.
  (C) even scientists would have trouble comprehending the universe.
  (D) people should give up trying to understand the universe.

2. Which of the following would be strange to a scientist?

  (A) The dissolution of energy

  (B) The concealment of ultimate things
  (C) Time-space shifts
  (D) All of the above

3. The author implies, but does not directly state, that

  (A) Einstein was a very strange man.
  (B) people were drawn to Einstein's work because it was so controversial.
  (C) relativity is the final word in physics.
  (D) man will never prove that God exists.

Questions 4 - 7

In the early 1930's a new religious voice burst on the American scene, that of Reinhold Niebuhr. Soon he became the most influential thinker in American Protestantism. Niebuhr had watched national and international developments from his pastorate in Detroit in a mood of growing disenchantment. The war had horrified him. The facts of industrial life in Detroit convinced him that it was fruitless to preach sermons about love and kindness, for the actual conditions of survival made it impossible for people to be always loving and kind.

4. Reinhold Niebuhr must have been

  (A) an antiwar activist.

  (B) a theologian.
  (C) a disenchanted rebel.
  (D) a cynic.

228   **Reading Targets**

5. Niebuhr came to prominence from

(A) a European background.
(B) his Protestant background.
(C) an American religious post.
(D) an undistinguished post.

6. The event which horrified Niebuhr must have been

(A) World War I.
(B) the actual conditions of survival.
(C) the Great Depression.
(D) the downfall of American Protestantism.

7. The writer implies, but does not directly state, that

(A) Niebuhr converted to a different religion.
(B) Niebuhr urged men to be loving and kind.
(C) Niebuhr stopped being loving and kind.
(D) Niebuhr gave up the idea that man could always be loving and kind.

EDUCATION

Questions 1 - 5

It is true that as a social organization moves from the simple to the complex, so does the organization through which it educates its children. Growth and change are vital if education is to meet new needs and demands. In a very simple social order it may suffice to have the parents carry on the education of their children. However, as will be shown later in more detail, such a method may become entirely untenable, and special individuals are entrusted with the task. These may be hired privately at first, but soon the social group -- the church, village, and the like -- will be responsible for education. Eventually, special training is required for those who do the teaching, and an agency to control this training is needed. Thus the influence of the local governmental unit, such as the town, township, and later the state or the province, becomes necessary. It was generally considered simpler to use as a unit the already existing local unit.

1. The closest restatement of the first sentence is

(A) The more complex a social organization becomes, the more complex the educational system becomes.
(B) The complexity of a social organization depends on the complexity of the educational system.
(C) Social organizations are truly as complex as they need to be for educational purposes.
(D) Our society must be complex if we want our education sytem to serve our children's educational requirements.

2. The writer would probably argue for

(A) more parental influence in education.
(B) an educational system which takes social complexity into account.
(C) strict state control of education.
(D) more special training for teachers.

3. The method which the author says might become entirely untenable is

(A) the method of social organization.
(B) parental education of children.
(C) a simple social order.
(D) the entrustment of education to special individuals.

4. According to the passage, the reason why the local governmental unit becomes influential is that

(A) teachers become too powerful.
(B) enrollment increases.
(C) a need arises to control the education of teachers.
(D) the church or village lacks the ability to oversee education.

5. The author promises to explain

(A) the necessity of the local governmental unit.
(B) why it is easier to use the government to control education.
(C) the responsibility of the social group.
(D) why parents should not teach their children.

Questions 6 - 9

The kindergarten child will develop many interests in the world around him and the teacher can use field trips to the schoolground or around the block to arouse interests to the point of having projects grow out of these experiences. For example, a story about buildings or pets, plus a walk around the schoolyard with the teacher pointing out the things described in a story, can generate ideas for many pictures done with crayons or paints. The child is thus developing ways of communicating. He uses his picture and talks about his experience. The regular routine of the days in kindergarten helps children establish certain patterns of living. Going to the toilet, washing hands, and getting drinks all help in establishing habits of orderly living. All of these things are part of a maturity schedule which prepare a child for his next stage of growth.

6. The main idea of this passage concerns

(A) the development of kindergarten children.
(B) communication patterns of young children.
(C) the maturation of children.
(D) living patterns of children.

7. The field trips referred to in the passage would be

(A) rather long trips.
(B) confined to the vicinity of the school.
(C) good opportunities to get out of the classroom.
(D) part of the regular routine.

8. Habits established in kindergarten should

(A) be changed by the parents.
(B) be carefully monitored by the teacher.
(C) generate ideas about life.
(D) get a child ready for the next growth period.

9. The value of field trips is that

(A) that the child will gain ideas for future school projects.
(B) that the child will learn to be independent.
(C) that the child will meet new friends.
(D) none of the above.

BUSINESS

Questions 1 - 5

Cotton was not the nation's only agribusiness before the Civil War. The tobacco, rice, sugar, livestock, lumbering, and wheat industries accounted for more dollar income than cotton, but not one of them alone before 1860, or even 1900, approached the dollar value of cotton. Each of these commodities involved hundreds of middlemen for every single producer, creating an intricate web of trade and commerce that stretched across North America to Europe. The cotton plantation employing slave labor marked only the first stage in the business of producing, marketing, and distributing cotton products.

1. The agribusiness with the highest dollar value in the United States between 1860 and 1900 was

   (A) cotton.
   (B) tobacco.
   (C) livestock.
   (D) wheat.

2. The cotton plantation was involved in which of the following activities?

   (A) Marketing cotton products
   (B) Distributing cotton products
   (C) Producing cotton products
   (D) The enslavement of black workers

3. The dollar income of cotton exceeded the dollar income of

   (A) tobacco.
   (B) sugar.
   (C) lumbering.
   (D) all of the above.

4. The commodities mentioned in the paragraph were marketed in

   (A) Europe and the United States.
   (B) Europe and Canada.
   (C) Canada and the United States.
   (D) America, Canada, and Europe.

5. Which of the following statements is true?

   (A) The dollar value of cotton did not approach the dollar value of sugar.
   (B) Each agribusiness required middlemen and slaves.
   (C) U.S. agribusiness prior to 1900 depended on the participation of many individuals.
   (D) The cotton plantation stopped employing slave labor after 1800.

Questions 6 - 10

Although the Constitution organized the American states into what was then the largest free-trade zone in the world, geographical constraints sorely inhibited trade and commerce. Enormous physical obstacles and great distances divided the republic. Henry Adams wrote, "No civilized country had yet been required to deal with physical difficulties so serious, nor did experience warrant the conviction that such difficulties could be overcome." From colonial times to the beginning of the 19th century, the movement of goods from the places of production to the points of sale continued to be a major problem for merchants and consumers alike. Throughout much of the nation, goods were transported by water from coastal port to coastal port and along navigable rivers and streams. Some freight moved over primitive, rutted roads, but in many areas the absence of roads meant that commodities could be transported only by pack horse. The cost of shipping items in such fashion often exceeded their value. Conditions for travelers were equally as bad. A 5-day trip north from Philadelphia would take a traveler only as far as Connecticut. The political and economic leaders of the country recognized the obstacles to commerce that distance and geographical barriers presented. Entrepreneurs and politicians proposed many internal development schemes to improve transportation. In most instances these involved local and state improvements, and the projects called invariably for the expenditure of substantial amounts of capital.

6. Which statement most accurately restates the main idea of this paragraph?

   (A) The U.S. Constitution was responsible for restrictions on business during colonial times.
   (B) The size and physical nature of the U.S. prevented the expansion of trade and commerce from colonial times to the early 1800's.
   (C) Businessmen and politicians were successful in their attempts to improve transportation.
   (D) Transportation projects were extremely expensive before 1800.

7. The quote from Henry Adams implies, but does not directly state, that

   (A) the U.S. was the first civilized country with physical difficulties.
   (B) the Americans believed that they could overcome their physical difficulties.
   (C) many Americans doubted that geographical constraints could be overcome.
   (D) Henry Adams was opposed to the expansion of trade and commerce.

8. Which of the following statements is true?

   (A) It was more expensive to ship items by water than by land.
   (B) Shipping items by water was less costly than shipping by land.
   (C) The cost of shipping items by pack horse was frequently more expensive than the goods which were being supplied.
   (D) Pack horses were necessary in areas where there was no water.

9. Traveling was

   (A) much easier than shipping.
   (B) more difficult than shipping.
   (C) just as difficult as shipping.
   (D) necessary if you wanted to buy goods.

10. The passage implies, but does not directly state, that

   (A) transportation problems prior to 1800 caused many businessmen to give up.
   (B) improvement of trade and commerce in early U.S. history required hard work and imagination by enterpreneurs and businessmen.
   (C) small countries have fewer economic problems than big countries.
   (D) big countries with no geographic constraints have few commercial problems.

SCIENCE

Questions 1 - 4

The basic idea of spontaneous generation can be easily understood. If food is allowed to stand for some time, it putrefies, and when the putrefied material is examined microscopically, it is found to be teeming with bacteria. Where do these bacteria come from, since they are not seen in fresh food? Some people said they developed from seeds or germs that entered the food from the air, whereas others said that they arose spontaneously.

Spontaneous generation would mean that life could arise from something nonliving, and many people could not imagine something so complex as a living cell arising spontaneously from dead materials. The most powerful opponent of spontaneous generation was the French chemist Louis Pasteur, whose work on this problem was the most exacting and convincing.

1. Spontaneous generation is defined as

   (A) the process by which food gets rotten.
   (B) the microscopic examination of bacteria.
   (C) the view that bacteria grow from seeds or germs in the air.
   (D) not enough information.

2. Louis Pasteur was an advocate of the view that

   (A) germs arose spontaneously.
   (B) germs entered food from the atmosphere.
   (C) life could arise from dead materials.
   (D) food should be examined microscopically for bacteria.

3. The author's view of Pasteur's work is that

   (A) Pasteur convinced everyone that he was correct.
   (B) Pasteur was quite careful and precise.
   (C) Pasteur made some basic mistakes.
   (D) Pasteur spent hours perfecting his experiments.

4. The reason why many people tended to agree with Pasteur is that

   (A) the alternative view seemed outrageous.
   (B) Pasteur rarely made mistakes.
   (C) his explanation was consistent with their religious views.
   (D) Pasteur was the greatest scientist of his day.

Questions 5 - 8

Ecology's roots extend to the origins of humanity itself. Our ancestors had to have been students of their environment, else our species would have been extinguished. Conscious observations of their surroundings can be traced to ancient civilizations, especially in matters of agriculture, but more formal and systematic study began in the third and fourth centuries B.C. Among the early natural historians were Aristotle and, most notable, his student and successor as head of the Lyceum, Theophrastus. In the best natural history writing then and since, there is careful attention to detail, precise recording of information, recognition and interpretation of variables, and awareness of the contributions of others.

Although studies on natural history of plants and animals formed and still serve as a cornerstone for modern ecology, they lacked the unifying focus that is critical to the development of concepts and theories. While definitions of a field of inquiry do not necessarily eliminate all ambiguities, they do set boundaries, sharpen perspectives, and give direction. The introduction and evolution of the meaning of the term "ecology" have done just that.

5. The science of ecology

   (A) began in the third and fourth centuries B.C.
   (B) began when people started to observe their environment.
   (C) was invented by Aristotle.
   (D) helped prevent the human race from being extinguished.

6. According to the author, one condition which guides the scientific writing of natural history is

   (A) knowing what others have done.
   (B) conscious attention to the environment.
   (C) mass collection of information.
   (D) being able to interpret every single variable.

7. The history of the term "ecology" has

(A) eliminated all ambiguities.
(B) depended on studies of natural history.
(C) helped focus efforts to resolve ambiguities.
(D) been long and interesting.

8. The author probably continues the essay with

(A) an attempt to define "ecology" once and for all.
(B) an analysis of the work done by Theophrastus.
(C) quotations from ancient ecological texts.
(D) an account of the first use of the term "ecology."

APPLIED SCIENCE

Questions 1 - 4

We now define "psychology" as the study of human behavior by scientific methods. "Behavior," as used here, refers to more than conduct, deportment, or manner. It includes all normal and abnormal activities of the whole organism, even those of the mentally retarded and mentally ill. The purposes of this study are to explore the roles of behavior in self-discovery and the varied beneficent behavioral patterns the individual can develop. The aims of applied psychology are the description, prediction, and control of human activities in order that we may understand and intelligently direct our own lives and influence the lives of others.

1. The main purpose of this passage is to

(A) explain behavior.
(B) introduce the scientific method.
(C) define some key terms.
(D) define applied psychology.

2. The primary difference between the ordinary use of the term "behavior" and its special sense here is that the

(A) ordinary use is broader.
(B) ordinary use is narrower.
(C) special sense is more useful.
(D) special sense is more correct.

3. The writer's use of the term "beneficent" suggests that he or she

(A) believes that psychology can do some good for mankind.
(B) wants mankind to be better.
(C) plans to delineate a new theory.
(D) believes that psychology has its limits.

4. One of the subjects which an applied psychologist would not be directly interested in would be

(A) behavior modification.
(B) thought control.
(C) animal behavior.
(D) the description of normal human activity.

Questions 5 - 7

We want to learn to think of human behavior in its dynamic aspects -- strivings, motivations, and adjustments to problems. These, of course, cannot be observed directly but they can be correctly inferred if we study behavior systematically.

The human being operates in as natural a manner as do other parts of the physical world. Every human act could be understood if we knew all the pertinent facts.

True, we do not know all the important facts needed to understand each person, but we believe that a person's behavior can be understood on the basis of principles that can be learned.

5. The writer believes that

   (A) motivation can be studied directly by trained observers.
   (B) a systematic approach to behavior is necessary in order to learn about human motivation.
   (C) human beings behave systematically.
   (D) all the pertinent facts about human behavior are open to inspection.

6. The reason why the author believes we need to collect pertinent facts about human behavior is that

   (A) we cannot learn anything without facts.
   (B) behavior can be reduced to facts.
   (C) the development of psychology demands more facts.
   (D) important principles can be inferred from facts.

7. When the author refers to the dynamic aspects of human behavior, he or she is contrasting aspects like motivation with aspects which

   (A) are easier to understand.
   (B) are more difficult to understand.
   (C) do not change.
   (D) do not concern psychologists.

RESTATEMENTS

Select the statement that most nearly matches the original statement. Many of the statements are true, but only one is a restatement of the original.

1. She reminded him to recommend her brother for the position.

   (A) He recommended that her brother apply for the position after she reminded him to do so.
   (B) Her brother was to be recommended for the job.
   (C) She told him that he should remember to recommend her brother for the position.
   (D) Her brother recommended her for the position.

2. The family entered the room, fearful of the news which the doctor would give them.

   (A) As they entered the room, the family felt uneasy as the doctor prepared to reveal the fearful news.
   (B) The doctor gave the family the bad news as they entered the room.
   (C) The doctor gave the news prior to the family's entrance.
   (D) Entering the room, the family felt a sense of dread with respect to the news which the doctor was going to disclose.

3. Working as a pediatrician has certain disadvantages which are far outweighed by the advantages.

   (A) The disadvantages of being a pediatrician far outweigh the advantages.
   (B) Working pediatricians have far greater disadvantages than advantages.
   (C) There are some negative aspects about the pediatrician's work; however, the positive aspects are far greater.
   (D) Baby doctors have both advantages and disadvantages with the former far greater.

4. The finest guitars are made in our workshop, where the craftsmen still use only the finest wood.

   (A) Our fine guitars are made by craftsmen who use only choice wood.
   (B) Our craftsmen make fine guitars out of the choicest wood.
   (C) Our workshop is the home of the finest guitars -- guitars made of the choicest wood.
   (D) In our workshop, where craftsmen continue to use only the choicest wood, the finest guitars are produced.

5. Psychology can be defined as the scientific study of human behavior.

   (A) Psychology is the study of human behavior.
   (B) Psychologists study human behavior scientifically.
   (C) One way to define psychology is to call it the scientific study of human behavior.
   (D) The scientific study of human behavior is psychology.

6. Rapid dissemination of information is undoubtedly the hallmark of the computer age.

   (A) Nobody doubts that news travels quickly in the computer age.
   (B) Undoubtedly, the computer age is most noteworthy for the rapid dissemination of data.
   (C) Computers store great amounts of information; this is why the computer age is so notorious.
   (D) The age of the computer came into its own with the undoubtedly rapid dissemination of information.

7. Wisdom is the chief goal of the true philosopher.

   (A) The true philosopher is interested in wisdom, nothing else.
   (B) A philosopher who is honest takes wisdom as his only goal.

   (C) The primary pursuit of the true philosopher is wisdom.
   (D) Among the philosopher's many goals, none is truer than the chief goal of wisdom.

8. In order to meet her deadline, the journalist set aside several less pressing assignments.

   (A) The reason why the journalist held several less urgent jobs in abeyance was that she had a deadline to meet.
   (B) Provided that her deadline can be met, other important assignments can be finished.
   (C) Her reason for meeting the deadline was the journalist's excuse for not attending to other less pressing assignments.
   (D) Meeting her deadline required that the journalist delegate several less pressing jobs.

9. Our town is famous for its theater, even though its theater district is now a hotbed of crime.

   (A) Crime is rampant in our town's theater district.
   (B) In addition to its hotbed of crime, our town has a well-known theater area.
   (C) Our town is known for theater, although criminal activity is rampant in its theater district.
   (D) Our town's famous theaters are surrounded by robbers.

10. The room fell into silence when the President appeared to make his announcement.

   (A) The President's announcement appeared to cause silence in the room.
   (B) The noise in the room abated when the President walked in to announce the news.
   (C) The President waited for silence before he entered the room to give the news.
   (D) Silence fell over the room as the President seemed to speak.

READING TARGET ANSWER KEY

INTRODUCTION

1. (C)	7. (C)	13. (B)	19. (D)
2. (A)	8. (C)	14. (B)	20. (A)
3. (B)	9. (C)	15. (C)	21. (A)
4. (A)	10. (B)	16. (A)	22. (A)
5. (D)	11. (D)	17. (D)	23. (C)
6. (B)	12. (A)	18. (A)	24. (C)

GENERAL READING

Announcements	*Advertisements*	*Instructions*
1. (C) - main idea	4. (A) - main idea	8. (D) - fact
2. (A) - fact	5. (C) - fact	9. (C) - fact
3. (C) - inference	6. (B) - fact	10. (B) - fact
	7. (A) - fact	

HUMANITIES

1. (A) - inference	3. (C) - inference	5. (B) - inference
2. (A) - skim	4. (B) - paraphrase	6. (D) - fact
		7. (C) - fact

HISTORY

1. (C) - paraphrase	3. (B) - inference	5. (C) - vocabulary
2. (D) - inference	4. ˥(B) - inference	6. (A) - fact
		7. (D) - inference

EDUCATION

1. (A) - paraphrase	4. (C) - inference	7. (B) - inference
2. (B) - inference	5. (D) - inference	8. (D) - fact
3. (B) - fact	6. (A) - main idea	9. (A) - paraphrase

BUSINESS

1. (A) - fact	4. (D) - inference	7. (C) - inference
2. (B) - inference	5. (C) - paraphrase	8. (C) - fact
3. (D) - fact	6. (B) - main idea	9. (C) - fact
		10. (B) - inference

SCIENCE

1. (D) - definition	4. (A) - inference	7. (C) - skim
2. (B) - inference	5. (B) - paraphrase	8. (D) - inference
3. (B) - vocabulary	6. (A) - paraphrase	

APPLIED SCIENCE

1. (C) - main idea	3. (A) - inference	5. (B) - inference
2. (B) - inference	4. (C) - inference	6. (D) - fact
		7. (C) - vocabulary

RESTATEMENTS

1. (C)	4. (D)	7. (C)
2. (D)	5. (C)	8. (A)
3. (C)	6. (B)	9. (C)
		10. (B)

ESSAY TARGETS

INTRODUCTION

July 11, 1986 -- First TOEFL Essay

As the result of numerous requests from college and university officials and teachers, the TOEFL Program has decided to institute an essay exam on the TOEFL. The Essay section will add a fourth section to the exam.

You will be required to write a 250 to 300 word essay in 30 minutes. You will not have a choice of topic. You will be given a topic that you must develop into a cohesive, grammatical essay in the allotted time.

Your essay will be read by 2 experienced, trained evaluators who will each give your essay a score of 1 to 6. The average of these two scores will be your score. If the readers' interpretations of your essay differ by more than 2 points, a third evaluator will read your essay.

The institutions that receive your score reports will not receive a copy of your essay. They will receive only the TOEFL score report with the essay score 1 to 6.

6	Excellent
5	Very Good
4	Good
3	Needs improvement
2	Needs improvement
1	Needs improvement

The descriptive interpretation above is not an official TOEFL Program interpretation, and those descriptions will not accompany the scores. The descriptions (*Excellent, Good, Needs Improvement*) are to help you understand the ranking. Each institution receiving the score will interpret it using its own guidelines.

The essay graders will be evaluating the following:
1. Appropriate development of topic
2. Clear, succinct presentation
3. Logical organization
4. Fluent Style
5. Appropriate vocabulary
6. Coherent structure
7. Standard spelling and punctuation

PREPARING FOR THE ESSAY SECTION

Organizing the Content
Different cultures have different organizational styles. English uses a linear style of organization. It is important to learn how to write in the linear style common to most English essays. A good way to become familiar with a linear style of organization is to practice outlining. In the reading passages in the **Super TOEFL Book**, try to find the general statements and the facts that support those statements. After you have outlined them, rewrite them (paraphrase them). This will give you practice in outlining, writing, and paraphrasing. A model of an outline may be seen in the essay exercise section which follows.

The most important part of any essay is to think and plan *before* you begin to write. Before you make any attempt to write the essay itself, you should have decided what you are going to say and what facts will support your arguments.

Organizing the Essay
It is more important to write an essay that is well organized and paragraphs that are well developed than to try to use complicated grammatical structures and "big" words. You should try to use the structures and the words you know well even if they would seem simple if translated in your own language. Written English is very straight forward. Try to express your ideas as simply as possible.

A typical 250 to 300 word essay is made up of three distinct parts:

Introduction	Alert your readers to what you intend to say
Body	Tell them about your subject
Conclusion	Remind them what you said

Generally the introduction and conclusion are each one paragraph long. The body of the essay may be several paragraphs long.

Organizing the Paragraph
A typical paragraph is made up of one *General Statement* followed by several *Supporting Statements (Facts)*.

General Statement
Inner city neighborhoods are noisy.

Supporting Statements
Trucks and buses run along the streets all day long.
Children play games in their yards until evening.
Radios and TV can be heard from open windows.
Airplanes fly low overhead.

The general statements are often paraphrased and combined in the introduction to prepare (alert) the reader; the introduction states the writer's intentions. The general statements are often paraphrased and combined again in the conclusion of the essay to remind the reader of the author's intentions.

Checking you own work
You should learn to be your own critic. You should allow a few minutes before the end of the 30 minutes to review and revise you work. You should look for misspellings, grammatical errors, and errors in organizational style.

Essay Topics
You will have no choice of topic on the Essay section. But there are several discourse styles in English that you should be aware of.
Comparing and Contrasting
Describing a Chart or Graph
Stating a Personal Opinion
Stating a Case

Below are lists of vocabulary and grammar patterns often associated with these four discourse styles. If you become familiar with these styles and the vocabulary associated with these styles, you will be better prepared to develop your essay. The essay question on the TOEFL may combine two or more of these styles.

Comparing and Contrasting

Contrast	Contrast	Compare
but . . . than	and . . . than	and
than	instead of	like
unlike	but . . . as	as . . . as
more	-er	but . : .than
and	-est	more . . .-er

Describing a Chart or Graph

bottom	circle	right hand side
top	square	left hand side
data	figure	table
increased	extend	begin
decreased	stop	last until

Stating A Personal Opinion
Personal opinions are not necessarily facts and are often expressed using vocabulary and grammatical structures that suggest supposition.

The passive voice
> It is thought that the family is less important as a social unit today than it was 50 years ago.

Personal nouns and pronouns *I, you, he, she, we, they, it*
> We support the free trade movement, but they do not.
> Gandhi believed conflicts should be resolved peacefully.

Adverbial qualifiers *probably, likely, maybe, usually,* and so forth.
> The future is likely to be more difficult for me than for the next generation.

Verbs *believe, think, seem, consider, agree, content, claim, suppose,* and so forth.
> I agree with the main tenets of the proposal.

Prepositional Phrases: *In my view, in my opinion, according to me,* and so forth.
> In my opinion, the law should be rescinded.

Stating a Case
In making an argument, you may have to describe a situation at the present time (*description*); how it might be changed (*process*); and what effect the change might cause (*cause and effect/prediction*).

Description
The vocabulary used for this section will depend, of course, on what is being described. You should practice for this section by writing physical descriptions of people, buildings, and cities. In addition, you should practice writing descriptions of ideas (for example, *What is the Theory of Relativity?*).

Process

first	then	during
second	next	while
third	before	when

Cause and Effect

the consequence	accordingly	that is why
as a result	if	for
therefore	by	cause
for this reason	so	make
thus	because of	provided
because	through	unless
result in	bring about	ensues
hence	when	as

Prediction

predict (that)	in the future	in the foreseeable future
projected	It is likely that...	most likely consequences
foresee	inevitable outcome	the future implications
the next step	subsequent move	the end result
probability of	plan to	presume

Practice

To be a good reader, you must read, read, and read. Similarly, to be a good writer, you must write, write, and write. Try to combine your reading practice with your writing practice. After you finish one of the reading passages in this book, you should formulate a question similar to the sample questions in this section and then write a response to your question.

Additional practice is found in the sample questions on the following pages. You should develop an essay from each one of the questions. On the left hand side of the book, prepare an outline for your essay. After you have prepared the outline, write the essay and revise it on the right hand side.

You may do a couple of the questions to practice organizing your thoughts without timing yourself. But you should soon begin to limit yourself to 30 minutes.

This timetable will help you organize your time.

8 minutes	Prepare an outline
5 minutes	Write the introduction
7 minutes	Write the body
5 minutes	Write the conclusion
5 minutes	Review and revise

For more help with your writing, refer to one of the Prentice-Hall writing texts listed in the back of this book.

ESSAY EXERCISE

INTRODUCTION:

_____

_____

_____

BODY:
(You may have more or less than 3 General Statements: you may have more or less than 3 Facts.)

General Statement 1: _____

    Fact 1: _____

    Fact 2: _____

    Fact 3: _____

General Statement 2: _____

    Fact 1: _____

    Fact 2: _____

    Fact 3: _____

General Statement 3: _____

    Fact 1: _____

    Fact 2: _____

    Fact 3: _____

CONCLUSION:

_____

_____

_____

Directions for the Essay Section:
You are to write a cohesive, grammatically correct essay on the following topic. You will have 30 minutes to compose a 250 to 300 word essay.

Question:
There are advantages and disadvantages to living and working in either a small town or a large city. Give one or two advantages and disadvantages of living in either. In which would you prefer to live and why?

Now, using the same format as the previous two pages, answer the following essay questions.

COMPARING AND CONTRASTING

Question:
People choose to have large families for many reasons. What are the advantages and disadvantages of a large family? Which would you prefer and why?

Question:
In U.S. universities and colleges, students sometimes are obliged to share a room with a stranger or live by themselves. Describe briefly what you think are the negative and postive aspects of sharing a room with a stranger or living by yourself. Which living arrangement would you prefer and why?

DESCRIBING A GRAPH

Question:
Compare the two graphs and write a few sentences comparing the figures in each.

Is there a correlation between your study habits and your grades? What is your best subject? Why is it your best subject?

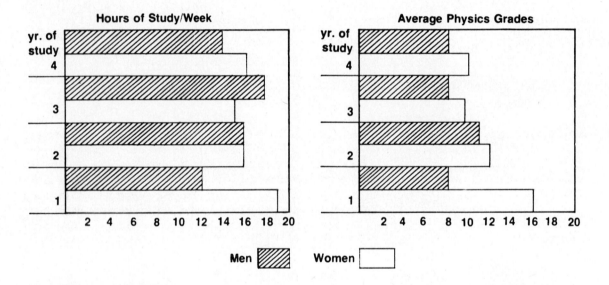

Question:
Compare the two graphs and write a few sentences comparing the findings of each.

Describe what you know about your own country's literacy rate and your government's expenditures on education.

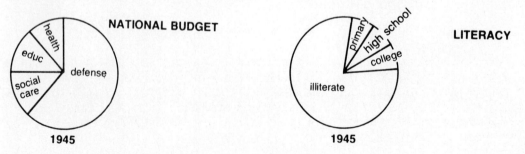

Question:
Compare the two graphs and write a few sentences comparing the figures in each.

What do you know about the rate of cancer and the number of smokers in your country? What conclusions can you draw from the graph about your own health?

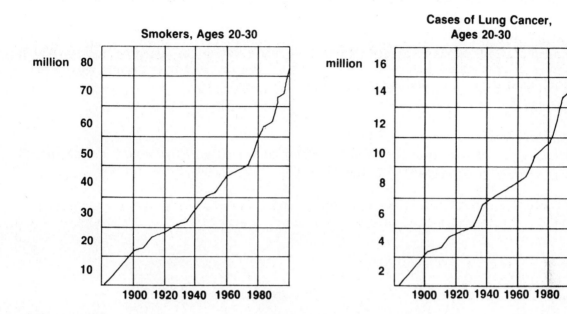

Smokers, Ages 20-30

Cases of Lung Cancer, Ages 20-30

STATING A CASE

Question:
Zoning regulations in the city prohibit buildings over three stories tall. A developer has applied to the city to build a six story building. The six story building would displace many low-income families and would be different from the buildings in the neighborhood. The developer has promised to add a much needed community center and other public services. As a citizen of the community, you must decide whether or not you support the developer and write your reasons to the city council.

Question:
Country X has little arable land. Country Z has lush vegetation and borders a sea. A river flows through Country X to Country Z and the sea. Country Z plans to divert the river to provide more water for its arid lands. State the arguments for and against the diversion. Tell which side you support and why.

Question:
The government has decided to build a new international airport that is much larger than the present one. It will create more jobs and allow bigger and more planes to land, thus increasing trade potential. The airport will be two hours away from the city center and will be built in the middle of a traditional farming community. Give the arguments both pro and con for the airport and tell why you favor one side.

Question:
Continuing your education in a foreign country away from your family may create
hardships for you and your family. What are some of the hardships? What are some
of the rewards you expect from your education away from home?

Question:
Radio stations have a variety of programs for a variety of listeners' tastes. Which
shows do you enjoy listening to or which do you not like to listen to? Why or why
not? What does your choice depend on?

Question:
Many cultures interpret the term *friendship* differently. How would you define it?
What are some of the qualities you expect to find in your close friends?

TAPESCRIPTS

DIAGNOSTIC TEST 1

PART A: STATEMENTS

Example 1: The candidate will not be beat.
Example 2: She never pays attention to the details.

1. My son is not skilled at adding sums, but my daughter is an excellent mathematician.

2. Flight 818 departs on the 18th at 20 of 8 in the evening.

3. I don't remember telling George that he couldn't leave home.

4. The lack of rain caused an increase in food prices.

5. If further efforts to raise money fail, the project will be disbanded.

6. Twelve students wanted to skip history class, but only two-thirds were given permission.

7. It is critical that trainees pay close attention to detail in the assignment.

8. The guard on finding the briefcase gave it to the principal who immediately recognized it belonged to the new teacher.

9. More books were on display this year although major publishers boycotted the fair.

10. Seeing the car crash, I telephoned for help and raced to the scene to find the police were already there.

11. Bill sipped his drink slowly to enjoy the taste.

12. Half of our crowd went to the movies, but only three of us could afford the tickets, so four went home disappointed.

13. The participants were seated around an oval table.

14. The first payment for $49.14 is due on the 4th of this month.

15. Our professor said he would never change his mind, but we didn't believe him.

16. The school boy missed catching the ball, so it hit the window and broke it.

17. My father's brother came to visit last summer.

18. If it rains, we'll cancel the picnic and eat at a restaurant instead.

19. The conductor waved his signal, then ran to the train, climbing aboard at the last minute.

20. The budget for defense is greater than the budget for education, which is less than that for health.

PART B: CONVERSATIONS

Example:
Woman: Why not finish watching the program?
Man: This show was on TV last week. I'm going to study.
Third Voice: What is the man going to do next?

21. Man: Is that a new pair of shoes?
    Woman: Yes, do you think the color is right?
    Third Voice: What did the woman do?

22. Woman: If George doesn't come to dinner, I'll have 13.
    Man: Let's invite two more just in case.
    Third Voice: If everyone comes, how many will have dinner?

23. Man: The block measures 16 by 6 by 60.
    Woman: Isn't that an odd length?
    Third Voice: What is the bigest dimension?

24. Man: I can't find my pen. I need to write a letter.
    Woman: I'll look for it later. Right now I need your help fixing this shelf before I paint it.
    Third Voice: What will they do first?

25. Man: This isn't the worst hotel that I've been in.
    Woman: It's nothing like what I'd imagined.
    Third Voice: What does the woman think?

26. Woman: If everyone runs for President, who'll run for the other offices?
    Man: Of the six candidates, only two are not running for President.
    Third Voice: How many people are running for President?

27. Woman: Be careful of the ice on the bridge.
    Man: I'll slow down when I get there.
    Third Voice: What is the potential problem?

28. Man: If I pass this test, I can go to the college of my choice.
    Woman: If not, you can work for your father.
    Third Voice: What happens if the man passes the test?

29. Man: When I was a child, I thought mice were cute, but now I think they're pests.
    Woman: I still like them, despite their reputation.
    Third Voice: What does the man think of mice now?

30. Man: Tonight I'm leaving home for a 10-day cruise.

Woman:	I envy your long holiday. Mine is four days long.
Third Voice:	Which statement is true?

31.
Woman:	Is there a dog in the house?
Man:	I hope not. How can I stay here if there is?
Third Voice:	Why is the man concerned?

32.
Woman:	The charity appeal raised only half of what it expected.
Man:	One quarter of a million is respectable, however.
Third Voice:	How much money did they expect to raise?

33.
Man:	Are you catching the 11:15 train to Washington?
Woman:	Yes. I thought I'd get a cab at 11th Street and 5th Avenue in about 15 minutes.
Third Voice:	When will the woman catch the cab?

34.
Man:	I used to collect rare volumes, but now I barely look at them.
Woman:	That's a pity. I'm always rereading my books.
Third Voice:	Which sentence describes the situation?

35.
Man:	I won't ever go there again.
Woman:	I can't promise I won't return, but I'll try not to.
Third Voice:	Which is true?

PART C: MINI-TALKS

Example:
The planets, in order from the sun, are Mercury, Venus, Earth, Mars, Jupiter, Saturn, Uranus, Neptune, and Pluto. Mars is known as "the red planet" because of its reddish appearance in the sky; Venus is, of course, the planet of mystery, shrouded in vaporous mists; and Mercury, the fastest sun-orbiting planet, is named for the messenger of the gods, although the planet, which circles the sun every 88 days, is lifeless and cratered, much like our moon.

Which planet is fifth from the earth?
Which planet resembles our moon?

Mini-Talk 1
Man: Excuse me, but have you seen my little gray dog as you were walking through the park?
Woman: No, I'm sorry, but I'll look before I leave. What's his name?
Man: Her name, actually. I call her Cinders because she's the color of soot.
Woman: Why isn't she on a leash?
Man: She saw a squirrel and broke away before I could catch her.

36. What word best describes the dog?
37. Where does the conversation take place?
38. Why did the dog run away?
39. What would the woman recommend?
40. What do soot and the dog have in common?

Mini-Talk 2

Ladies and gentlemen, we regret to announce that this evening's performance of Shakespeare's *Hamlet* must be postponed due to the failure of our electrical system. Those people wishing a refund of their money may go to the box office after this announcement. Members of the audience who wish to exchange their tickets for the rescheduled performance next Tuesday evening should appear at the box office tomorrow morning between 8:30 and 10 o'clock.

41. Why is there no performance?
42. When will tickets be exchanged?
43. To whom is this message addressed?

Mini-Talk 3

Dateline New York City. Yesterday afternoon, a special session of the United Nations produced a resolution calling for establishment of a select committee to study the problem of earthquakes in Japan, California, and around the globe. The committee would be charged with compiling data and interviewing leading international experts in the field as groundwork for a policy aimed at standardizing building methods, early warning systems, and relief procedures in the event of major earthquake activity.

44. Where does the report originate?
45. What is the main subject?
46. What will the study affect?
47. What does the committee recommend building methods should be?

Mini-Talk 4

Today we will be studying about King Charles the Second. Despite his position as claimant to the English throne after the execution of his father, Charles the First, Charles the Second was without a single drop of what we would call English blood in his veins, being one-quarter Scottish, one-quarter French, one-quarter German, and one-quarter Welsh. Nonetheless, by the time England had wearied of the protectorate established by Cromwell's forces, it welcomed Charles back as if he were the only child of the realm.

48. Who established the protectorate?
49. What happened to the father of Charles the Second?
50. What blood was not in the veins of Charles the Second?

DIAGNOSTIC TEST 2

PART A: STATEMENTS

Example 1: The candidate will not be beat.
Example 2: She never pays attention to the details.

1. The accountant can't be trusted because he hasn't got much sense.

2. The soccer team walked a total of 30 miles, but the coach walked only half as far as the team.

3. The 13 boys will meet the teacher at 9 o'clock to take the test.

4. The memorial was dedicated by the widows of the victims.

5. The landlord couldn't understand why the tenant wouldn't continue to rent the house from him.

6. Everyone but the engineer agreed that the building plans should be submitted to the city planner.

7. The nurse's clock was broken, so she overslept and was late for duty.

8. If I married a prince, I'd be a princess.

9. After the athlete ate dinner, she went running, but her roommate had already exercised before breakfast.

10. The engine noise on the newer jets is less than on the older ones even though the jets are larger.

11. The highway department needed more men to complete the road widening work by winter.

12. Before opening the cover to the vat, you must turn off the electricity and put on protective clothing.

13. If the exchange student had studied, she would have gotten an A.

14. The door was left open, so the wind blew the vase off the table.

15. Concerned citizens' groups keep a close watch on the activities of the mayor and his council.

16. The manager never leaves the door open, as he doesn't like drafts.

17. The lecturer's closing remarks left us speechless with amazement, and it was hours before we could talk.

18. Thirteen of us went to the show, but only eight of us could get in, so the rest went home.

19. I woke at 8:30 knowing the appointment was at 9:45, but despite all my plans, I still got there at 10.

20. The prime minister's speech was not well received by the restless crowd.

PART B: CONVERSATIONS

Example:
Woman:	Why not finish watching the program?
Man:	This show was on TV last week. I'm going to study.
Third Voice:	What is the man going to do next?

21.
Man:	Could you bear it if I opened the window and the curtains? We need some fresh air.
Woman:	We also need to keep it quiet in here.
Third Voice:	Which is true?

22. Man: Why did you get up at 6? I thought your meeting wasn't until 10.
    Woman: I wanted to visit the park before I left. It's the first time I've seen it.
    Third Voice: How much time did she have between waking and her meeting?

23. Woman: How much did the 50 envelopes cost?
    Man: Oh, about 25 cents each. They came stamped.
    Third Voice: How much did the envelopes cost?

24. Woman: These are simply delicious grapes.
    Man: You're certainly eating them heartily enough.
    Third Voice: How is she eating her food?

25. Man: I don't like the prices on this menu. They always seems too high.
    Woman: You never want to eat anywhere else, though.
    Third Voice: What does the man like?

26. Man: Where is the umbrella that was in the closet? I have to return it to my boss.
    Woman: I gave it to your brother. I'll get it back.
    Third Voice: Whose umbrella does the brother have?

27. Woman: You rowed hard today and won the race.
    Man: Yes, I practiced a lot and didn't eat much yesterday.
    Third Voice: Why did the man win?

28. Woman: If I go to Paris, will you meet me there? We can visit my cousin's new home.
    Man: I have to go to London, but if I have time, I'll meet you there on the weekend.
    Third Voice: What will the man do?

29. Man: Did you go to the store before or after you took a nap this afternoon?
    Woman: After. First, I took a nap, and then I took a walk. I did the shopping before I had dinner.
    Third Voice: What did the woman do second?

30. Man: I don't think this washing machine will fit in this space.
    Woman: It must. It's supposed to be the same size as the old one.
    Third Voice: What describes the machine?

31. Woman: I'll never learn this language properly. I'm always thinking I know a word, but I don't.
    Man: That isn't a crime. Giving up is.
    Third Voice: Which is true?

32. Man: I can hardly hear you.
     Woman: I was only complaining about his decision. It wasn't just.
     Third Voice: What describes the decision?

33. Woman: When does the express train leave? At 8:45?
     Man: No, at 9:30, I believe.
     Third Voice: When does the express train leave?

34. Woman: I thought the boat only held four. How did you reserve five
                      seats?
     Man: They've enlarged it to carry six. I'll reserve the last seat for
                      you.
     Third Voice: If the woman comes, how many people are going on the boat?

35. Man: Did you hear about the man next door? He lost all his hair
                      overnight.
     Woman: What? It was always so thick.
     Third Voice: What did the man lose?

PART C: MINI-TALKS

Example:
The planets, in order from the sun, are Mercury, Venus, Earth, Mars, Jupiter, Saturn, Uranus, Neptune, and Pluto. Mars is known as "the red planet" because of its reddish appearance in the sky; Venus is, of course, the planet of mystery, shrouded in vaporous mists; and Mercury, the fastest sun-orbiting planet, is named for the messenger of the gods, although the planet, which circles the sun every 88 days, is lifeless and cratered, much like our moon.

Which planet is fifth from the earth?
Which planet resembles our moon?

Mini-Talk 1
Teacher: Does everyone understand the directions? Blacken the letters completely.
Student: Do we use pencil or pen on the answer sheet?
Teacher: I prefer you to use pencil, even though these are just practice tests.
Student: How much will they count towards our final grade?
Teacher: They're worth nothing at the moment. Practice tests are just for practice in
        this classroom.

36. How does the teacher prefer the students to mark their answer sheets?
37. What percentage of the grade do the tests represent?
38. What kind of test is it?
39. Which statement would the teacher likely agree with?

Mini-Talk 2
In Josef Albers' theory of color, the intensity of a color will alter as the other colors surrounding it alter. Thus, no color is absolute in hue, but relies for its brilliant or muted tone on the colors next to it, which resonate with it and may actually appear to change its intensity completely. For example, a violet placed next

to orange will appear quite different from the same shade of violet placed next to white or deep blue.
40. Which statement is true?
41. Who invented this theory?
42. What alters the intensity of color?

Mini-Talk 3

Last year the snowfall in our area was 15 inches. This year, however, scientists are predicting that this total will more than double. The responsibility lies with the changes in weather patterns which have occurred in the last two years, partly as a worldwide climatic change, and partly as the fallout from weapons testing, industrial pollution, volcanic eruptions, and other man-made and natural phenomena.

43. How much snow is expected this season?
44. Who predicts this snowfall?
45. What does not cause climatic conditions to change?
46. Where have these climatic changes occurred?

Mini-Talk 4

Will Mr. Hill report to the information desk in the main lobby, please? Will Mr. Leonard Hill please come to the information desk as soon as possible? We have an urgent message for Mr. Hill from his company director. Will Mr. Hill please contact the information desk immediately, either in person or by using the courtesy phones in the lobby?

47. Where is Mr. Hill to report?
48. Which applies to the lobby phones?
49. Who sent the message?
50. What would describe the message?

Diagnostic Test 3

PART A: STATEMENTS

Example 1: The candidate will not be beat.
Example 2: She never pays attention to the details.

1. I beat the rug to get it clean, but the dust flew in my hair.

2. Eleven boys started the course, but only two didn't finish.

3. I asked for 15 cards, but the clerk only had 13.

4. I had no intention of hitting the pedestrian, but he wouldn't get out of the way.

5. Never in his life had the geologist seen anything like the canyon.

6. The sports equipment that belongs to the school must be returned to the trainer at the end of the session.

7. Because the door was open, the cat escaped into the tree-lined yard.

8. If the firemen had been called, they could have put out the fire.

9. After I ate, I went to the movies, but Jim had already seen it, so he went to the store instead.

10. The insurance coverage of Plan A is not as complete as that of Plan B but is more comprehensive than Plan C.

11. The widest part of the river is a few miles from here.

12. The bus pulled away from the curb before the attendant loaded the bags.

13. If the absentee votes were not counted, the election is invalid.

14. The batteries had been in the camera too long, and now the flash won't work.

15. Having worked with that technician before, we were reluctant to give her more responsibility.

16. This error would never have occurred if the rules hadn't been ignored.

17. The problem wouldn't have become so serious if it had been dealt with sooner.

18. We established a camp of 30 tents between 10 and 11 at night.

19. Even if I only walk 13 miles and you only walk 10, together we still will have walked twice as far as those two did.

20. The grain of the wood was gray, but I polished it anyway till it shone.

PART B: CONVERSATIONS

Example:
Woman:	Why not finish watching the program?
Man:	This show was on TV last week. I'm going to study.
Third Voice:	What is the man going to do next?

21.
Man:	Couldn't you walk any faster?
Woman:	This is the fastest I've ever walked.
Third Voice:	What does the man believe?

22.
Woman:	Where have you been since I saw you at the movies?
Man:	I went for a stroll, then decided to call on some friends.
Third Voice:	What did the man do first?

23.
Woman:	If you had listened to me, we'd be at the party. Move over. I'll drive.
Man:	I was sure I knew the way there. I'll turn around.
Third Voice:	What's the problem?

24.
Man:	I gave the man full payment when he asked for it.
Woman:	No wonder he hasn't finished the job yet.
Third Voice:	Who are they talking about?

25.
Woman:	Your nose is like your mother's.

Man: Yours is like your father's. My eyes are like my grandfather's!
Third Voice: Whose nose does the woman's nose resemble?

26. Man: Hand me the papers from my briefcase.
    Woman: Is that your briefcase there, next to the typewriter?
    Third Voice: What does he want?

27. Man: What classes are you taking?
    Woman: I've decided to take only one course and try to find a job.
    Third Voice: What will the woman do?

28. Woman: If your dog is 8, that's about 80 in human terms, right?
    Man: No, it's seven years to each dog year.
    Third Voice: How old is the dog in human terms?

29. Man: I gave you two dollars. You've given me back 50 cents.
    Woman: I had to buy milk.
    Third Voice: How much was the milk?

30. Man: Those shoes you're wearing are a beautiful color.
    Woman: I know. It's your favorite. You always choose it, for ties, shirts, suits . . . everything.
    Third Voice: What did the man like?

31. Woman: You never should have gone out in the rain.
    Man: I wouldn't have, but they were expecting me.
    Third Voice: What should the man have done?

32. Man: You look much slimmer.
    Woman: I stopped eating bread last week.
    Third Voice: What happened to the woman?

33. Man: If I were older, would I have a chance at this job?
    Woman: You have the experience, the degrees, and the good looks. It's up to fate.
    Third Voice: What does the man think he lacks?

34. Woman: According to this history book, the cotton embargo preceded the War Between the States.
    Man: I thought it was done in retaliation for the secession.
    Third Voice: What can be said for the cotton embargo?

35. Woman: If these prices get any higher, I'll have to go on a diet.
    Man: You should anyway.
    Third Voice: What is the woman referring to?

PART C: MINI-TALKS

Example:
The planets, in order from the sun, are Mercury, Venus, Earth, Mars, Jupiter, Saturn, Uranus, Neptune, and Pluto. Mars is known as "the red planet" because of

its reddish appearance in the sky; Venus is, of course, the planet of mystery, shrouded in vaporous mists; and Mercury, the fastest sun-orbiting planet, is named for the messenger of the gods, although the planet, which circles the sun every 88 days, is lifeless and cratered, much like our moon.

Which planet is fifth from the earth?
Which planet resembles our moon?

Mini-Talk 1
Man: Do you know if this is the first time this piece of music's been performed?
Woman: It's the first time I've heard it, but I believe it's been played elsewhere.
Man: It's quite modern, isn't it? I'm not certain I like it.
Woman: Oh, I think it's quite wonderful. So strong and loud!

36. Why does the woman like the music?
37. How often has the woman heard the piece?
38. How does the man feel about the music?

Mini-Talk 2
Ladies and Gentleman, Ringling Brothers and Barnum and Bailey Circus, The Greatest Show on Earth, will begin its afternoon performance as soon as crew members finish taking down the safety net under the Big Top. When we say "death-defying" acts, ladies and gentlemen, we mean precisely that. All the thrills you've ever hoped for from the circus will be yours for the next two hours. So let the show begin!

39. When does this performance take place?
40. Why are the acts called "death-defying"?
41. What adjective describes the show?

Mini-Talk 3
Special to the Des Moines Register, January 2, 1986. Art curators at the Ottumwa Museum announced today that the Brandenburg Venus, previously believed to have been a clever forgery from the 19th century, has been confirmed as an original. The Venus is a wall relief depicting the goddess of love and her attendants preparing for the wedding of one of the minor Hapsburg princes of the 15th century. The relief is remarkable for the clarity of its detailing and the brilliance of its coloration.

Board Chairman Matthew Wilby said, "Being told this piece is original puts our holdings in 15th century German sculpture in the forefront of international collections."

42. Where is the art museum located?
43. What is the Brandenburg Venus?
44. What did people wrongly believe about the piece?
45. Who made the announcement?
46. What characterizes the coloration?

Mini-Talk 4
The National Weather Service forecast for Hartford and vicinity: showers today, clearing towards nightfall, with chance of precipitation recurring in the early morning hours. Lows today in the 70's with a possible high of 80 in midafternoon. Long-range forecast: a high pressure area moving in from Canada will sweep across southern New England late Friday night, continuing the week's trend.

47. What is the weather at the moment?
48. When will the highest temperature be reached?
49. Where is the high pressure area coming from?
50. How long has this kind of weather persisted?

Diagnostic Test 4

PART A: STATEMENTS

Example 1: The candidate will not be beat.
Example 2: She never pays attention to the details.

1. The fisherman had not rowed the boat back that night.

2. At 11 o'clock we tried to call, but it was 30 minutes later that we got through to the six of them.

3. The anxious woman tore her dress when she sat down.

4. We went to bed at 6:30, but we'd promised to waken two hours later to meet your 9 o'clock train.

5. The flight from Brazil was due at 6:10, but we only heard them call out flights 16, 60, and 600 while we waited.

6. I rose at 8:30 to catch flight number 813, which left from an airport 50 minutes away.

7. I threw the blanket over the car to keep it dry.

8. The anger he displayed showed he'd not listen to reason.

9. I have never heard a story about orphans that didn't make me want to weep.

10. The committee presented prizes to the best dressed man and the worst dressed woman.

11. The grain embargo was only one of the bills occupying the senator's attention.

12. The strong gusts caused the speaker to hold onto his papers.

13. The magazine was sent to the printer before it was approved by the editor.

14. Unless electric consumption is reduced, the city will have to triple its power generation capacity by next year.

15. If there had been greater support, the motion would have been approved.

16. The commander gave the enlisted men their awards, promoting two to a higher rank.

17. The shuttle could have orbited longer had the pump not malfunctioned.

18. The cat chased the mouse and then climbed the tree where the bird had abandoned the nest.

19. My gas tank is larger than the one on my old car, but the gas was less expensive for my old car than it is now.

20. The exam would not have been as easy if I hadn't studied.

Part B: Conversations

Example:
Woman:	Why not finish watching the program?
Man:	This show was on TV last week. I'm going to study.
Third Voice:	What is the man going to do next?

21.
Woman:	I'm going to the doctor. I have something wrong with my eyes.
Man:	I never have anything wrong with my eyes.
Third Voice:	Where is she going?

22.
Woman:	Do you get up at 5 every morning?
Man:	Yes, and I need seven hours of sleep. I should go to bed earlier, I guess.
Third Voice:	When should the man go to bed?

23.
Woman:	The 5:18 bus is more expensive but faster.
Man:	To save 80 cents, I'll wait 20 minutes for the 5:28.
Third Voice:	What bus does the man take?

24.
Man:	I'm exhausted today. I can't talk anymore.
Woman:	We still have to visit the retired general.
Third Voice:	What describes the man?

25.
Man:	If you hadn't mentioned their dinner party, I could have gone home.
Woman:	That would have been the third time you've disappointed them this month.
Third Voice:	What's he going to do?

26.
Man:	Mrs. Smith, have you, your husband, or any members of your family suffered from any form of mental illness?
Woman:	No, but my father's family has a history of heart problems.
Third Voice:	Who suffers from heart disease?

27.
Woman:	I could be ready sooner if you'd help me take out the trash.
Man:	There isn't enough to fill the bag.
Third Voice:	What does the woman want?

28.
Woman:	Be glad you aren't at the other restaurant. They serve the biggest meals.
Man:	This is more than I can eat. Even you can't finish it all.
Third Voice:	Which statement is true?

29.	Man:	First thing after taking my car to be repaired, I'll go to my office.
	Woman:	Please stop for groceries on the way home if you have time.
	Third Voice:	What will the man do first?

30.	Woman:	My shoes are too new. I even wore thick socks and I got blisters.
	Man:	Perhaps you walked too far. You should wear new shoes only an hour a day.
	Third Voice:	What caused the blisters?

31.	Man:	My headaches are terrible. Maybe I need more sleep.
	Woman:	Actually, you need less sun and some aspirin. Plus it would help if you wore a hat. The sun is too bright.
	Third Voice:	What caused his headache?

32.	Woman:	Annie invited me to Bill's house for Joe's birthday.
	Man:	You haven't forgotten my dinner party, have you?
	Third Voice:	Whose house is the birthday party at?

33.	Man:	You're a good height. Just a little plump.
	Woman:	I wish I were taller. My hair would look longer if I were taller.
	Third Voice:	What describes this woman?

34.	Man:	I always begin my lectures with a joke. That puts the audience at ease.
	Woman:	Then they laugh to put you at ease.
	Third Voice:	How does the man like to begin?

35.	Woman:	This is the silliest book I have ever read. It's plain ridiculous.
	Man:	I've read duller books, though, but not one so long.
	Third Voice:	What does the man feel about the book?

PART C: MINI-TALKS

Example:
The planets, in order from the sun, are Mercury, Venus, Earth, Mars, Jupiter, Saturn, Uranus, Neptune, and Pluto. Mars is known as "the red planet" because of its reddish appearance in the sky; Venus is, of course, the planet of mystery, shrouded in vaporous mists; and Mercury, the fastest sun-orbiting planet, is named for the messenger of the gods, although the planet, which circles the sun every 88 days, is lifeless and cratered, much like our moon.

Which planet is fifth from the earth?
Which planet resembles our moon?

Mini-Talk 1
As the weather map shows, this Fourth of July weekend looks glorious across the country. In New England and New York, temperatures are expected to soar into the 90's. We had a taste of that here in New York City with yesterday's record-breaking high of 96, which beat the previous mark of 95 set in 1868. These temperatures will

hold steady through the weekend. On the west coast, the usual balmy weather. No threat of mudslides for a while, I'd say.

36. What would produce mud slides on the West Coast?
37. Where is the weatherman located?
38. What is characteristic of steady temperatures?

Mini-Talk 2
Today we are going to consider design trends in history. The teapot did not emerge until the 16th century in China, when it was modeled after the wine ewer that had all the necessary requirements -- handle, spout, cover. It was made of clay to maintain heat.

A 1685 English pot resembles its ancient prototype. It is a silver melon-shaped pot. Many early pots were no more than 5 inches tall and would brew only one cup of tea. The reason for this was tea's relative rarity. It was a very precious commodity for centuries.

Complete tea services were developed in the 18th century. A set was considered a statement of one's refinement since it was in full view of guests while the tea was brewing.

39. What is the focus of the talk?
40. When did the first tea pot come to exist?
41. Why was tea valued?
42. According to the lecture, which is not true of teapots?
43. What was an advantage to using clay?

Mini-Talk 3
Computer keyboard and disk drive covers enhance equipment reliability. Both covers help prevent maintenance problems caused when dust and dirt get into the delicate components. A disk drive cover is custom designed to seal off disk drive areas. A keyboard cover will protect any keyboard with a working area no larger than 17 inches by 5 inches. To protect the diskettes, compact rolltop files are a convenient way to store up to 100 diskettes. Such files take up very little space and may be divided according to any system you prefer.

44. What would improve your equipment performance?
45. What area can be covered by a keyboard cover?
46. What characterizes compact files?
47. What is a custom designed drive cover?

Mini-Talk 4
Student: Geometry is not my favorite subject.
Teacher: You must take the course anyway.
Student: Can't I substitute another subject?
Teacher: If you do so, you won't be able to graduate.
Student: But I'm a senior!
Teacher: That makes no difference. A requirement is a requirement.
Student: Even if I'm an English major?
Teacher: You could major in cooking for all I care. You must take this course.

48. What is the student's main area of study?
49. Why is he taking the course?
50. What year of study is he?

LISTENING TARGETS

STATEMENTS: MINIMAL PAIRS

1. There were 10 in the car when I looked.

2. We put the books on the seat near the door.

3. Going to bed early is a habit of his.

4. Given his health, he cannot work overtime.

5. Keeping close to her, he was able to hear their conversation.

6. The ice on the lake will melt in this heat.

7. A dog and a cat may get along if raised together.

8. Dinner at home was quite a good meal.

9. They look so much alike they could be doubles.

10. The boat sank fairly quickly in the storm.

STATEMENTS: COMPUTATION

1. A dozen of us went to the movie, but only five went to the reception.

2. I told him to meet me at quarter to 4, but he was 20 minutes late.

3. The group consisted of 30 men, 22 women, and 4 children.

4. John said he understood the directions, but we drove 15 miles one way, then 6 another, before we asked for help.

5. We must leave at 8:30 to get home by 9:15.

6. I told my sister to come at 8, but she was 10 minutes late.

7. The car went 60 miles an hour despite the speed limit of 55.

8. The show begins an hour earlier tonight, so if it takes 2 hours, we'll be out by 9:30.

9. We counted on a drive of 3 hours, but forgot that traffic would delay us 45 minutes more.

10. Nineteen members of the volleyball team went to the tournament, but six stayed at school.

STATEMENTS: NUMBER DISCRIMINATION

1. Open your books to page 16.

2. Flight 13 to Madrid leaves at 8:30.

3. Eighteen of us expect to graduate on the 8th.

4. We were asked to review column 4 on page 19.

5. The 70-year-old man gets up each morning at 7:15.

6. John was born in 1985 on the 30th of June.

7. At 20 of 9, teams began to appear on the field.

8. Fifteen percent of the class understood all six questions.

9. The clerk guaranteed that 60 of us would get on the 6:15 train to New York.

10. George counted the 2 flights of steps and found there were 90 steps, not counting the 13 at the top.

STATEMENTS: SYNONYMS

1. She was barely able to lift the package.

2. John seemed markedly distant during her explanation.

3. Practically all bears outside their natural habitat are kept in cages.

4. Only extremely rational people seem to enjoy playing this word game.

5. We lost sight of them in the enveloping mist.

6. The river was too high for the raft trip we'd planned.

7. In either case, whether we stay or go depends on the timing.

8. She'd just recovered from a bout of flu when she was called away on business.

9. He's finally discovered that she tires easily.

10. The boy was loyal through it all.

STATEMENTS: NEGATION

1. I didn't think she wanted any books on the table.

2. We don't think any of the boys were invited to go along with them.

3. Left to herself, she has no problems staying amused.

4. Last year at this time there were no mosquitoes.

5. There were not enough chairs for those who did not come on time.

6. I wouldn't blame anyone who couldn't stay awake for this performance.

7. Larry and Bill want no recognition for their feat.

8. Anytime he calls me, I pretend I am out.

9. We were told we could not have bananas to sell.

10. Marjorie had no reason to buy the book.

STATEMENTS: CONTEXTUAL REFERENCE

1. Frank let Louise use his car, but she loaned it to me without his permission.

2. Claire and Ann found their route was more direct and consequently faster than mine.

3. Loretta and I donated our old clothes to a charity, but the charity workers took some home to their families.

4. Richard gave me his knife, and I cut some roses for my sister.

5. Ronald handed back my ball, and I threw it to Laurie, who was playing nearby.

6. Although Bill liked his cousin Paul, he was fonder of his brother Jim.

7. If Chris had told his sister the truth, she would have warned us.

8. I let my mother take George's car to pick up his laundry.

9. My father and his brother visited my sister at camp.

10. Even when I tell John the answers, he still asks Karen for hers.

STATEMENTS: CAUSE AND EFFECT

1. Since the taxi was caught in traffic, I missed the plane.

2. The meal cost a dime more than I had, so I went without eating.

3. Because it rained, the birds stopped singing.

4. As I lost my compass, I could not find the path.

5. She was ill that day and had to miss the exam.

6. As he said he was going to be traveling that week, we only brought food for the four of us.

7. She disagreed with him and began to call him names.

8. I smiled at him, and he began to talk more openly.

9. When she knew of his presence in the program, she changed her plans.

10. Loren came to say goodbye before he left so we would know he was moving.

STATEMENTS: CONDITIONALS

1. If the sailors had been able to drink fresh milk, they would have had stronger bones.

2. If the rain had abated, we could have left sooner.

3. If the importation of goods decreases, the economy will be paralyzed.

4. If the computer memory fails, the system must be momentarily turned off.

5. If only the television repairmen would arrive, I could leave and return to work.

6. If you close the door, the noise will decrease.

7. If I were younger, I would not make the same mistakes.

8. If the regulations are not rescinded, there will be civil disobedience.

9. If more complaints are registered, the product will be recalled.

10. If she arrives before dusk, we'll go for a long walk.

STATEMENTS: CHRONOLOGICAL ORDER

1. After the sun set, the first stars came out.

2. When the diners were finished with their trays, the waitress took them away.

3. The second time I saw him was after the performance had ended.

4. The third child went home before the other two finished playing.

5. After we went skiing, we relaxed by the fire they had ready when we returned.

6. Before they got married, they arranged for a reception at the second biggest hall in town.

7. First we went to the store, then we cooked dinner, and at last we went to bed.

8. When he told us he was coming, we began to paint the guest room.

9. She stopped by the party first, before going to the concert.

10. The first thing he remembered after his fall was her crying.

STATEMENTS: COMPARISON

1. The engineer insisted that the bridge be made wider.

2. Cliff does better than Joe on these tests, I think.

3. The growth of the suburbs has made it more difficult for small urban stores.

4. I write more beautifully than George but not as nicely as Kate.

5. The runway of the new airport is the longest in the Eastern Hemisphere, but not in the world.

6. Lynn thinks faster than we do when she has to.

7. The days in winter are shorter than in the summer.

8. The narrow balcony was more crowded with plants than people.

9. The old man eats more dinner than his wife, but less than I give him to eat.

10. I gave Christine more money than I lent Rob.

CONVERSATIONS: MINIMAL PAIRS

1. Woman: Stop me if you've heard this one.
   Man: Please, we can't take any more of your humor.
   Third Voice: What is the woman going to do?

2. Man: I wouldn't take any bets that horse would win.
   Woman: Really? I was going to say he looks like he could beat them all.
   Third Voice: What does the man think?

3. Man: Do we have to go far?
   Woman: The farm is just a mile away. Would you like to rest now?
   Third Voice: What does the woman suggest?

4. Woman: Is he the best batter?
   Man: He hasn't hit anything yet. Should I ask the reporter who is better?
   Third Voice: What does the reporter know?

5. Man: Why did you cry to see him tear up the card?
   Woman: Does it bother you to see me in tears?

Third Voice: What is the woman doing?

6. Woman: How can you believe his lies?
   Man: Don't you think he has honest eyes? I do.
   Third Voice: What does the man think of the other man?

7. Man: Is it the wind or you making that noise?
   Woman: It's the flapping curtain. Close the window.
   Third Voice: What causes the sound?

8. Man: Their home is near the bakery on Lake Drive. Do you know where that is?
   Woman: If you follow your nose, it will lead you to the bakery.
   Third Voice: Where does the man want to go?

9. Woman: Don't you like the dark?
   Man: I'd prefer the light. Can you find the switch?
   Third Voice: What does the man want?

10. Man: Is this what you planned? It seems all wrong to me.
    Woman: This group of plants belongs here. Where would you put them?
    Third Voice: What are they discussing?

CONVERSATIONS: COMPUTATION

1. Man: I left home at 8:00. What time is it now?
   Woman: Just half past 9.
   Third Voice: How long ago did the man leave?

2. Woman: I sent three of the girls to bring six chairs.
   Man: Won't we need four more chairs?
   Third Voice: How many chairs will they need?

3. Woman: Is it true you only spent $32 on two dinners?
   Man: No, I only spent half of that on the two meals.
   Third Voice: How much did each dinner cost?

4. Woman: The plane leaves at 6:15. Do we have time to eat first?
   Man: No. We've only got 40 minutes until departure time.
   Third Voice: What time is it now?

5. Woman: Although we usually wake at 6, I overslept 15 minutes.
   Man: And I woke up 20 minutes earlier than usual.
   Third Voice: How much longer did the woman sleep than the man?

6. Man: The room is a rectangle 10 feet long and 6 feet wide.
   Woman: I thought its perimeter would be less than 30 feet.
   Third Voice: How big is the perimeter of the room?

7. Woman: The shoes were a bargain. I got them for half price!
   Man: You mean you only paid $40 for them?
   Third Voice: How much did the shoes cost originally?

8. Man: Six of us started to the movies, but only one-third of us actually made it to the theater.
   Woman: Then you could have asked four more people.
   Third Voice: How many went to the movies?

9. Woman: I waited until 9:20 for you.
   Man: I must have arrived 6 minutes after you left.
   Third Voice: What time did the man arrive?

10. Man: The radio cost $40, but I only have $30.
    Woman: I have $16. Would you like to borrow it?
    Third Voice: How much money do they have between them.

CONVERSATIONS: NUMBER DISCRIMINATION

1. Man: Are we supposed to leave at 8:13?
   Woman: I'm not sure. All I remember is that the flight number is 833.
   Third Voice: What time does the man think they'll leave?

2. Man: There are only 13 chairs for 14 of us.
   Woman: Why not find another, then?
   Third Voice: How many chairs are there?

3. Woman: Roberta took 22 minutes to dress and didn't arrive until 4.
   Man: Fortunately, we didn't start until 4:15.
   Third Voice: When did Roberta arrive?

4. Man: If 16 of us go now, then the others will have to wait until the 6:15 shift begins to have dinner.
   Woman: I couldn't wait another minute.
   Third Voice: How many people will go now?

5. Woman: The flight leaves on the 8th at 8:15.
   Man: That seems a long time from now.
   Third Voice: What day does the flight leave?

6. Man: I gave out 68 balloons at the party, and in less than 18 minutes the children took them all.
   Woman: That's too bad. I wanted to save six to eight of them for next year.
   Third Voice: How many balloons did the man hand out?

7. Woman: One of her grades was 90, and another was 50.
   Man: Her work is very uneven.
   Third Voice: What was the girl's low grade?

8. Man: The shotgun requires two .50 caliber bullets. I only have .22 caliber bullets.
   Woman: Are you sure you are ready for this hunting trip?
   Third Voice: How many bullets does his gun require?

9. Man: The temperature is supposed to reach 88 today and go down to 60 this evening.

| Woman: | Isn't that more than 18 degrees difference? |
| Third Voice: | What is the evening temperature forecast? |

10.
Woman:	I gave 30 cents to the 3 children next door.
Man:	You mean those living in apartment 13-B?
Third Voice:	How much money did she give away?

CONVERSATIONS: SYNONYMS

1.
Man:	The grooming of the horse's mane and tail is very well done.
Woman:	I always pay attention to details.
Third Voice:	What describes the woman?

2.
Man:	There was a great deal of sleet last night. Did you hear the wind?
Woman:	That's why I couldn't sleep. The wind was so strong.
Third Voice:	What did they experience last night?

3.
Woman:	I love the beach when the sand is fine and the water is just barely making waves.
Man:	I prefer an angry sea. That makes me feel better whenever I'm sad.
Third Voice:	What does the man like?

4.
Woman:	Sometimes I think you have no heart.
Man:	Just because I laughed at your breadmaking efforts? If it's too hard, you can always buy it.
Third Voice:	What does the man recommend the woman do?

5.
Man:	Will you have dinner with me on the boat?
Woman:	I thought you might launch her earlier, and then we could have lunch instead, with dinner in port.
Third Voice:	What has the woman planned?

6.
Woman:	The predominant factor is my need for relaxation.
Man:	There must be other alternatives to early retirement.
Third Voice:	What is the woman going to do?

7.
Man:	Did something scare you just then?
Woman:	Funny, I never thought you cared how I acted. No, nothing frightens me.
Third Voice:	Which statement describes the situation?

8.
Woman:	I wish you hadn't told me the end of the mystery.
Man:	I'm sorry I ruined your fun, but now you can start another.
Third Voice:	How does the man feel?

9.
Woman:	There are so many children at the school, I wonder how the teacher keeps track of them?
Man:	I used to get cold feet at the thought of teaching a class of 100. That's a fact.
Third Voice:	What is the man's attitude toward teaching?

10. Woman: She implored me to continue singing, but I was becoming hoarse.
    Man: Yes, you must conserve your voice.
    Third Voice: What was the problem?

CONVERSATIONS: NEGATION

1. Man: Isn't that a new book you're reading?
   Woman: This isn't the first time you've seen me with it.
   Third Voice: What does the woman imply?

2. Man: I can't believe you have never seen a giraffe.
   Woman: I haven't been to the zoo or to Africa. It's not surprising I haven't seen one before.
   Third Voice: What would not describe the woman?

3. Man: I'm not prepared for the test. Are you nervous?
   Woman: No, I'm not. I studied.
   Third Voice: Which is true?

4. Man: Isn't that the book I loaned you a while ago?
   Woman: I'm afraid I'm very bad at returning things.
   Third Voice: What describes the woman's emotion?

5. Man: I never drink water without ice.
   Woman: Don't you think that's bad for your stomach?
   Third Voice: What would be the woman's advice?

6. Woman: You aren't going to sleep, are you?
   Man: I've not had a good day. You can't blame me for trying to rest.
   Third Voice: What will the man do next?

7. Man: Wasn't that a good way to see the show?
   Woman: I think we could have had better seats.
   Third Voice: Where were they?

8. Woman: It's always difficult to decide what not to do, isn't it?
   Man: It isn't, if you think of what to do, not what to avoid.
   Third Voice: What would describe the man?

9. Woman: I don't believe we've ever met before, have we?
   Man: We've been introduced at other parties. Don't you remember?
   Third Voice: What does the man imply?

10. Man: The ice is not cold if you fall on a patch covered with snow. Did you know that?
    Woman: No, but I don't think it makes any difference. If I fall in the snow, I'll be cold.
    Third Voice: Where are they speaking?

CONVERSATIONS: CONTEXTUAL REFERENCE

1. Woman: Please take this package and give it to Kate to give to her brother.

Man:	Kate's not here. I'll take care of it.	
Third Voice:	Who is to get the package ultimately?	

2.
Man:	This desk used to belong to me, but I gave it to Sam.
Woman:	And now Sam's sister has given it to me.
Third Voice:	Who owns the desk now?

3.
Woman:	Did Louise tell you that John is coming to visit tomorrow?
Man:	Yes, she told me yesterday that he'd be here by the weekend.
Third Voice:	When does John arrive?

4.
Man:	I bought a scarf for Laura at the store Joan owns.
Woman:	Is it like the one I have?
Third Voice:	To whom is the man giving the scarf?

5.
Man:	I was running with two men when four dogs passed us.
Woman:	My friends Robin and Joan saw it happen.
Third Voice:	Who passed the man?

6.
Woman:	My left shoe fell off as I climbed over the hedge to reach the lake.
Man:	You should have used the gate or tied your shoelaces.
Third Voice:	Where was the woman going?

7.
Man:	I sent my book to Carol's college, but the dean returned it to me.
Woman:	That's odd. They've kept the four books I've sent them.
Third Voice:	Whose book was returned?

8.
Woman:	George and his sister are planning to live in your old family house.
Man:	No one's been there since grandfather died.
Third Voice:	Who will live in the house?

9.
Man:	My grades are higher than Susan's and lower than Sidney's.
Woman:	And mine are higher than Sidney's.
Third Voice:	Whose grades are the lowest?

10.
Man:	I sent a check for two dollars to George to donate to his favorite charity.
Woman:	I only give to my children.
Third Voice:	Who was the final recipient of the man's contribution?

CONVERSATIONS: CAUSE AND EFFECT

1.
Man:	Because I was late, they would not let me take the test.
Woman:	What will you do now? Take a job?
Third Voice:	How did being late affect the man?

2.
Woman:	The flowers are full of blossoms.
Man:	That's the result of all the rain last month when we expected to have a dry spell.
Third Voice:	What's responsible for the blossoms?

3. Man: Because of the recent flooding, we're going to have to take a detour.
    Woman: Not over more gravel roads, I hope.
    Third Voice: What is the problem?

4. Man: Why are you eating that apple?
    Woman: It's the only food in the house.
    Third Voice: Why did the woman choose the apple?

5. Woman: Because I wore red, they seemed to think I was one of the models.
    Man: That's right, the designer's dresses were either red or purple.
    Third Voice: What effect did wearing red produce?

6. Man: I can't stand buttermilk. It makes me sick.
    Woman: I'm afraid that's all we have to drink. Are you hungry?
    Third Voice: What won't the man do?

7. Man: My feet swell in the heat, and then my shoes get tight.
    Woman: Have you tried stretching them with solvent? I understand it works.
    Third Voice: What does the heat affect?

8. Woman: When I clean out my refrigerator, all the ice cream must be put in a cooler or it melts.
    Man: Why don't you just eat it?
    Third Voice: What does the man suggest?

9. Man: When I go on a diet, I eat only grapefruit and that takes off weight quickly.
    Woman: I prefer to eat whatever I want and then run to lose weight.
    Third Voice: What causes the man's weight loss?

10. Man: Because I love autumn, I take my vacations during that time of year.
    Woman: Isn't it cold and wet most of the season? I would be bothered by that.
    Third Voice: What season is the man referring to?

CONVERSATIONS: CONDITIONALS

1. Man: If I go to the store, will you make dinner for us tonight?
    Woman: Bring back enough food.
    Third Voice: What happens if the man shops?

2. Man: It would be easier to drive if there were no other cars on the road.
    Woman: Did you bring your license this time?
    Third Voice: What would the man prefer?

3. Woman: If you're going there anyway, would you change my travelers' checks at the bank?

Man:	It depends on whether or not they'll accept my passport as identification.
Third Voice:	Where is the man going?

4.
Man:	A record crop depends on whether or not it rains in June and is dry in August.
Woman:	Can't they just harvest it in July?
Third Voice:	What are they referring to?

5.
Woman:	If you spill ink on the tablecloth, what then?
Man:	I'll buy you another one.
Third Voice:	What word describes the man?

6.
Man:	If you don't wear a sweater when you go hiking, you will end up with a chill.
Woman:	My sweater is so thin and ugly, though.
Third Voice:	What does the man want the woman to do?

7.
Woman:	I promise to bring my boss home for dinner if he gives me a raise this afternoon.
Man:	Just let me know so I can be here when he comes.
Third Voice:	What does the man plan to do?

8.
Man:	The doctor said if I kept smoking, I would increase my chances of having a heart attack.
Woman:	Did he suggest losing some weight, too?
Third Voice:	How does the woman perceive the man?

9.
Woman:	I promised my sister I would attend the show if I didn't have work due the next day.
Man:	Why not take me along?
Third Voice:	Why will the woman go to the show?

10.
Man:	Next time I see George, I'll ask him if he's forgotten he owes me money.
Woman:	Why not just ask him to repay you?
Third Voice:	What will the man do to George?

CONVERSATIONS: CHRONOLOGICAL ORDER

1.
Man:	When I came home, I saw the fire had gone out.
Woman:	I must not have used enough kindling when I started it.
Third Voice:	When was the fire built?

2.
Woman:	After I sent Paula the report, I expected her to write me a letter, but instead she called.
Man:	She wrote me before she got your report, I believe.
Third Voice:	Who received a letter first?

3.
Woman:	I'm going to sleep after putting out the lights.
Man:	I'm going to take a walk first.
Third Voice:	When will the woman sleep?

4. Woman: When Sally arrives in an hour, we can go shopping.

Man: Let's finish the dishes now, and then we can talk until she comes.

Third Voice: When will they wash the dishes?

5. Man: First I went canoeing, then I went sailing, and finally I had dinner.

Woman: You should have gone hiking first.

Third Voice: What was the order of his activities?

6. Woman: When I travel, I like to get up, tour museums, walk through the town, and rest in the afternoons.

Man: And you never eat until evening?

Third Voice: What does the woman do after she gets up?

7. Man: Who would have thought that by the time he arrived, we'd have left?

Woman: I feel badly. I said we'd wait for him.

Third Voice: Why is the woman unhappy?

8. Man: I'll invite you to our country house as soon as I finish my thesis.

Woman: At the rate you write, that may be next year.

Third Voice: When is she invited?

9. Man: Before Charlotte built her house, she was living on a boat, and then in a tent.

Woman: Don't forget that just before she moved in, she stayed at the hotel.

Third Voice: Where did Charlotte live first?

10. Woman: I remember seeing the lions, then the elephants, and finally the walruses at the zoo when I visited it last May.

Man: I was there more recently than that.

Third Voice: What did the woman see first at the zoo?

CONVERSATIONS: COMPARISONS

1. Man: My coat is smaller than my brother's.

Woman: Really? He always seemed much shorter than you.

Third Voice: How does the man's coat compare to his brother's?

2. Man: I gave the job to Mary because your prices are too high.

Woman: I don't charge as much as John.

Third Voice: Who charges the second highest price?

3. Woman: This light shines more brightly than the one upstairs.

Man: It's the same wattage. It must be the color of the shade, then.

Third Voice: What makes the light seem brighter?

4. Man: The mountain seems higher. It makes me dizzy to climb it this year, but it's worth it for the view.

Woman:	The mountain may not be higher, but we're older.
Third Voice:	What has changed since last year?

5.
Woman:	The current deficit is the greatest this country's seen.
Man:	Next year it will be even bigger.
Third Voice:	What are they talking about?

6.
Man:	My suit is darker than I remembered. Is it as dark as Gill's?
Woman:	It's lighter than Gill's. I think yours is just fine.
Third Voice:	What does the woman think of his suit?

7.
Man	I think this exercise program has made me stronger.
Woman	You look better, and I'm sure you feel better.
Third Voice:	What has the man been doing?

8.
Man:	This Shore Line is the worst deal I've been involved in. You told me it was better than Eastern Sea.
Woman:	That's before I compared it to the Blue Company and Grey Express ventures. That made me see the difference.
Third Voice:	Which deal is worst?

9.
Woman:	I can see the bridge from here and the big tree beyond it.
Man:	The tree is on the opposite shore.
Third Voice:	Where is the bridge in relation to the trees?

10.
Man:	This is the longest play I've ever seen. It's 3 hours long now, and we have another act to go.
Woman:	It's shorter than the 8-hour play we saw last year.
Third Voice:	How do the plays compare?

MINI-TALKS: OVERHEARD CONVERSATIONS

Mini-Talk 1

Man:	Are you sure you want to go there now?
Woman:	I told you. I like nothing better than to visit museums.
Man:	But this is going to make us late for dinner.
Woman:	Then I suggest you stay home and pick me up at the main entrance on your way to the restaurant.

1. Why is the man concerned?
2. What does the woman suggest the man do?
3. Where is she going first?

Mini-Talk 2

Woman:	These peas are not very sweet. I'll have to ask the cook to shop at another market.
Man:	Why don't we ever have corn?
Woman:	I told you that it makes me sick.

4. How often do they eat corn?

5. What is wrong with the peas?
6. How could the couple be described?

Mini-Talk 3

Man: Do you recall where I put the checkbook?
Woman: Have you lost it?
Man: No, I'm only saying I can't locate it at the moment, and I need to enter some checks.
Woman: Well, I hope you haven't dropped it somewhere.

7. What is the conversation about?
8. What is the woman's attitude?
9. Why does the man need the book?

Mini-Talk 4

Woman: I love riding in the country, especially when the fall air is as crisp as it is today.
Man: It's too bad the horse doesn't seem as happy about this outing as you.
Woman: I know that once we get further away from the stable, he'll be content.

10. Where does this scene take place?
11. When does it take place?
12. What are they doing?
13. How does the woman feel?

Mini-Talk 5

Man: Are you certain you locked the car door?
Woman: Why do you ask?
Man: Because I thought I left my briefcase on the back seat.
Woman: Look in the trunk. You may have put it in there.

14. Where does the man think he left his briefcase?
15. What did the woman do?
16. Where does she direct him to look?

Mini-Talk 6

Woman: The children are bringing home friends to spend the night.
Man: Does this mean I have to hide in the bedroom to avoid being seen?
Woman: Don't be silly. I'm sure they'll want us around.
Man: They'll end up giggling all night long, and I'll never get to sleep.

17. Whose friends are spending the night?
18. What does the woman think of the man's attitude?
19. What do we know the children are doing?
20. What will the children do all night?

Mini-Talk 1
Ladies and Gentlemen, your attention please. Pan American Flight 588 for Madrid is now boarding at Gate 36 in the B concourse.

  1. Where is the plane going?
  2. Whom is the announcement addressing?
  3. To what does the number 588 refer?

Mini-Talk 2
The management wishes to announce that there will be a substitution of actors for this evening's performance of *MacBeth*. The role of Macduff, usually played by Douglas Cole, will be performed by Mr. Cole's understudy, Harold Zimmer.

  4. Where is the announcement being made?
  5. Whom is Zimmer playing?
  6. Who is making the announcement?
  7. Whom did the audience expect to see in the role?

Mini-Talk 3
Will the person who left the red wallet in the grocery cart at the end of the corridor please come to the store manager's office immediately? Thank you.

  8. What is someone missing?
  9. What color was the missing article?
10. Where should the owner go?

Mini-Talk 4
Paging Mr. Jones. Paging Mr. Jones. Will Alan Jones please come to the customer service desk in the main lobby of the hotel?

11. Where is Mr. Jones staying?
12. What is the tone of the announcement?
13. Why is he being paged?

Mini-Talk 5
It is my pleasure to announce to you the winner of this year's Sportsman of the Year award, given annually to that athlete who, in the opinion of the distinguished panel of sports writers and commentators, has shown both talent and determination in his achievements. This year's recipient shines in two sports: baseball and football. Please welcome him.

14. Whom does the award honor?
15. Who chooses the winner?
16. How often is the award given?

Mini-Talk 6
Due to circumstances beyond our control, this evening's broadcast of *The World We Live In* will not be seen in color. Do not adjust your sets. We hope to resume color transmission within the next 24 hours. Till then, the station apologizes for the inconvenience to our viewers. We repeat, tonight's broadcast, scheduled as a color

presentation, has been reduced to black and white due to circumstances beyond our control.

17. What is the problem?
18. What does the station advise?
19. How long will the situation last?
20. When is the broadcast scheduled?

MINI-TALKS: ADVERTISEMENTS

Mini-Talk 1
Now on sale: our complete selection of men's overcoats and raincoats, in a variety of plaids, checks, and tweeds, direct from the factory, so the savings go on to you! Come in today and see for yourself! Barney's will not be beat. You can't do better than buy at Barney's, where we double the power of your money.

1. What is being sold?
2. Where are they being sold?
3. What does Barney offer to do?

Mini-Talk 2
Coming soon to a theater near you: *Greenstoke, The Legend of Marzipan.* This magnificent film takes you from the wilds of Africa to the drawing rooms of Britain's stately homes and shows you the heart of darkness and the darkness in the hearts of civilized men. Don't miss the adventure! Be there!

4. What is being advertised?
5. When will it be available?
6. What does it offer?
7. Where can the viewer see it?

Mini-Talk 3
It is with the greatest pride that Harrison and Company, manufacturers of the world's finest furniture, invites you to preview our newest line of 19th century reproductions, now on display in our Maryland, Virginia, and West Virginia showrooms.

These superbly crafted pieces, polished to perfection by skilled craftsmen's hands, are available this fall for your enjoyment. What could be more satisfying than a magnificent suite of furniture from Harrison and Company? Stop by our showrooms today and see the difference quality makes.

8. What kind of furniture do they sell?
9. How is the furniture made?

Mini-Talk 4
Summer Sale! All prices slashed in half! Choose now from an inventory of boots and shoes, originally $100 to $200, now yours for only $50 to $100! Hundreds of styles and colors to choose from. Hurry today -- sale ends tomorrow. No narrow or half sizes in stock, but shelves of regular sizes still remain! You can't afford to pass up this opportunity!

10. What was the original price range?
11. What is the reduction?

12. How many half sizes remain?
13. What is the time of year?

Mini-Talk 5
It's that time of year again! Your local Toyota Dealer has slashed prices on trucks, offering 8.8 percent financing and no money down, with up to 4 years to pay. You can't afford to let this opportunity go by. Not only are we offering the lowest rates it town, but the widest selection of colors and styles, ready to be driven away today! So come by and see for yourself! Nobody does it better than we do.

14. What is being advertised?
15. What is the financing rate offered?
16. How much money is required as a down payment?
17. When can the customer take delivery?

Mini-Talk 6
Safeway announces a special on vegetables in their Chicago stores only. Due to the truckers' strike, our local area farms cannot ship beyond the city. This means an overload of inventory for us, and substantial savings for you. Just look at these prices: corn, 29 cents a dozen, squash, 10 pounds for 15 cents; tomatoes, 1 bushel for 50 cents. Come in today and you will receive a free sack of green beans. Our loss is your gain. Remember, this offer applies in Chicago stores only.

18. How much does the corn cost?
19. What is the free gift?
20. Why are the vegetables so cheap?

MINI-TALKS: NEWS REPORTS

Mini-Talk 1
Three men accused of last month's abduction of diplomat Herbert C. Case were arraigned in court yesterday. The three pleaded not guilty to the charge.

Case, taken at gunpoint from his car just moments after it had left the White House grounds, was held for 3 weeks in a downtown Washington hotel only 3 blocks from where the kidnapping took place.

Delicate negotiations between the FBI and the kidnappers led to a list of demands which included the release of members of the kidnappers' families serving jail terms in the United States on drug charges. A tap on the call to the State Department led agents to the hotel room, where an early morning raid freed the ambassador.

1. How many kidnappers were involved in the plot?
2. How did the agents locate the ambassador?
3. Where did the kidnapping take place?

Mini-Talk 2
King Benson, whose recent ventures into Manhattan's real estate market have aroused speculation that he would soon be moving to the United States, announced today through his spokesman that Dallas, and not New York, would be the site of his next residence.

The King, whose wealth is reportedly in the billions of dollars, is supposed to have chosen Dallas because of the television program of the same name, an international favorite.

Asked if the King would be commuting between his European palaces and Texas on a regular basis, the spokesman declined to answer, saying that plans were still in the formative stages. The only certainty is that a ranch has been bought in the Dallas vicinity, but no further particulars were available.

4. Why is the King choosing Dallas?
5. Where will he live?
6. Where else in the United States does the King own property?

Mini-Talk 3
Lowell County's Board of Supervisors decided Saturday night, in a 3 to 5 decision, not to allow horse racing within the county limits. The issue has long been opposed by citizens' groups that claim the income generated will not offset the increased expenditures in terms of police, fire, and other public services.

County Supervisor McLean maintained that increased revenue would exceed any new expenditures. He was opposed by Supervisor Walsh, who presented figures proving her point that a lottery would be a preferable scheme.

Discussion of the lottery has been placed on the agenda for next month's Board meeting in September.

7. Who opposed horse racing?
8. When will a lottery be discussed?
9. Why was the horse racing defeated?
10. What month did this meeting take place?

Mini-Talk 4
Mayor Marin Gill announced today that he will not run for reelection due to failing health. "It's very simple. He has a heart condition and would like to take it easy," said Joan Barry, Gill's press secretary. According to Barry, Gill's doctor advised him not to run last time, but the mayor decided it was in the city's interest that he continue.

Paul Morrisey, long-time critic of Gill, and now head of the city council, was skeptical of Barry's statements. "If he has a heart condition, I, for one, have seen no evidence of it."

Morrisey led a bitter battle last month to defeat Gill's proposals to cut hospital services in the city. His victory on that issue was seen by many as an indication that Gill's influence with the Council members is waning.

11. Who said Gill was retiring?
12. What was Morrisey's reaction?
13. What plan of Gill's did Morrisey oppose?
14. What did Morrisey's victory mean for Gill?

Mini-Talk 5
Girl Scout Ruth Ann Mayhew was awarded the coveted Merit Scout Medal for her role in the rescue of a 5-year-old boy from the Missouri River last fall.

The boy, who had attempted to swim into the center of the river to retrieve a ball, was caught in the swift undertow and pulled under. Mayhew pushed a long tree branch across the narrow current, giving the child a handhold while older rescue workers improvised a safety net from an abandoned tent screen.

The child was one of four people who survived the river last year. Fifteen adults and children perished while swimming and boating.

15. When did the rescue take place?
16. What did Mayhew use in the rescue?
17. How many people died in the river last year?

Mini-Talk 6
George Panderos, President of Realty Trust, Inc., announced today that his firm would offer new banking hours to service the off-hours working person.

Realty Trust, which specializes in mortgages and development packages, is the first city bank to switch its hours of operation to evening and weekends while keeping its regular 9 a.m. to 3 p.m. schedule. Starting June 1, bank patrons will be able to use the facility from 5 p.m. to 11 p.m. weekdays and from noon to 9 p.m. on Saturdays and Sundays.

18. How many hours will Realty Trust be open on weekdays?
19. What kind of loan is the bank's specialty?
20. Who announced the new hours?

MINI-TALKS: WEATHER REPORTS

Mini-Talk 1
Good evening. As those who have been outside in the past 3 hours know, yesterday's forecast for a sunny and warm Thursday evening has been proved wrong. That front of Canadian air moving across the midwest has finally caught up with us here in New York. The result? An awful blend of rain, hail, and cold winds, with temperatures in the low 40's this evening rising to a high of 62 tomorrow afternoon. Things don't look much better for us tomorrow. The cold front may pass, but a second wave is following just behind that. Looks as if it might bring us some unseasonable snow. Imagine, snow in June. Better get out those sweaters again, folks.

1. What time of day is it?
2. What will the temperature be tomorrow?
3. What is odd about the June weather?

Mini-Talk 2
This morning's temperature was 32 degrees at Dulles International Airport and 42 degrees in Washington, D.C., with a wind chill factor of 10 degrees. Presently, the sky is overcast and snow mixed with freezing rain is anticipated towards nightfall. A traveler's advisory is in effect for Northern Virginia, D.C., and Maryland, with a blizzard watch possible in the early hours of the morning.

4. What was the chill factor?
5. How many degrees colder was it at the airport?
6. What is the early morning prediction?
7. What is the weather at present?

Mini-Talk 3
A thunderstorm watch is in effect until 10 o'clock tonight with the possibility of a tornado watch taking effect during the evening rush hour. The area has been plagued by hail storms with hail measuring 3 inches in diameter falling near Great Falls. The last reported tornado in this section of the county was 7 years ago when a

twister destroyed Oldsfield school and town center leaving $3 million damage in its wake.

8. When was the last tornado?
9. How big was the hail?
10. How much damage did the tornado do?

Mini-Talk 4
The weekend forecast, brought to you by Castleton and Mire Realty Company, is happy to tell all of you that it looks like a fine weekend coming up. Thursday is going to be clear and sunny with temperatures in the high 80's and a humidity factor of only 64 percent. The outlook remains encouraging through Friday evening with high 80's predicted again and a chance of rain around 20 percent. Saturday things may cloud up a bit, but no rain is predicted until Sunday night when you are all in your cars coming back from the beach. You might want to check your air conditioning Saturday and Sunday though because we are showing a possible 98 percent humidity from Saturday afternoon through that Sunday evening shower.

11. When is there a chance the sky may become overcast?
12. What is Friday's chance of rain?
13. What will happen Sunday evening?

Mini-Talk 5
The National Weather Service forecast for today: Rain and thunderstorms will be scattered in the plateau region and northern Texas to the Mississippi and Ohio Valleys to the southern Atlantic Coast states. Some showers are expected over the Great Plains region and the midwestern states as warm weather continues around the rest of the nation. The Eastern Seaboard will have temperatures in the high 70's while temperatures will be in the 60's along the California coast and from Western Pennsylvania to northern New England. The temperature in the desert southwest will reach 100 degrees.

14. Where will it rain?
15. What is the highest predicted temperature?
16. What is the general temperature for the country?

Mini-Talk 6
Yesterday's weather: Rain and thunderstorms raged over the western states, in lower Michigan, and on the Gulf Coast. Storms were heaviest around central Arizona. A tornado in parts of Wisconsin blew down trees, and heavy winds caused power failures and property damage in Louisiana. One person was killed by lightning in Missouri, which experienced golf-ball sized hail during thunderstorms. Temperatures at 2 p.m. ranged from 59 degrees at Cody, Wyoming, to 100 degrees at Hill City, Kansas.

17. Where did the tornado appear?
18. What caused property damage in Louisiana?
19. Where were storms heaviest?
20. What was the low temperature at 2 p.m. ?

MINI-TALKS: ACADEMIC LECTURES

Mini-Talk 1
In 1600 the inking of type was done by what were called *balls*. These were similar to those used by etchers to spread the *ground*. They continued to be used until 1810, when the ink roller was introduced. Balls consisted of cotton or hair pads, circular

and covered with a material such as leather. They were provided with a stick that projected at right angles for use as a handle. The ink was initially spread on a stone and then taken up by the ink balls and spread on the type. A printer always used two ink balls at a time.

1. What replaced ink balls?
2. What material was used in their construction?
3. Where was ink spread first?

Mini-Talk 2
The earliest origins of romance novels are obscure, but certainly the songs of the 11th century troubadors, with their accent on chivalry and love that does not run smooth, predict the advent of the romantic novel.

Indeed, the very term romance from the French *roman*, or fiction, indicates that romance was regarded as a fabulous state not quite based in reality.

While today literary experts may deplore the turning of major publishing houses towards the mass market of romance readers, the publishers are supporting a time-honored tradition. Let us not forget that the novels of Sir Walter Scott, for example, are shameless romances made respectable by means of thin veils of history. The gothic novel of the late 18th century sent sufficient ghosts and ruined temples through the imaginations of its readers to have fathered a whole host of second and third generation romance authors. Both the historical and the gothic romance are alive and well today, thanks to the readership's avid appetite for the fabulous, the supernatural, and the lovelorn.

4. What did early readers consider romance novels to be?
5. What does a gothic novel contain?
6. Who publishes romance novels these days?
7. When did the gothic novel appear?

Mini-Talk 3
The English Romantic poets were distinguished by a naturalness of style hitherto unknown in the classically pure, rigidly formulated work of the Enlightenment authors. Difficult as it is for us to comprehend now, when his language appears stilted, even flowery, to the modern ear, Wordsworth's earliest poems were considered radical inspirations to a whole generation.

In fact, to write a simple poem about seeing daffodils was a thing unheard of in the lofty ranks of England's serious poets of the time. Wordsworth's focus on a common experience, remembered and related without recourse to hyperbole, immediately set him apart from the rest. He was followed of course by Coleridge, then Shelly and Byron, and finally Keats -- the latter three of whom were to make fun of their hero as he became more famous, more respectable, and finally more labored in his verse.

Still, Wordsworth's contributions freed his successors forever from the need to create in labored language on subjects of suitable importance. He was a revolutionary, no matter what his sentiments became in later life.

8. Who were Wordsworth's colleagues and followers?
9. What distinguished his verse?
10. What did his poetry do for his colleagues?

Mini-Talk 4
In art the term *pentimento* refers to the faint ghost of a painting that over time bleeds through the surface of whatever is painted over it so that several images of unrelated work are visible at once.

The effect of this action can be unsettling. I remember distinctly a painting that hung in the dining hall of my preparatory college where a peaceful woodland scene was undercut by the appearance, thanks to pentimento, of a fierce Indian whose hatchet looked ready to cleave the scalp of the young maid sleeping quietly beneath a tree, while on the opposite side of the picture a troop of cavalry thundered towards a couple walking along a winding path.

It was obvious that the artist had taken an old canvas on which no doubt he had painted a thrilling Indian fight and covered it with this more palatable idyll.

11. What appears to us in a pentimento?
12. In the example of the lecture, what was the underpainting?
13. Where did the lecturer see this picture?

Mini-Talk 5
Jackson Pollock and David Smith stand as two giants of the contemporary postwar art world. Indeed their contibutions to painting and sculpture may be said to be responsible for the shift in focus from Europe to the United States -- specifically the New York Abstract expressionists and their colleagues. This dominance of the international art scene lasted for the next three decades and only recently has reversed, as the European Expressionists have once again captured critical attention.

Under Pollock painting became an interior journey, a turning away from the external horrors of war, its false heroics and nationalistic fervor. Like others of his generation, he was disillusioned with the experiences of the last two decades. His art became a way to transcend that anger and dismay.

14. What was Pollock's medium?
15. Who has recently captured critical attention?
16. What was the impulse for Pollock's paintings?
17. What is Pollock's style?

Mini-Talk 6
The new American cuisine is really an adaptation of European, Eastern, and Latin American recipes to the ingredients occurring naturally in the United States. With a heightened public consiousness about fats, carbohydrates, and food additives, American cuisine of this new type has become synonymous with lower calories, smaller portions beautifully served, unusual treatment of vegetables and fresh fish, and an emphasis on the healthful side of each meal.

While many maintain that this standard grew up on the West Coast during the late 1960's and early 1970's, a few students of cuisine point out that this consciousness has been with us far longer, and is responsible for several excellent, long recognized restaurants on the East Coast as well.

18. Does the lecturer believe there is an indigenous American cuisine?
19. What is associated with American cuisine?
20. Where do most believe American cuisine originated?

Mini-Talk 1
There are twelve sign of the zodiac and each is purported to impart certain characteristics to those born under it. Aries, the youngest of the zodiacal year, is aggressive, creative, and self-centered. Gemini, the sign of the twins, is changeable and mercurial, while Cancer can be timid, home-loving, and devoted to family. Scorpios are proud and stubborn, Sagittarians exceptionally honest and spirited.

1. What is the first sign of the zodiac?
2. What sign is the most changeable?
3. According to this mini-talk, which is the most stubborn?

Mini-Talk 2
The language of flowers once so well known has passed out of use. This is a shame since the use of blossoms to convey deep emotions from love to hatred is a pretty convention and one that should be revived. Consider the following:

If you send someone a lotus flower, it indicates estranged love. The birch stands for meekness, ivy for friendship, and a cabbage rose is an ambassador of love. The anemone means you are forsaken while the wild tansy says "I declare war on you."

4. What shows love?
5. Which flower indicates meekness?
6. How is the language of flowers used today?

Mini-Talk 3
There are a number of well-known inns in Connecticut, primarily along the coastline and the upper northwest of the state. The Griswold Inn at Essex is among the most famous, located at the end of the Main Street in Essex, a quaint seaport town filled evey summer with yachtsmen and tourists. Close by in Old Lyme is the Bee and Thistle whose colonial cooking is renowned. You cannot order ahead at the Bee and Thistle, but must take what the owners, two delightful older women, decide their pantry will produce that day. The Griswold Inn, on the other hand, has an extensive menu that even includes the Cajun recipes of the first owner's wife, who came north in the early 1800's.

7. Where does one often find the inns?
8. At which inn can one find Cajun food?
9. How long has the Griswold Inn been in existence?

Mini-Talk 4
Agatha Christie, called the Queen of mystery writers, is known to mystery fans not so much for her characterizations as for her elaborate plots that often depend on coincidence, psychology, and a number of misleading clues or red herrings. Readers are divided among her detectives, each having his or her own distinct following. There are Hercule Poirot, the dapper Belgian and Miss Marple, who knits and solves murders in St. Mary Mead. Mr. Harley Quinn and a host of other more minor sleuths fill out her books.

10. What is Agatha Christie noted for?
11. What is a red herring?
12. What nationality is Hercule Poirot?

Mini-Talk 5
The planets in order from the sun are Mercury, Venus, Earth, Mars, Jupiter, Saturn, Uranus, Neptune, and Pluto. Mars is known as the "red planet" because of its reddish appearance in the sky; Venus is, of course, the planet of mystery, shrouded in vaporous mists; and Mercury, the fastest sun-orbiting planet, is named for the messenger of the gods, although the planet, which circles the sun every 88 days, is lifeless and cratered, much like our moon.

13. Which planet is farthest from the earth?
14. How many days does Mercury's sun revolution require?
15. Which planet resembles our moon?

MINI-TALKS: CLASS DISCUSSIONS

Mini-Talk 1

Man:	Susan, name some words considered negatives.
Woman:	*Not* and *never*.
Man:	Anyone else?
Woman:	Wait! What about *none*?
Man:	Yes, that's another one. Anyone else?

1. Which of the following is not a negative?
2. What does a negative word do?
3. What kind of class is this?

Mini-Talk 2

Man:	Who knows who wrote *Moby Dick*?
Woman:	Herman Mellville.
Man:	Right. And what did he base his book on?
Woman:	His experience on whaling ships.
Man:	Was Melville a popular writer?
Woman:	Probably.
Man:	Why do you think he stopped writing?
Woman:	I don't know. Bad reviews?

4. Who is Herman Melville?
5. What had Melville done besides write novels?
6. Why did he stop writing?

Mini-Talk 3

Woman:	Have you seen or used a slide rule?
Man:	I've never used one, but my father is an engineer. He still uses his.
Woman:	What do you use?
Man:	A calculator. I use it for everything.

7. What is the man's father?
8. Who uses a slide rule?
9. How does the student add and subtract?

Mini-Talk 4

Man:	I can't wait to see the zoo. What time will the bus come?
Woman:	I think it's supposed to arrive around noon.
Man:	When are we supposed to eat?
Woman:	On the bus. Didn't you remember to bring your lunch?

Man:	No one told me to.
Woman:	That's not true. The teacher told us Friday.
Man:	I wasn't here then.

10. Where is the class going?
11. What did the students need to bring?
12. Why didn't the man have food?

Mini-Talk 5

Man:	Grammar is harder to learn than math.
Woman:	I agree.
Man:	I used to think I was good at languages.
Woman:	And now?
Man:	I'm afraid to open my mouth -- I'll make a mistake.
Woman:	That's silly. You need to practice, like music or sports.
Man:	I'd rather be perfect.

13. What does the man think is hard to learn?
14. Why is the man timid about speaking?
15. What does the woman think of his attitude?

ANSWER SHEET FOR DIAGNOSTIC TEST 1

(Tear This Sheet Out and Use It to Mark Your Answers)

SECTION I
LISTENING COMPREHENSION

1 Ⓐ Ⓑ Ⓒ Ⓓ	26 Ⓐ Ⓑ Ⓒ Ⓓ	
2 Ⓐ Ⓑ Ⓒ Ⓓ	27 Ⓐ Ⓑ Ⓒ Ⓓ	
3 Ⓐ Ⓑ Ⓒ Ⓓ	28 Ⓐ Ⓑ Ⓒ Ⓓ	
4 Ⓐ Ⓑ Ⓒ Ⓓ	29 Ⓐ Ⓑ Ⓒ Ⓓ	
5 Ⓐ Ⓑ Ⓒ Ⓓ	30 Ⓐ Ⓑ Ⓒ Ⓓ	
6 Ⓐ Ⓑ Ⓒ Ⓓ	31 Ⓐ Ⓑ Ⓒ Ⓓ	
7 Ⓐ Ⓑ Ⓒ Ⓓ	32 Ⓐ Ⓑ Ⓒ Ⓓ	
8 Ⓐ Ⓑ Ⓒ Ⓓ	33 Ⓐ Ⓑ Ⓒ Ⓓ	
9 Ⓐ Ⓑ Ⓒ Ⓓ	34 Ⓐ Ⓑ Ⓒ Ⓓ	
10 Ⓐ Ⓑ Ⓒ Ⓓ	35 Ⓐ Ⓑ Ⓒ Ⓓ	
11 Ⓐ Ⓑ Ⓒ Ⓓ	36 Ⓐ Ⓑ Ⓒ Ⓓ	
12 Ⓐ Ⓑ Ⓒ Ⓓ	37 Ⓐ Ⓑ Ⓒ Ⓓ	
13 Ⓐ Ⓑ Ⓒ Ⓓ	38 Ⓐ Ⓑ Ⓒ Ⓓ	
14 Ⓐ Ⓑ Ⓒ Ⓓ	39 Ⓐ Ⓑ Ⓒ Ⓓ	
15 Ⓐ Ⓑ Ⓒ Ⓓ	40 Ⓐ Ⓑ Ⓒ Ⓓ	
16 Ⓐ Ⓑ Ⓒ Ⓓ	41 Ⓐ Ⓑ Ⓒ Ⓓ	
17 Ⓐ Ⓑ Ⓒ Ⓓ	42 Ⓐ Ⓑ Ⓒ Ⓓ	
18 Ⓐ Ⓑ Ⓒ Ⓓ	43 Ⓐ Ⓑ Ⓒ Ⓓ	
19 Ⓐ Ⓑ Ⓒ Ⓓ	44 Ⓐ Ⓑ Ⓒ Ⓓ	
20 Ⓐ Ⓑ Ⓒ Ⓓ	45 Ⓐ Ⓑ Ⓒ Ⓓ	
21 Ⓐ Ⓑ Ⓒ Ⓓ	46 Ⓐ Ⓑ Ⓒ Ⓓ	
22 Ⓐ Ⓑ Ⓒ Ⓓ	47 Ⓐ Ⓑ Ⓒ Ⓓ	
23 Ⓐ Ⓑ Ⓒ Ⓓ	48 Ⓐ Ⓑ Ⓒ Ⓓ	
24 Ⓐ Ⓑ Ⓒ Ⓓ	49 Ⓐ Ⓑ Ⓒ Ⓓ	
25 Ⓐ Ⓑ Ⓒ Ⓓ	50 Ⓐ Ⓑ Ⓒ Ⓓ	

SECTION II
STRUCTURE AND WRITTEN EXPRESSION

1 Ⓐ Ⓑ Ⓒ Ⓓ	26 Ⓐ Ⓑ Ⓒ Ⓓ
2 Ⓐ Ⓑ Ⓒ Ⓓ	27 Ⓐ Ⓑ Ⓒ Ⓓ
3 Ⓐ Ⓑ Ⓒ Ⓓ	28 Ⓐ Ⓑ Ⓒ Ⓓ
4 Ⓐ Ⓑ Ⓒ Ⓓ	29 Ⓐ Ⓑ Ⓒ Ⓓ
5 Ⓐ Ⓑ Ⓒ Ⓓ	30 Ⓐ Ⓑ Ⓒ Ⓓ
6 Ⓐ Ⓑ Ⓒ Ⓓ	31 Ⓐ Ⓑ Ⓒ Ⓓ
7 Ⓐ Ⓑ Ⓒ Ⓓ	32 Ⓐ Ⓑ Ⓒ Ⓓ
8 Ⓐ Ⓑ Ⓒ Ⓓ	33 Ⓐ Ⓑ Ⓒ Ⓓ
9 Ⓐ Ⓑ Ⓒ Ⓓ	34 Ⓐ Ⓑ Ⓒ Ⓓ
10 Ⓐ Ⓑ Ⓒ Ⓓ	35 Ⓐ Ⓑ Ⓒ Ⓓ
11 Ⓐ Ⓑ Ⓒ Ⓓ	36 Ⓐ Ⓑ Ⓒ Ⓓ
12 Ⓐ Ⓑ Ⓒ Ⓓ	37 Ⓐ Ⓑ Ⓒ Ⓓ
13 Ⓐ Ⓑ Ⓒ Ⓓ	38 Ⓐ Ⓑ Ⓒ Ⓓ
14 Ⓐ Ⓑ Ⓒ Ⓓ	39 Ⓐ Ⓑ Ⓒ Ⓓ
15 Ⓐ Ⓑ Ⓒ Ⓓ	40 Ⓐ Ⓑ Ⓒ Ⓓ
16 Ⓐ Ⓑ Ⓒ Ⓓ	
17 Ⓐ Ⓑ Ⓒ Ⓓ	
18 Ⓐ Ⓑ Ⓒ Ⓓ	
19 Ⓐ Ⓑ Ⓒ Ⓓ	
20 Ⓐ Ⓑ Ⓒ Ⓓ	
21 Ⓐ Ⓑ Ⓒ Ⓓ	
22 Ⓐ Ⓑ Ⓒ Ⓓ	
23 Ⓐ Ⓑ Ⓒ Ⓓ	
24 Ⓐ Ⓑ Ⓒ Ⓓ	
25 Ⓐ Ⓑ Ⓒ Ⓓ	

SECTION III
READING COMPREHENSION AND VOCABULARY

1 Ⓐ Ⓑ Ⓒ Ⓓ	26 Ⓐ Ⓑ Ⓒ Ⓓ	51 Ⓐ Ⓑ Ⓒ Ⓓ
2 Ⓐ Ⓑ Ⓒ Ⓓ	27 Ⓐ Ⓑ Ⓒ Ⓓ	52 Ⓐ Ⓑ Ⓒ Ⓓ
3 Ⓐ Ⓑ Ⓒ Ⓓ	28 Ⓐ Ⓑ Ⓒ Ⓓ	53 Ⓐ Ⓑ Ⓒ Ⓓ
4 Ⓐ Ⓑ Ⓒ Ⓓ	29 Ⓐ Ⓑ Ⓒ Ⓓ	54 Ⓐ Ⓑ Ⓒ Ⓓ
5 Ⓐ Ⓑ Ⓒ Ⓓ	30 Ⓐ Ⓑ Ⓒ Ⓓ	55 Ⓐ Ⓑ Ⓒ Ⓓ
6 Ⓐ Ⓑ Ⓒ Ⓓ	31 Ⓐ Ⓑ Ⓒ Ⓓ	56 Ⓐ Ⓑ Ⓒ Ⓓ
7 Ⓐ Ⓑ Ⓒ Ⓓ	32 Ⓐ Ⓑ Ⓒ Ⓓ	57 Ⓐ Ⓑ Ⓒ Ⓓ
8 Ⓐ Ⓑ Ⓒ Ⓓ	33 Ⓐ Ⓑ Ⓒ Ⓓ	58 Ⓐ Ⓑ Ⓒ Ⓓ
9 Ⓐ Ⓑ Ⓒ Ⓓ	34 Ⓐ Ⓑ Ⓒ Ⓓ	59 Ⓐ Ⓑ Ⓒ Ⓓ
10 Ⓐ Ⓑ Ⓒ Ⓓ	35 Ⓐ Ⓑ Ⓒ Ⓓ	60 Ⓐ Ⓑ Ⓒ Ⓓ
11 Ⓐ Ⓑ Ⓒ Ⓓ	36 Ⓐ Ⓑ Ⓒ Ⓓ	
12 Ⓐ Ⓑ Ⓒ Ⓓ	37 Ⓐ Ⓑ Ⓒ Ⓓ	
13 Ⓐ Ⓑ Ⓒ Ⓓ	38 Ⓐ Ⓑ Ⓒ Ⓓ	
14 Ⓐ Ⓑ Ⓒ Ⓓ	39 Ⓐ Ⓑ Ⓒ Ⓓ	
15 Ⓐ Ⓑ Ⓒ Ⓓ	40 Ⓐ Ⓑ Ⓒ Ⓓ	
16 Ⓐ Ⓑ Ⓒ Ⓓ	41 Ⓐ Ⓑ Ⓒ Ⓓ	
17 Ⓐ Ⓑ Ⓒ Ⓓ	42 Ⓐ Ⓑ Ⓒ Ⓓ	
18 Ⓐ Ⓑ Ⓒ Ⓓ	43 Ⓐ Ⓑ Ⓒ Ⓓ	
19 Ⓐ Ⓑ Ⓒ Ⓓ	44 Ⓐ Ⓑ Ⓒ Ⓓ	
20 Ⓐ Ⓑ Ⓒ Ⓓ	45 Ⓐ Ⓑ Ⓒ Ⓓ	
21 Ⓐ Ⓑ Ⓒ Ⓓ	46 Ⓐ Ⓑ Ⓒ Ⓓ	
22 Ⓐ Ⓑ Ⓒ Ⓓ	47 Ⓐ Ⓑ Ⓒ Ⓓ	
23 Ⓐ Ⓑ Ⓒ Ⓓ	48 Ⓐ Ⓑ Ⓒ Ⓓ	
24 Ⓐ Ⓑ Ⓒ Ⓓ	49 Ⓐ Ⓑ Ⓒ Ⓓ	
25 Ⓐ Ⓑ Ⓒ Ⓓ	50 Ⓐ Ⓑ Ⓒ Ⓓ	

ANSWER SHEET FOR DIAGNOSTIC TEST 2

(Tear This Sheet Out and Use It to Mark Your Answers)

SECTION I
LISTENING COMPREHENSION

1 Ⓐ Ⓑ Ⓒ Ⓓ	26 Ⓐ Ⓑ Ⓒ Ⓓ	
2 Ⓐ Ⓑ Ⓒ Ⓓ	27 Ⓐ Ⓑ Ⓒ Ⓓ	
3 Ⓐ Ⓑ Ⓒ Ⓓ	28 Ⓐ Ⓑ Ⓒ Ⓓ	
4 Ⓐ Ⓑ Ⓒ Ⓓ	29 Ⓐ Ⓑ Ⓒ Ⓓ	
5 Ⓐ Ⓑ Ⓒ Ⓓ	30 Ⓐ Ⓑ Ⓒ Ⓓ	
6 Ⓐ Ⓑ Ⓒ Ⓓ	31 Ⓐ Ⓑ Ⓒ Ⓓ	
7 Ⓐ Ⓑ Ⓒ Ⓓ	32 Ⓐ Ⓑ Ⓒ Ⓓ	
8 Ⓐ Ⓑ Ⓒ Ⓓ	33 Ⓐ Ⓑ Ⓒ Ⓓ	
9 Ⓐ Ⓑ Ⓒ Ⓓ	34 Ⓐ Ⓑ Ⓒ Ⓓ	
10 Ⓐ Ⓑ Ⓒ Ⓓ	35 Ⓐ Ⓑ Ⓒ Ⓓ	
11 Ⓐ Ⓑ Ⓒ Ⓓ	36 Ⓐ Ⓑ Ⓒ Ⓓ	
12 Ⓐ Ⓑ Ⓒ Ⓓ	37 Ⓐ Ⓑ Ⓒ Ⓓ	
13 Ⓐ Ⓑ Ⓒ Ⓓ	38 Ⓐ Ⓑ Ⓒ Ⓓ	
14 Ⓐ Ⓑ Ⓒ Ⓓ	39 Ⓐ Ⓑ Ⓒ Ⓓ	
15 Ⓐ Ⓑ Ⓒ Ⓓ	40 Ⓐ Ⓑ Ⓒ Ⓓ	
16 Ⓐ Ⓑ Ⓒ Ⓓ	41 Ⓐ Ⓑ Ⓒ Ⓓ	
17 Ⓐ Ⓑ Ⓒ Ⓓ	42 Ⓐ Ⓑ Ⓒ Ⓓ	
18 Ⓐ Ⓑ Ⓒ Ⓓ	43 Ⓐ Ⓑ Ⓒ Ⓓ	
19 Ⓐ Ⓑ Ⓒ Ⓓ	44 Ⓐ Ⓑ Ⓒ Ⓓ	
20 Ⓐ Ⓑ Ⓒ Ⓓ	45 Ⓐ Ⓑ Ⓒ Ⓓ	
21 Ⓐ Ⓑ Ⓒ Ⓓ	46 Ⓐ Ⓑ Ⓒ Ⓓ	
22 Ⓐ Ⓑ Ⓒ Ⓓ	47 Ⓐ Ⓑ Ⓒ Ⓓ	
23 Ⓐ Ⓑ Ⓒ Ⓓ	48 Ⓐ Ⓑ Ⓒ Ⓓ	
24 Ⓐ Ⓑ Ⓒ Ⓓ	49 Ⓐ Ⓑ Ⓒ Ⓓ	
25 Ⓐ Ⓑ Ⓒ Ⓓ	50 Ⓐ Ⓑ Ⓒ Ⓓ	

SECTION II
STRUCTURE AND WRITTEN EXPRESSION

1 Ⓐ Ⓑ Ⓒ Ⓓ	26 Ⓐ Ⓑ Ⓒ Ⓓ
2 Ⓐ Ⓑ Ⓒ Ⓓ	27 Ⓐ Ⓑ Ⓒ Ⓓ
3 Ⓐ Ⓑ Ⓒ Ⓓ	28 Ⓐ Ⓑ Ⓒ Ⓓ
4 Ⓐ Ⓑ Ⓒ Ⓓ	29 Ⓐ Ⓑ Ⓒ Ⓓ
5 Ⓐ Ⓑ Ⓒ Ⓓ	30 Ⓐ Ⓑ Ⓒ Ⓓ
6 Ⓐ Ⓑ Ⓒ Ⓓ	31 Ⓐ Ⓑ Ⓒ Ⓓ
7 Ⓐ Ⓑ Ⓒ Ⓓ	32 Ⓐ Ⓑ Ⓒ Ⓓ
8 Ⓐ Ⓑ Ⓒ Ⓓ	33 Ⓐ Ⓑ Ⓒ Ⓓ
9 Ⓐ Ⓑ Ⓒ Ⓓ	34 Ⓐ Ⓑ Ⓒ Ⓓ
10 Ⓐ Ⓑ Ⓒ Ⓓ	35 Ⓐ Ⓑ Ⓒ Ⓓ
11 Ⓐ Ⓑ Ⓒ Ⓓ	36 Ⓐ Ⓑ Ⓒ Ⓓ
12 Ⓐ Ⓑ Ⓒ Ⓓ	37 Ⓐ Ⓑ Ⓒ Ⓓ
13 Ⓐ Ⓑ Ⓒ Ⓓ	38 Ⓐ Ⓑ Ⓒ Ⓓ
14 Ⓐ Ⓑ Ⓒ Ⓓ	39 Ⓐ Ⓑ Ⓒ Ⓓ
15 Ⓐ Ⓑ Ⓒ Ⓓ	40 Ⓐ Ⓑ Ⓒ Ⓓ
16 Ⓐ Ⓑ Ⓒ Ⓓ	
17 Ⓐ Ⓑ Ⓒ Ⓓ	
18 Ⓐ Ⓑ Ⓒ Ⓓ	
19 Ⓐ Ⓑ Ⓒ Ⓓ	
20 Ⓐ Ⓑ Ⓒ Ⓓ	
21 Ⓐ Ⓑ Ⓒ Ⓓ	
22 Ⓐ Ⓑ Ⓒ Ⓓ	
23 Ⓐ Ⓑ Ⓒ Ⓓ	
24 Ⓐ Ⓑ Ⓒ Ⓓ	
25 Ⓐ Ⓑ Ⓒ Ⓓ	

SECTION III
READING COMPREHENSION AND VOCABULARY

1 Ⓐ Ⓑ Ⓒ Ⓓ	26 Ⓐ Ⓑ Ⓒ Ⓓ	51 Ⓐ Ⓑ Ⓒ Ⓓ
2 Ⓐ Ⓑ Ⓒ Ⓓ	27 Ⓐ Ⓑ Ⓒ Ⓓ	52 Ⓐ Ⓑ Ⓒ Ⓓ
3 Ⓐ Ⓑ Ⓒ Ⓓ	28 Ⓐ Ⓑ Ⓒ Ⓓ	53 Ⓐ Ⓑ Ⓒ Ⓓ
4 Ⓐ Ⓑ Ⓒ Ⓓ	29 Ⓐ Ⓑ Ⓒ Ⓓ	54 Ⓐ Ⓑ Ⓒ Ⓓ
5 Ⓐ Ⓑ Ⓒ Ⓓ	30 Ⓐ Ⓑ Ⓒ Ⓓ	55 Ⓐ Ⓑ Ⓒ Ⓓ
6 Ⓐ Ⓑ Ⓒ Ⓓ	31 Ⓐ Ⓑ Ⓒ Ⓓ	56 Ⓐ Ⓑ Ⓒ Ⓓ
7 Ⓐ Ⓑ Ⓒ Ⓓ	32 Ⓐ Ⓑ Ⓒ Ⓓ	57 Ⓐ Ⓑ Ⓒ Ⓓ
8 Ⓐ Ⓑ Ⓒ Ⓓ	33 Ⓐ Ⓑ Ⓒ Ⓓ	58 Ⓐ Ⓑ Ⓒ Ⓓ
9 Ⓐ Ⓑ Ⓒ Ⓓ	34 Ⓐ Ⓑ Ⓒ Ⓓ	59 Ⓐ Ⓑ Ⓒ Ⓓ
10 Ⓐ Ⓑ Ⓒ Ⓓ	35 Ⓐ Ⓑ Ⓒ Ⓓ	60 Ⓐ Ⓑ Ⓒ Ⓓ
11 Ⓐ Ⓑ Ⓒ Ⓓ	36 Ⓐ Ⓑ Ⓒ Ⓓ	
12 Ⓐ Ⓑ Ⓒ Ⓓ	37 Ⓐ Ⓑ Ⓒ Ⓓ	
13 Ⓐ Ⓑ Ⓒ Ⓓ	38 Ⓐ Ⓑ Ⓒ Ⓓ	
14 Ⓐ Ⓑ Ⓒ Ⓓ	39 Ⓐ Ⓑ Ⓒ Ⓓ	
15 Ⓐ Ⓑ Ⓒ Ⓓ	40 Ⓐ Ⓑ Ⓒ Ⓓ	
16 Ⓐ Ⓑ Ⓒ Ⓓ	41 Ⓐ Ⓑ Ⓒ Ⓓ	
17 Ⓐ Ⓑ Ⓒ Ⓓ	42 Ⓐ Ⓑ Ⓒ Ⓓ	
18 Ⓐ Ⓑ Ⓒ Ⓓ	43 Ⓐ Ⓑ Ⓒ Ⓓ	
19 Ⓐ Ⓑ Ⓒ Ⓓ	44 Ⓐ Ⓑ Ⓒ Ⓓ	
20 Ⓐ Ⓑ Ⓒ Ⓓ	45 Ⓐ Ⓑ Ⓒ Ⓓ	
21 Ⓐ Ⓑ Ⓒ Ⓓ	46 Ⓐ Ⓑ Ⓒ Ⓓ	
22 Ⓐ Ⓑ Ⓒ Ⓓ	47 Ⓐ Ⓑ Ⓒ Ⓓ	
23 Ⓐ Ⓑ Ⓒ Ⓓ	48 Ⓐ Ⓑ Ⓒ Ⓓ	
24 Ⓐ Ⓑ Ⓒ Ⓓ	49 Ⓐ Ⓑ Ⓒ Ⓓ	
25 Ⓐ Ⓑ Ⓒ Ⓓ	50 Ⓐ Ⓑ Ⓒ Ⓓ	

ANSWER SHEET FOR DIAGNOSTIC TEST 3

(Tear This Sheet Out and Use It to Mark Your Answers)

SECTION I

LISTENING COMPREHENSION

1 Ⓐ Ⓑ Ⓒ Ⓓ	26 Ⓐ Ⓑ Ⓒ Ⓓ
2 Ⓐ Ⓑ Ⓒ Ⓓ	27 Ⓐ Ⓑ Ⓒ Ⓓ
3 Ⓐ Ⓑ Ⓒ Ⓓ	28 Ⓐ Ⓑ Ⓒ Ⓓ
4 Ⓐ Ⓑ Ⓒ Ⓓ	29 Ⓐ Ⓑ Ⓒ Ⓓ
5 Ⓐ Ⓑ Ⓒ Ⓓ	30 Ⓐ Ⓑ Ⓒ Ⓓ

6 Ⓐ Ⓑ Ⓒ Ⓓ	31 Ⓐ Ⓑ Ⓒ Ⓓ
7 Ⓐ Ⓑ Ⓒ Ⓓ	32 Ⓐ Ⓑ Ⓒ Ⓓ
8 Ⓐ Ⓑ Ⓒ Ⓓ	33 Ⓐ Ⓑ Ⓒ Ⓓ
9 Ⓐ Ⓑ Ⓒ Ⓓ	34 Ⓐ Ⓑ Ⓒ Ⓓ
10 Ⓐ Ⓑ Ⓒ Ⓓ	35 Ⓐ Ⓑ Ⓒ Ⓓ

11 Ⓐ Ⓑ Ⓒ Ⓓ	36 Ⓐ Ⓑ Ⓒ Ⓓ
12 Ⓐ Ⓑ Ⓒ Ⓓ	37 Ⓐ Ⓑ Ⓒ Ⓓ
13 Ⓐ Ⓑ Ⓒ Ⓓ	38 Ⓐ Ⓑ Ⓒ Ⓓ
14 Ⓐ Ⓑ Ⓒ Ⓓ	39 Ⓐ Ⓑ Ⓒ Ⓓ
15 Ⓐ Ⓑ Ⓒ Ⓓ	40 Ⓐ Ⓑ Ⓒ Ⓓ

16 Ⓐ Ⓑ Ⓒ Ⓓ	41 Ⓐ Ⓑ Ⓒ Ⓓ
17 Ⓐ Ⓑ Ⓒ Ⓓ	42 Ⓐ Ⓑ Ⓒ Ⓓ
18 Ⓐ Ⓑ Ⓒ Ⓓ	43 Ⓐ Ⓑ Ⓒ Ⓓ
19 Ⓐ Ⓑ Ⓒ Ⓓ	44 Ⓐ Ⓑ Ⓒ Ⓓ
20 Ⓐ Ⓑ Ⓒ Ⓓ	45 Ⓐ Ⓑ Ⓒ Ⓓ

21 Ⓐ Ⓑ Ⓒ Ⓓ	46 Ⓐ Ⓑ Ⓒ Ⓓ
22 Ⓐ Ⓑ Ⓒ Ⓓ	47 Ⓐ Ⓑ Ⓒ Ⓓ
23 Ⓐ Ⓑ Ⓒ Ⓓ	48 Ⓐ Ⓑ Ⓒ Ⓓ
24 Ⓐ Ⓑ Ⓒ Ⓓ	49 Ⓐ Ⓑ Ⓒ Ⓓ
25 Ⓐ Ⓑ Ⓒ Ⓓ	50 Ⓐ Ⓑ Ⓒ Ⓓ

SECTION II

STRUCTURE AND WRITTEN EXPRESSION

1 Ⓐ Ⓑ Ⓒ Ⓓ	26 Ⓐ Ⓑ Ⓒ Ⓓ
2 Ⓐ Ⓑ Ⓒ Ⓓ	27 Ⓐ Ⓑ Ⓒ Ⓓ
3 Ⓐ Ⓑ Ⓒ Ⓓ	28 Ⓐ Ⓑ Ⓒ Ⓓ
4 Ⓐ Ⓑ Ⓒ Ⓓ	29 Ⓐ Ⓑ Ⓒ Ⓓ
5 Ⓐ Ⓑ Ⓒ Ⓓ	30 Ⓐ Ⓑ Ⓒ Ⓓ

6 Ⓐ Ⓑ Ⓒ Ⓓ	31 Ⓐ Ⓑ Ⓒ Ⓓ
7 Ⓐ Ⓑ Ⓒ Ⓓ	32 Ⓐ Ⓑ Ⓒ Ⓓ
8 Ⓐ Ⓑ Ⓒ Ⓓ	33 Ⓐ Ⓑ Ⓒ Ⓓ
9 Ⓐ Ⓑ Ⓒ Ⓓ	34 Ⓐ Ⓑ Ⓒ Ⓓ
10 Ⓐ Ⓑ Ⓒ Ⓓ	35 Ⓐ Ⓑ Ⓒ Ⓓ

11 Ⓐ Ⓑ Ⓒ Ⓓ	36 Ⓐ Ⓑ Ⓒ Ⓓ
12 Ⓐ Ⓑ Ⓒ Ⓓ	37 Ⓐ Ⓑ Ⓒ Ⓓ
13 Ⓐ Ⓑ Ⓒ Ⓓ	38 Ⓐ Ⓑ Ⓒ Ⓓ
14 Ⓐ Ⓑ Ⓒ Ⓓ	39 Ⓐ Ⓑ Ⓒ Ⓓ
15 Ⓐ Ⓑ Ⓒ Ⓓ	40 Ⓐ Ⓑ Ⓒ Ⓓ

| 16 Ⓐ Ⓑ Ⓒ Ⓓ |
| 17 Ⓐ Ⓑ Ⓒ Ⓓ |
| 18 Ⓐ Ⓑ Ⓒ Ⓓ |
| 19 Ⓐ Ⓑ Ⓒ Ⓓ |
| 20 Ⓐ Ⓑ Ⓒ Ⓓ |

| 21 Ⓐ Ⓑ Ⓒ Ⓓ |
| 22 Ⓐ Ⓑ Ⓒ Ⓓ |
| 23 Ⓐ Ⓑ Ⓒ Ⓓ |
| 24 Ⓐ Ⓑ Ⓒ Ⓓ |
| 25 Ⓐ Ⓑ Ⓒ Ⓓ |

SECTION III

READING COMPREHENSION AND VOCABULARY

1 Ⓐ Ⓑ Ⓒ Ⓓ	26 Ⓐ Ⓑ Ⓒ Ⓓ	51 Ⓐ Ⓑ Ⓒ Ⓓ
2 Ⓐ Ⓑ Ⓒ Ⓓ	27 Ⓐ Ⓑ Ⓒ Ⓓ	52 Ⓐ Ⓑ Ⓒ Ⓓ
3 Ⓐ Ⓑ Ⓒ Ⓓ	28 Ⓐ Ⓑ Ⓒ Ⓓ	53 Ⓐ Ⓑ Ⓒ Ⓓ
4 Ⓐ Ⓑ Ⓒ Ⓓ	29 Ⓐ Ⓑ Ⓒ Ⓓ	54 Ⓐ Ⓑ Ⓒ Ⓓ
5 Ⓐ Ⓑ Ⓒ Ⓓ	30 Ⓐ Ⓑ Ⓒ Ⓓ	55 Ⓐ Ⓑ Ⓒ Ⓓ

6 Ⓐ Ⓑ Ⓒ Ⓓ	31 Ⓐ Ⓑ Ⓒ Ⓓ	56 Ⓐ Ⓑ Ⓒ Ⓓ
7 Ⓐ Ⓑ Ⓒ Ⓓ	32 Ⓐ Ⓑ Ⓒ Ⓓ	57 Ⓐ Ⓑ Ⓒ Ⓓ
8 Ⓐ Ⓑ Ⓒ Ⓓ	33 Ⓐ Ⓑ Ⓒ Ⓓ	58 Ⓐ Ⓑ Ⓒ Ⓓ
9 Ⓐ Ⓑ Ⓒ Ⓓ	34 Ⓐ Ⓑ Ⓒ Ⓓ	59 Ⓐ Ⓑ Ⓒ Ⓓ
10 Ⓐ Ⓑ Ⓒ Ⓓ	35 Ⓐ Ⓑ Ⓒ Ⓓ	60 Ⓐ Ⓑ Ⓒ Ⓓ

11 Ⓐ Ⓑ Ⓒ Ⓓ	36 Ⓐ Ⓑ Ⓒ Ⓓ
12 Ⓐ Ⓑ Ⓒ Ⓓ	37 Ⓐ Ⓑ Ⓒ Ⓓ
13 Ⓐ Ⓑ Ⓒ Ⓓ	38 Ⓐ Ⓑ Ⓒ Ⓓ
14 Ⓐ Ⓑ Ⓒ Ⓓ	39 Ⓐ Ⓑ Ⓒ Ⓓ
15 Ⓐ Ⓑ Ⓒ Ⓓ	40 Ⓐ Ⓑ Ⓒ Ⓓ

16 Ⓐ Ⓑ Ⓒ Ⓓ	41 Ⓐ Ⓑ Ⓒ Ⓓ
17 Ⓐ Ⓑ Ⓒ Ⓓ	42 Ⓐ Ⓑ Ⓒ Ⓓ
18 Ⓐ Ⓑ Ⓒ Ⓓ	43 Ⓐ Ⓑ Ⓒ Ⓓ
19 Ⓐ Ⓑ Ⓒ Ⓓ	44 Ⓐ Ⓑ Ⓒ Ⓓ
20 Ⓐ Ⓑ Ⓒ Ⓓ	45 Ⓐ Ⓑ Ⓒ Ⓓ

21 Ⓐ Ⓑ Ⓒ Ⓓ	46 Ⓐ Ⓑ Ⓒ Ⓓ
22 Ⓐ Ⓑ Ⓒ Ⓓ	47 Ⓐ Ⓑ Ⓒ Ⓓ
23 Ⓐ Ⓑ Ⓒ Ⓓ	48 Ⓐ Ⓑ Ⓒ Ⓓ
24 Ⓐ Ⓑ Ⓒ Ⓓ	49 Ⓐ Ⓑ Ⓒ Ⓓ
25 Ⓐ Ⓑ Ⓒ Ⓓ	50 Ⓐ Ⓑ Ⓒ Ⓓ

ANSWER SHEET FOR DIAGNOSTIC TEST 4

(Tear This Sheet Out and Use It to Mark Your Answers)

SECTION I

LISTENING
COMPREHENSION

1 Ⓐ Ⓑ Ⓒ Ⓓ	26 Ⓐ Ⓑ Ⓒ Ⓓ	
2 Ⓐ Ⓑ Ⓒ Ⓓ	27 Ⓐ Ⓑ Ⓒ Ⓓ	
3 Ⓐ Ⓑ Ⓒ Ⓓ	28 Ⓐ Ⓑ Ⓒ Ⓓ	
4 Ⓐ Ⓑ Ⓒ Ⓓ	29 Ⓐ Ⓑ Ⓒ Ⓓ	
5 Ⓐ Ⓑ Ⓒ Ⓓ	30 Ⓐ Ⓑ Ⓒ Ⓓ	
6 Ⓐ Ⓑ Ⓒ Ⓓ	31 Ⓐ Ⓑ Ⓒ Ⓓ	
7 Ⓐ Ⓑ Ⓒ Ⓓ	32 Ⓐ Ⓑ Ⓒ Ⓓ	
8 Ⓐ Ⓑ Ⓒ Ⓓ	33 Ⓐ Ⓑ Ⓒ Ⓓ	
9 Ⓐ Ⓑ Ⓒ Ⓓ	34 Ⓐ Ⓑ Ⓒ Ⓓ	
10 Ⓐ Ⓑ Ⓒ Ⓓ	35 Ⓐ Ⓑ Ⓒ Ⓓ	
11 Ⓐ Ⓑ Ⓒ Ⓓ	36 Ⓐ Ⓑ Ⓒ Ⓓ	
12 Ⓐ Ⓑ Ⓒ Ⓓ	37 Ⓐ Ⓑ Ⓒ Ⓓ	
13 Ⓐ Ⓑ Ⓒ Ⓓ	38 Ⓐ Ⓑ Ⓒ Ⓓ	
14 Ⓐ Ⓑ Ⓒ Ⓓ	39 Ⓐ Ⓑ Ⓒ Ⓓ	
15 Ⓐ Ⓑ Ⓒ Ⓓ	40 Ⓐ Ⓑ Ⓒ Ⓓ	
16 Ⓐ Ⓑ Ⓒ Ⓓ	41 Ⓐ Ⓑ Ⓒ Ⓓ	
17 Ⓐ Ⓑ Ⓒ Ⓓ	42 Ⓐ Ⓑ Ⓒ Ⓓ	
18 Ⓐ Ⓑ Ⓒ Ⓓ	43 Ⓐ Ⓑ Ⓒ Ⓓ	
19 Ⓐ Ⓑ Ⓒ Ⓓ	44 Ⓐ Ⓑ Ⓒ Ⓓ	
20 Ⓐ Ⓑ Ⓒ Ⓓ	45 Ⓐ Ⓑ Ⓒ Ⓓ	
21 Ⓐ Ⓑ Ⓒ Ⓓ	46 Ⓐ Ⓑ Ⓒ Ⓓ	
22 Ⓐ Ⓑ Ⓒ Ⓓ	47 Ⓐ Ⓑ Ⓒ Ⓓ	
23 Ⓐ Ⓑ Ⓒ Ⓓ	48 Ⓐ Ⓑ Ⓒ Ⓓ	
24 Ⓐ Ⓑ Ⓒ Ⓓ	49 Ⓐ Ⓑ Ⓒ Ⓓ	
25 Ⓐ Ⓑ Ⓒ Ⓓ	50 Ⓐ Ⓑ Ⓒ Ⓓ	

SECTION II

STRUCTURE AND
WRITTEN EXPRESSION

1 Ⓐ Ⓑ Ⓒ Ⓓ	26 Ⓐ Ⓑ Ⓒ Ⓓ
2 Ⓐ Ⓑ Ⓒ Ⓓ	27 Ⓐ Ⓑ Ⓒ Ⓓ
3 Ⓐ Ⓑ Ⓒ Ⓓ	28 Ⓐ Ⓑ Ⓒ Ⓓ
4 Ⓐ Ⓑ Ⓒ Ⓓ	29 Ⓐ Ⓑ Ⓒ Ⓓ
5 Ⓐ Ⓑ Ⓒ Ⓓ	30 Ⓐ Ⓑ Ⓒ Ⓓ
6 Ⓐ Ⓑ Ⓒ Ⓓ	31 Ⓐ Ⓑ Ⓒ Ⓓ
7 Ⓐ Ⓑ Ⓒ Ⓓ	32 Ⓐ Ⓑ Ⓒ Ⓓ
8 Ⓐ Ⓑ Ⓒ Ⓓ	33 Ⓐ Ⓑ Ⓒ Ⓓ
9 Ⓐ Ⓑ Ⓒ Ⓓ	34 Ⓐ Ⓑ Ⓒ Ⓓ
10 Ⓐ Ⓑ Ⓒ Ⓓ	35 Ⓐ Ⓑ Ⓒ Ⓓ
11 Ⓐ Ⓑ Ⓒ Ⓓ	36 Ⓐ Ⓑ Ⓒ Ⓓ
12 Ⓐ Ⓑ Ⓒ Ⓓ	37 Ⓐ Ⓑ Ⓒ Ⓓ
13 Ⓐ Ⓑ Ⓒ Ⓓ	38 Ⓐ Ⓑ Ⓒ Ⓓ
14 Ⓐ Ⓑ Ⓒ Ⓓ	39 Ⓐ Ⓑ Ⓒ Ⓓ
15 Ⓐ Ⓑ Ⓒ Ⓓ	40 Ⓐ Ⓑ Ⓒ Ⓓ
16 Ⓐ Ⓑ Ⓒ Ⓓ	
17 Ⓐ Ⓑ Ⓒ Ⓓ	
18 Ⓐ Ⓑ Ⓒ Ⓓ	
19 Ⓐ Ⓑ Ⓒ Ⓓ	
20 Ⓐ Ⓑ Ⓒ Ⓓ	
21 Ⓐ Ⓑ Ⓒ Ⓓ	
22 Ⓐ Ⓑ Ⓒ Ⓓ	
23 Ⓐ Ⓑ Ⓒ Ⓓ	
24 Ⓐ Ⓑ Ⓒ Ⓓ	
25 Ⓐ Ⓑ Ⓒ Ⓓ	

SECTION III

READING COMPREHENSION AND
VOCABULARY

1 Ⓐ Ⓑ Ⓒ Ⓓ	26 Ⓐ Ⓑ Ⓒ Ⓓ	51 Ⓐ Ⓑ Ⓒ Ⓓ
2 Ⓐ Ⓑ Ⓒ Ⓓ	27 Ⓐ Ⓑ Ⓒ Ⓓ	52 Ⓐ Ⓑ Ⓒ Ⓓ
3 Ⓐ Ⓑ Ⓒ Ⓓ	28 Ⓐ Ⓑ Ⓒ Ⓓ	53 Ⓐ Ⓑ Ⓒ Ⓓ
4 Ⓐ Ⓑ Ⓒ Ⓓ	29 Ⓐ Ⓑ Ⓒ Ⓓ	54 Ⓐ Ⓑ Ⓒ Ⓓ
5 Ⓐ Ⓑ Ⓒ Ⓓ	30 Ⓐ Ⓑ Ⓒ Ⓓ	55 Ⓐ Ⓑ Ⓒ Ⓓ
6 Ⓐ Ⓑ Ⓒ Ⓓ	31 Ⓐ Ⓑ Ⓒ Ⓓ	56 Ⓐ Ⓑ Ⓒ Ⓓ
7 Ⓐ Ⓑ Ⓒ Ⓓ	32 Ⓐ Ⓑ Ⓒ Ⓓ	57 Ⓐ Ⓑ Ⓒ Ⓓ
8 Ⓐ Ⓑ Ⓒ Ⓓ	33 Ⓐ Ⓑ Ⓒ Ⓓ	58 Ⓐ Ⓑ Ⓒ Ⓓ
9 Ⓐ Ⓑ Ⓒ Ⓓ	34 Ⓐ Ⓑ Ⓒ Ⓓ	59 Ⓐ Ⓑ Ⓒ Ⓓ
10 Ⓐ Ⓑ Ⓒ Ⓓ	35 Ⓐ Ⓑ Ⓒ Ⓓ	60 Ⓐ Ⓑ Ⓒ Ⓓ
11 Ⓐ Ⓑ Ⓒ Ⓓ	36 Ⓐ Ⓑ Ⓒ Ⓓ	
12 Ⓐ Ⓑ Ⓒ Ⓓ	37 Ⓐ Ⓑ Ⓒ Ⓓ	
13 Ⓐ Ⓑ Ⓒ Ⓓ	38 Ⓐ Ⓑ Ⓒ Ⓓ	
14 Ⓐ Ⓑ Ⓒ Ⓓ	39 Ⓐ Ⓑ Ⓒ Ⓓ	
15 Ⓐ Ⓑ Ⓒ Ⓓ	40 Ⓐ Ⓑ Ⓒ Ⓓ	
16 Ⓐ Ⓑ Ⓒ Ⓓ	41 Ⓐ Ⓑ Ⓒ Ⓓ	
17 Ⓐ Ⓑ Ⓒ Ⓓ	42 Ⓐ Ⓑ Ⓒ Ⓓ	
18 Ⓐ Ⓑ Ⓒ Ⓓ	43 Ⓐ Ⓑ Ⓒ Ⓓ	
19 Ⓐ Ⓑ Ⓒ Ⓓ	44 Ⓐ Ⓑ Ⓒ Ⓓ	
20 Ⓐ Ⓑ Ⓒ Ⓓ	45 Ⓐ Ⓑ Ⓒ Ⓓ	
21 Ⓐ Ⓑ Ⓒ Ⓓ	46 Ⓐ Ⓑ Ⓒ Ⓓ	
22 Ⓐ Ⓑ Ⓒ Ⓓ	47 Ⓐ Ⓑ Ⓒ Ⓓ	
23 Ⓐ Ⓑ Ⓒ Ⓓ	48 Ⓐ Ⓑ Ⓒ Ⓓ	
24 Ⓐ Ⓑ Ⓒ Ⓓ	49 Ⓐ Ⓑ Ⓒ Ⓓ	
25 Ⓐ Ⓑ Ⓒ Ⓓ	50 Ⓐ Ⓑ Ⓒ Ⓓ	

ANSWER SHEET FOR LISTENING TARGET EXERCISE

(Tear This Sheet Out and Use It to Mark Your Answers)

Statements:

Minimal pairs	Computation	Number Discrimination	Synonyms	Negatives
1 Ⓐ Ⓑ Ⓒ Ⓓ	1 Ⓐ Ⓑ Ⓒ Ⓓ	1 Ⓐ Ⓑ Ⓒ Ⓓ	1 Ⓐ Ⓑ Ⓒ Ⓓ	1 Ⓐ Ⓑ Ⓒ Ⓓ
2 Ⓐ Ⓑ Ⓒ Ⓓ	2 Ⓐ Ⓑ Ⓒ Ⓓ	2 Ⓐ Ⓑ Ⓒ Ⓓ	2 Ⓐ Ⓑ Ⓒ Ⓓ	2 Ⓐ Ⓑ Ⓒ Ⓓ
3 Ⓐ Ⓑ Ⓒ Ⓓ	3 Ⓐ Ⓑ Ⓒ Ⓓ	3 Ⓐ Ⓑ Ⓒ Ⓓ	3 Ⓐ Ⓑ Ⓒ Ⓓ	3 Ⓐ Ⓑ Ⓒ Ⓓ
4 Ⓐ Ⓑ Ⓒ Ⓓ	4 Ⓐ Ⓑ Ⓒ Ⓓ	4 Ⓐ Ⓑ Ⓒ Ⓓ	4 Ⓐ Ⓑ Ⓒ Ⓓ	4 Ⓐ Ⓑ Ⓒ Ⓓ
5 Ⓐ Ⓑ Ⓒ Ⓓ	5 Ⓐ Ⓑ Ⓒ Ⓓ	5 Ⓐ Ⓑ Ⓒ Ⓓ	5 Ⓐ Ⓑ Ⓒ Ⓓ	5 Ⓐ Ⓑ Ⓒ Ⓓ
6 Ⓐ Ⓑ Ⓒ Ⓓ	6 Ⓐ Ⓑ Ⓒ Ⓓ	6 Ⓐ Ⓑ Ⓒ Ⓓ	6 Ⓐ Ⓑ Ⓒ Ⓓ	6 Ⓐ Ⓑ Ⓒ Ⓓ
7 Ⓐ Ⓑ Ⓒ Ⓓ	7 Ⓐ Ⓑ Ⓒ Ⓓ	7 Ⓐ Ⓑ Ⓒ Ⓓ	7 Ⓐ Ⓑ Ⓒ Ⓓ	7 Ⓐ Ⓑ Ⓒ Ⓓ
8 Ⓐ Ⓑ Ⓒ Ⓓ	8 Ⓐ Ⓑ Ⓒ Ⓓ	8 Ⓐ Ⓑ Ⓒ Ⓓ	8 Ⓐ Ⓑ Ⓒ Ⓓ	8 Ⓐ Ⓑ Ⓒ Ⓓ
9 Ⓐ Ⓑ Ⓒ Ⓓ	9 Ⓐ Ⓑ Ⓒ Ⓓ	9 Ⓐ Ⓑ Ⓒ Ⓓ	9 Ⓐ Ⓑ Ⓒ Ⓓ	9 Ⓐ Ⓑ Ⓒ Ⓓ
10 Ⓐ Ⓑ Ⓒ Ⓓ	10 Ⓐ Ⓑ Ⓒ Ⓓ	10 Ⓐ Ⓑ Ⓒ Ⓓ	10 Ⓐ Ⓑ Ⓒ Ⓓ	10 Ⓐ Ⓑ Ⓒ Ⓓ

Contextual References	Cause and Effect	Conditionals	Chronological Order	Comparison
1 Ⓐ Ⓑ Ⓒ Ⓓ	1 Ⓐ Ⓑ Ⓒ Ⓓ	1 Ⓐ Ⓑ Ⓒ Ⓓ	1 Ⓐ Ⓑ Ⓒ Ⓓ	1 Ⓐ Ⓑ Ⓒ Ⓓ
2 Ⓐ Ⓑ Ⓒ Ⓓ	2 Ⓐ Ⓑ Ⓒ Ⓓ	2 Ⓐ Ⓑ Ⓒ Ⓓ	2 Ⓐ Ⓑ Ⓒ Ⓓ	2 Ⓐ Ⓑ Ⓒ Ⓓ
3 Ⓐ Ⓑ Ⓒ Ⓓ	3 Ⓐ Ⓑ Ⓒ Ⓓ	3 Ⓐ Ⓑ Ⓒ Ⓓ	3 Ⓐ Ⓑ Ⓒ Ⓓ	3 Ⓐ Ⓑ Ⓒ Ⓓ
4 Ⓐ Ⓑ Ⓒ Ⓓ	4 Ⓐ Ⓑ Ⓒ Ⓓ	4 Ⓐ Ⓑ Ⓒ Ⓓ	4 Ⓐ Ⓑ Ⓒ Ⓓ	4 Ⓐ Ⓑ Ⓒ Ⓓ
5 Ⓐ Ⓑ Ⓒ Ⓓ	5 Ⓐ Ⓑ Ⓒ Ⓓ	5 Ⓐ Ⓑ Ⓒ Ⓓ	5 Ⓐ Ⓑ Ⓒ Ⓓ	5 Ⓐ Ⓑ Ⓒ Ⓓ
6 Ⓐ Ⓑ Ⓒ Ⓓ	6 Ⓐ Ⓑ Ⓒ Ⓓ	6 Ⓐ Ⓑ Ⓒ Ⓓ	6 Ⓐ Ⓑ Ⓒ Ⓓ	6 Ⓐ Ⓑ Ⓒ Ⓓ
7 Ⓐ Ⓑ Ⓒ Ⓓ	7 Ⓐ Ⓑ Ⓒ Ⓓ	7 Ⓐ Ⓑ Ⓒ Ⓓ	7 Ⓐ Ⓑ Ⓒ Ⓓ	7 Ⓐ Ⓑ Ⓒ Ⓓ
8 Ⓐ Ⓑ Ⓒ Ⓓ	8 Ⓐ Ⓑ Ⓒ Ⓓ	8 Ⓐ Ⓑ Ⓒ Ⓓ	8 Ⓐ Ⓑ Ⓒ Ⓓ	8 Ⓐ Ⓑ Ⓒ Ⓓ
9 Ⓐ Ⓑ Ⓒ Ⓓ	9 Ⓐ Ⓑ Ⓒ Ⓓ	9 Ⓐ Ⓑ Ⓒ Ⓓ	9 Ⓐ Ⓑ Ⓒ Ⓓ	9 Ⓐ Ⓑ Ⓒ Ⓓ
10 Ⓐ Ⓑ Ⓒ Ⓓ	10 Ⓐ Ⓑ Ⓒ Ⓓ	10 Ⓐ Ⓑ Ⓒ Ⓓ	10 Ⓐ Ⓑ Ⓒ Ⓓ	10 Ⓐ Ⓑ Ⓒ Ⓓ

Conversations:

Minimal Pairs	Computation	Number Discrimination	Synonyms	Negation
1 Ⓐ Ⓑ Ⓒ Ⓓ	1 Ⓐ Ⓑ Ⓒ Ⓓ	1 Ⓐ Ⓑ Ⓒ Ⓓ	1 Ⓐ Ⓑ Ⓒ Ⓓ	1 Ⓐ Ⓑ Ⓒ Ⓓ
2 Ⓐ Ⓑ Ⓒ Ⓓ	2 Ⓐ Ⓑ Ⓒ Ⓓ	2 Ⓐ Ⓑ Ⓒ Ⓓ	2 Ⓐ Ⓑ Ⓒ Ⓓ	2 Ⓐ Ⓑ Ⓒ Ⓓ
3 Ⓐ Ⓑ Ⓒ Ⓓ	3 Ⓐ Ⓑ Ⓒ Ⓓ	3 Ⓐ Ⓑ Ⓒ Ⓓ	3 Ⓐ Ⓑ Ⓒ Ⓓ	3 Ⓐ Ⓑ Ⓒ Ⓓ
4 Ⓐ Ⓑ Ⓒ Ⓓ	4 Ⓐ Ⓑ Ⓒ Ⓓ	4 Ⓐ Ⓑ Ⓒ Ⓓ	4 Ⓐ Ⓑ Ⓒ Ⓓ	4 Ⓐ Ⓑ Ⓒ Ⓓ
5 Ⓐ Ⓑ Ⓒ Ⓓ	5 Ⓐ Ⓑ Ⓒ Ⓓ	5 Ⓐ Ⓑ Ⓒ Ⓓ	5 Ⓐ Ⓑ Ⓒ Ⓓ	5 Ⓐ Ⓑ Ⓒ Ⓓ
6 Ⓐ Ⓑ Ⓒ Ⓓ	6 Ⓐ Ⓑ Ⓒ Ⓓ	6 Ⓐ Ⓑ Ⓒ Ⓓ	6 Ⓐ Ⓑ Ⓒ Ⓓ	6 Ⓐ Ⓑ Ⓒ Ⓓ
7 Ⓐ Ⓑ Ⓒ Ⓓ	7 Ⓐ Ⓑ Ⓒ Ⓓ	7 Ⓐ Ⓑ Ⓒ Ⓓ	7 Ⓐ Ⓑ Ⓒ Ⓓ	7 Ⓐ Ⓑ Ⓒ Ⓓ
8 Ⓐ Ⓑ Ⓒ Ⓓ	8 Ⓐ Ⓑ Ⓒ Ⓓ	8 Ⓐ Ⓑ Ⓒ Ⓓ	8 Ⓐ Ⓑ Ⓒ Ⓓ	8 Ⓐ Ⓑ Ⓒ Ⓓ
9 Ⓐ Ⓑ Ⓒ Ⓓ	9 Ⓐ Ⓑ Ⓒ Ⓓ	9 Ⓐ Ⓑ Ⓒ Ⓓ	9 Ⓐ Ⓑ Ⓒ Ⓓ	9 Ⓐ Ⓑ Ⓒ Ⓓ
10 Ⓐ Ⓑ Ⓒ Ⓓ	10 Ⓐ Ⓑ Ⓒ Ⓓ	10 Ⓐ Ⓑ Ⓒ Ⓓ	10 Ⓐ Ⓑ Ⓒ Ⓓ	10 Ⓐ Ⓑ Ⓒ Ⓓ

Contextual Reference	Cause and Effect	Conditionals	Chronological Order	Comparisons
1 Ⓐ Ⓑ Ⓒ Ⓓ	1 Ⓐ Ⓑ Ⓒ Ⓓ	1 Ⓐ Ⓑ Ⓒ Ⓓ	1 Ⓐ Ⓑ Ⓒ Ⓓ	1 Ⓐ Ⓑ Ⓒ Ⓓ
2 Ⓐ Ⓑ Ⓒ Ⓓ	2 Ⓐ Ⓑ Ⓒ Ⓓ	2 Ⓐ Ⓑ Ⓒ Ⓓ	2 Ⓐ Ⓑ Ⓒ Ⓓ	2 Ⓐ Ⓑ Ⓒ Ⓓ
3 Ⓐ Ⓑ Ⓒ Ⓓ	3 Ⓐ Ⓑ Ⓒ Ⓓ	3 Ⓐ Ⓑ Ⓒ Ⓓ	3 Ⓐ Ⓑ Ⓒ Ⓓ	3 Ⓐ Ⓑ Ⓒ Ⓓ
4 Ⓐ Ⓑ Ⓒ Ⓓ	4 Ⓐ Ⓑ Ⓒ Ⓓ	4 Ⓐ Ⓑ Ⓒ Ⓓ	4 Ⓐ Ⓑ Ⓒ Ⓓ	4 Ⓐ Ⓑ Ⓒ Ⓓ
5 Ⓐ Ⓑ Ⓒ Ⓓ	5 Ⓐ Ⓑ Ⓒ Ⓓ	5 Ⓐ Ⓑ Ⓒ Ⓓ	5 Ⓐ Ⓑ Ⓒ Ⓓ	5 Ⓐ Ⓑ Ⓒ Ⓓ
6 Ⓐ Ⓑ Ⓒ Ⓓ	6 Ⓐ Ⓑ Ⓒ Ⓓ	6 Ⓐ Ⓑ Ⓒ Ⓓ	6 Ⓐ Ⓑ Ⓒ Ⓓ	6 Ⓐ Ⓑ Ⓒ Ⓓ
7 Ⓐ Ⓑ Ⓒ Ⓓ	7 Ⓐ Ⓑ Ⓒ Ⓓ	7 Ⓐ Ⓑ Ⓒ Ⓓ	7 Ⓐ Ⓑ Ⓒ Ⓓ	7 Ⓐ Ⓑ Ⓒ Ⓓ
8 Ⓐ Ⓑ Ⓒ Ⓓ	8 Ⓐ Ⓑ Ⓒ Ⓓ	8 Ⓐ Ⓑ Ⓒ Ⓓ	8 Ⓐ Ⓑ Ⓒ Ⓓ	8 Ⓐ Ⓑ Ⓒ Ⓓ
9 Ⓐ Ⓑ Ⓒ Ⓓ	9 Ⓐ Ⓑ Ⓒ Ⓓ	9 Ⓐ Ⓑ Ⓒ Ⓓ	9 Ⓐ Ⓑ Ⓒ Ⓓ	9 Ⓐ Ⓑ Ⓒ Ⓓ
10 Ⓐ Ⓑ Ⓒ Ⓓ	10 Ⓐ Ⓑ Ⓒ Ⓓ	10 Ⓐ Ⓑ Ⓒ Ⓓ	10 Ⓐ Ⓑ Ⓒ Ⓓ	10 Ⓐ Ⓑ Ⓒ Ⓓ

Mini-Talks:

Overheard Conversations	Announcements	Advertisements	News Reports
1 Ⓐ Ⓑ Ⓒ Ⓓ	1 Ⓐ Ⓑ Ⓒ Ⓓ	1 Ⓐ Ⓑ Ⓒ Ⓓ	1 Ⓐ Ⓑ Ⓒ Ⓓ
2 Ⓐ Ⓑ Ⓒ Ⓓ	2 Ⓐ Ⓑ Ⓒ Ⓓ	2 Ⓐ Ⓑ Ⓒ Ⓓ	2 Ⓐ Ⓑ Ⓒ Ⓓ
3 Ⓐ Ⓑ Ⓒ Ⓓ	3 Ⓐ Ⓑ Ⓒ Ⓓ	3 Ⓐ Ⓑ Ⓒ Ⓓ	3 Ⓐ Ⓑ Ⓒ Ⓓ
4 Ⓐ Ⓑ Ⓒ Ⓓ	4 Ⓐ Ⓑ Ⓒ Ⓓ	4 Ⓐ Ⓑ Ⓒ Ⓓ	4 Ⓐ Ⓑ Ⓒ Ⓓ
5 Ⓐ Ⓑ Ⓒ Ⓓ	5 Ⓐ Ⓑ Ⓒ Ⓓ	5 Ⓐ Ⓑ Ⓒ Ⓓ	5 Ⓐ Ⓑ Ⓒ Ⓓ
6 Ⓐ Ⓑ Ⓒ Ⓓ	6 Ⓐ Ⓑ Ⓒ Ⓓ	6 Ⓐ Ⓑ Ⓒ Ⓓ	6 Ⓐ Ⓑ Ⓒ Ⓓ
7 Ⓐ Ⓑ Ⓒ Ⓓ	7 Ⓐ Ⓑ Ⓒ Ⓓ	7 Ⓐ Ⓑ Ⓒ Ⓓ	7 Ⓐ Ⓑ Ⓒ Ⓓ
8 Ⓐ Ⓑ Ⓒ Ⓓ	8 Ⓐ Ⓑ Ⓒ Ⓓ	8 Ⓐ Ⓑ Ⓒ Ⓓ	8 Ⓐ Ⓑ Ⓒ Ⓓ
9 Ⓐ Ⓑ Ⓒ Ⓓ	9 Ⓐ Ⓑ Ⓒ Ⓓ	9 Ⓐ Ⓑ Ⓒ Ⓓ	9 Ⓐ Ⓑ Ⓒ Ⓓ
10 Ⓐ Ⓑ Ⓒ Ⓓ	10 Ⓐ Ⓑ Ⓒ Ⓓ	10 Ⓐ Ⓑ Ⓒ Ⓓ	10 Ⓐ Ⓑ Ⓒ Ⓓ
11 Ⓐ Ⓑ Ⓒ Ⓓ	11 Ⓐ Ⓑ Ⓒ Ⓓ	11 Ⓐ Ⓑ Ⓒ Ⓓ	11 Ⓐ Ⓑ Ⓒ Ⓓ
12 Ⓐ Ⓑ Ⓒ Ⓓ	12 Ⓐ Ⓑ Ⓒ Ⓓ	12 Ⓐ Ⓑ Ⓒ Ⓓ	12 Ⓐ Ⓑ Ⓒ Ⓓ
13 Ⓐ Ⓑ Ⓒ Ⓓ	13 Ⓐ Ⓑ Ⓒ Ⓓ	13 Ⓐ Ⓑ Ⓒ Ⓓ	13 Ⓐ Ⓑ Ⓒ Ⓓ
14 Ⓐ Ⓑ Ⓒ Ⓓ	14 Ⓐ Ⓑ Ⓒ Ⓓ	14 Ⓐ Ⓑ Ⓒ Ⓓ	14 Ⓐ Ⓑ Ⓒ Ⓓ
15 Ⓐ Ⓑ Ⓒ Ⓓ	15 Ⓐ Ⓑ Ⓒ Ⓓ	15 Ⓐ Ⓑ Ⓒ Ⓓ	15 Ⓐ Ⓑ Ⓒ Ⓓ
16 Ⓐ Ⓑ Ⓒ Ⓓ	16 Ⓐ Ⓑ Ⓒ Ⓓ	16 Ⓐ Ⓑ Ⓒ Ⓓ	16 Ⓐ Ⓑ Ⓒ Ⓓ
17 Ⓐ Ⓑ Ⓒ Ⓓ	17 Ⓐ Ⓑ Ⓒ Ⓓ	17 Ⓐ Ⓑ Ⓒ Ⓓ	17 Ⓐ Ⓑ Ⓒ Ⓓ
18 Ⓐ Ⓑ Ⓒ Ⓓ	18 Ⓐ Ⓑ Ⓒ Ⓓ	18 Ⓐ Ⓑ Ⓒ Ⓓ	18 Ⓐ Ⓑ Ⓒ Ⓓ
19 Ⓐ Ⓑ Ⓒ Ⓓ	19 Ⓐ Ⓑ Ⓒ Ⓓ	19 Ⓐ Ⓑ Ⓒ Ⓓ	19 Ⓐ Ⓑ Ⓒ Ⓓ
20 Ⓐ Ⓑ Ⓒ Ⓓ	20 Ⓐ Ⓑ Ⓒ Ⓓ	20 Ⓐ Ⓑ Ⓒ Ⓓ	20 Ⓐ Ⓑ Ⓒ Ⓓ

Weather Reports	Academic Lectures	Informative Talks	Class Discussions
1 Ⓐ Ⓑ Ⓒ Ⓓ	1 Ⓐ Ⓑ Ⓒ Ⓓ	1 Ⓐ Ⓑ Ⓒ Ⓓ	1 Ⓐ Ⓑ Ⓒ Ⓓ
2 Ⓐ Ⓑ Ⓒ Ⓓ	2 Ⓐ Ⓑ Ⓒ Ⓓ	2 Ⓐ Ⓑ Ⓒ Ⓓ	2 Ⓐ Ⓑ Ⓒ Ⓓ
3 Ⓐ Ⓑ Ⓒ Ⓓ	3 Ⓐ Ⓑ Ⓒ Ⓓ	3 Ⓐ Ⓑ Ⓒ Ⓓ	3 Ⓐ Ⓑ Ⓒ Ⓓ
4 Ⓐ Ⓑ Ⓒ Ⓓ	4 Ⓐ Ⓑ Ⓒ Ⓓ	4 Ⓐ Ⓑ Ⓒ Ⓓ	4 Ⓐ Ⓑ Ⓒ Ⓓ
5 Ⓐ Ⓑ Ⓒ Ⓓ	5 Ⓐ Ⓑ Ⓒ Ⓓ	5 Ⓐ Ⓑ Ⓒ Ⓓ	5 Ⓐ Ⓑ Ⓒ Ⓓ
6 Ⓐ Ⓑ Ⓒ Ⓓ	6 Ⓐ Ⓑ Ⓒ Ⓓ	6 Ⓐ Ⓑ Ⓒ Ⓓ	6 Ⓐ Ⓑ Ⓒ Ⓓ
7 Ⓐ Ⓑ Ⓒ Ⓓ	7 Ⓐ Ⓑ Ⓒ Ⓓ	7 Ⓐ Ⓑ Ⓒ Ⓓ	7 Ⓐ Ⓑ Ⓒ Ⓓ
8 Ⓐ Ⓑ Ⓒ Ⓓ	8 Ⓐ Ⓑ Ⓒ Ⓓ	8 Ⓐ Ⓑ Ⓒ Ⓓ	8 Ⓐ Ⓑ Ⓒ Ⓓ
9 Ⓐ Ⓑ Ⓒ Ⓓ	9 Ⓐ Ⓑ Ⓒ Ⓓ	9 Ⓐ Ⓑ Ⓒ Ⓓ	9 Ⓐ Ⓑ Ⓒ Ⓓ
10 Ⓐ Ⓑ Ⓒ Ⓓ	10 Ⓐ Ⓑ Ⓒ Ⓓ	10 Ⓐ Ⓑ Ⓒ Ⓓ	10 Ⓐ Ⓑ Ⓒ Ⓓ
11 Ⓐ Ⓑ Ⓒ Ⓓ	11 Ⓐ Ⓑ Ⓒ Ⓓ	11 Ⓐ Ⓑ Ⓒ Ⓓ	11 Ⓐ Ⓑ Ⓒ Ⓓ
12 Ⓐ Ⓑ Ⓒ Ⓓ	12 Ⓐ Ⓑ Ⓒ Ⓓ	12 Ⓐ Ⓑ Ⓒ Ⓓ	12 Ⓐ Ⓑ Ⓒ Ⓓ
13 Ⓐ Ⓑ Ⓒ Ⓓ	13 Ⓐ Ⓑ Ⓒ Ⓓ	13 Ⓐ Ⓑ Ⓒ Ⓓ	13 Ⓐ Ⓑ Ⓒ Ⓓ
14 Ⓐ Ⓑ Ⓒ Ⓓ	14 Ⓐ Ⓑ Ⓒ Ⓓ	14 Ⓐ Ⓑ Ⓒ Ⓓ	14 Ⓐ Ⓑ Ⓒ Ⓓ
15 Ⓐ Ⓑ Ⓒ Ⓓ	15 Ⓐ Ⓑ Ⓒ Ⓓ	15 Ⓐ Ⓑ Ⓒ Ⓓ	15 Ⓐ Ⓑ Ⓒ Ⓓ
16 Ⓐ Ⓑ Ⓒ Ⓓ	16 Ⓐ Ⓑ Ⓒ Ⓓ		
17 Ⓐ Ⓑ Ⓒ Ⓓ	17 Ⓐ Ⓑ Ⓒ Ⓓ		
18 Ⓐ Ⓑ Ⓒ Ⓓ	18 Ⓐ Ⓑ Ⓒ Ⓓ		
19 Ⓐ Ⓑ Ⓒ Ⓓ	19 Ⓐ Ⓑ Ⓒ Ⓓ		
20 Ⓐ Ⓑ Ⓒ Ⓓ	20 Ⓐ Ⓑ Ⓒ Ⓓ		

ANSWER SHEET FOR STRUCTURE TARGET EXERCISE

(Tear This Sheet Out and Use It to Mark Your Answers)

Active-Passive I	Active-Passive II	Articles I	Articles II	Comparisons I

1 Ⓐ Ⓑ Ⓒ Ⓓ
2 Ⓐ Ⓑ Ⓒ Ⓓ
3 Ⓐ Ⓑ Ⓒ Ⓓ
4 Ⓐ Ⓑ Ⓒ Ⓓ
5 Ⓐ Ⓑ Ⓒ Ⓓ

6 Ⓐ Ⓑ Ⓒ Ⓓ
7 Ⓐ Ⓑ Ⓒ Ⓓ
8 Ⓐ Ⓑ Ⓒ Ⓓ
9 Ⓐ Ⓑ Ⓒ Ⓓ
10 Ⓐ Ⓑ Ⓒ Ⓓ

Comparisons II	Conditionals I	Conditionals II	Conjunctions: Form I	Conjunctions: Form II

1 Ⓐ Ⓑ Ⓒ Ⓓ
2 Ⓐ Ⓑ Ⓒ Ⓓ
3 Ⓐ Ⓑ Ⓒ Ⓓ
4 Ⓐ Ⓑ Ⓒ Ⓓ
5 Ⓐ Ⓑ Ⓒ Ⓓ

6 Ⓐ Ⓑ Ⓒ Ⓓ
7 Ⓐ Ⓑ Ⓒ Ⓓ
8 Ⓐ Ⓑ Ⓒ Ⓓ
9 Ⓐ Ⓑ Ⓒ Ⓓ
10 Ⓐ Ⓑ Ⓒ Ⓓ

Conjunctions: Parallel Structures I	Conjunctions: Parallel Structures II	Prepositions I	Prepositions II	Pronouns: Agreement

1 Ⓐ Ⓑ Ⓒ Ⓓ
2 Ⓐ Ⓑ Ⓒ Ⓓ
3 Ⓐ Ⓑ Ⓒ Ⓓ
4 Ⓐ Ⓑ Ⓒ Ⓓ
5 Ⓐ Ⓑ Ⓒ Ⓓ

6 Ⓐ Ⓑ Ⓒ Ⓓ
7 Ⓐ Ⓑ Ⓒ Ⓓ
8 Ⓐ Ⓑ Ⓒ Ⓓ
9 Ⓐ Ⓑ Ⓒ Ⓓ
10 Ⓐ Ⓑ Ⓒ Ⓓ

Pronouns: Form	Pronouns: Extra Exercises	Redundancy: I	Redundancy: II

1 Ⓐ Ⓑ Ⓒ Ⓓ
2 Ⓐ Ⓑ Ⓒ Ⓓ
3 Ⓐ Ⓑ Ⓒ Ⓓ
4 Ⓐ Ⓑ Ⓒ Ⓓ
5 Ⓐ Ⓑ Ⓒ Ⓓ

6 Ⓐ Ⓑ Ⓒ Ⓓ
7 Ⓐ Ⓑ Ⓒ Ⓓ
8 Ⓐ Ⓑ Ⓒ Ⓓ
9 Ⓐ Ⓑ Ⓒ Ⓓ
10 Ⓐ Ⓑ Ⓒ Ⓓ

Subject:

Omission

| 1 (A) (B) (C) (D) |
| 2 (A) (B) (C) (D) |
| 3 (A) (B) (C) (D) |
| 4 (A) (B) (C) (D) |
| 5 (A) (B) (C) (D) |

| 6 (A) (B) (C) (D) |
| 7 (A) (B) (C) (D) |
| 8 (A) (B) (C) (D) |
| 9 (A) (B) (C) (D) |
| 10 (A) (B) (C) (D) |

Repetition

| 1 (A) (B) (C) (D) |
| 2 (A) (B) (C) (D) |
| 3 (A) (B) (C) (D) |
| 4 (A) (B) (C) (D) |
| 5 (A) (B) (C) (D) |

| 6 (A) (B) (C) (D) |
| 7 (A) (B) (C) (D) |
| 8 (A) (B) (C) (D) |
| 9 (A) (B) (C) (D) |
| 10 (A) (B) (C) (D) |

Agreement

| 1 (A) (B) (C) (D) |
| 2 (A) (B) (C) (D) |
| 3 (A) (B) (C) (D) |
| 4 (A) (B) (C) (D) |
| 5 (A) (B) (C) (D) |

| 6 (A) (B) (C) (D) |
| 7 (A) (B) (C) (D) |
| 8 (A) (B) (C) (D) |
| 9 (A) (B) (C) (D) |
| 10 (A) (B) (C) (D) |

Extra Exercises

| 1 (A) (B) (C) (D) |
| 2 (A) (B) (C) (D) |
| 3 (A) (B) (C) (D) |
| 4 (A) (B) (C) (D) |
| 5 (A) (B) (C) (D) |

| 6 (A) (B) (C) (D) |
| 7 (A) (B) (C) (D) |
| 8 (A) (B) (C) (D) |
| 9 (A) (B) (C) (D) |
| 10 (A) (B) (C) (D) |

Subjunctive:

I

II

Subordinate Clauses:

Noun Clauses

I

II

Adjective Clauses

I

II

Adverb Clauses

I

II

Reduced Adjective Clauses

I

II

Verb:

Reduced Adverb Clauses

I

II

Verb Omission

Unnecessary Word

Verb Agreement

Word Families:

Verb Tense	Extra Exercises	I	II

Verb Tense

1 Ⓐ Ⓑ Ⓒ Ⓓ
2 Ⓐ Ⓑ Ⓒ Ⓓ
3 Ⓐ Ⓑ Ⓒ Ⓓ
4 Ⓐ Ⓑ Ⓒ Ⓓ
5 Ⓐ Ⓑ Ⓒ Ⓓ

6 Ⓐ Ⓑ Ⓒ Ⓓ
7 Ⓐ Ⓑ Ⓒ Ⓓ
8 Ⓐ Ⓑ Ⓒ Ⓓ
9 Ⓐ Ⓑ Ⓒ Ⓓ
10 Ⓐ Ⓑ Ⓒ Ⓓ

Extra Exercises

1 Ⓐ Ⓑ Ⓒ Ⓓ
2 Ⓐ Ⓑ Ⓒ Ⓓ
3 Ⓐ Ⓑ Ⓒ Ⓓ
4 Ⓐ Ⓑ Ⓒ Ⓓ
5 Ⓐ Ⓑ Ⓒ Ⓓ

6 Ⓐ Ⓑ Ⓒ Ⓓ
7 Ⓐ Ⓑ Ⓒ Ⓓ
8 Ⓐ Ⓑ Ⓒ Ⓓ
9 Ⓐ Ⓑ Ⓒ Ⓓ
10 Ⓐ Ⓑ Ⓒ Ⓓ

I

1 Ⓐ Ⓑ Ⓒ Ⓓ
2 Ⓐ Ⓑ Ⓒ Ⓓ
3 Ⓐ Ⓑ Ⓒ Ⓓ
4 Ⓐ Ⓑ Ⓒ Ⓓ
5 Ⓐ Ⓑ Ⓒ Ⓓ

6 Ⓐ Ⓑ Ⓒ Ⓓ
7 Ⓐ Ⓑ Ⓒ Ⓓ
8 Ⓐ Ⓑ Ⓒ Ⓓ
9 Ⓐ Ⓑ Ⓒ Ⓓ
10 Ⓐ Ⓑ Ⓒ Ⓓ

II

1 Ⓐ Ⓑ Ⓒ Ⓓ
2 Ⓐ Ⓑ Ⓒ Ⓓ
3 Ⓐ Ⓑ Ⓒ Ⓓ
4 Ⓐ Ⓑ Ⓒ Ⓓ
5 Ⓐ Ⓑ Ⓒ Ⓓ

6 Ⓐ Ⓑ Ⓒ Ⓓ
7 Ⓐ Ⓑ Ⓒ Ⓓ
8 Ⓐ Ⓑ Ⓒ Ⓓ
9 Ⓐ Ⓑ Ⓒ Ⓓ
10 Ⓐ Ⓑ Ⓒ Ⓓ

Word Order:

Subject Verb Placement

1 Ⓐ Ⓑ Ⓒ Ⓓ
2 Ⓐ Ⓑ Ⓒ Ⓓ
3 Ⓐ Ⓑ Ⓒ Ⓓ
4 Ⓐ Ⓑ Ⓒ Ⓓ
5 Ⓐ Ⓑ Ⓒ Ⓓ

6 Ⓐ Ⓑ Ⓒ Ⓓ
7 Ⓐ Ⓑ Ⓒ Ⓓ
8 Ⓐ Ⓑ Ⓒ Ⓓ
9 Ⓐ Ⓑ Ⓒ Ⓓ
10 Ⓐ Ⓑ Ⓒ Ⓓ

Adjective and Adverb Placement

1 Ⓐ Ⓑ Ⓒ Ⓓ
2 Ⓐ Ⓑ Ⓒ Ⓓ
3 Ⓐ Ⓑ Ⓒ Ⓓ
4 Ⓐ Ⓑ Ⓒ Ⓓ
5 Ⓐ Ⓑ Ⓒ Ⓓ

6 Ⓐ Ⓑ Ⓒ Ⓓ
7 Ⓐ Ⓑ Ⓒ Ⓓ
8 Ⓐ Ⓑ Ⓒ Ⓓ
9 Ⓐ Ⓑ Ⓒ Ⓓ
10 Ⓐ Ⓑ Ⓒ Ⓓ

Adjective Placement

1 Ⓐ Ⓑ Ⓒ Ⓓ
2 Ⓐ Ⓑ Ⓒ Ⓓ
3 Ⓐ Ⓑ Ⓒ Ⓓ
4 Ⓐ Ⓑ Ⓒ Ⓓ
5 Ⓐ Ⓑ Ⓒ Ⓓ

6 Ⓐ Ⓑ Ⓒ Ⓓ
7 Ⓐ Ⓑ Ⓒ Ⓓ
8 Ⓐ Ⓑ Ⓒ Ⓓ
9 Ⓐ Ⓑ Ⓒ Ⓓ
10 Ⓐ Ⓑ Ⓒ Ⓓ

Adverb Placement

1 Ⓐ Ⓑ Ⓒ Ⓓ
2 Ⓐ Ⓑ Ⓒ Ⓓ
3 Ⓐ Ⓑ Ⓒ Ⓓ
4 Ⓐ Ⓑ Ⓒ Ⓓ
5 Ⓐ Ⓑ Ⓒ Ⓓ

6 Ⓐ Ⓑ Ⓒ Ⓓ
7 Ⓐ Ⓑ Ⓒ Ⓓ
8 Ⓐ Ⓑ Ⓒ Ⓓ
9 Ⓐ Ⓑ Ⓒ Ⓓ
10 Ⓐ Ⓑ Ⓒ Ⓓ

ANSWER SHEET FOR VOCABULARY TARGET EXERCISE

(Tear This Sheet Out and Use It to Mark Your Answers)

Usage	General	Prefixes
1 Ⓐ Ⓑ Ⓒ Ⓓ	1 Ⓐ Ⓑ Ⓒ Ⓓ	1 Ⓐ Ⓑ Ⓒ Ⓓ
2 Ⓐ Ⓑ Ⓒ Ⓓ	2 Ⓐ Ⓑ Ⓒ Ⓓ	2 Ⓐ Ⓑ Ⓒ Ⓓ
3 Ⓐ Ⓑ Ⓒ Ⓓ	3 Ⓐ Ⓑ Ⓒ Ⓓ	3 Ⓐ Ⓑ Ⓒ Ⓓ
4 Ⓐ Ⓑ Ⓒ Ⓓ	4 Ⓐ Ⓑ Ⓒ Ⓓ	4 Ⓐ Ⓑ Ⓒ Ⓓ
5 Ⓐ Ⓑ Ⓒ Ⓓ	5 Ⓐ Ⓑ Ⓒ Ⓓ	5 Ⓐ Ⓑ Ⓒ Ⓓ
6 Ⓐ Ⓑ Ⓒ Ⓓ	6 Ⓐ Ⓑ Ⓒ Ⓓ	6 Ⓐ Ⓑ Ⓒ Ⓓ
7 Ⓐ Ⓑ Ⓒ Ⓓ	7 Ⓐ Ⓑ Ⓒ Ⓓ	7 Ⓐ Ⓑ Ⓒ Ⓓ
8 Ⓐ Ⓑ Ⓒ Ⓓ	8 Ⓐ Ⓑ Ⓒ Ⓓ	8 Ⓐ Ⓑ Ⓒ Ⓓ
9 Ⓐ Ⓑ Ⓒ Ⓓ	9 Ⓐ Ⓑ Ⓒ Ⓓ	9 Ⓐ Ⓑ Ⓒ Ⓓ
10 Ⓐ Ⓑ Ⓒ Ⓓ	10 Ⓐ Ⓑ Ⓒ Ⓓ	10 Ⓐ Ⓑ Ⓒ Ⓓ
11 Ⓐ Ⓑ Ⓒ Ⓓ	11 Ⓐ Ⓑ Ⓒ Ⓓ	11 Ⓐ Ⓑ Ⓒ Ⓓ
12 Ⓐ Ⓑ Ⓒ Ⓓ	12 Ⓐ Ⓑ Ⓒ Ⓓ	12 Ⓐ Ⓑ Ⓒ Ⓓ
13 Ⓐ Ⓑ Ⓒ Ⓓ	13 Ⓐ Ⓑ Ⓒ Ⓓ	13 Ⓐ Ⓑ Ⓒ Ⓓ
14 Ⓐ Ⓑ Ⓒ Ⓓ	14 Ⓐ Ⓑ Ⓒ Ⓓ	14 Ⓐ Ⓑ Ⓒ Ⓓ
15 Ⓐ Ⓑ Ⓒ Ⓓ	15 Ⓐ Ⓑ Ⓒ Ⓓ	15 Ⓐ Ⓑ Ⓒ Ⓓ
16 Ⓐ Ⓑ Ⓒ Ⓓ	16 Ⓐ Ⓑ Ⓒ Ⓓ	16 Ⓐ Ⓑ Ⓒ Ⓓ
17 Ⓐ Ⓑ Ⓒ Ⓓ	17 Ⓐ Ⓑ Ⓒ Ⓓ	17 Ⓐ Ⓑ Ⓒ Ⓓ
18 Ⓐ Ⓑ Ⓒ Ⓓ	18 Ⓐ Ⓑ Ⓒ Ⓓ	18 Ⓐ Ⓑ Ⓒ Ⓓ
19 Ⓐ Ⓑ Ⓒ Ⓓ	19 Ⓐ Ⓑ Ⓒ Ⓓ	19 Ⓐ Ⓑ Ⓒ Ⓓ
20 Ⓐ Ⓑ Ⓒ Ⓓ	20 Ⓐ Ⓑ Ⓒ Ⓓ	20 Ⓐ Ⓑ Ⓒ Ⓓ
21 Ⓐ Ⓑ Ⓒ Ⓓ		
22 Ⓐ Ⓑ Ⓒ Ⓓ		
23 Ⓐ Ⓑ Ⓒ Ⓓ		
24 Ⓐ Ⓑ Ⓒ Ⓓ		
25 Ⓐ Ⓑ Ⓒ Ⓓ		

ANSWER SHEET FOR READING TARGET EXERCISE

(Tear This Sheet Out and Use It to Mark Your Answers)

Introduction

1 Ⓐ Ⓑ Ⓒ Ⓓ
2 Ⓐ Ⓑ Ⓒ Ⓓ
3 Ⓐ Ⓑ Ⓒ Ⓓ
4 Ⓐ Ⓑ Ⓒ Ⓓ
5 Ⓐ Ⓑ Ⓒ Ⓓ

6 Ⓐ Ⓑ Ⓒ Ⓓ
7 Ⓐ Ⓑ Ⓒ Ⓓ
8 Ⓐ Ⓑ Ⓒ Ⓓ
9 Ⓐ Ⓑ Ⓒ Ⓓ
10 Ⓐ Ⓑ Ⓒ Ⓓ

11 Ⓐ Ⓑ Ⓒ Ⓓ
12 Ⓐ Ⓑ Ⓒ Ⓓ
13 Ⓐ Ⓑ Ⓒ Ⓓ
14 Ⓐ Ⓑ Ⓒ Ⓓ
15 Ⓐ Ⓑ Ⓒ Ⓓ

16 Ⓐ Ⓑ Ⓒ Ⓓ
17 Ⓐ Ⓑ Ⓒ Ⓓ
18 Ⓐ Ⓑ Ⓒ Ⓓ
19 Ⓐ Ⓑ Ⓒ Ⓓ
20 Ⓐ Ⓑ Ⓒ Ⓓ

21 Ⓐ Ⓑ Ⓒ Ⓓ
22 Ⓐ Ⓑ Ⓒ Ⓓ
23 Ⓐ Ⓑ Ⓒ Ⓓ
24 Ⓐ Ⓑ Ⓒ Ⓓ

General

1 Ⓐ Ⓑ Ⓒ Ⓓ
2 Ⓐ Ⓑ Ⓒ Ⓓ
3 Ⓐ Ⓑ Ⓒ Ⓓ
4 Ⓐ Ⓑ Ⓒ Ⓓ
5 Ⓐ Ⓑ Ⓒ Ⓓ

6 Ⓐ Ⓑ Ⓒ Ⓓ
7 Ⓐ Ⓑ Ⓒ Ⓓ
8 Ⓐ Ⓑ Ⓒ Ⓓ
9 Ⓐ Ⓑ Ⓒ Ⓓ
10 Ⓐ Ⓑ Ⓒ Ⓓ

Humanities

1 Ⓐ Ⓑ Ⓒ Ⓓ
2 Ⓐ Ⓑ Ⓒ Ⓓ
3 Ⓐ Ⓑ Ⓒ Ⓓ
4 Ⓐ Ⓑ Ⓒ Ⓓ
5 Ⓐ Ⓑ Ⓒ Ⓓ

6 Ⓐ Ⓑ Ⓒ Ⓓ
7 Ⓐ Ⓑ Ⓒ Ⓓ

History

1 Ⓐ Ⓑ Ⓒ Ⓓ
2 Ⓐ Ⓑ Ⓒ Ⓓ
3 Ⓐ Ⓑ Ⓒ Ⓓ
4 Ⓐ Ⓑ Ⓒ Ⓓ
5 Ⓐ Ⓑ Ⓒ Ⓓ

6 Ⓐ Ⓑ Ⓒ Ⓓ
7 Ⓐ Ⓑ Ⓒ Ⓓ

Education

1 Ⓐ Ⓑ Ⓒ Ⓓ
2 Ⓐ Ⓑ Ⓒ Ⓓ
3 Ⓐ Ⓑ Ⓒ Ⓓ
4 Ⓐ Ⓑ Ⓒ Ⓓ
5 Ⓐ Ⓑ Ⓒ Ⓓ

6 Ⓐ Ⓑ Ⓒ Ⓓ
7 Ⓐ Ⓑ Ⓒ Ⓓ
8 Ⓐ Ⓑ Ⓒ Ⓓ
9 Ⓐ Ⓑ Ⓒ Ⓓ

Business

1 Ⓐ Ⓑ Ⓒ Ⓓ
2 Ⓐ Ⓑ Ⓒ Ⓓ
3 Ⓐ Ⓑ Ⓒ Ⓓ
4 Ⓐ Ⓑ Ⓒ Ⓓ
5 Ⓐ Ⓑ Ⓒ Ⓓ

6 Ⓐ Ⓑ Ⓒ Ⓓ
7 Ⓐ Ⓑ Ⓒ Ⓓ
8 Ⓐ Ⓑ Ⓒ Ⓓ
9 Ⓐ Ⓑ Ⓒ Ⓓ
10 Ⓐ Ⓑ Ⓒ Ⓓ

Science

1 Ⓐ Ⓑ Ⓒ Ⓓ
2 Ⓐ Ⓑ Ⓒ Ⓓ
3 Ⓐ Ⓑ Ⓒ Ⓓ
4 Ⓐ Ⓑ Ⓒ Ⓓ
5 Ⓐ Ⓑ Ⓒ Ⓓ

6 Ⓐ Ⓑ Ⓒ Ⓓ
7 Ⓐ Ⓑ Ⓒ Ⓓ
8 Ⓐ Ⓑ Ⓒ Ⓓ

Applied Science

1 Ⓐ Ⓑ Ⓒ Ⓓ
2 Ⓐ Ⓑ Ⓒ Ⓓ
3 Ⓐ Ⓑ Ⓒ Ⓓ
4 Ⓐ Ⓑ Ⓒ Ⓓ
5 Ⓐ Ⓑ Ⓒ Ⓓ

6 Ⓐ Ⓑ Ⓒ Ⓓ
7 Ⓐ Ⓑ Ⓒ Ⓓ

Restatements

1 Ⓐ Ⓑ Ⓒ Ⓓ
2 Ⓐ Ⓑ Ⓒ Ⓓ
3 Ⓐ Ⓑ Ⓒ Ⓓ
4 Ⓐ Ⓑ Ⓒ Ⓓ
5 Ⓐ Ⓑ Ⓒ Ⓓ

6 Ⓐ Ⓑ Ⓒ Ⓓ
7 Ⓐ Ⓑ Ⓒ Ⓓ
8 Ⓐ Ⓑ Ⓒ Ⓓ
9 Ⓐ Ⓑ Ⓒ Ⓓ
10 Ⓐ Ⓑ Ⓒ Ⓓ

PERSONAL STUDY PLAN

LISTENING TARGETS	DIAGNOSTIC TESTS			
STATEMENTS	**1**	**2**	**3**	**4**
Minimal Pairs				
Computation				
Number Discrimination				
Synonyms				
Negation				
Contextual Reference				
Cause and Effect				
Conditionals				
Chronological Order				
Comparisons				

CONVERSATIONS	**1**	**2**	**3**	**4**
Minimal Pairs				
Computation				
Number Discrimination				
Synonyms				
Negation				
Contextual Reference				
Cause and Effect				
Conditionals				
Chronological Order				
Comparisons				

MINI-TALKS	**1**	**2**	**3**	**4**
Overheard Conversations				
Announcements				
Advertisements				
News Reports				
Weather Reports				
Academic Lectures				
Informative Talks				
Class Discussions				

STRUCTURE	1	2	3	4
Active-Passive Verbs				
Articles				
Comparisons				
Conditionals				
Conjunctions: Form				
Conjunctions: Parallel Structure				
Prepositions				
Pronouns: Agreement				
Pronouns: Form				
Redundancy				
Subject: Agreement				
Subject: Repetition				
Subject: Omission				
Subjunctive				
Subordinate Clauses: Noun				
Subordinate Clauses: Adjective				
Subordinate Clauses: Adverb				
Subordinate Clauses: Reduced Adjective				
Subordinate Clauses: Reduced Adverb				
Verb: Omission				
Verb: Unnecessary Form				
Verb: Agreement				
Verb: Tense				
Word Families				
Word Order: Subject-Verb				
Word Order: Adjective-Adverb				
Word Order: Adjective				
Word Order: Adverb				